Phonology in Protolanguage and Interlanguage

Studies in Phonetics and Phonology
Edited by Martin J. Ball, Bangor University, and Pascal van Lieshout, University of Toronto

The aim of this series is to provide both accessible and relevant texts to students of linguistics, phonetics and speech sciences, and to publish more advanced texts and edited collections. The textbooks aim to cover a wide variety of topics relevant for such an audience, and to introduce these topics in a practical way to enable students to undertake a range of analysis procedures. The more advanced books will present state-of-the-art research in the topic concerned.

While we intend to cover a wide range of topics in phonetics and phonology, there will be an emphasis on phonetic studies of under-reported languages, or the bringing of new data to explore phonetic characteristics on the one hand, and on phonological studies that employ more psycholinguistic, cognitive and functional approaches on the other (and, of course, on the interaction between phonetics and phonology). The recent increase in interest in laboratory phonology we see as particularly to be welcomed. Each volume will be authored by leading authorities in the field, who have a grasp of both the theoretical issues and the practical requirements of the area and, further, are at the forefront of current research and practice.

Published:

Challenging Sonority: Cross-Linguistic Evidence
Edited by Martin J. Ball and Nicole Müller

Romance-Germanic Bilingual Phonology
Edited by Mehmet Yavaş, Margaret Kehoe and Walcir Cardoso

Forthcoming:

Prosodic Variation (with)in Languages: Intonation, Phrasing and Segments
Edited by Marisa Cruz, Pedro Oliveira and Sónia Frota

Phonology in Protolanguage and Interlanguage

Edited by
Elena Babatsouli and David Ingram

SHEFFIELD UK BRISTOL CT

Published by Equinox Publishing Ltd.

UK: Office 415, The Workstation, 15 Paternoster Row, Sheffield, South Yorkshire S1 2BX
USA: ISD, 70 Enterprise Drive, Bristol, CT 06010

www.equinoxpub.com

First published 2018

British Library Cataloguing-in-Publication Data

A catalogue record for this book is available from the British Library.
ISBN-13 978 1 78179 564 4 (hardback)

Library of Congress Cataloging-in-Publication Data

Names: Babatsouli, Elena, editor. | Ingram, David, 1944- editor.
Title: Phonology in protolanguage and interlanguage / edited by Elena Babatsouli and David Ingram.
Description: Sheffield, UK ; Bristol, CT : Equinox Publishing Ltd, 2018. | Series: Studies in phonetics and phonology | Includes bibliographical references and index.
Identifiers: LCCN 2017023833 (print) | LCCN 2017044089 (ebook) | ISBN 9781781796481 (ePDF) | ISBN 9781781795644 (hardcover)
Subjects: LCSH: Language acquisition. | Grammar, Comparative and general—Phonology.
Classification: LCC P118 (ebook) | LCC P118 .P487 2018 (print) | DDC 401/.93—dc23
LC record available at https://lccn.loc.gov/2017023833

Typeset by S.J.I. Services, New Delhi
Printed and bound by Lightning Source Inc. (La Vergne, TN), Lightning Source UK Ltd. (Milton Keynes), Lightning Source AU Pty. (Scoresby, Victoria)

Contents

Preface vii

Prologue 1
Elena Babatsouli and David Ingram

PROTOLANGUAGE

1. Are speech sound disorders phonological or articulatory? A spectrum approach 27
David Ingram, A. Lynn Williams and Nancy Scherer

2. Crosslinguistic interaction in early bilingual phonology: A critical review 49
Margaret Kehoe

3. German-Spanish bilinguals' phonological grammars: Permeable or resilient? 76
Conxita Lleó

4. Acquired singleton fricatives and lateral in cluster development: A bilingual child case 109
Elena Babatsouli

5. The production of selected phonemically short versus long Hungarian vowel pairs by 5-, 6- and 7-year-olds 139
Ferenc Bunta, Tilda Neuberger, Judit Bóna, Alexandra Markó and Ágnes Jordanidisz

6. Phonological development and language proficiency of bilingual children who learn Greek as a second language 162
Eleni Morfidi and Eleni Samsari

Synopsis on Protolanguage 192
The Authors and Editors

INTERLANGUAGE

7. Schwa productions in Spanish-English bilingual adults — 201
Kelly Millard and Mehmet Yavaş

8. Identification and discrimination of initial voiceless stops by Catalan and Portuguese learners of English: The role of formal instruction and L2 exposure — 231
Angélica Carlet and Anabela Rato

9. The impact of production complexity in German L2 by French native speakers: Focus on /h/ and vowel duration contrast — 255
Jane Wottawa, Martine Adda-Decker and Frédéric Isel

10. The acquisition of second dialect speech: An acoustic examination of the production of Ecuadorian Spanish assibilated rhotics by Andalusian speakers of Spanish — 286
Esparanza Ruiz-Peña, Diego Sevilla and Yasaman Rafat

11. The perceptual weight of word stress, quantity and tonal word accent in Swedish — 316
Åsa Abelin and Bosse Thorén

Synopsis on Interlanguage — 342
The Authors and Editors

Index — 347

Preface

'Every thing must have a beginning...; and that beginning must be linked to something that went before' (Mary Shelley, Introduction to *Frankenstein*, 1831). Assuming that new projects entail a dosage of invention, then it has been admitted that invention 'does not consist in creating out of void, but out of chaos' (ibid). This edited volume is accordingly linked to actions past, present and those yet to come, and its brief preface will serve the function of elucidating some of these links.

Though it is not easy to identify where the genesis of this project lies, one could say that it stemmed from a lay mother's question: *Children exposed to a mother tongue learn to speak it; will this child of mine also speak if she is exposed to my non-native tongue which I feel I am comfortably fluent in?* The initial question led to actions, and on to securing the circumstances that would allow a more systematic research endeavour, which consequently led to more specialized hypotheses on language acquisition. The child's acquisition of the second language, exposed to it through a single person's second-language input in a foreign context, turned out to be somewhat of a scarce phenomenon. So, which term best describes such a case in language acquisition: L1, L2, bilingual? What is the role of accent in the input? Is there accent in toddlers' speech or is it just baby speech? Answers to such questions are core themes in language acquisition literature and have also formed the thematic background of the current volume.

On the occasion of a visit to Arizona State University, the editors of this volume met with Roy Major, whose work needs no introduction among second-language acquisition (SLA) phonologists. During that casual meeting, there was not much discussion on language acquisition with the exception of Professor Major's question: 'Is there transfer [in the child's speech]?', that was followed by: 'Yes, but whose transfer is it?' One may have a preference that leans more towards researching L1 rather than L2, or vice versa, but for others this may not be true. As simply as that, and one ends up involuntarily mixing language-acquisition themes across childhood and adulthood in a language-acquisition research community, where it is not unlikely to hear that *child* and *adult* are different, and ought not to be viewed as a whole or directly compared. However, isn't a child much like an adult if one puts aside their fundamental differences relating to maturity?

These arguments have led to the idea that a more holistic viewpoint could be advocated with regard to researching language acquisition, since the dividing boundaries on what constitutes monolingual, bilingual and second-language phonology are not necessarily and unquestionably distinct. On more practical grounds, a conference was initiated whose purpose was to assist in cutting across dividing boundaries between language sub-fields: first language, second language, bilingual, multilingual; child or adult; normal or disordered. The *International Symposium on Monolingual and Bilingual Speech*, inaugurated in 2015, aspired to encourage investigations that widen existing horizons and perspectives, kindle a holistic viewpoint and seek to foster collaborations across the board.

We are grateful to the contributing authors of this volume, who responded to our invitation and made the book possible by submitting to it written articles based on their *ISMBS 2015* presentations. We are also thankful to the reviewers for their thorough and timely work which assisted in the process of preparing these studies for publication.

This edited volume becomes a coherent collection because its papers help advance research in diverse aspects in the acquisition of first- and second-language phonology in general, and within the specific context of mechanisms in language learning and use, as employed by children (monolingual or bilingual) and adults (in a first or second language), in particular. By bringing together research contributions into the production, perception and evaluation of developmental speech in childhood or adulthood, the ultimate goal of the book is to assist towards delineating precise descriptions of similarities and/or dissimilarities in the course of language acquisition across children and adults, in diverse contexts of learning, and across languages. There is a fairly equal division in this volume between child phonology studies and adult phonology studies. We do not feel that the volume is all-inclusive or exhaustive, but see it as a small stride towards what will be more work in the future that will perhaps incorporate direct comparisons between children and adults on aspects relating to language acquisition. This approach may provide more insights on the extent of their convergence or divergence.

Finally, we wish to express our gratitude to Martin J. Ball and Pascal van Lieshout who graciously accepted this volume as part of the book series *Studies in Phonetics and Phonology* at Equinox Publishing. Special thanks go to Martin J. Ball who, as the corresponding editor, has generously, expertly and in a timely manner supported this endeavour.

Elena Babatsouli and David Ingram

Prologue

Elena Babatsouli and David Ingram

What is the longest word in the English language? An instant online inquiry easily provides answers to this question. The longest technical term, referring to the chemical name of a human protein, starts with '*methionylthreonylthreonylglutaminylalanyl...*', finishes with '*...oleucine*' and contains 189,819 characters. Given that this is, arguably, not a *real* word, the next candidate is the nontechnical and, thus, unchallenged *floccinaucinihilipilification*/ˌflɒksɪˌnɔːsɪˌnaɪhɪlɪˌpɪlɪfɪˈkeɪʃən/, a humorous neologism with just 29 characters that refers to the act of looking upon something as unimportant or having no value. We learn language by learning to say words, but does not knowing *floccinaucinihilipilification* mean that one has not acquired the English language?

Children know by experience that long words and neologisms, such as the ones just mentioned, are not common in the everyday use of language and that, when they occur, they are specialized and often carry certain sociolinguistic prominence. Disney's musical film *Mary Poppins* has popularized the concept with the English 1940s coinage: *supercalifragilisticexpialidocious,* which is defined as 'something to say when you have nothing to say'. The argument in the song is that 'Even though the sound of it/Is something quite atrocious/If you say it loud enough/You'll always sound precocious.' Adults know, also by experience, that an English-speaking child will soon be able to sing *supercalifragilisticexpialidocious,* just by watching the movie a couple of times. In learning *new words,* the length of the word is not the only determinant for the ease or difficulty involved in the learning process. Unusual (in terms of structure) and less frequent words also pose difficulty in acquisition. A monolingual 10-year-old may have difficulty pronouncing a novel (to him) term, like *στιλπνή* /stil.ˈpni/ 'shining, bright', when first encountering it in Greek, thus producing [stiɾpfni]. Does this mean that the child has not acquired his language?

However, this volume is not concerned with long words, neologisms or even advanced vocabularies. It is, rather, concerned with how and whether people, young and older, acquire language *accurately,* when comparison is made to the known norms of a targeted linguistic system. Ever since its original use, as *dnghu* 'tongue' in the Proto-Indo-European (PIE) lexicon, language refers to 'words, what is said, conversation, talk' (*Online Etymology Dictionary* 2016). The PIE mother-language has given birth to several hundred related languages and dialects, of which only about 445 are still living (e.g. Babatsouli forthcoming a; *Ethnologue* 2016). But, let's assume that the words for language in some of these offspring-languages, i.e. *língua, lingua, langue, llenguatge, lenguaje, jazyk, lingvo, lingwa, cànan, keel, kieli, γλώσσα, nyelv, taal, teanga, valoda, језик, jazyk, jezik, gjuhe,* could be viewed as productions targeting /dnghu/. Using standard phonological theory, could one support the validity of these 'productions' as probable attempts at *dnghu*?

The aural/oral component of language is what makes acquisition of phonology the most fundamental function in language learning. Phonemic awareness (relating to perception of speech) and phonetic skill (relating to production of speech) are the driving forces in phonological acquisition. As a result, the presence or lack of the former crucially determines the outcome of the latter. This inescapably becomes a common thread that interweaves developmental phonology (i.e. the acquisition of sound systems) in both childhood and adulthood. Whether phonological acquisition precedes or follows a 'critical period' (Lenneberg 1967) of human cognitive and physical maturation, research on it has substantially relied on the same theoretical sources: universalist/markedness theory (e.g. Chomsky and Halle 1968; Ingram 1989; Jakobson 1941/1968; Prince and Smolensky 2004), biological theory (Lenneberg 1967; Locke 1983), natural phonology theory (Stampe 1979), cognitive/perceptual models (e.g. Best 1995; Best and Tyler 2007; Macken and Ferguson 1987) etc. Issues in children's sound speech disorders are also addressed in a similar manner (e.g. Ingram 2015).

With such thoughts in mind, the present volume forms an assembly of studies on the acquisition of phonology in childhood and adulthood, supporting a holistic approach across these sub-fields and hoping to further encourage a more avid exchange of information across language acquisition sub-disciplines. A study on atypical development of phonology (Chapter 1: Ingram, Williams and Scherer) has also been included as a reminder that the typical and atypical are integrally related (e.g. Babatsouli, Ingram and Müller 2017; Paradis, Genesee and Crago 2010). The title of the volume, *Phonology in Protolanguage and Interlanguage,* is meant as an epitome of these ideas. The volume also proposes that *protolanguage* and *interlanguage* are adapted as broad, all-encompassing terms to refer to developmental language in children and adults, respectively. In other words, the semantic scope of *protolanguage* and *interlanguage* (terms already present in language acquisition research) is opened out like an umbrella to contain all forms of language acquisition/learning, thus, only differentiating between the young and those no longer so young.

The processes that evolve during the development of phonology in any language acquired in isolation or in combination with others, either simultaneously or successively, are very revealing for our understanding of language acquisition. The existing build-up of categories and subcategories in language acquisition literature (more below) aims and serves to untangle these overt or underlying processes. The intention of the volume to propose broadening the terminology is not to underestimate the significance of thorough and detailed classifications. It mostly advocates for the merit of seeing language acquisition as a cohesive whole. An occasional bird's eye view could further widen our perspective.

The concept in the present work that focuses on phonology complements and continues in the line of other similar stances in the literature (e.g. MacWhinney 2015; Unsworth, Parodi, Sorace and Young-Scholten 2006; Yavaş 1994). There are numerous books on child language acquisition, monolingual and bilingual (Lust 2006; Grosjean 2010; Bhatia and Ritchie 2014), as well as on second-language acquisition (e.g. Van Patten and Williams 2014; Gass, Behney and Plosnky 2013; Lightbown and Spada 2013) that present clear and concise introductions to main concepts, issues and debates. Several recent books also deal with child language phonological acquisition from different thematic points (e.g. Davis and Bedore 2013; Tessier 2016; Vihman 2014; Vihman and Keren-Portnoy 2013). There are two edited books on second-language acquisition (SLA) whose titles include the term 'interlanguage' (Han and Tarone 2014; Ioup and Weinberger 1987) but only the latter one is specific to the acquisition of L2 phonology in adults. There are no books in the language acquisition literature that use the term *protolanguage*, or that relate it to *interlanguage*.

The remaining part of this introductory chapter will provide a brief overview of themes that commonly underlie phonological acquisition in childhood and adulthood, which justifies the concept of grouping the two together. This edited volume comprises example studies that contribute towards this. Both the overview here and the collection of the example studies support the main aim of the volume to view the development of phonology in all its facets, including end states, as one whole; they also provide justification for what is suggested to be a need to expand the semantics of the terms *protolanguage* and *interlanguage* beyond their current usage. What follows is divided into two main sections: 'Language acquisition: An overview'; 'Protolanguage and Interlanguage'. How the contributed chapters fit within language acquisition research is discussed alongside the arguments below.

Beyond this prologue, the entire book is further divided into two main sections and two summary sections. The main sections are named 'Protolanguage' and 'Interlanguage', respectively. The summary section following each main section discusses what each chapter in the volume contributes to language acquisition literature, and how each one relates to the theme of the book. The summary sections form the combined write-up of the contributing authors and the editors of this book.

Language acquisition: An overview

Linguistic competence is a primary attribute that differentiates humankind from the animal kingdom. The neurological foundations of language date back to a change, some 300,000–400,000 years ago, of a gene called FoxP2 in the DNA of primates (e.g. Lai, Fisher, Hurst, Vargha-Khadem and Monaco 2001). Humans acquire the language of their environment seemingly effortlessly when they are young. What's even more wondrous is that humans acquire language in a general sense, involving more than just one linguistic system as the phenomenon of contemporary multilingualism attests. Knowledge of language is the result of a complicated process of human learning, the acquisition of language. There is, however, a crucial distinction made in the literature between *learning* (conscious and explicit) and *acquisition* (unconscious and implicit).

By arguing that linguistic knowledge is a type of cognitive learning, there is a difference between *implicit* and *explicit* learning (e.g. Ellis 1994). Implicit learning is defined as an unconscious, 'automatic process whereby the structural nature of the stimulus environment is mapped into the mind of the attentive subject' (Reber and Allen 1978: 191). Explicit learning is an active, conscious and selective mode of learning in which learning products are accessible to metacognitive processes (Reber 1993). Weinert (2009: 242) argues that 'implicit compared to explicit learning processes are rather independent of age and thus available' to all, and that 'explicit learning processes are predominantly focused on semantic and conceptual aspects of the environment, while implicit learning is equally functional in learning phonological and conceptual regularities.' In second-language acquisition (SLA) theory, the differentiation between implicit and explicit becomes *acquisition* versus *learning* (Krashen 1982). The 'monitor hypothesis' (Krashen 1987) states that the acquired system produces language focusing on meaning, whereas the learned system serves as an 'inspector' of the acquired system, that is, a monitor of the actual grammar. The majority of the studies in this volume are investigating *acquisition*, though Chapter 11 (Abelin and Thorén) aims at enhancing *learning* practices.

First-language acquisition (FLA), as opposed to SLA, is equated with naturalistic input beginning in infancy. The constructionist approach emphasizes the gradual building-up of knowledge through steps by advocating that a new 'stage *n* will consist of everything at stage *n* plus the new feature(s) of stage *n+1*' (Ingram 1989: 73). Like most theoretical approaches pertinent in FLA, this approach has also found relevance in SLA. Krashen (1982) referred to this as the 'i+1' level of knowledge with regard to L2 learning in instructional settings. In 1987, he also acknowledged the manifestation of an 'affective filter' in L2 acquisition, meaning that factors like motivation, self-confidence and anxiety play important roles. Such factors were subsequently found to be enacting in child bilingual acquisition, as well (e.g. Montrul 2014).

Major themes in language acquisition

Speech perception and production

Speech perception and production play a primary role in the acquisition of phonology, with the left hemisphere of the human brain being responsible for comprehension (Wernicke's area) and for articulation (Broca's area), thus guiding speech functions (e.g. Gerschwind 2004). Perception facilitates comprehension that leads to the eventual ability to produce language. Parallel to mapping a speech signal onto meaning, the language acquirer (monolingual, bilingual, infant, child or adult) is expected to have the ability to segment the speech stream heard into isolated meaningful units. This proves to be especially difficult because the acoustic signal in speech is not broken up into noticeably distinct sections, as if in a Morse signal, whereby each section corresponds at all times to a particular word. If language is to be mastered through exposure to speech, co-articulation (e.g. Liberman, Copper, Shankweiler and Studdert-Kennedy 1967), or the overlapping of speech sounds, needs to be disentangled, segmenting fluent speech into discrete parts.

This is achieved with categorical perception: the ability to identify speech sounds as belonging to specific category boundaries embedded in speech contexts, not simply discriminating between them acoustically. Categorical perception is known to be compromised in adult listeners of speech (e.g. Liberman et al. 1967) because the ability to discriminate universal speech-sound contrasts is minimized very early in life. Babies turn into 'language bound listeners' much before their first birthdays (Kuhl 2000: 979). That is, infants become increasingly more sensitive to the distributions and statistics of their native language, which results in the perception of the sound system in the environment becoming very language-specific. Chapter 5 of this volume is an example study in child monolingual acquisition of phonology. In a nutshell, 'native language phonetic performance is indicative of neural commitment to the native language', while 'non-native phonetic performance' (ibid.) reveals the opposite. The majority of the chapters in this volume provide further evidence of this in bilingual children (Chapters 2, 3: Kehoe, Lleó), bilingual adults (Chapter 7: Millard and Yavaş), second-language (L2) learners (Chapters 8, 9: Carlet and Rato; Wottawa, Adda-Decker and Isel), and second-dialect (D2) learners (Chapter 10: Ruiz-Peña, Sevilla and Rafat).

Steered by perception, the production of speech (see Levelt 1989) is hardly automatic in infants, whose articulatory skill is subject to the outgrowth of biological constraints relating to maturation (e.g. Gleitman 1981), or in adults who enter into learning an additional language, with mature, already formed articulatory habits (e.g. Major 2001, 2008). For a discussion and schematic representation of the differences between infant and adult vocal tracts, a biological model of perceptual and motor factors in phonological development, and a description of the anatomy and physiology involved in adult speech, see e.g. Gut (2009), Kent (1992) and Vihman (2014). Ease of articulation, or 'the principle of least effort' (Schultze 1880/1971), is a decisive element in the understanding of developing phonologies, which is customarily interpreted in terms of markedness and universals in phonological theory (Jakobson 1941/1968), in terms of child vs. adult, or L1 vs. L2 levels of representation (Best 1995; Best and Tyler 2007; Flege 1991; Ingram 1974; Kiparsky and Menn 1977; Stampe 1979), and in the psychological terms of allocation of knowledge (Major 2008).

The mental lexicon

In spite of knowing that perception and production are differentiated in human brain anatomy, the brain seems 'to have no single location where language is created or stored' but rather 'many different cerebral centers' (e.g. Abutalebhi, Cappa and Perani 2005: 498). Mental lexicon in linguistics refers to the function of the brain to catalogue and process *words* and how *grammatical rules* apply on words for the purpose of speech (e.g. Babatsouli forthcoming b). The significance of the mental lexicon in language acquisition is well known, with various theoretical models differentiating between monolingual, bilingual and L2 lexicon, as well as between child and adult lexicon (Ingram 1974; Kiparsky and Menn 1977; Pavlenko 2008; Singleton 1999; Wright, Piske and Young-Scholten in preparation). Following a long debate, with the majority of theoretical stances ranging between single and separated lexicons for speakers of more than one language (i.e. child and adult bilinguals and L2 adult speakers), current theoretical stances assume distinct lexicons that are, however, variably interconnected on many levels (e.g. Li and MacWhinney 2012; Vihman 2015). Due to the significance of the lexicon in language acquisition, related studies (including those here) rely on actual word productions, both naturalistic and task-elicited. Thus, one's knowing or not of a word, like *floccinaucinihilipilification*, does highlight that language is something potentially learned (and even unlearned) throughout one's life-span (e.g. Babatsouli, Ingram and Müller 2017; Köpke, Schmid, Keijzer and Dostert 2007), though not critical for one's communication skills.

Input and the 'critical period'

Why child monolinguals attain global competence and performance in the target language (TL) faster than everyone else is the riddle underlying the 'logical problem of language acquisition' (Chomsky 1986). Words and speech sounds are acquired via imitation of linguistic input (e.g. Bloomfield 1933; Skinner 1957). Input is necessary for gaining linguistic knowledge, but 'input alone may not be sufficient in metalinguistic tasks' (Gierut 1996: 47). Together with input itself, age and timing of exposure play a crucial role in attaining native competence and performance, often referred to as *nativeness* or *native-likeness*. The 'critical period' (Lenneberg 1967) recognizes the existence of an upper age limit in neurological development, set inconclusively somewhere between pre- and post-puberty, beyond which humans progressively lose the fundamental capacity for acquiring novel grammatical contrasts and, in extreme cases, even the capacity for language itself (Curtiss 1977).

There are universal patterns observed in the acquisition of phonology between monolingual and bilingual children (e.g. Bunta, Fabiano-Smith, Goldstein and Ingram 2009; Lleó and Kehoe 2002). Complete acquisition of a grammatical system is known to take place between the 4th and 5th year of life but, subject to individual variation, it may exceed that for a couple of years (e.g. Ingram 1989; Meisel 2010). Meisel (2010: 225) states that an 'onset between age 3 and 4' is a necessary, though not sufficient, condition for acquiring native competence. It is also argued that the critical period 'should be understood as a cluster of sensitive periods, each defined in terms of an optimal period for the development of specific features of grammar' (ibid.); 'subcomponents of phonology seem to fade out at different points of development' with the peak beginning shortly before the 2nd birthday, gradually declining by age 5 and ending sometime between ages 7 and 10. Late effects in the acquisition of child monolingual and bilingual phonology are represented in this volume by Chapter 5 (Bunta, Neuberger, Bóna, Markó and Jordanidisz) and Chapter 6 (Morfidi and Samsari), respectively.

Knowledge of the processes involved in FLA is commonly a yardstick for deciphering SLA (e.g. Ioup and Weinberger 1987; Major 2008) though the two are known to differ at least in terms of the outcome of acquisition and the length of the developmental path. Dialectal contacts, as the one studied by Ruiz-Peña, Sevilla and Rafat (Chapter 10 this volume), are equally challenging in deciphering acquisition, although the focus is on the acquisition of language variety rather than language itself. Though native competence is the outcome of FLA, critical period effects in SLA lead to a 'global foreign accent' (Major 2001: 18) in L2 speakers (both children and adults), which makes itself evident in the inconsistency of production with regard to individual sound segments, their combinations and prosodic features. In other words, a lack of mastery of any or all three phonological levels results in a foreign accent. The 'ontogeny phylogeny model' (ibid.) compared SLA to FLA and discussed the developmental path of SLA longitudinally. It claimed that there are similar phenomena in L1 and L2, such as the presence of universals, but the developmental path in SLA is slower, with universals playing a smaller role in the process, and transfer shrinking as L2 gradually progresses towards native-likeness. Subsequent theoretical postulations and insights that deal with aspects of child and adult language in development focus on chaos and dynamic systems theory (e.g. Babatsouli 2016; De Bot, Lowie and Verspoor 2007).

Because of the length involved in the developmental paths of language, which involves years of data collection and thorough analysis, there are relatively few studies that provide actual insights on the development of language in individual children longitudinally. Interestingly, the majority of children in such studies were exposed to more languages than one – of which one is second-language English (e.g. Babatsouli 2017; Leopold 1949; Schnitzer and Krasinski 1994), coming from at least one of the child's parents (Babatsouli 2015; Major 1977; Smith 1973); the fact that in every four speakers of English three are non-native (Babatsouli forthcoming a, and references therein) may explain this. Because of longer developmental paths and methodological limitations, longitudinal investigations in SLA are even rarer (e.g. Munro and Derwing 2008), involving groups rather than case studies, where *longitudinal* refers to length of residence (LOR) in the country where the target language is spoken (e.g. Riney and Flege 1998) or span of intermitted data collection (e.g. Carlisle and Cutillas Espinosa 2015) rather than length of uninterrupted data collection and assessment.

Thus, in both child bilingualism and SLA theory, the quality and quantity of input (e.g. Müller and Hulk 2001; Piske and Young-Scholten 2009) are important factors in determining ultimate attainment and native-like competence, and can also play a fundamental role in L2 instruction settings (e.g. Abelin and Thorén this volume). Such effects differentiate between acquisition of language in monolinguals, and acquisition of a second language in child bilinguals, adult L2 learners/acquirers and second-dialect (D2) learners. In spite of such evidence, there are theoretical advancements arguing that native-like competence is possible in speakers of an L2, as a result of cognitive (i.e. neural), socio-psychological, behavioral and environmental changes in the span of an individual's life (e.g. De Bot, Lowie and Verspoor 2006).

Child bilingualism: L1 or L2?

The notion of two (or more) languages developing in infancy and childhood, as if each one were a first language originally appeared in Swain (1972). Deuchar and Quay (2000: 1) characterize bilingualism as the 'acquisition of two languages in childhood'. A clear distinction has often been made between 'simultaneous' and 'successive' bilingualism (McLauglin 1978), i.e. between a set of languages developing concurrently with exposure to input beginning at birth until about age 3, and a set of languages whose acquisition is in a successive order (e.g. L1 exposure before age 3 and L2 exposure any time afterwards). Several other terms, like bilingual first language, bilingual second language, dual-language, sequential, consecutive, incipient, balanced, additive, subtractive, heritage language acquisition, and their variable gradations, like early and late sequential, early second-language acquisition, and so on, have been advanced in the literature (see e.g. Bhatia and Ritchie 2014; Gass and Selinker 2008 for reviews). Their purpose has been to classify child bilinguals based on different variables like exact age and timing of exposure, sociolinguistic contexts, language status and dominance, etc. (e.g. Babatsouli and Ingram 2015).

Regardless of these, case and group studies in child bilingualism, including child bidialectalism (e.g. Grohmann, Kambanaros, Leivada and Rowe 2016) provide vital evidence that languages in bilingualism are both like and unlike L1 and L2, irrespective of other variables. Grosjean's (1989) statement that 'the bilingual is not two monolinguals in one' has further supported the earlier theoretical advances on how languages in contact interact; terms like 'transfer' and 'interference' (Weinreich 1953) have been at the heart of the literature on the acquisition of a second language in early childhood and subsequently. Two of the chapters in this volume are representative of these themes, one initiating a look across phonological development in children and adults (Chapter 2: Kehoe), and the other discussing 'crosslinguistic interaction' in child bilingualism (Chapter 3: Lleó). Interestingly, the notion of 'transfer' has come to be interpreted somewhat differently in child bilingualism when compared to SLA (see e.g. Kehoe 2015, also this volume, for review). It is however a major construct in the acquisition of L2 in childhood and adulthood, as it relies on the psychological notion that previously-acquired knowledge influences subsequently-acquired skill (Major 2008). Lastly, transfer has been argued to be a culprit for the compromised input a learner may receive in child bilingualism (Babatsouli 2015; Major 1977; Paradis 2000; Place and Hoff 2011) and in foreign-language instruction settings (e.g. Gass and Selinker 2008).

SLA vs. FLA vs. Bilingualism

The acquisition of a first and of a second language involve similar notions, in that acquisition, rather than learning, takes place in a naturalistic setting with the language being picked up as a matter of course in social interaction, rather than being learned in an educational setting through formal instruction or through a combination of both. Ellis (2008) has argued that factors that 'affect L2 acquisition differ according to social context' and setting: 'Natural settings' are distinguished into those where the second language is: (I) the native language of the majority, (II) an official language when the majority speaks another or (III) a language used in heterogeneous settings. 'Educational settings' involve: (I) 'segregation' (L2 is learned separately from the majority group), (II) 'mother tongue maintenance' (the minority group's first language is being taught), (III) 'submersion' (the L2 is taught where the L1 is dominant), (IV) 'immersion' (native input is available either in natural or instruction settings) and (V) 'foreign language classrooms.'

A principle dictum in SLA is that an L2 is being acquired or learned after the L1 is well-established. The 'fundamental difference hypothesis' (FDH) has argued that the adult L2 acquirer does not have the same potential for language acquisition as child L1 acquirers (Bley-Vroman 1989) or bilingual child acquirers (Montrul 2009), especially so for simultaneous bilinguals; this is due to 'critical period' effects and the 'acquisition' vs. 'learning' hypothesis (Krashen 1982). Skilled adult bilinguals are known to employ different cognitive processes than those of adult L2 speakers (e.g. Kroll and Sunderman 2003), but adult fluent L2 speakers are also sometimes referred to as bilinguals (e.g. Haugen 1953; Bhatia 2006). Interestingly, there are opposing arguments with regard to attaining native competence in both of these speaker groups (e.g. De Bot et al. 2006; Gut 2009; Kroll and Sunderman 2003; Millard and Yavaş this volume). Overall, target language competence does not seem to be the de facto outcome either in adult L2 speech resulting from SLA contexts, or in adult L2 speech resulting from bilingual exposure in early childhood. Attaining native-like competence in either of these contexts is not always possible, and undeveloped forms may 'fossilize' (Selinker 1972) even after years of exposure and use (e.g. Lightbown and Spada 2013).

Consequently, bilingual competence should not be described and evaluated in terms of fluency and balance in the bilingual's languages, and the monolingual speaker ought not to be the model of the 'normal speaker-hearer' against which bilingualism must be measured (Grosjean 1985: 470). Because 'bilinguals find themselves at various points along a situation continuum which induce different language modes' (Grosjean 2001), there is constant competition between the languages (e.g. Marian and Spivey 2003). Similarly, speech acquired in SLA contexts is equally known to exhibit a dynamic and variable nature (e.g. De Bot, Lowie, Thorne and Verspoor 2013), whereby there is an ongoing ebb and flow between the languages (McLaughlin 1995).

Protolanguage and interlanguage

As seen from this very brief, and certainly neither complete nor thorough, overview of language acquisition research, child speech and adult speech in the course of development have a lot to share, while still constituting separate linguistic systems in their own right. They are intermediate states whose endpoint is (or ought to be) mastery of the targeted speech either in a first or a second language. Using terms already present in the literature, these intermediate states are referred to here as *protolanguage* and *interlanguage* respectively, and they will be elaborated in more detail next.

Protolanguage

The child's linguistic system is 'in the process of build-up' (Jakobson 1941/1968) but there is, to our knowledge, no single term of reference to it in the literature. Prior to mastery of adult speech, 'each child must construct his or her own version of the adult system' (Menn and Matthei 1992: 222). Given that children are not aware of their errors (Ervin and Miller 1963) and that their speech is often unintelligible to adults, the child's linguistic system is an *early* but *different* form of the adult language. This early developing linguistic system from babbling, to first meaningful forms to acquisition of the adult system is referred to as *protolanguage* here. The term is coined from *proto* meaning 'first, early' and *language*, and is also found in Halliday (1979) who used it in a narrower sense to refer to children's first stable word productions. Such early word productions, or 'proto-words', appear during the transition from babbling to speech but lack the form and meaning of the adult model (e.g. Bates 1976; Menn 2013; Vihman 2014). Protolanguage, in the sense introduced here, has a broader definition that covers the entire span of child linguistic development including all various language acquisition types in childhood (monolingual, bilingual/multilingual; dialectal/multilectal); the only determining factor is that linguistic development refers to the cognitive and articulatory immaturity evidenced in children, prior to the end of critical period effects. It is further suggested here that protolanguage also includes child speech delay and disorders (see Bowen 2015), which are known to exhibit child language characteristics in an amplified, thus atypical, manner.

By using the 'atrocious' term *protolanguage*, the intention here is not to suggest that *protolanguage* is not language. *Oxford Living Dictionaries* (2016) defines *language* as 'the method of human communication, either spoken or written, consisting of the use of words in a structured or conventional way'. The same holds for protolanguage (PL), only that protolanguage is the language of infants, toddlers and children in the process of growth rather than the typical, target-language of grown-ups, whose phonological skill is arguably in a fairly balanced and steady state. It goes without saying that there is systematicity and universal patterning in the developing speech of monolingual and bilingual children (e.g. Bunta, Fabiano-Smith, Goldstein and Ingram 2009; Ingram 1981, 1989; Jakobson 1941/1968; Lleó and Kehoe 2002; Vihman and Keren-Portnoy 2013), that also incorporates the evidenced systematicity of child-specific and crosslinguistic variation (e.g. Goad and Ingram 1987; Pye, Ingram and List 1987). Protolanguage is represented in this volume by Chapter 1 (Ingram, Williams and Scherer) discussing the atypical, Chapters 2 and 3 (Kehoe; Lleó) representing bilingual crosslinguistic interaction, Chapter 4 (Babatsouli) with a longitudinal case study in protolanguage phonology, and finally, Chapters 5 (Bunta, Neuberger, Bóna, Markó and Jordanidisz) and 6 (Morfidi and Samsari) with examples of near-end states in monolingualism and bilingualism, respectively.

A parenthesis is made at this stage to take notice of the following two points. Firstly, it is not argued here that target language, as the outcome of protolanguage, is a static medium but rather one that, like a living organism (e.g. Anderson and Lightfoot 2000), is subject to change (Van Geert 1994), instigated by a multiplicity of speaker internal and external factors. Hohenberger and Peltzer-Karpf (2009) have argued that throughout and beyond development, plasticity (i.e. the brain's ability to re-organize in response to external factors) should be made responsible for the '(in)determinism of language'. Secondly, because there is not yet enough evidence from studies in protolanguage phonology within individual languages as well as crosslinguistically to allow for a thorough labelling of universals, it is not sensible to attempt to define exactly when protolanguage becomes language. This will become possible after we have determined when specific protolanguage(s) become(s) the targeted language(s) in monolingualism, bilingualism or multilingualism. This is especially true in the case of bilingual (and multilingual) children, where protolanguage also involves *interlanguage* aspects.

Interlanguage

'Interlanguage' is a term coined by Selinker (1972) to describe an individual speaker's idiolect when learning (and thus using) a non-native language, or L2. Though L2 speech was initially referred to as a 'learner-language' system (Sampson and Richards 1973) or an 'approximative' system (Nemser 1971), interlanguage (IL) is widely used these days to refer to the adult learner's transitional linguistic system during acquisition of a second language, i.e. after the native language has been acquired. Like child developmental speech, interlanguage is in the process of developing (e.g. Selinker, Swain and Dumas 1975), and it includes variable degrees of linguistic skill from beginner to native-like. Selinker (1972) postulated that speech in the adult L2 learner has a distinctive grammatical system that differs from those in the L1 and targeted L2. The autonomy of IL as an intermediate linguistic system is evidenced in the systematicity that underlies the developmental sequence by learners from different native language backgrounds (e.g. Han and Tarone 2014).

Interlanguage phonology is typically recognized in L2 speech as foreign accent. Several factors are corollaries for the extent of accent in both adult and child L2 speakers. Among the most decisive ones are the amount and type of exposure, and the amount of L2 use involving interaction with native speakers (Major 2008), thus differentiating between native input and accented input in homeland and foreign settings. The 'interlanguage hypothesis' (Selinker 1972) claimed that, like Lenneberg's (1967) 'latent psychological structure' as part of the critical period hypothesis (CPH), there is in SLA an age-sensitive 'latent language structure' which becomes active after puberty, and which is known to affect linguistic competence in the L2. Though IL customarily refers to the post-CPH L2, it also includes the IL of child learners, who get exposed to an L2 after certain phonological constructs have already been acquired in their L1. This is clearly exemplified in the interlanguage of children learning foreign languages in school, with accent being caused both system-internally and system-externally by compromised input. It has also been claimed that the IL hypothesis also extends to child L2 in the case of unbalanced bilingual acquisition (e.g. Selinker et al. 1975; Schlyter 1993) when the weaker language behaves less like an L1, and also in the absence of native input as in the 'interlanguage ambiguity hypothesis' (e.g. Paradis 2000). Such IL phenomena as 'fossilization', which is reminiscent of 'frozen forms' (Ferguson and Farewell 1975) in protolanguage, are also argued to be typical of incomplete acquisition in bilingualism (Montrul 2014).

Interlanguage is represented in this volume by Chapter 7 (Millard and Yavaş) investigating bilingual adults' speech, Chapters 8 and 9 (Carlet and Rato; Wottawa, Adda-Decker and Isel) on aspects of adult L2 speech and formal instruction in SLA contexts, Chapter 10 (Ruiz-Peña, Sevilla and Rafat) studying second-dialect (D2) acquisition, and finally Chapter 11 (Abelin and Thorén) exemplifying how the perceptual weight of phonemic contrasts in an L1 may have interesting implications for SLA teaching practices. In the way of conclusive remarks, if interlanguage is something that is triggered by exposure to a novel linguistic system (a new language or dialect), then this approximative system or learner language (that is neither like what is already acquired nor what is targeted) could be argued to account for all learner/acquirer systems, irrespective of the timing of exposure to those systems. This would mean that, given the known patterns of crosslinguistic interference, a child's protolanguage in simultaneous bilingualism is also a form of interlanguage, albeit at an infant state. An example of that on the level of lexicon may come from a bilingual child's production [ˈnoʃi] at 2;10, resulting from a combination of targeted English *no* and targeted Greek *όχι* /ˈoxi/ → [ˈoçi] 'no'. In a sense, therefore, protolanguage includes aspects of interlanguage. In simultaneous bilinguals (with earlier exposure to L2 when L1 is still immature), the patterns of crosslinguistic interference may be of a different type than those found in sequential bilinguals, where exposure to the L2 occurs at a later stage. In spite of these observations, it is suggested that all 'pre-critical period' developmental language systems are treated as protolanguage, and all post-'critical-period' developmental language systems are treated as interlanguage.

Native competence is the outcome of typical monolingual PL. Native competence as the end state of IL is also possible in humans, assuming that all the necessary facilitating factors are guaranteed. Interestingly, linguistic diversity has been the norm in human history for thousands of years; in today's globalized and multilingual world, languages are also in contact in society and within individuals. Thus, one could be permitted to think that *interlanguage* may just be *language* going about its business of diachronic change. Interlanguages may be the reason that *língua, llenguatge, teanga, jezik, gjuhe,* etc. are no longer *dnghu.*

References

Abutalebhi, J., Cappa, S. and Perani, D., 2005, 'What can functional neuroimaging tell us about the bilingual brain?', in J. Kroll and A. De Groot (eds.), *Handbook of bilingualism: Psycholinguistic perspectives,* pp. 497–515, Oxford, UK: Oxford University Press.

Anderson, S.R. and Lightfoot, D.W., 2000, 'The human language faculty as an organ', *Annual Review of Physiology* 62, 697–722.

Babatsouli, E., 2015, 'Technologies for the study of speech: Review and an application', *Themes in Science and Technology Education* 8(1), 17–32.

Babatsouli, E., 2016, 'Chaos in monolingual and bilingual speech', in C.H. Skiadas and C. Skiadas (eds.), *Handbook of applications of chaos theory,* pp. 789–890, London: CRC Press. https://doi.org/10.1201/b20232-51

Babatsouli, E., 2017, 'Bilingual development of *theta* in a child', *Poznan Studies in Contemporary Linguistics* 53(2), 157–92. https://doi.org/10.1515/psid-2017-0007

Babatsouli, E., forthcoming a, 'Multilingualism', in M.J. Ball and J.S. Damico (eds.), *The Sage encyclopedia of human communication sciences and disorders,* Thousand Oaks, CA: Sage Publications.

Babatsouli, E., forthcoming b, 'Lexicon', in M.J. Ball and J.S. Damico (eds.), *The Sage encyclopedia of human communication sciences and disorders,* Thousand Oaks, CA: Sage Publications.

Babatsouli, E. and Ingram, D., 2015, 'What bilingualism tells us about phonological acquisition', in R.H. Bahr and E.R. Silliman (eds.), *Routledge handbook of communication disorders,* pp. 173–82, Routledge: Taylor & Francis.

Babatsouli, E., Ingram D. and Müller, N. (2017), 'Introduction', in E. Babatsouli, D. Ingram and N. Müller (eds.), *Crosslinguistic encounters in language acquisition: Typical and atypical development*, Bristol, UK: Multilingual Matters.

Bates, E., 1976, *Language and context: The acquisition of pragmatics*, New York, NY: Academic Press.

Best, C., 1995, 'A direct realist view of cross-language speech perception', in W. Strange (ed.), *Speech perception and linguistic experience: Issues in cross-language research*, pp. 171–204, Timonium, MD: York Press.

Best, C.T. and Tyler, M.D., 2007, 'Nonnative and second-language speech perception: Commonalities and complementarities', in O.S. Bohn and M.J. Munro (eds.), *Language experience in second language speech learning: In honour of James Emil Flege*, pp. 13–34, Amsterdam: John Benjamins. https://doi.org/10.1075/lllt.17.07bes

Bhatia, T.K., 2006, 'Introduction to part I', in T. Bhatia and W. Ritchie (eds.), *The handbook of bilingualism*, pp. 5–7, Malden, MA: Blackwell. https://doi.org/10.1002/9780470756997

Bhatia, T.K. and Ritchie, W.C. (eds.), 2014, *The handbook of bilingualism and multilingualism* (2nd edn.), Chichester, UK: Wiley-Blackwell.

Bley-Vroman, R., 1989, 'What is the logical problem of foreign language learning?', in S. Gass and J. Schachter (eds.), *Linguistic perspectives on second language acquisition*, pp. 41–68, New York, NY: City University Press. https://doi.org/10.1017/CBO9781139524544.005

Bloomfield, L., 1933, *Language*, New York, NY: Holt.

Bowen, C. (ed.), 2015, *Children's speech sound disorders* (2nd edn.), Oxford, UK: John Wiley & Sons.

Bunta, F., Fabiano-Smith, L., Goldstein, B.A. and Ingram, D., 2009, 'Phonological wholeword measures in three-year-old bilingual children and their age-matched monolingual peers', *Clinical Linguistics and Phonetics* 23, 156–75. https://doi.org/10.1080/02699200802603058

Carlisle, R.S. and Cutillas Espinosa, J.A., 2015, 'The production of /.sC/ onsets in a markedness relationship', in M. Yavaş (ed.), *Unusual productions in phonology: Universals and language-specific considerations*, pp. 183–205, New York, NY: Psychology Press.

Chomsky, N., 1986, *Knowledge of language: Its nature, origins, and use*, New York: Praeger.

Chomsky, N. and Halle, M., 1968, *The sound pattern of English*, New York: Harper & Row.

Curtiss, S., 1977, *Genie: A psychological study of a modern-day 'wild child'*, New York: Academic Press.

Davis, B.L. and Bedore, L.M., 2013, *An emergence approach to speech acquisition: Doing and knowing*, New York, NY: Psychology Press.

De Bot, K., Lowie, W. and Verspoor, M.H., 2006, *Second language acquisition: An advanced resource book*, London/New York: Routledge.

De Bot, K., Lowie, W. and Verspoor, M.H., 2007, 'A dynamic systems theory approach to second language acquisition', *Bilingualism: Language and Cognition* 10, 7–21. https://doi.org/10.1017/S1366728906002732

De Bot, K., Lowie, W., Thorne, S.L. and Verspoor, M.H., 2013, 'DST as a comprehensive theory of second language development', in M.G.M. Del Pilar, M.J.G. Mangado and M. Martínez Adrián (eds.), *Contemporary approaches to second language acquisition*, pp. 199–220, Amsterdam/Philadelphia: John Benjamins. https://doi.org/10.1075/aals.9.13ch10

Deuchar, M. and Quay, S., 2000, *Bilingual acquisition: Theoretical implications of a case study*, Oxford, UK: Oxford University Press.

Ellis, N., 1994, *Implicit and explicit learning of languages*, New York, NY: Academic Press.

Ellis, R., 2008, *The study of second language acquisition*, Oxford, UK: Oxford University Press.

Ervin, S.M. and Miller, W.R., 1963, 'Language development', in H.W. Stevenson (ed.), *Child psychology, NSSEY*, pp. 108–43, Chicago, IL: Chicago University Press. https://doi.org/10.1037/13101-004

Ethnologue: Languages of the world (2016), retrieved from https://www.ethnologue.com/.

Ferguson, C. and Farewell, C., 1975, 'Words and sounds in early language acquisition: Initial consonants in the first fifty words', *Language* 51, 419–39. https://doi.org/10.2307/412864

Flege, J.E., 1991, 'Perception and production: The relevance of phonetic input to L2 phonological learning', in T. Huemner and C.A. Ferguson (eds.), *Cross currents in second language acquisition and linguistic theories*, pp. 249–69, Amsterdam/Philadelphia: John Benjamins. https://doi.org/10.1075/lald.2.15fle

Gass, S.M., Behney, J. and Plosnky, L., 2013, *Second language acquisition: An introductory course*, New York, NY: Routledge.

Gass, S.M. and Selinker, L., 2008, *Second language acquisition: An introductory course*, New York, NY: Routledge.

Gerschwind, N., 2004, 'Language and the brain', in B.C. Lust and C. Foley (eds.), *First language acquisition: The essential readings*, pp. 108–22, Oxford, UK: Blackwell Publishers.

Gierut, J.A., 1996, 'Featural categories in English phonemic acquisition', in B. Bernhardt, D. Ingram and J. Gilbert (eds.), *Proceedings of the UBC International Conference on Phonological Acquisition*, pp. 42–52, Somerville, MA: Cascadilla Press.

Gleitman, L.R., 1981, 'Maturational determinants of language growth', *Cognition* 10, 103–14. https://doi.org/10.1016/0010-0277(81)90032-9

Goad, H. and Ingram, D., 1987, 'Individual variation and its relevance to a theory of phonological acquisition', *Journal of Child Language* 14, 419–32. https://doi.org/10.1017/S0305000900010217

Grohmann, K., Kambanaros, M., Leivada, E. and Rowe, C., 2016, 'A developmental approach to diglossia: Bilectalism on a gradient scale of linguality', in E. Babatsouli and D. Ingram (guest-eds.), Special issue on *Monolingual and bilingual speech across languages, Poznan Studies in Contemporary Linguistics* 52(4), 629–62. https://doi.org/10.1515/psicl-2016-0025

Grosjean, F., 1985, 'The bilingual as a competent but specific speaker-hearer', *Journal of Multilingual and Multicultural Development* 4(6), 467–77. https://doi.org/10.1080/01434632.1985.9994221

Grosjean, F., 1989, 'Neurolinguists, beware! The bilingual is not two monolinguals in one person', *Brain and Language* 36, 3–15. https://doi.org/10.1016/0093-934X(89)90048-5

Grosjean, F., 2001, 'The bilingual's language modes', in J. Nicol (ed.), *One mind, two languages: Bilingual language processing*, pp. 1–22, Oxford, UK: Blackwell.

Grosjean, F., 2010, *Bilingual: Life and reality*, Cambridge, MA: Harvard University Press. https://doi.org/10.4159/9780674056459

Gut, U., 2009, *Introduction to English phonetics and phonology*, Frankfurt: Peter Lang. https://doi.org/10.3726/978-3-653-04390-7

Halliday, M.A.K., 1979, 'One child's protolanguage', in M. Bullowa (ed.), *Before speech: The beginnings of interpersonal communication*, pp. 179–90, Cambridge, UK: Cambridge University Press.

Han, Z.-H. and Tarone, E. (eds.), 2014, *Interlanguage: Forty years later*, Amsterdam/Philadelphia: John Benjamins.

Haugen, E., 1953, *The Norwegian language in America*, Philadelphia: University of Pennsylvania Press.

Hohenberger, A. and Peltzer-Karpf, A., 2009, 'Language learning from the perspective of nonlinear dynamic systems', *Linguistics* 47(2), 481–511. https://doi.org/10.1515/LING.2009.017

Ingram, D., 1974, 'Phonological rules in young children', *Journal of Child Language* 1, 49–64. https://doi.org/10.1017/S0305000900000076

Ingram, D., 1981, 'The emerging phonological system of an Italian-English bilingual child', *Journal of Italian Linguistics* 2, 955–1113.

Ingram, D., 1989, *First language acquisition: Method, description and explanation*, Cambridge, UK: Cambridge University Press.

Ingram, D., 2015, 'The role of theory in SSD', in C. Bowen (ed.), *Children's speech sound disorders* (2nd edn.), pp. 28–31, Oxford, UK: John Wiley & Sons.

Ioup, G. and Weinberger, S.H., 1987, 'Introduction', in G. Ioup and S.H. Weinberger (eds.), *Interlanguage phonology: The acquisition of a second language sound system*, pp. 3–22, Cambridge, MA: Newbury House.

Jakobson, R., 1941/1968, *Child language, aphasia and phonological universals* (trans. A. Keiler), The Hague: Mouton. Original work published in 1941 as *Kindersprache, aphasie und allgemeine Lautgesetze*.

Kehoe, M., 2015, 'Cross-linguistic interaction: A retrospective and prospective view', in E. Babatsouli and D. Ingram (eds.), *Proceedings of the International Symposium on Monolingual and Bilingual Speech 2015*, pp. 141–67, ISBN: 978-618-82351-0-6. Retrieved from http://ismbs.eu/publications.

Kent, R.D., 1992, 'The biology of phonological development', in C.A. Ferguson, L. Menn, and C. Stoel-Gammon (eds.), *Phonological development: Models, research, implications*, pp. 65–90, Timonium, MD: York Press.

Kiparsky, P. and Menn, L., 1977, 'On the acquisition of phonology', in J. MacNamara (ed.), *Language learning and thought*, pp. 47–78, New York, NY: Academic Press.

Köpke, M., Schmid, M., Keijzer, M. and Dostert, S. (eds.), 2007, *Language attrition: Theoretical perspectives*, pp. 83–98, Amsterdam: John Benjamins.

Krashen, S.D., 1982, 'Acounting for child-adult differences in second language rate and attainment', in S.D. Krashen, R. Scarcella and M.H. Long (eds.), *Child-adult differences in second language acquisition*, pp. 202–26, Rowley, MA: Newbury House.

Krashen, S.D., 1987, *Principles and practice in second language acquisition*, New York, NY: Prentice Hall.

Kroll, J. F., and Sunderman, G., 2003, 'Cognitive processes in second language learners and bilinguals: The development of lexical and conceptual representations', in C. Doughty and M.H. Long (eds.), *The handbook of second language acquisition*, pp. 104–29, Cambridge, MA: Blackwell. https://doi.org/10.1002/9780470756492.ch5

Kuhl, P.K., 2000, 'A new view of language acquisition', *Proceedings of the National Academy of Science* 97, 11850–57. https://doi.org/10.1073/pnas.97.22.11850

Lai, C.S.L., Fisher, S.E., Hurst, J.A., Vargha-Khadem, F. and Monaco, A.P., 2001, 'A fork head domain gene is mutated in a severe speech and language disorder', *Nature* 413, 519–23. https://doi.org/10.1038/35097076

Lenneberg, E., 1967, *Biological foundations of language*, New York, NY: Wiley.

Leopold, W.F., 1949, *Speech development of a bilingual child: A linguist's record*, Evanston, IL: Northwestern University Press.

Levelt, W.J.M., 1989, *Speaking: From intention to articulation.* Cambridge, MA: MIT Press.

Li, P. and MacWhinney, B., 2012, 'The competition model', in C.A. Chapelle (ed.), *The encyclopedia of applied linguistics*, Malden, MA: Wiley. https://doi.org/10.1002/9781405198431.wbeal0168

Liberman, A.M., Copper, F.S., Shankweiler, D.P. and Studdert-Kennedy, M.G., 1967, 'Perception of the speech code', *Psychological Review* 74, 431–61. https://doi.org/10.1037/h0020279

Lightbown, P.M. and Spada, N., 2013, *How languages are learned*, Oxford, UK: Oxford University Press.

Lleó, C. and Kehoe, M., 2002, 'On the interaction of phonological systems in child bilingual acquisition', *International Journal of Bilingualism* 6, 233–37. https://doi.org/10.1177/13670069020060030101

Locke, J.L., 1983, *Phonological acquisition and change*, New York, NY: Academic.

Lust, B., 2006, *Child language: Acquisition and growth*, Cambridge: Cambridge University Press. https://doi.org/10.1017/CBO9780511803413

Macken, M.A. and Ferguson, C.A., 1987, 'Phonological universals in language acquisition', in G. Ioup and S.H. Weinberger (eds.), *Interlanguage phonology: The acquisition of a second language sound system*, pp. 3–22, Cambridge, MA: Newbury House.

MacWhinney, B., 2015, 'A unified model of first and second language learning', in M. Hickmann and M. Kail (eds.), *Language acquisition*, New York: John Benjamins.

Major, R.C., 1977, 'Phonological differentiation of a bilingual child', *Papers in Psycholinguistics and Sociolinguistics, Working Papers in Linguistics* 22, 88–122.

Major, R.C., 2001, *Foreign accent: The ontogeny and phylogeny of second language phonology*, Hillsdale, NJ: Lawrence Erlbaum.

Major, R.C., 2008, 'Transfer in second language phonology', in J.G.H. Edwards and M.L. Zampini (eds.), *Phonology and second language acquisition*, pp. 63–94, Philadelphia/Amsterdam: John Benjamins. https://doi.org/10.1075/sibil.36.05maj

Marian, V. and Spivey, M., 2003, 'Competing activation in bilingual language processing: Within- and between language competition', *Bilingualism: Language and Cognition* 6(2), 97–115. https://doi.org/10.1017/S1366728903001068

McLaughlin, B., 1978, *Second language acquisition in childhood*, Hillsdale, NJ: Lawrence Erlbaum.

McLaughlin, B., 1995, *Fostering second language development in young children: Principles and practices*, NCRCDSLL Educational Practice Reports, Online: http://escholarship.org/uc/item/23s607sr.

Meisel, J.M., 2010, 'Age of onset in successive acquisition of bilingualism: Effects on grammatical development', in M. Kail and M. Hickman (eds.), *Language acquisition across linguistic and cognitive systems*, pp. 225–47, Amsterdam: John Benjamins. https://doi.org/10.1075/lald.52.16mei

Menn, L., 2013, 'Development of articulatory, phonetic, and phonological capabilities', in M.M. Vihman and T. Keren-Portnoy (eds.), *The emergence of phonology: Whole-word approaches and cross-linguistic evidence*, pp. 168–214, Cambridge, UK: Cambridge University Press. https://doi.org/10.1017/CBO9780511980503.009

Menn, L. and Matthei, E., 1992, 'The "Two-Lexicon" account of child phonology looking ahead', in C.A. Ferguson, L. Menn and C. Stoel-Gammon (eds.), *Phonological development: Models, research, implications*, pp. 211–47, Timonium, MD: York Press.

Montrul, S.A., 2009, 'Re-examining the fundamental difference hypothesis: What can early bilinguals tell us?', *Studies in Second Language Acquisition* 31(2), 225–57. https://doi.org/10.1017/S0272263109090299

Montrul, S.A., 2014, *Incomplete acquisition in bilingualism: Re-examining the age factor*, Amsterdam/Philadelphia: John Benjamins.

Müller, N. and Hulk, A., 2001, 'Crosslinguistic influence in bilingual acquisition: Italian and French as recipient languages', *Bilingualism: Language and Cognition* 4, 1–21. https://doi.org/10.1017/s1366728901000116

Munro, M.J. and Derwing, T.M., 2008, 'Segmental acquisition in adult ESL learners: A longitudinal study of vowel production', *Language Learning* 58(3), 479–502. https://doi.org/10.1111/j.1467-9922.2008.00448.x

Nemser, W., 1971, 'Approximate systems of foreign language learners', *International Review of Applied Linguistics* 9, 115–24.

Online Etymology Dictionary, 2016, retrieved from http://www.etymonline.com/index. php?term=language, December 8, 2016.

Oxford Living Dictionaries, 2016, retrieved from https://en.oxford dictionaries. com/definition/language, December 10, 2016.

Paradis, J., 2000, 'Beyond "One system or two": Degrees of separation between languages of French-English bilingual children', in S. Döpke (ed.), *Cross-linguistic structures in simultaneous bilingualism*, pp. 175–200, Amsterdam/Philadelphia: John Benjamins.

Paradis, J., Genesee, F. and Crago, M.B., 2010, *Dual language development and disorders*, Baltimore: Paul H. Brookes Publishing Company.

Pavlenko, A. (ed.), 2008, *The bilingual mental lexicon: Interdisciplinary approaches*, Clevedon, UK: Multilingual Matters.

Piske, T., and Young-Scholten, M. (eds.), 2009, *Input matters in SLA*, Clevedon, UK: Multilingual Matters.

Place, S. and Hoff, E., 2011, 'Properties of dual language exposure that influence 2-year olds' bilingual proficiency', *Child Development* 82(6), 1834–49. https://doi.org/10.1111/j.1467-8624.2011.01660.x

Prince, A. and Smolensky, P., 2004, *Optimality theory: Constraint interaction in generative grammar*, Oxford, UK: Basil Blackwell. https://doi.org/10.1002/9780470759400

Pye, C., Ingram, D. and List, H., 1987, 'A comparison of initial consonant acquisition in English and Quiche', in K.E. Nelson and A. van Kleeck (eds.), *Children's language*, Hillsdale, NJ: Lawrence Erlbaum.

Reber, A.S., 1993, *Implicit learning and tacit knowledge: An essay on the cognitive unconscious*, New York, NY: Oxford.

Reber, A.S. and Allen, R., 1978, 'Analogic and abstraction strategies in synthetic grammar learning: A functionalist interpretation', *Cognition* 6, 189–221. https://doi.org/10.1016/0010-0277(78)90013-6

Riney, T.J. and Flege, J.E., 1998, 'Changes over time in global foreign accent and liquid identifiability and accuracy', *Studies in Second Language Acquisition* 20, 213–43. https://doi.org/10.1017/S0272263198002058

Sampson, G.P. and Richards, J.C., 1973, 'Learner language systems', *Language Sciences* 19, 18–25.

Schlyter, S., 1993, 'The weaker language in bilingual Swedish-French children', in K. Hyltenstam and A. Viberg (eds.), *Progression and regression in language*, Cambridge, UK: Cambridge University Press.

Schnitzer, M.L., and Krasinski, E., 1994. The development of segmental phonological production in a bilingual child, *Journal of Child Language* 21, 585–622. https://doi.org/10.1017/S0305000900009478

Schultze, F., 1880/1971, 'The speech of the child', in A. Bar-Adon and F. Leopold (eds.), *Child language: A book of readings*, pp. 187–215, Englewood Cliffs, NJ: Prentice Hall.

Selinker, L., 1972, 'Interlanguage', *International Review of Applied Linguistics* 10, 209–31. https://doi.org/10.1515/iral.1972.10.1-4.209

Selinker, L., Swain, M. and Dumas, G., 1975, 'The interlanguage hypothesis extended to children', *Language Learning* 25(1), 139–52. https://doi.org/10.1111/j.1467-1770.1975.tb00114.x

Singleton, D., 1999, *Exploring the second language mental lexicon*, Cambridge, UK: Cambridge University Press. https://doi.org/10.1017/CBO9781139524636

Skinner, B.F., 1957, *Verbal behavior*, Englewood Cliffs, NJ: Prentice Hall. https://doi.org/10.1037/11256-000

Smith, N.V., 1973, *The acquisition of phonology: A case study*, Cambridge Studies in Linguistics 25, Cambridge, UK: Cambridge University Press.

Stampe, D., 1979, *A dissertation on natural phonology*, New York, NY: Garland.

Swain, M., 1972, *Bilingualism as a first language*, unpublished doctoral dissertation, University of California, Irvine, USA.

Tessier, A-M., 2016, *Phonological acquisition: Child language and constraint-based grammar*, London: Palgrave Macmillan. https://doi.org/10.1007/978-1-137-54306-6

Unsworth, S., Parodi, T., Sorace, A. and Young-Scholten, M. (eds.), 2006, *Paths of development in L1 and L2 acquisition*, Amsterdam/Philadelphia: John Benjamins.

Van Geert, P., 1994, *Dynamic systems of development: Change between complexity and chaos*, New York, NY: Harvester Wheatsheaf.

Van Patten, B. and Williams, J., 2014, *Theories in second language acquisition* (2nd edn.), New York, NY: Routledge.

Vihman, M.M., 2014, *Phonological development: The first two years* (2nd edn.), Malden, MA: Wiley-Blackwell.

Vihman, M.M., 2015, 'Perception and production in phonological development', in B. MacWhinney and W. O'Grady (eds.), *Handbook of language emergence*, pp. 437–57, Malden, MA: Wiley-Blackwell. https://doi.org/10.1002/9781118346136.ch20

Vihman, M.M. and Keren-Portnoy, T. (eds.), 2013, *The emergence of phonology: Whole-word approaches and cross-linguistic evidence*, Cambridge, UK: Cambridge University Press.

Weinert, S., 2009, 'Implicit and explicit modes of learning: Similarities and differences from a developmental perspective', *Linguistics* 47(2), 241–71.

Weinreich, U., 1953, *Languages in contact: Findings and problems*, The Hague: Mouton.

Wright, C., Piske, T. and Young-Scholten, M. (eds.), in preparation, *Mind matters in SLA*, Bristol: Multilingual Matters.

Yavaş, M., 1994, *First and second language phonology*, San Diego: Singular Publishing Group.

Elena Babatsouli is the Director of the Institute of Monolingual and Bilingual Speech in Greece, whose purpose is the advancement and dissemination of scientific knowledge in monolingual and bilingual acquisition and use, typical and atypical. She has a BA in English from the University of London, an MA in Languages and Business from London South Bank University, and a

PhD in Linguistics from the University of Crete. Her publications and research interests are in language acquisition and use by children and adults, with a focus on phonology and morphology. She co-chaired the organization of the *International Symposium of Monolingual and Bilingual Speech 2015* and is co-editor of its *Proceedings* and of *Crosslinguistic encounters in language acquisition: Typical and atypical development* (Multilingual Matters, 2017).

David Ingram is Professor in the Department of Speech and Hearing Science at Arizona State University. He received his BS from Georgetown University and his PhD in Linguistics from Stanford University. His research interests are in language acquisition in typically developing children and children with language disorders, with a crosslinguistic focus. The language areas of interest are phonological, morphological and syntactic acquisition. He is the author of *Phonological disability in children* (1976) *Procedures for the phonological analysis of children's language* (1981) and *First language acquisition* (1989). His most recent work has focused on whole word measures of phonological acquisition.

PROTOLANGUAGE

1
Are speech sound disorders phonological or articulatory? A spectrum approach

David Ingram, A. Lynn Williams and Nancy Scherer

Introduction

In the beginning was the word, and the word was 'speech' (Van Riper 1939). The field of speech and hearing is appropriately labelled if we consider the origins of speech intervention and its focus on an inability to articulate, a focus that dominated for most of the first half of the 20th century. Meanwhile, in another universe populated by linguists, the attention was on typical articulation of language, and the field of child phonology emerged. One of the leaders of the early phonologists referred to as the Prague School, was Roman Jakobson. Jakobson was not just interested in the phonological structures of languages and the ways in which languages' speech sounds are articulated, but also in understanding how children acquire the phonological system of a language. The suggestion that phonological issues also needed to be considered in instances of speech difficulties began to appear in articles in the 1960s and 1970s, and that approach was the focus of *Phonological disability in children* (Ingram 1976).

The impact of having phonological assessments become part of the field of speech disorders created a conundrum concerning how to refer to children with them. In 1985, Stoel-Gammon and Dunn published *Normal and disordered phonology in children*, using the term 'phonology' in the title. Meanwhile, other works held to the previous focus on speech and articulation, as seen in the book *Articulation disorders* (Sommers 1983). In recent years, speech has made a comeback, as seen in the textbook *Children's speech sound disorders* (Bowen 2015). To be fair, Bowen emphasizes that 'speech sound disorders' is a generic term, one which is to be considered neutral regarding the extent to which a child's articulation difficulties are the result of an inability to articulate per se or an inability to establish a phonological system.

The return of speech to the forefront is the result of a complex of factors. For some, it may be a form of intransigence, in that speech to an extent is a more accessible concept, and speech problems for decades were seen as articulatory problems. Certain difficulties such as fluency appear to be very articulatory, as well as specific error patterns such as a child's inability to produce an [r], or an [s], the latter pattern traditionally referred to as lisping. There is a movement in the United States for oral motor speech intervention, in which children blow whistles, and do other exercises to manipulate and strengthen the articulators. The appeal of speech is also likely due to some extent to the more abstract and in turn nebulous nature of phonological assessment. It imposes another layer of assessment that does not always seem to add much to intervention. For example, Ingram (1992) discussed four distinct phonological analyses of why a child might show a phonological process of fronting velar stops, using alveolar stops in their place, e.g. 'go' as [do]. The clinical decision in each case, it was concluded, was to teach the child to say [k] and [g]. Such conclusions are not strong incentives for speech-language pathologists to rush off to their closest university to take courses in phonological theory.

Our purpose is to propose a more inclusive view of the interface between speech and phonology. The general idea, to be expanded and demonstrated below, is to consider the influence of articulation and phonological organization on a child's word productions as a spectrum, one in which articulation is on one end and phonology is on the other. (The reader is encouraged to view this spectrum in any perspective that works for them, for example horizontal or vertical, and with articulation and phonology at either end.) For example, a child whose speech is developing typically for all intents and purposes with high intelligibility, but with a specific problem with [r], would fall on one extreme of the spectrum. Another child, with very low intelligibility and multiple error patterns, is likely more toward the other end, where both articulatory and phonological patterns need to be identified.

The exposition of this proposal will proceed as follows. We will begin with a discussion of phonology, and provide the basic evidence of why in many cases phonological assessment is necessary. This will lead to a distinction between delay versus disorder, one that is of importance and interwoven with the contrast of articulation and phonology. Some preliminary results will be provided to show that the distinction is of clinical importance, and that articulatory factors lead to patterns suggestive of a phonological disorder, while phonological factors suggest patterns of delay. The central part of the chapter will follow with reports on two studies. One is a case study of a child with a speech sound disorder, in the sense of Bowen (2015). It will be shown that the child's error patterns are best understood by identifying those errors that are influenced by phonological factors versus those that are more articulatory. The analysis places the child along the articulation/phonology spectrum. The second study is a longitudinal group study of young children with clefts. These children could be anticipated to show primarily articulatory errors due to their anatomical anomalies. The results indicate that the children began speech development with a wide range of atypical patterns with great individual variation, while a year later they showed substantial advances and much more typical development. Their development is best understood by seeing the interaction of articulatory and phonological influences, with their development moving from the former end of the spectrum toward the other.

Phonology

The most influential early work on phonological development in children is the book *Child language, aphasia and phonological universals* by the Russian linguist Roman Jakobson, first published in German in 1941, and translated into English in 1968. Jakobson proposed that phonological factors are at play in the earliest words that children produce. The extent to which this is true has been challenged by some in the modern era, but this debate is not at stake for the purposes of the present discussion, given the age and stages of the children discussed. At the core of Jakobson's theory is the principle of 'maximal contrast', which proposes that children establish phonological distinctions that are distinct from the sounds that are articulated. (1) provides a hypothetical example of a child's acquisition of the non-labial stop consonants /t, k, d, g/.

(1) /t/ pronounced as [t] /k/ pronounced as [t] /g/ pronounced as [k]

From an articulation perspective, we might expect that the child would produce [t] first, and then later [k], though the identification of the articulatory factors at work is no simple matter. Jakobson proposed, however, that the underlying emerging phonological system influences the patterns of correctness or error, not the articulatory factors alone. In this example, the phonemes /t/ and /g/ are most distinct, since they differ in both place and voice. The child's goal, under the influence of maximal contrast, is to keep these two phonemes distinct by pronouncing them distinctly. The important point in the example is that the child can articulate [k], but does not do so for the target phoneme /k/. Jakobson gives examples of this kind, one from Russian and one from English. The Russian example is actually a real example of the hypothetical one just given involving /t, k, g/. The English example is from a British child who changed /l/ to [j], but deleted the phoneme /j/.

The importance of these kinds of substitution patterns should not be underestimated by their simplicity. It is not uncommon for children to be able to produce a sound, but not produce it for the corresponding phoneme in the language. A common pattern of this kind for English-speaking children, both typical and some with speech sound disorders, involves the English fricatives /s/ and /ʃ/. A hypothetical example would be saying the word *shoe* as [s], and the word *Sue* as [tu]. In the example, it can be said that the child can articulate an [s], but not for /s/. This is not to say that there may be children who cannot articulate an [s]. For these children, both *Sue* and *shoe* will be produced as stops, not as fricatives. It is important to understand that a substitution of a [t] for an /s/ can be articulatory for one child, and phonological for another. In the terminology of this chapter, the differences fall at different points on the articulation/phonology spectrum. Also importantly, a single child may show errors in some cases that are at the articulatory end, and other errors that are at the phonological end.

Phonological delay versus phonological disorder: A proposal

In a simple world, it might be reasonable to conclude at this point that maximal contrast may be a heuristic for distinguishing phonological delay from phonological disorder. Here, we will define phonological delay as an instance of a child who is typically developing except for their rate of acquisition (no easy matter by the way, given the extent of individual differences). This child might be expected to show instances of maximal contrast. Conversely, we can define phonological disorder as distinct from a delay, in that it is the result of some problem with the mechanisms that lead to typically developing patterns. There is no consensus on what underlies a phonological disorder, though two reasonable options come to mind. One is that it is a linguistic problem with the formulation of the underlying principles at work in acquiring the phonology, such as maximal contrast. The alternative is that there is no such thing, and that a phonological disorder is actually a more complex version of an articulatory disorder. For a child who has multiple errors for fricatives, /r/ and /l/, it could be interpreted as the child having a 'fricative problem', and a separate 'liquid problem'.

Is there an empirical way to decide between delay and disorder? The simple answer is not yet. An example of how difficult it can be to determine delay from disorder can be found in one of the earliest studies on a child with a speech sound disorder, this being Nice (1925). Margaret Nice studied the language acquisition of each of her five children (all girls), and reported various aspects of their language in several articles in the first half of the 20th century. In Nice (1925), she presented the data on four of her children, one of which, R, showed both a severe delay in word acquisition (approximately 50 spoken words by age 3), and a very atypical early phonological system. If we were to define Nice's daughter by her atypical speech, she would be considered a child with a phonological disorder. The happy ending of R's development is that she caught up with her sisters by age 4, acquiring vocabulary at a rate twice that of her sisters during that year. This is a result of great significance, for a core assumption for the speech-language pathologist is that such development is possible. For our purpose, her speech development caught up as well.

In the present chapter, we will pursue a definition of delay versus disorder based on preliminary research on whole word acquisition and consonant correctness. It has been observed but not always overtly stated that children show a relation between word complexity and consonant correctness. This observation can also be stated in the reverse order, which would be that children do not acquire phonemes spontaneously. That is, there is typically no point at which children go from not being able to correctly pronounce a phoneme immediately to a point where they produce it correctly in all the words that they know. The course of correct consonant acquisition is gradual, and the gradient is most visibly the impact of word complexity. The most apparent example of this relation is found in the acquisition of sounds that occur in consonant clusters. An English-speaking child may develop a correct [s] in simple CV words at an early age, but may take several years to acquire their correct production in clusters. Another example is cases of unstressed syllable deletions. It is less obvious in other instances, and those cases need more careful study.

Preliminary results on the relation between acquiring correct consonant production in relation to word complexity is reported in Ingram (2012) for typically developing English-speaking children, and in Ingram and Purinton (2014) for typically developing Spanish-speaking children. The details of this research are beyond the purpose of the present chapter, but basically they deal with the selection of categories of word complexity. The key is to select a range of categories that are large enough to show an effect on consonant correctness but not too large as to obscure the basic effect. In the above studies two dimensions have been used (as shown below in our group study on children with clefts), these being the number of syllables in a word and whether or not a word contains one or more consonant clusters. For English, most simply these dimensions lead to four categories, monosyllables with or without clusters, and multi-syllables with and without clusters.

To measure the relation with word complexity and consonant correctness, a measure has been developed by the first author to evaluate the accuracy of a child's words called the PCC/PWP Intersect (Ingram 2015). PCC stands for 'percentage of correct consonants' and is similar to, but not exactly the same as, the one developed by Shriberg and Kwiatkowski (1982). PWP stands for the percentage (or proportion) of whole word proximity, a measure first presented in Ingram (2002). To determine a child's PWP, it is necessary first to measure the child's pMLU, or 'phonological mean length of utterance' of his or her productions, and the pMLU of the target words. The pMLU examines three aspects of the child's words, which are consonant correctness, retention of syllables as measured by the number of vowels produced, and the number of incorrect consonants (usually referred to as substitutions). The PWP is a measure of the closeness of fit of the child's pMLU to the target words. The child's PWP is then determined by dividing the child's pMLU into the target pMLU. Words which are completely correct receive a score of 100%. When the child's word has mismatches due to consonant and vowel deletions or consonant substitutions, the percentages will be lower. The PCC/PWP Intersect compares the child's PCC and PWP across categories of word complexity.

As noted in Babatsouli, Ingram and Sotopoulos (2014), PCC and PWP are in a linear relationship since the latter measure contains the former. The intersect of the two measures occurs within a predictable upper and lower boundary for any group of words selected for analysis. In Ingram (2012), the PCC/PWP Intersect was measured separately for four categories, and the following scale from highest intersect to lowest scores was found: Monosyllables without Clusters > Multisyllables without Clusters > Multisyllables with Clusters > Monosyllables with Clusters. Figure 1.1 shows this result for a typically developing child Jennika at age 1;11.

Ingram (2012) also gave preliminary results on the use of the PCC/PWP Intersect with nine children with speech sound disorders reported in Hodson and Paden (1983, 1991). The use of the Hodson and Paden children provided a means to control the assessment since all the children were given the same articulation assessment (i.e. the same words), and

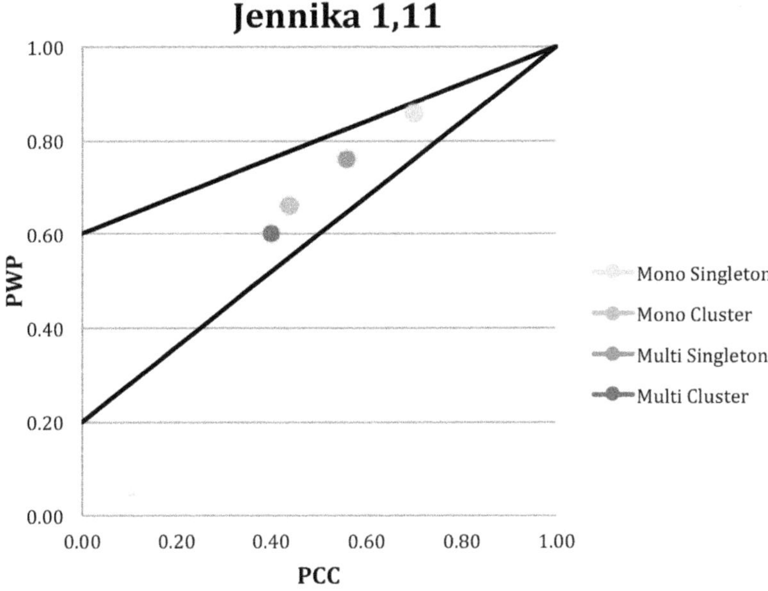

Figure 1.1. PCC/PWP Intersect for Jennika at 1;11.

transcribed in the same manner. The children fell into two groups. One group showed the correlation found for the typically developing children as shown for Jennika in Figure 1.1, though with some variation in the category ranking that needs further study. This finding is shown for participant Tim, age 5;0, in Figure 1.2. A second group, however, did *not* show the correlation. For these children the PCC ranges were very small, usually within a range of 10%. The children did, however, use consonant substitutions and retained vowels, aspects measured by PWP but not by PCC. This created a circular pattern of the plots, as shown in Figure 1.3 for participant Alan, age 5;11. For this group, the interpretation was that these children simply could not produce some consonants, regardless of word complexity. Using the notion of an articulation/phonology spectrum, these children would fall on the articulation side, while the children in the first group would be more toward the phonology side, since they showed the same correlation as found in the typically developing children. These results lead to the following hypothesis:

> (2) Hypothesis on *Delay* versus *Disorder*:
> Typically developing children and a subset of children with speech sound disorders show a correlation between consonant correctness and whole word complexity; they therefore should show patterns of phonological development distinct from an ability to produce particular speech sounds. Children who do not show a correlation between consonant correctness

and word complexity are showing primarily an articulation problem, i.e. there are specific sounds that they cannot say, regardless of the words in which they occur.

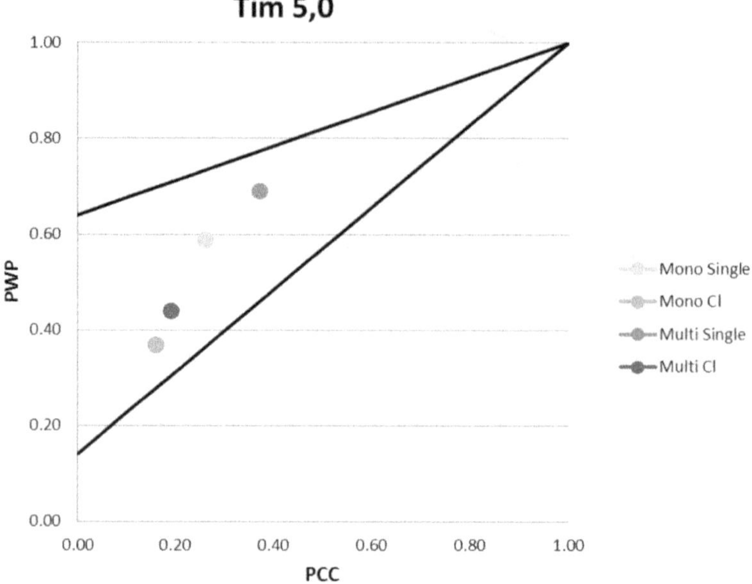

Figure 1.2. PCC/PWP Intersect for Tim at age 5;0.

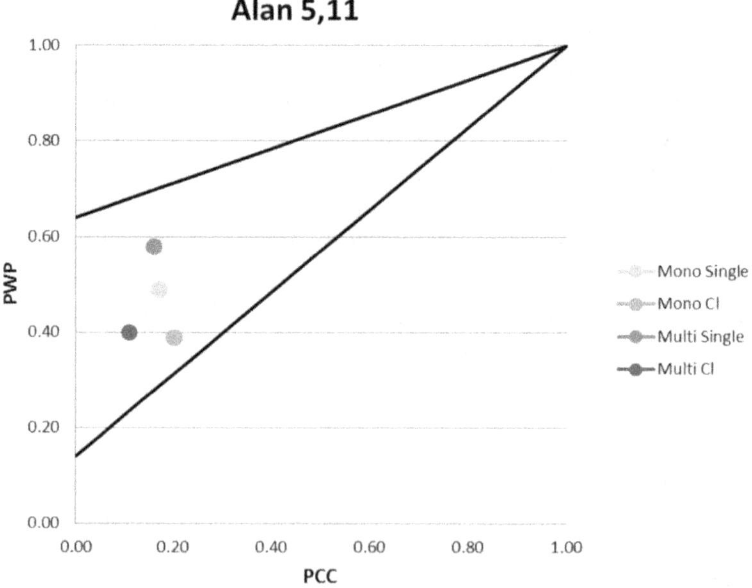

Figure 1.3. PCC/PWP Intersect for Alan at age 5;11.

CS: A case study

Our case study is a child CS who was identified as having a speech sound disorder. His speech was examined by having him produce 307 English words. The words were selected so that they provided opportunities to produce the full range of English consonants in all word positions as well as in consonant clusters. The largest group of words was for onset consonants, ranging from 10 to 20 words per phoneme. The instances for medial and final position were smaller but still ranged between 5 and 10 words per position. The present results are limited to single consonant productions in word-initial (onset) position.

The PCC was calculated for each word-initial consonant phoneme. Setting a criterion for correct usage proved to be a simple task. For consonants considered correct, they were correct 100% of the time, except for /j/ which was correct 80% (4 out of 5). Alternatively, for consonants which were not completely correct, the PCC ranged from 0.00 to 0.30. In other words, his inventory was basically two groups of phonemes, those which he could produce very well, and those which he rarely produced correctly. CS could correctly produce the following English onset consonants: /m, n, p, t, k, b, d, g, w, j, f, h/. He could not produce any other fricatives than /f/, nor affricates and liquids.

Since CS was so extreme in his rate of correct and incorrect consonants, an initial interpretation could be that he has an articulation disorder, in that he has a subset of consonants that he cannot produce correctly, regardless of word complexity. This fact also meets the definition given above about the difference between a phonological disorder versus articulation disorder based on the correlation between consonant correctness and word complexity. To confirm this hypothesis, an analysis was conducted comparable to the one that was done on the children discussed above and demonstrated in Figures 1.2 and 1.3. This was possible because the large list of words elicited from CS contained a subset of words that were the ones used by Hodson and Paden. These words were pulled from the sample and analysed in the same manner as the nine children taken from Hodson and Paden's study, as exemplified in Figures 1.2 and 1.3.

The hypothesis that CS has an articulation disorder was confirmed by the analysis (Figure 1.4). The range of PCC scores for the four categories of word complexity was very narrow, from 0.49 to 0.54. At the same time, CS was good at using consonant substitutions and syllable retention, leading to higher PWP scores, creating the circular pattern found for children with articulation difficulties.

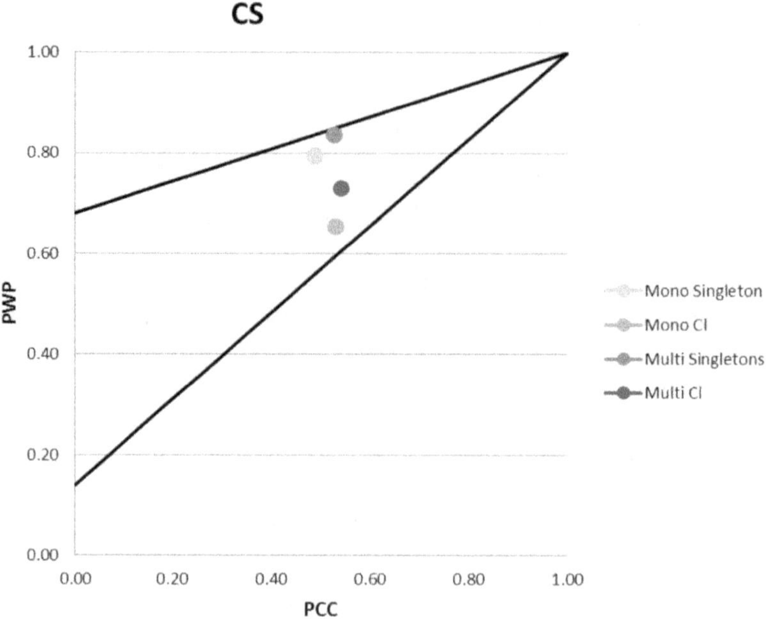

Figure 1.4. PCC/PWP Intersect for CS.

An examination of CS's substitution patterns, however, revealed that the use of the PCC/PWP Intersect does not identify a dichotomy between articulation versus phonology, but it rather indicates a strong *articulatory influence* on the child's patterns. This point can be seen by taking a look at CS's substitution patterns, which are shown in Table 1.1.

At first glance, an examination of CS's substitutions also showed evidence of the influence of articulation. For the phonemes /θ, ð, v, r, l/, CS

Table 1.1. CS's substitution patterns.

Target Phonemes	*Substitutions*	*Examples*
/s/, /ʃ/	[θ]	soup [θup], shoe [θu],
/z/	[ð]	zoo [ðu]
/tʃ/	[t] or [θ]	chalk [tɔk], chip [θɪp]
/dʒ/	[d] or [ð]	juice [duθ], juicy, [ðuθi]
/θ/	[f]	thumb [fʌm]
/ð/	[d]	that [dæt]
/v/, /r/, /l/	[w]	van [wæn], read [wid], light [wait]

substituted consonants that appear to be articulatorily simpler, based on the order in which children acquire speech sounds.

While it is the case that there is something very articulatory about CS's word productions, the conclusion that he solely had an articulation disorder runs into problems when his substitutions for the alveolar fricatives and affricates are addressed. If articulatory simplicity was the only factor at work, we would expect that the fricatives and affricates would be produced as stops, a word class normally thought to be unmarked in relation to them. CS correctly produces stop consonants, so stops are available to be the substitutions for the affricates and fricatives. This substitution occurred occasionally for the affricates, but not for the stops. Instead, CS produced the fricatives /s/, /ʃ/ as [θ] and the fricative /z/ as [ð]. For the affricates, the fricative substitutions varied with the stop substitutions. A further observation is that we have a substitution sequence that can be interpreted as an example of 'maximal contrast'. CS produced the phoneme /θ/ as an [f], but substituted a [θ] for the fricatives /s/, /ʃ/ (and substituted [ð] for [z]). This can be interpreted as a phonological series of substitutions, articulatorily marked from the perspective of markedness theory, that preserved in his words a distinction between alveolar stops and fricatives, albeit not with the correct fricatives.

The use of marked substitutions showed the influence of CS's underlying representations on his productions. The substitutions also showed that CS could articulate dental fricatives, but that he hadn't reached a stage where he did so for their phonemic targets. It is not the case, therefore, that the sole issue at stake is that there were speech sounds that he could not articulate. This leads us to a conclusion that CS showed strong articulation influences in his word productions, but also that phonological factors are operating and need to be recognized.

Children with clefts

The next study to be reported is one of the early speech development of young children with cleft lip and/or palate. These children are not a population who would be at risk for speech sound disorders, were it not for their clefts. As such, one might anticipate that, for the most part, their articulatory/phonological development would show normal sequences of development (though speech delay in onset and rate might be anticipated as well). Conversely, any speech problems could also be assumed to be traced back to their clefts. Using the focus and terminology of the present chapter, it would be a reasonable hypothesis that any speech difficulties that they show would be articulatory in nature. We have just seen, however, in the case of CS, that there were patterns in his speech that could only be accounted for by phonological factors, not articulatory ones. This can be interpreted as the result of the child attempting to establish phonological representations and phonological oppositions (i.e. phonemes) to overcome as much as possible the speech limitations. The group of children with clefts was studied to explore the same factors, that is, those speech developments that could be accounted for by articulation, and those, if any, that might show phonological organization.

The study is part of a broader study on the speech and language development of children with clefts being conducted by Nancy Scherer. The preliminary results to be discussed on speech involved 20 2-year-old children with cleft lip/palate. Two studies on the children will be reported separately. The first one concerned the children's speech relatively soon after the children's clefts had undergone repair, which will be referred to as Time 1. There were two aspects of the analyses conducted. One purpose was to examine the children's whole word development, using the PCC/PWP Intersect. The second purpose was an analysis of the phonological patterns in their samples, in particular, the extent to which the samples showed atypical patterns. As with CS, the question asked is the extent to which it can be said that their speech development was the result of articulatory factors, and the extent to which phonological factors, if any, were found. The second study examined second samples from a subset of 10 of the original children taken 7 to 10 months later (Time 2), to see if and how their speech changed.

Study 1: Time 1

The participants in the first study were 20 children with cleft lip/palate between the ages of 1;9 and 3;2, with a median age of 2;1. Each child was given a single-word, object-naming test, the *Profiles of Early Expressive Phonological Skills (PEEPS)* (Stoel-Gammon and Williams 2013), which consists of 39 words that are common in the vocabulary of 2-year-old children. The samples were first analysed using the PCC/PWP Intersect measure. Their overall PCC scores were calculated and used to place the children into four groups, five children per group, with the mean PCC scores ranging from a high of 63% for the highest performing group to 17% for the lowest one (Table 1.2). As can be seen, the children were very diverse in their abilities. Using the PCC differences between the groups,

Table 1.2. Four groups of children with clefts.

Group	*PCC (Range)*	*Age (Range)*
I	0.63 (0.66–0.55)	2,7 (3,2–2,1)
II	0.43 (0.47–0.40)	2,3 (2,8–2,0)
III	0.33 (0.39–0.27)	2,1 (2,8–1,11)
IV	0.17 (0.20–0.12)	2,0 (2,3–1,9)

we will refer to Group I as the high group, Groups II and III as the middle groups (as they were closer to each other than to the other groups), and Group IV as the low group.

Next, the children's samples were each broken into the five categories of word complexity, CV and VC words, CVC words, disyllables with clusters, CVCV words, and polysyllables (Table 1.3). This was done to examine a wider range of word categories the earlier studies reported. As mentioned earlier, the determination of word categories is somewhat arbitrary, and will vary based on the sample (test) used, as well by the language being studied. In this case, the PEEPS list is very heavy with CVC words, and all the other categories are much smaller. Articulation Tests vary greatly in their distribution of word categories. For example, the assessment used by Hodson and Paden has a much greater number of words with clusters than does the PEEPS.

The PCC/PWP measures for the four groups of children showed three patterns (Figures 1.5, 1.6, 1.7). Group IV, the one with the lowest PCC scores (mean of just 17%), showed no effect of word complexity on consonant correctness (Figure 1.5). These children looked like the subgroup from the analysis of the Hodson and Paden children (Figure 1.3), and the

Table 1.3. Five word categories of phonological complexity.

Monosyllabic Words with Single Consonants: CV, VC
cow, go, moo, shoe, toe, ear (6)

Monosyllabic Words with Final Consonants: CVC
ball, bed, bib, cheese, cup, dog, doll, duck, fish, foot, hair, hat, juice, light, mouse, mouth, nose, pig, rock, sock, woof (21)

Disyllable Words with Clusters
finger, hand, quack, truck (4)

Disyllable Words without Clusters: CVCV
baby, kitty, cookie, puppy, tummy (5)

Other: Polysyllables and Words with Non-initial Stress
balloon, banana, peekaboo (3)

analysis for CS (Figure 1.4). Based on the hypothesis in (2), these children showed a very strong influence of articulation. There were sounds the children could not say, leading to little influence of word complexity. Groups II and III were similar to each other and their results are combined for the subsequent discussion. This was not surprising since their PCCs were closer to each other than to those of the other groups. Groups II and III showed some correlation between PCC and word complexity, but the categories of word complexity collapsed into two groups. There were higher PCC scores for CV, VC and CVC words (just above 50%), and then lower PCC scores for CVC, disyllables with clusters, and polysyllables (clustering around 35% to 40%) (Figure 1.6). Lastly, the highest performing children, Group I, with a range of PCC scores across the five word categories, showed the influence of word complexity on consonant correctness (Figure 1.7). This pattern is the one that has been found for typically developing children (Figure 1.1), and one subgroup of the Hodson and Paden children (Figure 1.3).

Next, phonological analyses were conducted on each of the children's samples, following the multidimensional approach found in Ingram and Dubasik (2011). Preliminary analyses suggested that the samples from the individual children were quite varied, so a more detailed analysis was

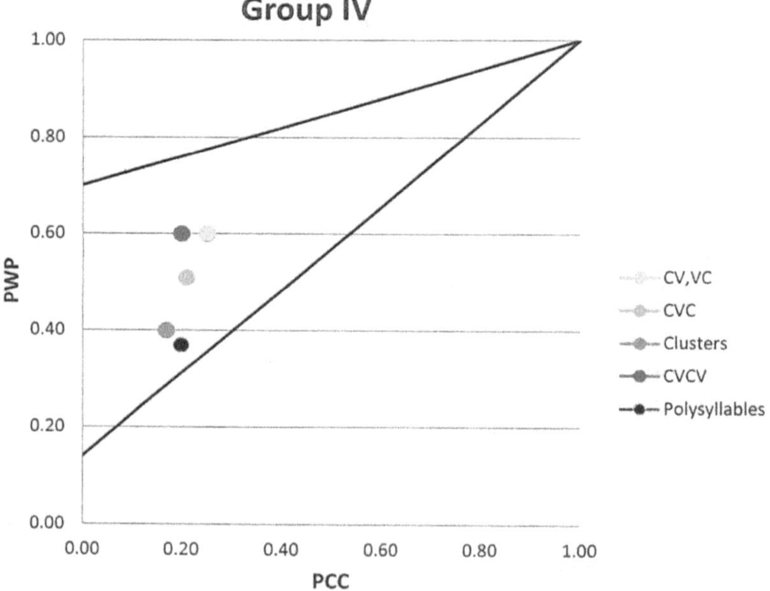

Figure 1.5. PCC/PWP Intersect for Group IV.

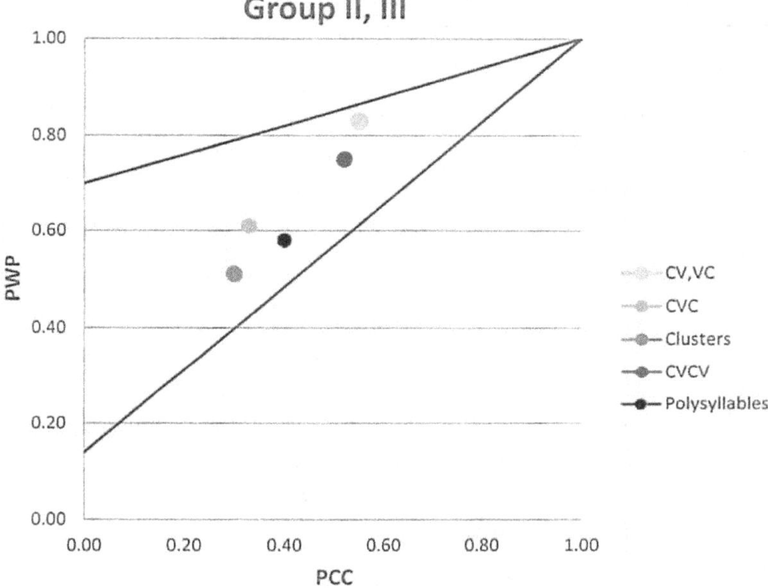

Figure 1.6. PCC/PWP Intersect for Groups II and III.

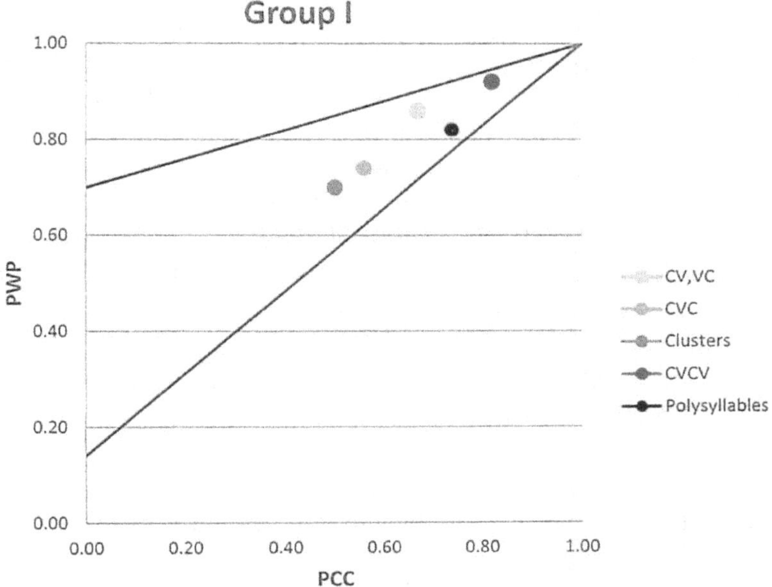

Figure 1.7. PCC/PWP Intersect for Group I.

Table 1.4. Patterns of atypical phonological development.

Gross Inclusion: Use of a single consonant substitution for multiple target phonemes (Grunwell 1981)
Backing/Fronting: Extended use of fronting velar consonants or backing alveolar consonants, resulting in a single place distinction (Ingram 1976)
Final Consonant Deletion: A lack of final consonants (Renfrew 1966)
Voice Before Place: Due to Backing/Fronting problems, child acquires the voice contrast in stops ahead of 3 place distinctions (Ingram 1997)

conducted to examine this aspect. There is no consensus on what constitutes atypical phonological development, and the literature is full of proposals. Four patterns of possible atypical development were chosen for closer analysis. These were patterns mentioned in the literature as possible markers of a phonological disorder that were also ones used by at least six of the 20 participants (Table 1.4).

The first three atypical patterns are well documented in the literature. The notion of 'Gross Inclusion' was first labelled by Grunwell (1981). We defined gross inclusion when the child used a single consonant (commonly [d]) for four or more target phonemes. Participant C1004, for example, used [d] for the target phonemes /b, p, d, s, dʒ, r/. The Backing/Fronting pattern refers to the situation in which the child is using only alveolar stops (Fronting) or velar stops (Backing) for either of the velar consonants. This pattern was assumed to be the case if 50% or more instances of the category underwent the process. Most of the children who used this pattern showed Fronting (10 of 12). Participant C1005, for example, changed /g/ to [d] (1/1 times), and /k/ to [t] 50% (2/4). Two children, however, showed a velar preference. Participant C1010 could match /p, t, k, b, g/ but changed /d/ to [g] (3/3 instances). Participant C2001 had the most striking use of Backing, in that the use of [k] as a substitute for /t, tʃ, k, s, ʃ, tʒ/ also met the criterion for Gross Inclusion. Since children normally show the deletion of some final consonants in the early stages of acquisition, Final Consonant Deletion here refers to excessive use of the process. The occurrence of this pattern as a possible sign of a speech sound disorder was reported in Renfrew (1966). In the present study, a child was determined to show FCD as an atypical process if there were no final consonants or, at most, one final consonant class (for example final [m]). Participant C1002, for example, produced 11 onset consonants in the phonetic inventory, but only one final consonant, [t], which only was used for one production.

The last atypical process considered is Voice Before Place, a process discussed in Ingram (1997). The assumption is that in more typical phonological development in English, the three places of the English stops, labial, alveolar and velar are acquired before the corresponding voice contrasts for all three. Voice Before Place describes a pattern in children who are using either Fronting or Backing, that is resulting in their using just two places of articulation, and who are also acquiring at least one voice contrast. Voice is ahead of place in the sense that a voicing feature has been acquired before the features underlying three places of articulation are acquired. The most dramatic case of Voice Before Place was reported years ago to the first author by a colleague. He had assessed a child who only had two consonants /t, d/, and [t] was used for all voiceless consonants and [d] was used for all voiced ones. A more common example of such a system would be /p, b, t, d/ with the velars undergoing Fronting. The following stop consonant inventories of the children with clefts met this pattern: [b, p], [b, p, d], [b, d, t], [b, p, t, d], [d, t, g, k].

The results of the identification of atypical patterns found that 17 of the 20 children showed at least one atypical pattern of development. The usage of atypical patterns varied across the four groups based on PCC. The number of atypical patterns decreased as PCC increased. The distribution of each of the four patterns is given in Table 1.5. Their distribution varied across the four groups of children. The children with the lowest PCC scores, Groups III and IV, used two patterns more than the advanced groups, these being Gross Inclusion and Final Consonant Deletion. The Backing/Fronting pattern occurred across all four groups. Lastly, the Voice Before Place pattern was found more frequently in the higher performing Groups I and II. Also, the actual patterns varied greatly by individual children. More detailed analysis would lead to a claim that virtually every child was unique.

The sequence of these patterns is important in understanding the articulation/phonology interface. The lowest groups have higher rates of the first three processes in Table 1.5. These processes are very articulatory in nature, and involve either deletion of a sound or using a sound they can

Table 1.5. Distribution of four atypical patterns.

Pattern	I	II	III	IV
Gross Inclusion	0	2	4	4
Backing/Fronting	4	1	3	4
Final Consonant Deletion	0	0	4	4
Voice Before Place	2	2	2	0
Totals	6	5	13	12

make for one that they cannot. Voice Before Place, however, can be seen as more phonological in nature. The child who is having Backing/Fronting problems continues their phonological acquisition by adding a new phonological feature, Voice. This pattern was twice as frequent for the two higher groups.

Summary

The results of Study 1 indicate that the children with clefts cannot be said uniformly to be undergoing either typical or atypical development. Their typicality depended on where they were in their speech development. The children in the lowest group looked like atypical children showing a speech sound disorder. They did not show a relationship between consonant correctness and word complexity. In other words, there were many sounds that they simply couldn't say. At the other extreme, the children in the highest group looked typically developing in that they did show a relationship between word complexity and consonant correctness. They were doing well with CV, VC and polysyllables, with PCC scores around 80%. They were doing less well with CVC words and words with clusters, where PCC scores dropped to around 55%. The middle groups were in between, and showed a pattern suggesting that they were transitioning from the articulatory restrictions of the lowest group toward the typical pattern of the highest group.

Study 2: Time 2

Given the results of Study 1, a second study was undertaken to discover how the three group patterns in Study 1 developed over time. Two basic questions were formulated: one, did the three groups develop similarly or not, and two, what was the rate of development for each group? To explore these questions, children were selected from each group who had follow-up samples taken within 7 to 10 months of the first samples. At least two children from each of the four groups was selected. Ten children from Study 1 were subsequently selected and their phonological samples assessed at the later time. Sample information is found in Table 1.6.

The children in all groups showed marked gains in their PCC from Sample 1 to Sample 2: Group I: 21%; Group II: 32%; Group III: 40%; Group IV: 66%. There was a correlation between PCC at Time 1 and Time 2 based on the size of PCC at Time 1. The lower the PCC at Time 1, the greater increase was found at Time 2. The increases in consonant correctness also took place in all five of the categories of word complexity. The differences

Table 1.6. Number of children, mean age, mean PCC for four groups.

	(n)	*Sample 1*		*Sample 2*	
		Age	*PCC*	*Age*	*PCC*
I	(3)	2,10	0.62	3,6	0.83
II	(3)	2,3	0.44	3,1	0.76
III	(2)	2,5	0.36	3,1	0.76
IV	(2)	2,1	0.17	2,8	0.83

between the categories were small, since the overall PCC scores were so high, yet they showed similar variations as discussed above for typically developing children. The words with CV, VC, and CVCV shapes showed the highest levels of consonant correctness. Slightly below were the percentages for words with clusters and final consonants (see Figure 1.8).

None of the 10 children at Time 2 showed any atypical patterns. The children at this point had all acquired velar consonants, a number of final consonants, and voicing in stop consonants. In addition, they all had acquired a range of fricatives. Their consonant inventories were similar to those of typically developing children.

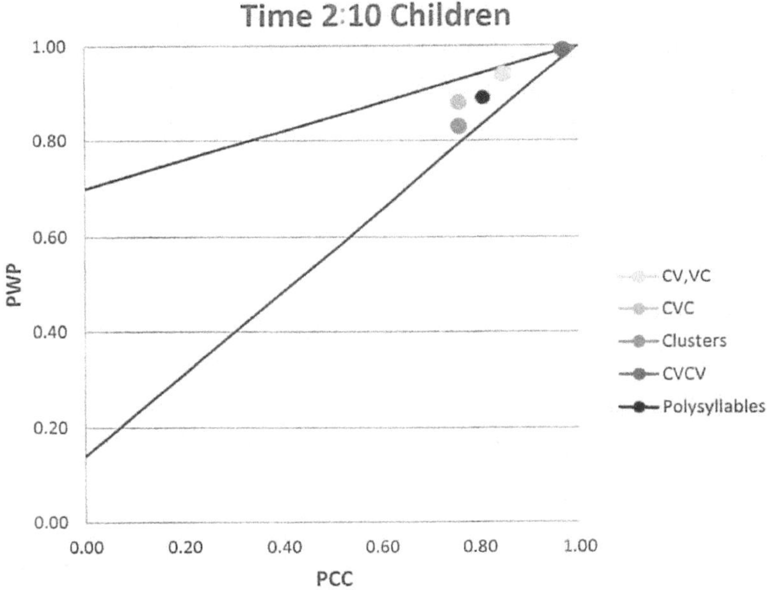

Figure 1.8. PCC/PWP Intersect for 10 children of Study 2.

Summary

We have presented the case that speech sound disorders should not be viewed as either the result of an articulatory problem or a phonological problem. Instead, they are best understood if both factors are taken into consideration. The proposal is that speech sound disorders be assessed within a model that sees the interaction of articulation and phonology as a spectrum upon which both reside. For some children, the phonological patterns are clearly identifiable; for children at the articulatory end, when children 'can't say the word', they still exist except in the extreme cases such as motor speech disorders. The evidence of the value of this perspective was demonstrated by both a case study and a group study. The case study of CS showed that the child's speech errors were in some cases articulatory in nature, in that there were consonants that he was unable to say correctly, regardless of the words used to assess them. Some of the child's sound substitutions, however, were phonological in nature, in that the substitutions were not the replacement of one consonant by another that was simpler to articulate, but by one that maintained phonological contrasts. The group study involved the speech assessment of children with clefts. This population is one that might be anticipated to show articulation errors due to their clefts. The children were found to show extreme variation in their speech, and patterns that were best understood by consideration of both articulation and phonology. Despite having a clear articulation difficulty to overcome, they uniquely demonstrated phonological influences on their speech development. The longitudinal assessment of the children revealed that the atypical nature of their early speech developed within less than a year to a phonological system that much more appeared to be developing typically, with some speech delay.

References

Babatsouli, E., Ingram, D. and Sotopoulos, D., 2014, 'Phonological word complexity in child speech development', *Chaotic Modelling and Simulation (CMSIM)* 3, 295–313.

Bowen, C., 2015, *Children's speech sound disorders* (2nd edn.), Oxford: Wiley-Blackwell.

Grunwell, P., 1981, *The nature of phonological disability in children*, London: Academic Press.

Hodson, B. and Paden, E., 1983, *Targeting intelligible speech: A phonological approach to remediation*, San Diego: College-Hill Press.

Hodson, B. and Paden, E., 1991, *Targeting intelligible speech: A phonological approach to remediation* (2nd edn.), San Diego: College-Hill Press.

Ingram, D., 1976, *Phonological disability in children*, London: Edward.

Ingram, D., 1992, 'Diagnostic implications of phonological underspecification', Poster, *Annual Meeting of the American Speech-Language-Hearing Association*, San Antonio, Texas.

Ingram, D., 1997, 'The categorization of phonological impairment', in B. Hodson and M. Edwards (eds.), *Applied phonology: Theoretical perspectives and clinical implications*, pp. 19–41, Frederick, Maryland: Aspen.

Ingram, D., 2002, 'The measurement of whole-word productions', *Journal of Child Language* 29, 713–33. https://doi.org/10.1017/s0305000902005275

Ingram, D., 2012, 'A comparison of two measures of phonological assessment: PCC & PWP', Seminar, *Annual meeting of the American Speech-Language-Hearing Association*, Atlanta.

Ingram, D., 2015, 'Whole-word measures: Using the PCC-PWP Intersect to distinguish speech delay from speech disorder', in C. Bowen (ed.), *Children's speech sound disorders* (2nd edn.), pp. 100–04, Oxford: Wiley-Blackwell.

Ingram, D. and Dubasik, V., 2011, 'Multidimensional assessment of phonological similarity within and between children', *Clinical Linguistics & Phonetics* 25(11–12), 962–67. https://doi.org/10.3109/02699206.2011.617855

Ingram, D. and Purinton, K., 2014, 'The interaction of word complexity and consonant correctness in Spanish-speaking children', Paper, *International Child Language Conference*, Missoula, Montana.

Jakobson, R., 1941/1968, *Child language, aphasia and phonological universals*, The Hague: Mouton, translation by R. Keiler of original 1941 German version.

Nice, M.M., 1925, 'A child who would not talk', *Pedagogical Seminary* 25, 105–42. https://doi.org/10.1080/08856559.1925.10532320

Renfrew, C.E., 1966, 'Persistence of the open syllable in defective articulation', *Journal of Speech and Hearing Disorders* 31, 370–73. https://doi.org/10.1044/jshd.3104.370

Shriberg, L.D. and Kwiatkowski, J., 1982, 'Phonological disorders IIIA procedure for assessing severity of involvement', *Journal of Speech & Hearing Disorders* 47(3), 256–70. https://doi.org/10.1044/jshd.4703.256

Sommers, R., 1983, *Articulation disorders*, Englewood Cliffs, NJ: Prentice-Hall.

Stoel-Gammon, C. and Dunn, C., 1985, *Normal and disordered phonology in children*, Baltimore: University Park Press.

Stoel-Gammon, C. and Williams, A.L., 2013, 'Early phonological development: Creating an assessment test', *Clinical Linguistics & Phonetics* 27, 278–86. https://doi.org/10.3109/02699206.2013.766764

Van Riper, C., 1939, *The nature of stuttering, the treatment of stuttering and speech correction: Principles and methods*, Englewood Cliffs, NJ: Prentice-Hall.

David Ingram is Professor in the Department of Speech and Hearing Science at Arizona State University. He received his BS from Georgetown University and his PhD in Linguistics from Stanford University. His research interests are in language acquisition in typically developing children and children with language disorders, with a crosslinguistic focus. The language areas of interest are phonological, morphological and syntactic acquisition. He is the author of *Phonological disability in children* (1976), *Procedures for the phonological analysis of children's language* (1981) and *First language acquisition* (1989). His most recent work has focused on whole word measures of phonological acquisition.

A. Lynn Williams, PhD, CCC-SLP, is an Associate Dean for the College of Clinical and Rehabilitative Health Sciences and Professor in the Department of Audiology and Speech-Language Pathology at East Tennessee State University in Johnson City, Tennessee. Her research and practice have focused on developing assessment and intervention models that utilize linguistic methodology and principles to describe and treat disordered sound systems. Lynn is the author of several articles, book chapters and books, is the current Associate Editor of the *American Journal of Speech-Language Pathology*, a Fellow of ASHA, and ASHA Vice President for Academic Affairs in Speech-Language Pathology (2016–18).

Nancy Scherer is currently Professor and Chair in the Speech and Hearing Science Department at Arizona State University. Her research and clinical interests are in the areas of speech and language development and intervention for children with craniofacial conditions. Her research has focused on developing and validating intervention models including parent implemented intervention, telehealth delivery and training community health professionals in rural and international contexts with the goal of preventing long-term speech disorders. Her research funding includes grants from the National Institutes of Health (NIDCD) and Department of Education.

2 Crosslinguistic interaction in early bilingual phonology: A critical review

Margaret Kehoe

Introduction

During the last two to three decades, there has been considerable research investigating the phonetic and phonological abilities of young bilingual children. This research shows that bilingual children do not differ greatly from monolingual children in terms of global phonological ability (Fabiano-Smith and Goldstein 2010a; Goldstein and Washington 2001; Hambly, Wren, McLeod and Roulstone 2013); however, they may differ in qualitative and quantitative ways from monolingual children in specific linguistic areas, such as Voice Onset Time (VOT), production of coda consonants and onset clusters, and rhythm (Almeida, Rose and Freitas 2012; Bunta and Ingram 2007; Fabiano-Smith and Barlow 2010; Kehoe, Lleó and Rakow 2004; Lleó, Kuchenbrandt, Kehoe and Trujillo 2003; Mayr, Howells and Lewis 2015; Mok 2011, 2013; Tamburelli, Sanoudaki, Jones and Sowinska 2015). The presence of systematic differences between monolingual and bilingual speech suggests that there is interaction between the two linguistic systems of the bilingual, a phenomenon referred to as crosslinguistic interaction.

The aim of this chapter is to examine findings on crosslinguistic interaction in the phonetic and phonological development of young bilinguals. By 'young bilinguals,' we refer to children under the age of five years who are acquiring two or more languages. Our literature review shows that there is considerable variability across studies, meaning that many of the findings are not easily generalizable. The focus of this chapter is, then, to explore reasons for this lack of generalizability and to consider ways that it can be overcome. The chapter is divided into two main parts. The first part provides an overview and historical perspective of phonetic and phonological research in early bilingualism, followed by a closer examination of crosslinguistic interaction. The second part starts with a critical look at current research and the research model, and moves on to a presentation of new data.

Research in early bilingualism

Overview and historical perspective

Consistent with the theme of the current volume, we view the field of early bilingualism as sharing many commonalities with the larger fields of first- and second-language acquisition. Both first-language acquisition and early bilingualism are concerned with children who are in the process of developing their phonological representations, articulatory, acoustic-perceptual and higher-level, as well as their speech-motor control (Munson 2004; Munson, Edwards and Beckman 2005; Nittrouer 1992). Early bilingualism and second-language acquisition deal in both cases with language contact, and similar outcomes may arise from the typological characteristics of the two languages under contact, regardless of whether the two languages come together in a young head or an adult one.

If we examine speech production studies in early bilingualism from a historical perspective, two important landmarks can be discerned. The first is the idea promoted by Volterra and Taeschner (1978) that bilingual children speak a mixed sort of language at the beginning. The second is the notion of crosslinguistic interaction introduced by Paradis and Genesee (1996), who argue that bilingual children operate with two systems from the beginning but with the possibility of interaction between the two systems. Since that time, we have not seen any major change in the orientation of the research, although some recent studies suggest new developments, notably a study by Lleó and Cortés (2013) which attempts to model crosslinguistic interaction, and one by Vihman (2015) which takes a critical stance towards the Paradis and Genesee (1996) position, arguing that it is 'more programmatic than empirically testable'. Given an emergent view of phonology, Vihman (2015) points out that the question of whether there is one or two systems need not be asked. We do not focus on the first landmark since the view of a single system as proposed by Volterra and Taeschner (1978) has been severely criticized both empirically and methodologically (De Houwer 1990; Genesee 1989; Meisel 1989). We focus instead on the programme of research stimulated by Paradis and Genesee's (1996) article, in which the possibility of both separation and interaction was entertained.

Definition of crosslinguistic interaction

Paradis and Genesee (1996: 3) define crosslinguistic interaction (or interdependence) as 'the systemic influence of the grammar of one language on the grammar of the other language during acquisition, causing differences in a bilingual's patterns and rates of development in comparison with a monolingual's'. They consider three potential manifestations of crosslinguistic interaction, which are summarized below:

1. **Transfer**: the incorporation of a grammatical property into one language from the other;
2. **Acceleration**: the situation in which a certain property emerges in the grammar earlier than would be the norm in monolingual acquisition;
3. **Delay**: the situation in which a certain property emerges later than would be the norm in monolingual acquisition.[1]

In addition, the two grammars may not interact at all, in which case a bilingual's grammatical development would resemble that of two monolinguals. This is referred to as **autonomous development**.

Before we consider some classic examples of crosslinguistic interaction, some clarification of terminology is necessary. The use of 'transfer' here refers specifically to the presence of a non-native sound or structure in one of the bilingual's languages which comes from its presence in the other bilingual's language. It should not be confused with a more general employment of 'transfer' which is used synonymously with crosslinguistic interaction (e.g. positive and negative transfer). Rather than the term 'delay', Fabiano-Smith and Goldstein (2010b) recommend the term 'deceleration' since the former may have pejorative connotations suggesting impairment. For the purposes of this article, we maintain the original terms proposed by Paradis and Genesee (1996).

1 We characterize 'delay' as the opposite of acceleration. Paradis and Genesee (1996) suggest that the 'burden of acquiring two languages could slow down the acquisition process' which is an outdated interpretation of delay according to Tamburelli et al. (2015).

Examples of crosslinguistic interaction

The examples of crosslinguistic interaction presented below stem from studies conducted at the Research Centre for Multilingualism in Hamburg, Germany. Four simultaneous bilinguals were recorded from the onset of word production through to six years (Project B3/E3). Three other bilingual children were tested from word production through to two/three years of age (Project PEDSES). The bilinguals were children of Spanish-speaking mothers and German-speaking fathers. Each parent followed the 'une personne, une langue' rule by addressing the child in his/her respective language. In addition, four monolingual Spanish children were recorded in Madrid, Spain, and five monolingual German children were recorded in Hamburg, Germany, from the onset of words through to about three years (Project PAIDUS; see Lleó 2012, for a detailed description of the monolingual and bilingual corpora). All children were audio-recorded in their homes, while interacting with a parent and an experimenter. Sessions were phonetically transcribed by native speakers of the respective languages.

Acceleration

An example of acceleration comes from a study by Lleó et al. (2003) on the acquisition of syllable-final consonants or codas. An important phonological difference between German and Spanish is in the area of syllable structure. Spanish has less complex syllable structure than German. Spanish rhymes consist of a single vowel (e.g. *yo* [jo] 'I'), a diphthong (e.g. *ley* [leɪ] 'law') or a vowel plus consonant (e.g. *sol* [sol] 'sun'). Only a restricted set of consonants appear in coda position, namely coronals such as /n/, /r/, /l/, /s/, /ð/, /θ/ (Harris 1983). Complex codas do occur but they are rare. In contrast, the German rhyme allows many more possibilities. It consists minimally of two positions: a long vowel or diphthong (e.g. *tee* [teː] 'tea'; *Frau* [fʁaʊ] 'woman' or 'wife') or a vowel with a consonant (e.g. *bal* [bal] 'ball'). There are no restrictions on consonants in coda position. They may be labial, coronal or dorsal. The German rhyme may consist of more than two positions: a long vowel followed by a consonant (e.g. *hahn* [haːn] 'cock'), a short vowel followed by two consonants (e.g. *mund* [mʊnt] 'mouth') or a long vowel followed by two consonants (e.g. *mond* [moːnt] 'moon'). Frequency data reveal that Spanish has 27% syllables with codas compared to German which has 67% (Meinhold and Stock 1980). In sum, codas are more frequent in German and they are more complex.

Lleó et al. (2003) posited that two types of interaction effects may be observed in bilingual German-Spanish children acquiring codas. There may be acceleration of codas in Spanish due to their high frequency in German or delay of codas in German due to their low frequency in Spanish. They examined the structural presence of codas in the productions of three monolingual Spanish, three monolingual German, and five bilingual children from word onset to 2;4 years (1 child was only tested through to 1;9).

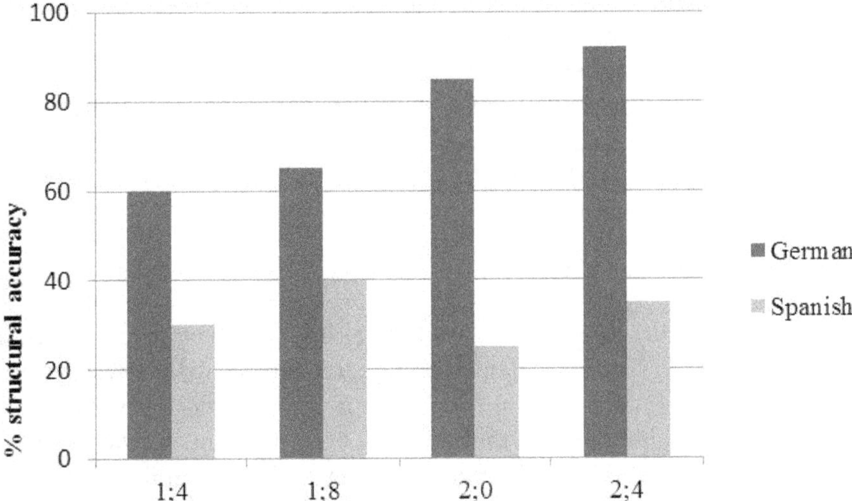

Figure 2.1. Coda production: monolinguals.

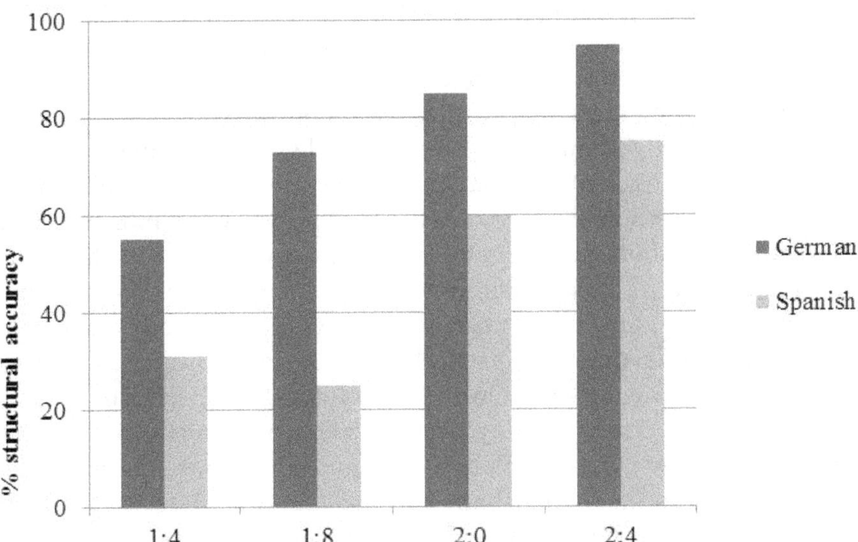

Figure 2.2. Coda production: bilinguals.

Figures 2.1 and 2.2, adapted from Lleó et al.'s (2003) study, present the findings on coda production for the monolingual and bilingual children respectively. Figure 2.1 shows that coda production was higher in German than in Spanish monolingual children at all time points, reaching over 90% at the last time point in German compared to 30 to 40% in Spanish. Figure 2.2 shows that the bilingual children started to produce relatively high percentages of codas in Spanish as of 2;0 years. Coda production remained always higher in German than in Spanish but, importantly, coda production in Spanish was higher in the bilinguals than in the monolinguals. Thus, of the two possible interaction effects predicted by Lleó et al. (2003), only one was found, namely that of acceleration of codas in Spanish. Lleó et al. (2003) hypothesize that the high frequency of codas in German influenced their production in Spanish.

Delay

An example of delay comes from a study by Kehoe (2002) on the acquisition of vowel length in German-Spanish bilinguals. The German vowel system is more complex than the Spanish one. It not only has more vowels, but it has a phonological opposition that does not exist in Spanish, vowel length, which is characterized by both quantity (phonetic length) and quality (formant frequency) differences between long and short vowels. In contrast, Spanish has a classic five-vowel system. Kehoe (2002) predicted that bilingual children might show a delay in their acquisition of vowel length. Her rationale was that vowel length is a marked phenomenon which requires a certain amount of positive evidence. In the bilingual situation, there is a dilution of this evidence leading to a possible delay in acquisition.

Kehoe (2002) conducted acoustic analyses of the word productions of three monolingual German and three bilingual German-Spanish children at two time periods: 1;10–2;0 and 2;3–2;6. The monolingual children produced long vowels significantly longer than short vowels in monosyllables and disyllables at both time periods. In contrast, the bilingual children did not produce long vowels significantly longer than short vowels in monosyllables and only some of the time in disyllables. Furthermore, the magnitude of the duration difference between long and short vowels was reduced compared to the one produced by the monolinguals (average ratio was 1.3 for bilinguals vs. 1.9 for monolinguals). This pattern is evident in Figure 2.3, which displays the duration values of long and short vowels in disyllables at 2;3–2;6 for the monolingual and bilingual children. In sum, the findings confirmed Kehoe's (2002) predictions: bilingual children experienced difficulty acquiring the marked system of German vowels. Importantly,

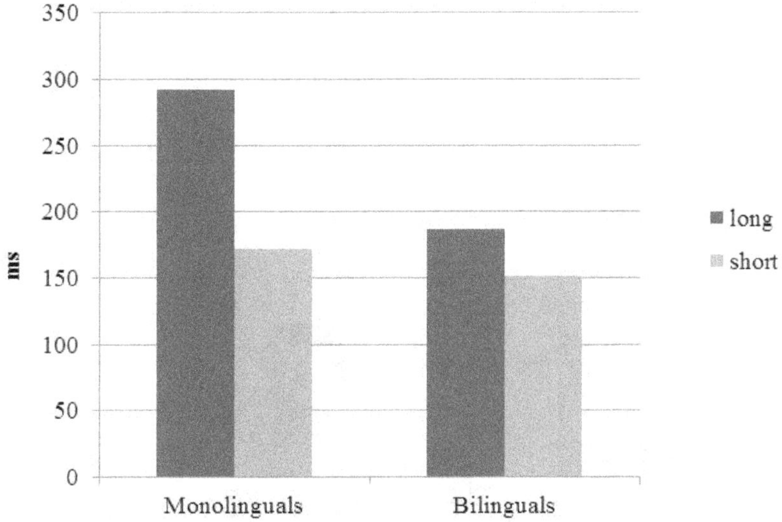

Figure 2.3. Short and long vowel duration in disyllables.

when Kehoe (2002) examined the children's acquisition of the five-vowel system in Spanish, differences between monolinguals and bilinguals were not observed.

Transfer

The final example, that of transfer, stems from a study of VOT by Kehoe et al. (2004). Both German and Spanish have voiced /b, d, g/ and voiceless /p, t, k/ stops but the phonetic basis underlying the voicing distinction is different in the two languages. In German, the opposition is between long and short lag, whereas in Spanish it is between short lag and lead voicing.

Kehoe et al. (2004) examined the acquisition of VOT in four bilingual children, aged 2;0 to 3;0 years. The bilinguals displayed several different patterns of acquisition; however, for the purposes of this section we concentrate on Nils, who, at 2;3 to 2;6, produced not only his German voiceless stops in the long lag region, but his Spanish ones were also produced with high VOT values (mean = 50 ms) (see Figure 2.4). Kehoe et al. (2004) interpreted this pattern as transfer of long lag voicing from German into Spanish. One of the possible reasons for this transfer was that Nils was becoming dominant in German due to his participation in a German kindergarten.

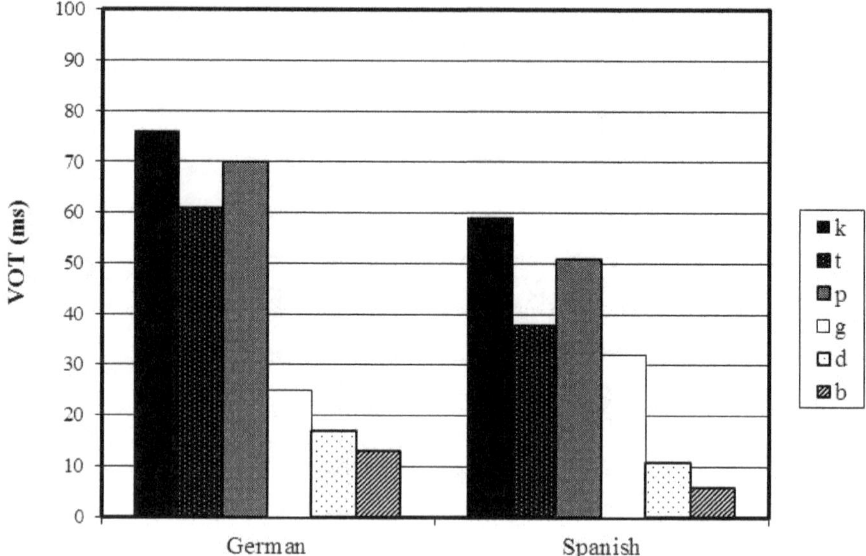

Figure 2.4. Voiceless stops produced by Nils.

In sum, findings on the same group of German-Spanish bilingual children revealed different patterns of crosslinguistic interaction: acceleration of codas in Spanish, delay of the vowel length distinction in German, and transfer of long lag voicing into Spanish.

Seeking generalizations across studies: Acquisition of codas

Having examined some classic examples of crosslinguistic interaction in the Hamburg data, we widen the literature base to look more closely at crosslinguistic interaction in other studies. We are interested in determining whether they have obtained similar results to Lleó et al. (2003) in the area of coda acquisition.

An analogous study to Lleó et al. (2003) would be that of Keffala, Barlow and Rose (2016) which examined syllable structure acquisition in Spanish-English bilinguals; English, like German, is a language which has many closed syllables. Gildersleeve-Neumann, Kester, Davis and Peña (2008) also examined Spanish-English bilinguals, although their study is limited by the fact that only the English of the bilinguals was examined. Nevertheless, we include it in the current list to see if their results were consistent with those of Lleó et al. (2003) at least for one of the languages. Apart from these two studies, we found few other studies which have examined coda production in children who are acquiring languages characterized by high and low frequencies of codas.[2] Thus, we also considered complexity or the distributional features of the codas. As mentioned above, codas are more restricted in Spanish, being only coronal, whereas in German (also English), they are more varied, allowing all places of articulation. German and English also contain coda clusters, whereas they are infrequent in Spanish. Using a criterion of restricted/low complexity versus less restricted/high complexity codas, studies by Almeida et al. (2012) on Portuguese-French[3] and Ezeizabarrena and Alegria (2015) on Basque-Spanish can be included. Portuguese has more restricted use of codas, analogous to Spanish. In contrast, French and Basque allow more segmental diversity in their codas, analogous to German and English. In terms of frequency, however, closed syllables are not frequent in any of these languages. Table 2.1 lists the above-mentioned studies.

Table 2.1. Studies examining crosslinguistic interaction in codas: Comparison involving languages with high frequency/unrestricted versus low frequency/restricted codas.

Investigators	*Languages*	*Results*
Keffala et al. (2016)	Spanish – low frequency/ restricted English – high frequency/ unrestricted	Acceleration in Spanish
Gildersleeve-Neumann et al. (2008)	Spanish – low frequency/ restricted English- high frequency/ unrestricted	Delay in English (Spanish not tested)
Almeida et al. (2012) (word-medial codas)	Portuguese – restricted French – unrestricted	Delay in French
Ezeizabarrena and Alegria (2015)	Spanish – restricted Basque – unrestricted	No difference

2 There are other studies which have measured coda production in bilinguals but they are not included here because the percentages of coda production were too high to allow a good differentiation between the bilingual's two languages (e.g. Goldstein and Washington 2001).

3 Almeida et al. (2012) focus on word-medial codas whereas the discussion of the other studies concern word-final codas.

This comparison does not take into consideration differences in methodology. Rather, we are concerned with whether a similar contact situation (i.e. high frequency/unrestricted codas coming into contact with low frequency/restricted codas) leads to similar outcomes in terms of crosslinguistic interaction. The findings appear to be equivocal. The most similar study to Lleó et al. (2003), namely Keffala et al. (2016) did find support for acceleration: bilinguals were more accurate than monolinguals in their production of codas (both in terms of structural and segmental accuracy) in Spanish. The authors also observed reduced coda production in the English of the bilinguals in comparison to the monolinguals; however, the differences were not significant. In contrast, Gildersleeve-Neumann et al. (2008) found significantly reduced coda production in the English of their bilinguals in comparison to the monolinguals, suggesting a delay effect. The other two studies in which frequency played a lesser role did not find an acceleration effect. Almeida et al. (2012) found delay in the language with the less restricted use of codas (i.e. French) similar to Gildersleeve-Neumann et al.'s (2008) findings for English. In contrast, Ezeizabarrena and Alegria (2015) found that their subject produced more codas in Basque than in Spanish, which led them to conservatively interpret their findings in terms of language-specific development, meaning that there was no interaction between the two languages. In sum, three different interaction effects (acceleration, delay and no difference) were documented in the current contact situation in which codas were examined.

One possible reason as to why few generalizations could be gleaned when examining similar contact situations is that we have ignored important methodological differences between studies. Some studies are based on small groups of bilinguals whereas others are single case studies. Some use word-naming tasks to elicit productions, whereas other are based on longitudinal naturalistic recordings. These factors may lead to different outcomes in terms of crosslinguistic interaction.

Critical look at the research

Methodology

A striking limitation of research on bilingual phonology is the lack of studies with large numbers of children. Hambly et al. (2013) in their review article on the speech production of young bilinguals point out that single or multiple case studies (29 out of the 66 studies reviewed) predominate in this field. Case studies provide important information in the field of early bilingualism, but they increase the risk that effects interpreted as crosslinguistic interaction are due to individual differences. The article by Hambly et al. (2013) also makes clear that much of what we know on bilingual speech acquisition pertains to the population of Spanish-English bilinguals (24 out of 66 studies) and that even well-known European languages, such as French and Italian, have not been strongly represented in early bilingual phonological research. Another limitation is that data on monolingual controls is not extensive for many languages of the world. A decision as to whether crosslinguistic interaction takes place can only be made when a study includes monolingual controls or when it refers to a solid base of monolingual data. There are other methodological limitations, including the fact that few are experimental, few are longitudinal, and few include extensive information on the language background of the children; however, the focus of this section is on another major limitation of current research, namely, the lack of a research model in early bilingualism.

The research model

One clear handicap of current approaches to early bilingual phonology is the lack of a research model specially designed to account for crosslinguistic interaction in speech production. In the overview to this chapter, we situated early bilingualism between the larger fields of first- and second-language acquisition. We noted that early bilingualism shares characteristics in common with both fields; however, it has not necessarily integrated these characteristics into a coherent model. If anything, early bilingualism has leant more towards the field of second language acquisition, but even in this respect, it has not adopted all aspects that could be useful to it. In the following sections, we expand upon findings in first- and second-language acquisition research which could be incorporated into current approaches to early bilingualism.

Looking towards second-language acquisition

One of the most well-known models in second-language research, the Speech Learning Model (SLM) of Flege (1995) has motivated some research in early bilingualism (Fabiano-Smith and Goldstein 2010b; Gildersleeve-Neumann and Wright 2010), although, strictly speaking, it is a model which is intended for children acquiring a second language after the age of five to six years (Flege 1997), and, thus, does not concern the majority of studies presented here. Central tenets of the SLM are, nevertheless, implicit in speech production research in early bilingualism, in particular, that the two linguistic systems share a common phonological space in which bi-directional interaction occurs. It also provides a taxonomy for classifying the relationship between L1 and L2 sounds, which is sadly absent in early bilingualism.

In the SLM, an L2 sound is new (i.e. differs acoustically and perceptually from the L1 sound), identical (i.e. there is no significant acoustic difference between the L1 and L2 sounds) or similar (i.e. there are significant and audible differences between the L1 and L2 sounds, but both sounds can be transcribed with the same IPA symbol) with respect to the L1 system. It is the similar (but not identical) sounds that create the most difficulty for second-language learners. Their acquisition often leads to two processes: perceptual assimilation or dissimilation. The acquisition of a similar L2 sound may result in equivalence classification which prevents a new L2 category from being formed and the categories of the L1 and L2 are merged. 'Merging' phenomena have been reported in the acquisition of VOT, whereby second-language learners produce stops in their L1 and L2 with similar VOT values (Flege 1987). The acquisition of a similar L2 sound may lead to an opposite phenomenon in which the two categories move away from each other to avoid crowding the phonetic space. These 'deflecting' phenomena have also been reported in the acquisition of VOT. Mack (1990) reports excessively high VOT values for English long lag stops (e.g. 108 ms) in a 10-year-old French-English bilingual child. Since the child produced French voiceless stops also in the long lag region (e.g. 66 ms), the very long VOTs in English allowed the child to maintain phonetic contrast between his L1 and L2 systems.

We mention 'merging' and 'deflecting' patterns in L2 acquisition because similar types of phenomena have been observed in young bilinguals. Kehoe and Lleó (2017) document merging patterns in the vowel reduction processes of German-Spanish bilingual children. They measured the ratios of stressed-to-unstressed syllable durations in German and Spanish. Differences between ratios of stressed-to-unstressed syllable durations were significant in the German versus Spanish monolingual children. The ratios were greater than 1.0 in the German monolingual children (1.4 in phrase-final and 1.7 in phrase-medial position), but close to 1.0 in the Spanish monolingual children (0.87 in phrase-final and 1.0 in phrase-medial position), reflecting the syllable-timed nature of Spanish, and the fact that German unstressed syllables are schwa syllables, leading to greater acoustic distances between stress and unstress. Differences between the ratios of stressed-to-unstressed syllables durations in German and Spanish were not significant in the bilingual children. The ratios were reduced in the case of German (1.32 in phrase-final and 1.24 in phrase-medial position) and similar or slightly increased in Spanish (0.98 in phrase-final and 1.04 in phrase-medial position), resulting in a less extreme contrast between the German and Spanish systems, that is, in a merging effect. Other examples of merging patterns have been reported in acoustic measures of rhythm in Spanish-English bilinguals (Kehoe, Lleó and Rakow 2011), intrinsic vowel duration in English-German bilinguals (Whitworth 2000) and in VOT (Watson 1990).

Dodane and Bijeljic-Babic (2017) present findings on acquisition of the acoustic correlates of stress in French-English bilinguals which are consistent with deflecting patterns. They measured duration, F_0 and intensity in the disyllabic productions of French and English monolingual children and in French-English bilingual children, aged 4;0 years. Here, we concentrate on their findings on duration and F_0 in the French productions of the monolingual and bilingual children. The monolingual children displayed a substantial final lengthening effect (the ratio of syllable 2 to syllable 1 was 1.72) and they produced no pitch accent on the first syllable, consistent with the language-specific stress pattern of French. The bilingual children also displayed a substantial final lengthening effect, but it was significantly larger than the one made by the monolingual children (the ratio of syllable 2 to syllable 1 was 2.29) and it was larger than the one made in their English words (ratio of syllable 2 to syllable 1 was 1.3), although they also produced a pitch accent on the first syllable suggesting the influence of English stress. What interests us is the exaggeration of the final lengthening effect in French allowing the bilinguals to make a maximal contrast between their two language systems. Another example of a deflecting pattern is the vowel development of a young Mandarin child acquiring English, aged 3;7, who drastically reduced the vowel space of English initially to achieve maximal contrast between his Mandarin and English vowels (Yang, Fox and Jacewicz 2015).

The current framework of crosslinguistic interaction, namely Paradis and Genesee's (1996) framework, reduces crosslinguistic interaction to three main patterns: transfer, acceleration and delay. It is possible that 'merging' is derived from the two basic patterns of delay and acceleration, and, as such, adding a new pattern is superfluous. However, we believe that enlarging the inventory of crosslinguistic patterns to incorporate 'merging' and 'deflecting' may provide a more accurate global depiction of what takes place when two languages come into contact in a young child.[4] In children,

4 Lleó (2015) has also recommended enlarging the set of interaction patterns proposed by Paradis and Genesee (1996).

'merging effects' may reflect a common speech-motor base which limits or constrains differences between developing phonological systems (see next section) and, as such, may have its origins in production and not just in perception as in Flege's (1995) model. We now turn to how approaches in first-language acquisition may complement a possible research model.

Looking towards first-language acquisition

Two themes central to first-language acquisition will be discussed here: (1) speech motor control; and (2) the developing lexicon. Phonological acquisition may be conceptualized as having two basic components: (1) a biologically based component associated with the development of speech-motor capacities; and (2) a cognitive-linguistic component associated with learning the phonological system of the ambient language (Stoel-Gammon 2011). While the cognitive-linguistic component may vary between a bilingual child's two languages, the speech motor skills which underlie the two phonological systems may not necessarily vary. In actual fact, we know little about the speech motor development of young bilinguals. However, studies on bilinguals with motor speech involvement (e.g. childhood apraxia of speech) show similar patterns across languages on motor-based tasks such as diadochokinetic tests or measures of production variability suggesting that aspects of motor control are language-neutral (Preston and Seki 2011). The fact that a bilingual child's phonological systems share a common speech motor base as well as have many segments and phonological structures in common may explain findings in the literature which show that a bilingual child's two phonologies approximate each other at certain levels. These findings include the presence of common templates (Vihman 2002, 2015; Kehoe 2015); merging patterns (see above); and similar orders of acquisition of phonological structures (Almeida et al. 2012; Lleó 2015).

Acquiring a phonological system also involves learning words. In emergent approaches to phonological development, acquiring phonological categories and learning words goes hand in hand (Edwards, Munson and Beckman 2011). Numerous studies have focused on the relationship between phonological and lexical development in monolingual children (see Stoel-Gammon 2011, for review). For example, studies on late talkers in English, Cypriot Greek, Italian and French consistently show that children with small vocabularies have less developed phonologies than children with large vocabularies (Bortolini and Leonard 2000; Kehoe, Chaplin, Mudry and Friend 2015; Petinou and Okalidou 2006; Paul and Jennings 1992; Rescorla and Ratner 1996). These findings support the presence of a bidirectional relationship between phonology and the lexicon. Only recently have researchers started to examine the relationship between lexical and phonological development in bilingual children (Kehoe 2011, 2015; Vihman 2002, 2015), although many aspects of this relationship remain unstudied. For example, we do not know whether a language-specific or a combined vocabulary score is most predictive of a bilingual child's phonological ability in each language.

Developing speech motor and lexical abilities are important components of phonological acquisition which need to be controlled since they may lead to considerable individual differences amongst children. Interestingly, they are factors that are rarely controlled in studies on bilingual phonological acquisition, with some rare exceptions. Scarpino (2011) examined which factors were the best predictors of phonological production (as measured by PCC and whole word proximity) in a large group of Spanish-English children (n = 199), aged 3;0 to 6;4 years. Important to the current discussion is that she found that the language-specific vocabulary scores and the phonological accuracy in the other language were highly predictive of phonological proficiency in both the English and Spanish of the bilingual children. Scarpino (2011) hypothesized that the predictive nature of the other language's phonological score reflected general developmental factors (articulatory maturation) and individual aptitude.

In sum, research in first-language acquisition highlights the importance of considering the child's developing speech motor and lexical abilities as crucial factors to be controlled in studies on early bilingualism. These factors lead to considerable individual differences amongst children which is inherent in the current state of research in the field. Varied models currently exist in first-language acquisition which may eventually be applied to speech production in young bilinguals. PRIMIR (Processing Rich Information from Multidimensional Interactive Representations) is a theoretical framework of early speech perception and word learning which has been extended to bilingual acquisition (Curtin, Byers-Heinlein and Werker 2011). One important feature of the model is, in addition to general statistical learning, that it includes a mechanism which aids the child in comparing and contrasting information across an array of representations, allowing her/him to separate the linguistic input. Such a mechanism could be important in aiding the child to separate his/her output as well. More specifically in the area of crosslinguistic interaction, Lleó and Cortés (2013) have developed a model which manipulates language-internal (e.g. markedness, frequency, complexity etc.) and -external factors (e.g. age, family language etc.) to account for phonological acquisition in bilingual children acquiring Spanish. This model is able to explain diverse interaction effects across an array of phonological phenomena (e.g. coda development, Spanish spirantization, vowel length) in the Spanish bilingual data, but additional research would be needed to determine whether it can explain findings across a broader range of studies.

Some new data: Coda acquisition in French bilinguals

As an attempt to tackle some of the limitations mentioned above in bilingual phonological research, we present preliminary findings of an investigation on young French-speaking bilinguals conducted at the University of Geneva in conjunction with Melanie Havy (Kehoe and Havy in preparation). The innovative aspect of this study is that it examines the language contact situation using multiple languages: the bilinguals stem from different linguistic backgrounds (e.g. Spanish, Italian, Portuguese, English, Romanian and Hungarian) and it includes detailed information on the lexical abilities of the children. The limitation of the study is that it focuses on the French productions of the bilinguals only, comparing them to a group of French-speaking monolinguals of the same age. Providing phonological information on the bilinguals' other languages would have been difficult given the multiple language backgrounds of the children. The study investigates the development of word-final codas, so some background on French codas is necessary to understand the predictions of this study.

Predictions of the study

Codas in French are of low frequency. According to Delattre and Olsen (1969), the percentage of closed syllables in French is 24% versus 60% in English. In child speech, codas may be even less frequent: Gayraud and Kern (2007) report that 90% of a French 2-year-old's lexicon is vowel-final. French differs, however, from languages with low percentages of codas, such as Spanish, by having no restrictions on coda position. Word-final codas may be coronal, labial and dorsal. They may be complex. Word-final codas are also situated in the salient stressed word-final syllable.

Given the characteristics of word-final consonants in French, we predict that there may be acceleration of codas in French if a bilingual's other language contains a high percentage of codas, such as in English or German. This would be similar to the findings by Lleó et al. (2003) and Keffala et al. (2016) in German-Spanish and, respectively, English-Spanish bilingual children. We predict the opposite, delay, if the bilingual's other language contains low frequency and restricted codas. This would be analogous to Almeida et al.'s (2012) study which found delay in French codas due to the influence of Portuguese; Portuguese having a more restricted set of codas than French. Due to the design of the study, we cannot determine if there is acceleration of codas in the other language. For example, a French-Spanish bilingual may display acceleration of codas in Spanish due to the presence of the less restricted, more complex codas in French.

Method

The participants were 13 monolinguals and 11 bilinguals aged 2;6 years growing up in Geneva, Switzerland. The monolinguals had no exposure to any other language, whereas the bilinguals had 40 up to 80% exposure to the *other* language. We tested 9 additional children who had limited exposure to a second language (10 to 20% exposure). These children are not included in the main analyses but in the correlational analyses at the end of this section. Parents were required to provide detailed information on the language exposure of their child and to complete an inventory of their child's expressive vocabulary skills in both languages.

All participants took part in an object and word naming task, which was designed to elicit productions of words containing word-final consonants. The stimuli were monosyllabic and disyllabic real words containing word-final consonants of different manners of articulation (e.g. stops: *crêpe* /kʁɛp/ 'crêpe', *lunettes* /ly'nɛt/ 'glasses'; fricatives: *cloche* /klɔʃ/ 'bell', *chemise* /ʃə'miz/ 'shirt'; nasals: *banane* /ba'nan/ 'banana'; liquids: *cheval* /ʃə'val/ 'horse', *fleur* /flœːʁ/ 'flower'; and glides: *soleil* /sɔ'lɛːj/ 'sun'). The average number of target words with word-final consonants produced by the monolinguals was 37 and by the bilinguals, 31. All productions were phonetically transcribed in Phon (Rose et al. 2006) by native French speakers. Transcribed data were coded in terms of structural (i.e. marking of coda position) and segmental accuracy (i.e. whether the produced coda was the same as the target coda; voicing errors were excluded) of the coda consonant. Three participants were re-transcribed by a second transcriber and high inter-transcriber reliability was obtained (95% on point-to-point consonant accuracy).

Results

We first present the group results for structural and segmental accuracy in the monolingual and bilingual children (see Figures 2.5 and 2.6). As can be seen, bilinguals as a group produced similar percentages of word-final codas as the monolinguals (bilinguals: 85% vs. monolinguals: 90%) and had similar degrees of segmental accuracy (bilinguals: 77% vs. monolinguals: 78%). Non-parametric statistical tests (Mann Whitney U tests) indicated no significant differences between the two groups of children in terms of structural and segmental accuracy of word-final codas in French (structural accuracy: $U = 70, p > 0.05$; segmental accuracy: $U = 71, p > 0.05$).

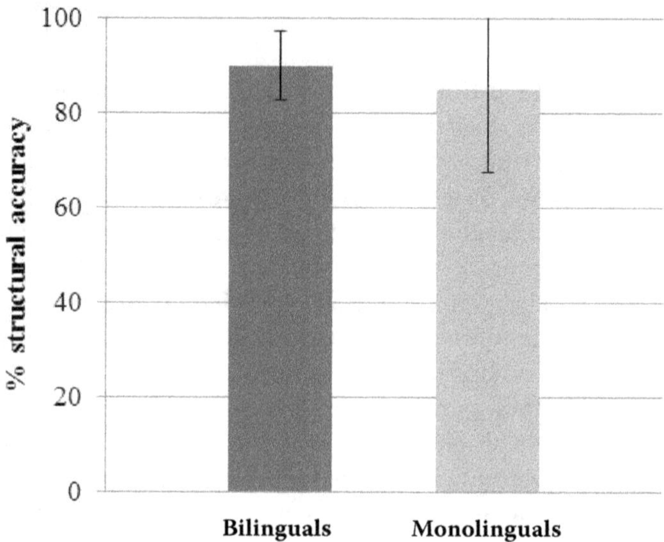

Figure 2.5. Structural accuracy.

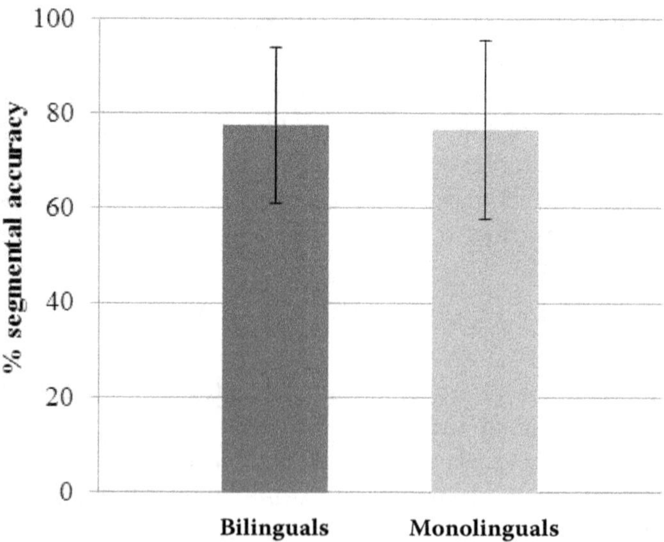

Figure 2.6. Segmental accuracy.

In the next analysis, we divide the bilingual group into those children who are speaking a language with a high frequency of codas (e.g. English) and those who are speaking a language with a low frequency of codas (e.g. Spanish and Italian). Unfortunately, there were not balanced numbers of

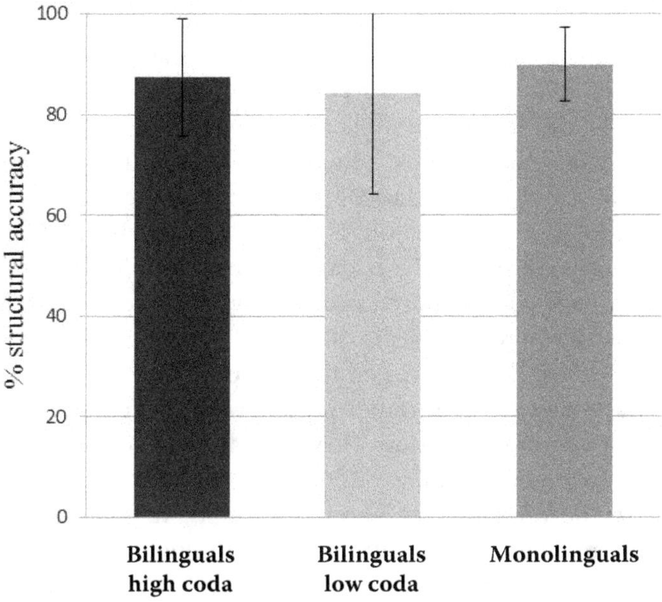

Figure 2.7. Coda structural accuracy.

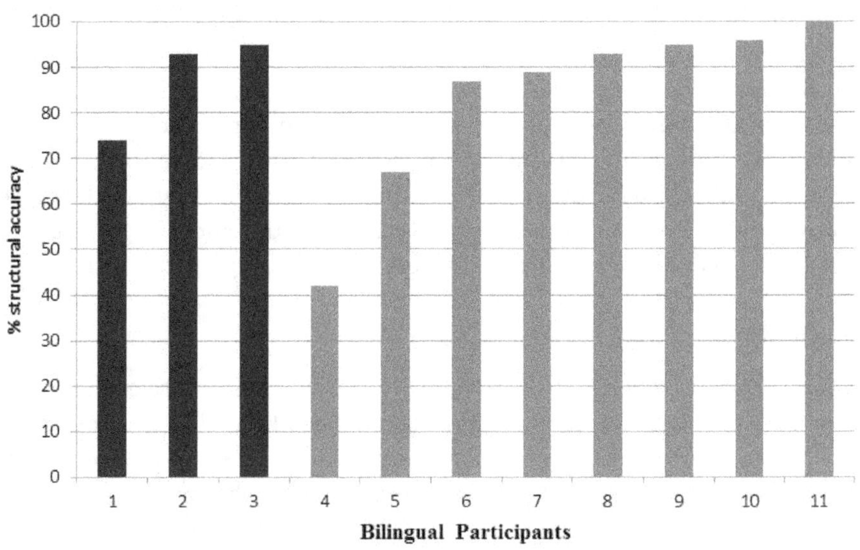

Figure 2.8. Bilingual participants' coda structural accuracy.

children in each group; there were more children in the low ($n = 8$) than in the high coda group ($n = 3$). Figure 2.7 presents the group results for coda structural accuracy in bilingual children speaking high and low percentages of codas in their other language; results for monolinguals are shown alongside. Figure 2.8 shows the individual results on coda structural accuracy for the 11 bilingual children, divided into high (1–3) and low (4–11) coda groups. The findings on coda segmental accuracy were comparable to those on structural accuracy and are not shown here.

The group findings indicate similar mean values for structural accuracy in the high and low coda groups, although the standard deviations are considerably greater in the low coda group. The greater inter-subject variability in the low coda group is evident in Figure 2.8, which shows the individual participant data. We observe that participants 4 and 5, who are Spanish- and Romanian-speaking children respectively, omit codas on many occasions in French, whereas subjects 10 and 11, who are also Spanish- and Romanian-speaking, hardly ever omit codas in French.

In the final analysis, we examined if there were other factors which were correlated with coda production. Here we used the entire group of bilingual children ($n = 20$), including the children who had limited exposure (i.e. 10 to 20%) to another language, and we examined the influence of lexicon size and percent language exposure on coda production. Results indicated a mild (but significant) correlation between number of words in the child's French vocabulary ($r = 0.35$, $p < 0.05$) and coda production, and a mild (but significant) relationship between percentage exposure to French and coda production ($r = 0.35$, $p < 0.05$). There was no significant relationship between total vocabulary and coda production ($r = 0.27$; $p = 0.12$), although this result may be hampered by the fact that there was missing data in some cases: not all parents were able to complete vocabulary checklists on both languages of the child. It is important to note that participants 1, 4 and 5 were the children with the lowest vocabulary scores in French (they also had the lowest Total Vocabularies) and participants 1 and 4 had low exposure levels to French (20 and 30% respectively).

Discussion

Several findings emerge from the above study, which are relevant to the themes of this chapter. First, monolingual and bilingual children did not differ from each other in terms of coda structural and segmental accuracy. This finding joins several other studies which show that monolingual and bilingual children attain comparable levels of phonological performance (Fabiano-Smith and Goldstein 2010a; Hambly et al. 2013); although, it differs from studies which have shown that bilinguals differ from monolinguals in the development of codas, due to crosslinguistic interaction (Lleó et al. 2003; Keffela et al. 2016). Given the presence of crosslinguistic interaction, we might have observed superior performance in coda production by the high coda group and inferior performance by the low coda group in comparison to the monolinguals; however, this was not the case. Why the findings in this study are different from other studies is not clear; however, the majority of children achieved high levels of coda production possibly suggesting ceiling effects. Word-final codas in French are low frequency; however, they are not restricted in distribution and they occur in the salient stressed word-final syllable; these factors may play a role in their high production rates.

Second, certain children in the low coda group (participants 4 and 5) did receive inferior results on coda production suggesting the possibility of crosslinguistic interaction for these children. These children also had low vocabulary levels (French and Total Vocabularies) and low exposure levels to French, suggesting that several factors individually or in combination may explain their low coda production. Unfortunately, the methodology of this study does not allow us to determine whether these children received low coda scores in their other language. This study does, however, highlight the individual differences that may arise even in the same language contact situation, as was suggested earlier in the chapter when reviewing studies on coda production.

Third, vocabulary scores in French were correlated with coda production implicating the role of the lexicon in bilingual phonological production. The relationship was relatively modest nevertheless, with some children achieving good coda scores although their vocabulary levels were low (in general, children with large vocabularies achieved good coda results as well). Kehoe et al. (2015) observed a strong relationship between the lexicon and the percentage of consonants correct in syllable-initial position in monolingual French-speaking children (aged 2;5 years) but not in syllable-final position, suggesting that growth of the lexicon may be less associated with this prosodic position in French than with other positions.

Finally, degree of input as determined by percent exposure levels was also mildly correlated with coda production. In other areas of language development (e.g. lexical and syntactic development), degree of input has been shown to be highly correlated with language performance in bilingual children (Hoff et al. 2012; Thordardottir 2011; Thordardottir and Brandeker 2013). In the area of phonology, there have been mixed findings: differentiated measures of dominance, such as parent-reported estimates of language experience (frequency of output and language use), are not always correlated with phonological scores (Goldstein et al. 2010; Goldstein, Fabiano and Washington 2005), suggesting that the role of input may play a lesser role in phonology than in other language domains.

Conclusion

Our review of the literature on crosslinguistic interaction leads to modest conclusions. Crosslinguistic interaction has been documented in numerous studies but it is still not well understood. Our attempt to seek generalizations across similar contact situations (e.g. high frequency of codas in one language vs. low frequency in the other) yielded diverse findings. Methodological limitations related to small subject numbers and to the lack of extensive monolingual data contribute to the poor generalizability of the findings. Our own study presented here on coda production also revealed diverse findings. Children with the same language contact conditions manifested with varying degrees of coda production indicating that lexical ability, language exposure levels and possibly other factors influence phonological performance. In sum, crosslinguistic interaction can only be assumed after many other diverse factors have been controlled.

We have argued that a new research model is sorely needed in early bilingualism. This is not only our conclusion but was one of the main recommendations of the review article by Hambly et al. (2013: 13):

> Developing models of cross-linguistic bilingual speech acquisition that take into account ... length and type of L2 exposure, capacity of perceptual and cognitive systems, individual variation ... is an enormous challenge but will assist practitioners as they assess the speech of bilingual children ....

This model needs to integrate important components from first- and second-language acquisition, as well as develop its own unique aspects. We recommend that it expands upon existing manifestations of crosslinguistic interaction and considers the role of developing articulatory capacities and lexical abilities as a way of controlling for individual differences amongst bilingual children. It may be the case that seeking generalizations in this field will never be easy, however, due to the inherent uniqueness of each bilingual child.

References

Almeida, L., Rose, Y. and Freitas, J., 2012, 'Prosodic influence in bilingual phonological development: Evidence from a Portuguese-French first language learner', in A. Biller, E. Chung, and A. Kimball (eds.), *Proceedings of the 36th Annual Boston University Conference on Language Development*, pp. 42–52, Somerville, MA: Cascadilla Press.

Bortolini, U. and Leonard, L.B., 2000, 'Phonology and children with specific language impairment: Status of structural constraints in two languages', *Journal of Communication Disorders* 33, 131–50. https://doi.org/10.1016/S0021-9924(99)00028-3

Bunta, F. and Ingram, D., 2007, 'The acquisition of speech rhythm by bilingual Spanish- and English-speaking 4- and 5-year-old children', *Journal of Speech, Language, and Hearing* 50, 999–1014. https://doi.org/10.1044/1092-4388(2007/070)

Curtin, S., Byers-Heinlein, K. and Werker, J., 2011, 'Bilingual beginnings as a lens for theory development: PRIMIR in focus', *Journal of Phonetics* 39, 492–504. https://doi.org/10.1016/j.wocn.2010.12.002

De Houwer, A., 1990, *The acquisition of two languages from birth: A case study*, Cambridge: Cambridge University Press. https://doi.org/10.1017/CBO9780511519789

Delattre, P. and Olsen, C., 1969, 'Syllable features and phonic impression in English, German, French, and Spanish', *Lingua* 22, 160–75. https://doi.org/10.1016/0024-3841(69)90051-5

Dodane, C. and Bijeljic-Babic, R., 2017, 'Cross-language influences in the productions of bilingual children: Separation or interaction', in M. Yavaş, M. Kehoe and W. Cardoso (eds.), *Romance-Germanic bilingual phonology*, pp. 38–55, Sheffield, UK: Equinox Publishing Ltd.

Edwards, J., Munson, B. and Beckman, M.E., 2011, 'Lexicon-phonology relationships and dynamics of early language development – A commentary on Stoel-Gammon's "Relationships between lexical and phonological development in young children"', *Journal of Child Language* 38, 35–40. https://doi.org/10.1017/S0305000910000450

Ezeizabarrena, M.-J. and Alegria, A., 2015, 'Early coda production in bilingual Spanish and Basque', in T. Judy and S. Perpiñán (eds.), *The acquisition of Spanish in understudied language pairings*, Amsterdam/Philadelphia: John Benjamins. https://doi.org/10.1075/ihll.3.04eze

Fabiano-Smith, L. and Barlow, J., 2010, 'Interaction in bilingual phonological acquisition: Evidence from phonetic inventories', *International Journal of Bilingual Education and Bilingualism* 13, 1–17.

Fabiano-Smith, L. and Goldstein, B., 2010a, 'Early, middle, and late developing sounds in monolingual and bilingual children: An exploratory study', *American Journal of Speech-Language Pathology* 19, 1–12. https://doi.org/10.1044/1058-0360(2009/08-0036)

Fabiano-Smith, L. and Goldstein, B., 2010b, 'Phonological acquisition in bilingual Spanish-English speaking children', *Journal of Speech, Language, and Hearing Research* 53, 1–19. https://doi.org/10.1044/1092-4388(2009/07-0064)

Flege, J., 1987, 'A critical period for learning to pronounce foreign languages?', *Applied Linguistics* 8, 162–77. https://doi.org/10.1093/applin/8.2.162

Flege, J., 1995, 'Second-language speech learning: Theory, findings, and problems', in W. Strange (ed.), *Speech perception and linguistic experience: Issues in cross-language research*, pp. 233–73, Timonium, MD: York Press.

Flege, J., 1997, 'English vowel productions by Dutch talkers: more evidence for the "similar" vs. "new" distinction', in A. James and J. Leather (eds.), *Second-language speech*, pp. 11–52, Berlin: Mouton de Gruyter. https://doi.org/10.1515/9783110882933.11

Gayraud, F. and Kern, S., 2007, 'Caractéristiques phonologiques des noms en fonction de l'âge d'acquisition', *Enfance* 59, 324–38. https://doi.org/10.3917/enf.594.0324

Genesee, F., 1989, 'Early bilingual development: One language or two?', *Journal of Child Language* 6, 161–79. https://doi.org/10.1017/S0305000900013490

Gildersleeve-Neumann, C., Kester, E., Davis, B. and Peña, E., 2008, 'English speech sound development in preschool-aged children from bilingual English-Spanish environments', *Language, Speech, and Hearing Services in Schools* 39, 314–28. https://doi.org/10.1044/0161-1461(2008/030)

Gildersleeve-Neumann, C. and Wright, K., 2010, 'English speech acquisition in 3- to 5-year-old children learning Russian and English', *Language, Speech, and Hearing Services in Schools* 41, 429–44. https://doi.org/10.1044/0161-1461(2009/09-0059)

Goldstein, B., Bunta, F., Lange, J., Rodriguez, J. and Burrows, L., 2010, 'The effects of measures of language experience and language ability on segmental accuracy in bilingual children', *American Journal of Speech-Language Pathology* 19, 238–47. https://doi.org/10.1044/1058-0360(2010/08-0086)

Goldstein, B., Fabiano, L. and Washington, P., 2005, 'Phonological skills in predominantly English-speaking, predominantly Spanish-speaking, and Spanish-English bilingual children', *Language, Speech, and Hearing Services in Schools* 36, 201–18. https://doi.org/10.1044/0161-1461(2005/021)

Goldstein, B. and Washington, P., 2001, 'An initial investigation of phonological patterns in typically developing 4-year-old Spanish English bilingual children', *Language, Speech, and Hearing Services in Schools* 32, 153–64. https://doi.org/10.1044/0161-1461(2001/014)

Hambly, H., Wren, Y., McLeod, S. and Roulstone, S., 2013, 'The influence of bilingualism on speech production: A systematic review', *International Journal of Language and Communication Disorders* 48, 1–24. https://doi.org/10.1111/j.1460-6984.2012.00178.x

Harris, J., 1983, *Syllable structure and stress in Spanish: A nonlinear analysis*, Cambridge, Massachusetts: MIT Press.

Hoff, E., Core, C., Place, S., Rumiche, R., Señor, M. and Parra, M., 2012, 'Dual language exposure and early bilingual development', *Journal of Child Language* 39, 1–27. https://doi.org/10.1017/S0305000910000759

Keffala, B., Barlow, J. and Rose, S., 2016, 'Interaction in Spanish-English bilinguals' acquisition of syllable structure', *International Journal of Bilingualism*. https://doi.org/10.1177/1367006916644687

Kehoe, M., 2002, 'Developing vowel systems as a window to bilingual phonology', *International Journal of Bilingualism* 6, 315–34. https://doi.org/10.1177/13670069020060030601

Kehoe, M., 2011, 'Relationships between lexical and phonological development: A look at bilingual children', *Journal of Child Language* 38, 75–81. https://doi.org/10.1017/S0305000910000474

Kehoe, M., 2015, 'Lexical-phonological interactions in bilingual children', *First Language* 35, 93–125. https://doi.org/10.1177/0142723715574398

Kehoe, M., Chaplin, E., Mudry, P. and Friend, M., 2015, 'La relation entre le développement du lexique et de la phonologie chez les enfants francophones', *Rééducation Orthophonique* 263, 61–85.

Kehoe, M. and Havy, M., in preparation, 'Bilingual phonological acquisition: The influence of language-internal and -external factors'.

Kehoe, M. and Lleó, C., 2017, 'Vowel reduction in German-Spanish bilinguals', in M. Yavaş, M. Kehoe and W. Cardoso (eds.), *Romance-Germanic bilingual phonology*, pp. 14–37, Sheffield, UK: Equinox Publishing Ltd.

Kehoe, M., Lleó, C. and Rakow, M., 2004, 'Voice onset time in bilingual German-Spanish children', *Bilingualism: Language and Cognition* 7, 71–88. https://doi.org/10.1017/S1366728904001282

Kehoe, M., Lleó, C. and Rakow, M., 2011, 'Speech rhythm in the pronunciation of German and Spanish monolingual and German-Spanish bilingual 3-year-olds', *Linguistische Berichte* 227, 323–51.

Lleó, C., 2012, 'Monolingual and bilingual phonoprosodic corpora of child German and child Spanish', in T. Schmidt and K. Wörner (eds.), *Multilingual corpora and multilingual corpus analysis: Hamburger Studies on Multilingualism 14*, pp. 107–22, Amsterdam/Philadelphia: John Benjamins. https://doi.org/10.1075/hsm.14.08lle

Lleó, C., 2015, 'On the permeability of German-Spanish bilinguals' phonological grammars', in E. Babatsouli and D. Ingram (eds.), *Proceedings of the International Symposium on Monolingual and Bilingual Speech 2015*, pp. 196–206, ISBN: 978-618-82351-0-6. http://ismbs.eu/publications.

Lleó, C. and Cortés, S., 2013, 'Modeling the outcome of language contact in the speech of German-Spanish and Catalan-Spanish bilingual children', *International Journal of the Sociology of Language* 221, 101–25. https://doi.org/10.1515/ijsl-2013-0025

Lleó, C., Kuchenbrandt, I., Kehoe, M. and Trujillo, C., 2003, 'Syllable final consonants in Spanish and German monolingual and bilingual acquisition', in N. Müller (ed.), *(Non)Vulnerable domains in bilingualism*, pp. 191–220, Amsterdam/Philadelphia: John Benjamins. https://doi.org/10.1075/hsm.1.08lle

Mack, M., 1990, 'Phonetic transfer in a French-English bilingual child', in P. Nelde (ed.), *Language attitides and language conflict*, Bonn, Germany: Dümmler.

Mayr, R., Howells, G. and Lewis, R., 2015, 'Asymmetries in phonological development: the case of word-final cluster acquisition in Welsh-English bilingual children', *Journal of Child Language* 42, 146–79. https://doi.org/10.1017/S0305000913000603

Meinhold, G. and Stock, E., 1980, *Phonologie der Deutschen degenwartssprache*, Leipzig: Bibliographisches Institut.

Meisel, J., 1989, 'Early differentiation of languages in bilingual children', in K. Hyltenstam and L. Obler (eds.), *Bilingualism across the lifespan: Aspects of acquisition, maturity and loss*, pp. 13–40, Cambridge: Cambridge University Press. https://doi.org/10.1017/CBO9780511611780.003

Mok, P., 2011, 'The acquisition of rhythm by three-year-old bilingual and monolingual children', *Bilingualism: Language and Cognition* 14, 458–72. https://doi.org/10.1017/S1366728910000453

Mok, P., 2013, 'Speech rhythm of monolingual and bilingual children at age 2;6: Cantonese amd English', *Bilingualism: Language and Cognition* 16, 693–703. https://doi.org/10.1017/S1366728912000636

Munson B., 2004, 'Variability in /s/ production in children and adults: Evidence from dynamic measures of spectral mean', *Journal of Speech, Language, and Hearing Research* 47, 58–69. https://doi.org/10.1044/1092-4388(2004/006)

Munson, B., Edwards, J. and Beckman, M.E., 2005, 'Phonological knowledge in typical and atypical speech–sound development', *Topics in Language Disorders* 25, 190. https://doi.org/10.1097/00011363-200507000-00003

Nittrouer S., 1992, 'Age-related differences in perceptual effects of formant transitions within syllables and across syllable boundaries', *Journal of Phonetics* 20, 1–32.

Paradis, J. and Genesee, F., 1996, 'Syntactic acquisition in bilingual children: Autonomous or inderdependent?', *Studies in Second Language Acquisition* 18, 1–25. https://doi.org/10.1017/S0272263100014662

Paul, R. and Jennings, P., 1992, 'Phonological behavior in toddlers with slow expressive language development', *Journal of Speech, Language, and Hearing Research* 35, 99–107. https://doi.org/10.1044/jshr.3501.99

Petinou, K. and Okalidou, A., 2006, 'Speech patterns in Cypriot-Greek late talkers', *Applied Psycholinguistics* 27, 335–53. https://doi.org/10.1017/S0142716406060309

Preston, J. and Seki, A., 2011, 'Identifying residual speech sound disorders in bilingual children: A Japanese-English case study', *American Journal of Speech-Language Pathology* 20, 73–85. https://doi.org/10.1044/1058-0360(2011/10-0057)

Rescorla, L. and Ratner, N.B., 1996, 'Phonetic profiles of toddlers with specific expressive language impairment (SLI-E)', *Journal of Speech, Language, and Hearing Research* 39, 153–65. https://doi.org/10.1044/jshr.3901.153

Rose, Y., MacWhinney, B., Byrne, R., Hedlund, G., Maddocks, K., O'Brien, P. and Wareham, T., 2006, 'Introducing Phon: A software solution for the study of phonological acquisition', in D. Bamman, T. Magnitskaia and C. Zaller (eds.),

Proceedings of the 30th Boston University Conference on Language Development, pp. 489–500, Somerville, MA: Cascadilla Press.

Scarpino, S., 2011, *The effects of language environment and oral language ability on phonological production proficiency in bilingual Spanish-English speaking children*, unpublished doctoral dissertation, Pennsylvania State University.

Stoel-Gammon, C., 2011, 'Relationships between lexical and phonological development in young children', *Journal of Child Language* 38, 1–34. https://doi.org/10.1017/S0305000910000425

Tamburelli, M., Sanoudaki, E., Jones, G. and Sowinska, M., 2015, 'Acceleration in the bilingual acquisition of phonological structure: Evidence from Polish-English children', *Bilingualism: Language and Cognition* 18, 713–25. https://doi.org/10.1017/S1366728914000716

Thordardottir, E., 2011, 'The relationship between bilingual exposure and vocabulary development', *International Journal of Bilingualism*15, 426–45. https://doi.org/10.1177/1367006911403202

Thordardottir, E. and Brandeker, M., 2013, 'The effect of bilingual exposure versus language impairment on nonword repetition and sentence imitation scores', *Journal of Communication Disorders* 46, 1–16. https://doi.org/10.1016/j.jcomdis.2012.08.002

Vihman, M., 2002, 'Getting started without a system: From phonetics to phonology in bilingual development', *The International Journal of Bilingualism* 6, 239–54. https://doi.org/10.1177/13670069020060030201

Vihman, M., 2015, 'Prosodic structures and templates in bilingual phonological development', *Bilingualism: Language and Cognition* 19, 1–20.

Volterra, V. and Taeschner, T., 1978, 'The acquisition and development of language by bilingual children', *Journal of Child Language* 5, 311–26. https://doi.org/10.1017/S0305000900007492

Watson, I., 1990, 'Acquiring the voicing contrast in French: A comparative study of monolingual and bilingual children', in J.N. Green and W. Ayres-Bennett (eds.), *Variation and change in French: Essays presented to Rebecca Posner on the occasion of her sixtieth birthday*, pp. 37–60, London: Routledge.

Whitworth, N., 2000, 'Acquisition of VOT, and vowel length by English-German bilinguals: A pilot study', *Leeds Working Papers in Linguistics and Phonetics* 8.

Yang, J., Fox, R. and Jacewicz, E., 2015, 'Vowel development in an emergent Mandarin-English bilingual child: A longitudinal study', *Journal of Child Language* 42, 1125–43. https://doi.org/10.1017/S0305000914000531

Margaret Kehoe is a senior lecturer at the University of Geneva. She is also a practising speech-language therapist who works with the international community in Geneva. She received her Bachelor in Speech Therapy (with Honors) from the University of Queensland, her MSc from the University of Arizona, and her PhD from the University of Washington. She has conducted research on phonetic and phonological acquisition in English-, German-, Spanish- and French-speaking children as well as in bilingual children. She is currently interested in the theme of crosslinguistic interaction in bilingual children.

3
German-Spanish bilinguals' phonological grammars: Permeable or resilient?

Conxita Lleó

Introduction

At the University of Hamburg, research on bilingualism and multilingualism was intensified in 1999 under a whole new set of circumstances: a Collaborative Research Center for Multilingualism (in German, Sonderforschungsbereich 538) was created with the support of the German Science Foundation (DFG) and coordinated by Dr Jürgen Meisel. The existence of the Center was limited to no more than 12 years, until June 2011. However, during those 12 years we had the opportunity to study many aspects of multilingualism. In my work and in the work of my collaborators, the focus was on phonology.

What rationale did our research follow? First, we tried to understand what the bilingual outcome of certain segments was, as for instance the VOTs of a child acquiring German and Spanish simultaneously, as short lag corresponds to voiced stops in German and to voiceless stops in Spanish (discussed here in a later section). Our segmental analyses also focused on properties that only occurred in one of the languages, like vowel length in German, developing in contact with Spanish, which does not distinguish vowels on duration grounds. We soon realized that prosody plays a crucial role in predicting the outcome of acquiring two languages simultaneously. In fact, vowel length itself is a property that is best understood as belonging both to segments and to prosody. Thus, we analysed cases of allophony as, for example, spirantization, place assimilation of nasals, or resyllabification. At the same time, we focused on stress, intonation and rhythm. Several corpora were compiled (Schmidt and Wörner 2012) and a wide range of phenomena were analysed, although there are data still waiting to be approached.

Multilingualism: numerous data, few theories

Babatsouli and Ingram (2015: 173) refer to the enormous task involved in the study of bilingual acquisition, given the great number of variables to take into consideration: numerous languages and language combinations, the contexts, simultaneous or sequential, number of participants etc., and they conclude: 'When the math is done, the number of possible bilingual studies approaches one million.' This conclusion can be discouraging if taken on the pessimistic side, but it can be received optimistically, too, as a challenge to begin by disentangling a minimum number of criteria leading to variables, which will allow us to better understand (some of) the outcomes of phonological acquisition.

Some researchers focus on structural variables, whereas others prefer to struggle with sociolinguistic ones. Thomason and Kaufman (1988: 35), for instance, declare: 'The starting point for our theory of linguistic interference is this: it is the sociolinguistic history of the speakers, and not the structure of their language that is the primary determinant of the linguistic outcome of language contact.' Although sociolinguistic variables may be essential, the intention of the present chapter is to consider the relevance of some structural and psycholinguistic factors, and to try to unify them with sociolinguistic ones. The ultimate goal is to explore possible ways to predict the outcome of various bilingual constellations. For instance, if with regard to rhythm, one of the languages is trochaic and the other one iambic, what will the simultaneous bilingual's stress systems of these languages look like, i.e. if there is interaction between the languages, in what direction will the influence go? Or, if one of the languages is syllable-timed and the other one is stress-timed, what will the learner's rhythmic structures of these languages look like, i.e. will there be interaction, and in what direction?

There are not enough studies trying to systematize crosslanguage interaction in a bilingual child acquiring two languages simultaneously. The best known proposal, often referred to in the field, is Paradis and Genesee (1996). They proposed three potential manifestations of crosslanguage interaction, which they called 'interdependence': *delay*, *acceleration* and *transfer*. In order to test the presence of these phenomena in their bilingual data, they observed three French-English bilinguals at ages 2;0, 2;6 and 3;0, growing up in Montreal. With regard to syntax (finiteness, negation and pronominal subjects), they found:

No delay – No acceleration – No transfer

However, they did not observe areas of grammar other than syntactic ones, while the literature on the simultaneous bilingual acquisition of phonology is, by now, full of studies showing crosslanguage interaction beyond any doubt. Thus, the main research question of this chapter is not whether the simultaneous acquisition of two languages by the child involves cross-language interaction, but rather how such interaction manifests itself: by delay, acceleration and transfer or by something else?

Manifestations of interaction: Six outcomes instead of three

Fabiano-Smith and Goldstein (2010) reviewed Paradis and Genesee's proposal and confirmed the three outcomes of interaction, namely delay, acceleration and transfer, but with a few modifications: (1) The term 'delay' is replaced by *deceleration*, as the former may evoke negative associations, which the latter should not. (2) *Acceleration* presupposes great speed in the bilingual condition, and is defined anew, because simultaneous bilingual acquisition already presupposes double speed in relation to monolinguals. (3) Regarding *transfer*, Fabiano and Goldstein (2005), as well as other studies stemming from Dr Goldstein's lab, hardly found any instances of prosodic or syllabic transfer, which led them to the conclusion that transfer is restricted to the segmental domain: segments of one language are used in the other language (e.g. German /R/ for Spanish /ɾ/ and /r/. But still, segmental transfer is minimal in their view.

Further additions to the Paradis and Genesee (1996) types of interaction have been proposed in Queen (2001) and Lleó (2006): (4) Queen (2001) discusses the notion of *fusion* in relation to intonation, which implies a two-way influence between two languages. Her example indicates that German-Turkish bilingual children use two rises both in German and Turkish, emerging from the interaction between the two languages: L*HH% (similar to a German contour), used for discourse cohesion, and L%H% (similar to a Turkish contour), used to signal continuation. This is comparable to further effects mentioned in the literature: compromise values, encountered in relation to the acquisition of VOT and rhythm (Kehoe, Lleó and Rakow 2004, 2011), and so-called bidirectional transfer, as the influence goes from L1 to L2 and from L2 to L1 (Kehoe, Lleó and Rakow 2011). (5) Lleó (2006) proposes a *different order of acquisition*: Two categories that are acquired in the order first A then B by monolinguals may be acquired as first B and then A by bilinguals in that same language. (6) Moreover, in some cases, *no crosslinguistic influence* can be attested, which is a possible outcome of language contact, as well. With these additions to Paradis and Genesee (1996) in mind, we will consider six types of interaction, which will be exemplified with grammatical phenomena of Spanish and German in contact with one another.

Aims of the present chapter

The literature on early bilingual acquisition has widely shown that children exposed to two languages from birth generally acquire them both, and that the outcome involves a lot of crosslanguage interaction or influence. However, in the opinion of Kehoe (2015), such interaction does not seem to be as consistent as some authors assume (e.g. Lleó and Cortés 2013). Thus, our goal here is to try to (1) discover what systematic rationale lies behind all these cases of interaction. In order to do that, we will apply the tenets of Optimality Theory to the results of studies dealing with bilingual phonological acquisition carried out in the Research Center on Multilingualism. Moreover, (2) we want to uncover those areas in phonology that are vulnerable to the influence of the bilingual child's other language. Finally, (3) we want to identify what factors have a stronger predictive force as to the outcome of language contact in phonology.

Studies under consideration

All studies considered were carried out in the Research Center for Multilingualism, focusing on German-Spanish simultaneous bilingual children acquiring various phonological phenomena, in both the segmental and prosodic domains.

Participants and data

Participants were the German-Spanish bilingual children and their monolingual controls (Table 3.1). The bilinguals lived in North Germany (Hamburg) and had a native Spanish-speaking mother (Peninsular Standard Spanish) and a native German-speaking father (North Standard German). The German-speaking controls were from the same German region as the bilinguals (North Germany), and the Spanish-speaking controls were from the Madrid area (Spain). The bilinguals were well balanced until about 3 years of age, thereafter with a slight dominance of German, the majority language. German became stronger as the bilinguals began to attend kindergarten. All data had been collected in the children's homes in semi-spontaneous situations, playing with and talking to the child. Utterances were transcribed and introduced into a database: EXMARaLDA, developed by Schmidt and Wörner (2012) at the Research Center for Multilingualism of the University of Hamburg. Topics to study were selected on the basis of similarities and differences between German and Spanish. Speech samples have been selected from three longitudinal corpora: PAIDUS (a monolingual corpus created at the University of Hamburg in the early 1990s, comprised five children acquiring German in Hamburg, Germany, and three acquiring Spanish in Madrid, Spain),[1] PEDSES (with data from 3 German-Spanish bilingual children from Hamburg), and PhonBLA (a bilingual corpus collected at the same Research Center for Multilingualism) with data from four German-Spanish simultaneous bilinguals.

These data have been complemented with cross-sectional data from a group of Spanish-German bilinguals from Madrid, out of which three 3-year-olds were selected. These children thus represented the mirror image of the bilinguals from Hamburg, with Spanish as the majority language. For a detailed description of these and further related corpora, see Lleó (2012). All utterances were digitized with a sampling rate of 44.1 KHz. The corpora are available at the Hamburger Zentrum für Sprachkorpora (HZSK, Hamburg Centre for Language Corpora) and recently from CHILDES. The pitch curves of the utterances were acoustically analysed.

Table 3.1. Children who participated in the project, with L1 Spanish and German, monolingual and bilingual.

Language	*Children*	*Age*	*Acquisition*	*Environment*
Spanish = L1	3	1;6–3;0	monolingual	Spain
Spanish = L1	7	1;6–3;0	bilingual	Germany
German = L1	5	1;6–3;0	monolingual	Germany
German = L1	7	1;6–3;0	bilingual	Germany
Spanish = L1	3	ca. 3;0	bilingual	Spain

1 There was a fourth child in the PAIDUS database, who was not included in most analyses, because his data were incomplete: they only reached up to 2;1 and the data could not be transferred to EXMARaLDA.

Observed phenomena and their outcomes

Listed below are the six bilingual effects of languages in contact, encountered in our research. Under each one of these effects, some phonological phenomena exemplifying them are specified.

Delay: Pretonic (unfooted) syllables in bilingual Spanish – Vowel length in bilingual German – Rising pitch accent in prefinal phrases in bilingual Spanish.
Order of acquisition: Prosodic Word structures in bilingual Spanish.
No effect: Bilingual Spanish vowels – Consonant clusters.
Acceleration: Syllable codas in Spanish.
Transfer: Voiced stops vs. spirants in bilingual Spanish
Fusion or *merger*: Monolingual German and bilingual Spanish VOT from 2;0 to 2;6 – Rhythm.

Results

This section summarizes our studies about the phonology of German-Spanish bilingual children and their comparison with monolinguals. Given the bilingual condition of the children studied, the languages in contact result in some type of influence or interaction, which will be described case by case.

Delay

Pretonic unfooted syllables in Spanish and German

Unfooted syllables are the underscored initial syllables of words like *melón*, 'melon' or *pelota*, 'ball' (Figure 3.1a). The former is iambic shaped and the latter amphibrachic shaped. The study reported here (Lleó 2002) focuses on the truncation of such unfooted syllables by three Spanish monolingual children (José, María and Miguel), three German monolingual children (Bernd, Marion and Thomas) and three German-Spanish bilingual children (Jens, Nils and Simon). Whereas monolingual Spanish-speaking children produce the first syllable of words like *pelota*, 'ball' very soon (between 1;3 and 1;6), German-Spanish bilinguals produce these or similar words by means of two syllables, i.e. as trochaic feet: e.g. ['lota] or ['pota]. Production in Spanish of the unfooted syllable takes place between 1;8 and 1;10 by the

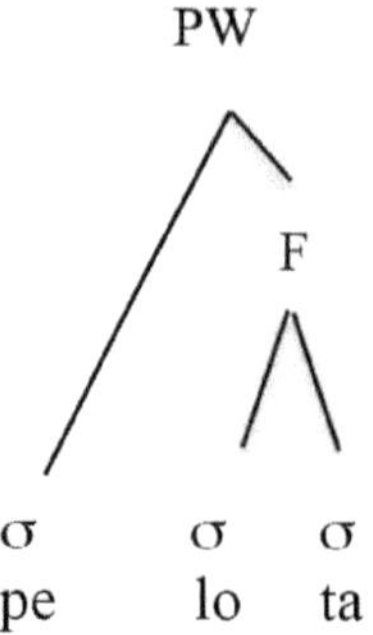

Figure 3.1a. Prosodic structure of Spanish *pelota*, 'ball'.

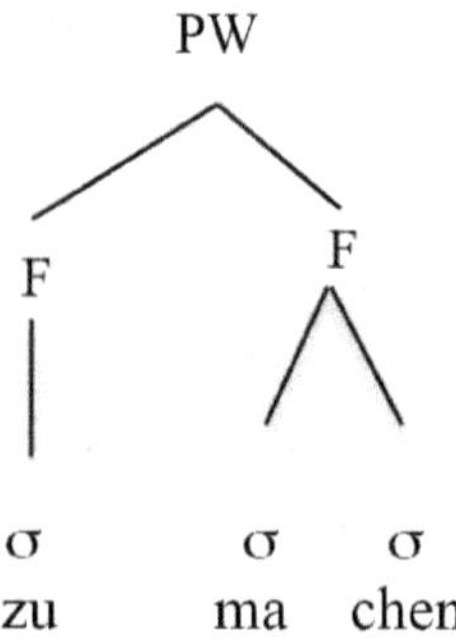

Figure 3.1b. Prosodic structure of German *zumachen*, 'close'.

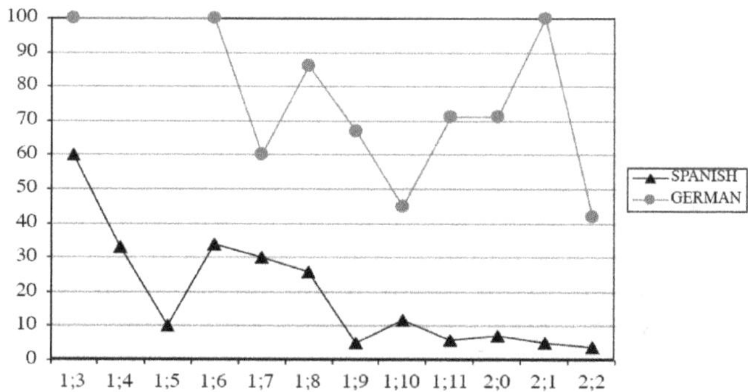

Figure 3.2a. Percentages of unfooted syllable truncation by Spanish and German monolinguals. (Adapted from Lleó 2002: p. 298, Fig. 1.)

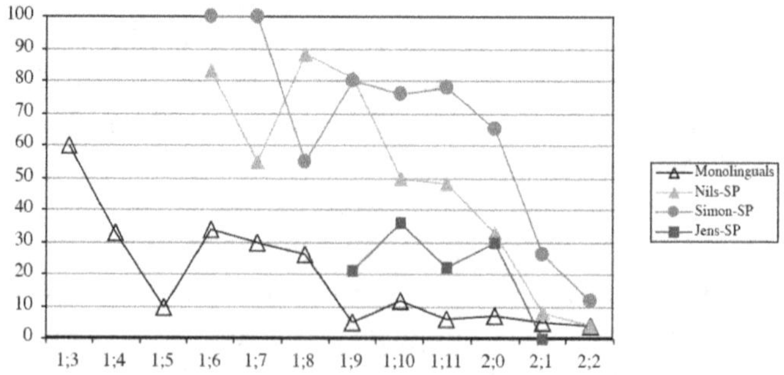

Figure 3.2b. Percentages of unfooted syllable truncation by Spanish monolinguals and three bilinguals in Spanish. (Adapted from Lleó 2002: p. 305, Fig. 2.)

Table 3.2. Examples of unfooted syllable production by monolingual Spanish-speaking children.

Written word	*Meaning*	*Phonetic word*	*Child form*	*Child*	*Child age*
conejo	'rabbit'	/koˈnexo/	[noˈnino]	José	(1;7,27)
			[toˈleto]		(1;11,23)
pelota	'ball'	/peˈlota/	[baˈpɔta]		(1;9,2)
sombrero	'hut'	/somˈbrero/	[baˈbɛlo]		(1;9,2)
zapato	'shoe'	/θaˈpato/	[paˈpapa]		(1;7,27)
			[pɐˈpɐto]		(1;9,2)
zapato	'shoe'	/θaˈpato/	[haˈpatʃa]	Miguel	(1;6,7)
bizcocho	'cookie'	/biθˈkotʃo/	[viˈkɔtʃɔ]		(1;7,26)
manzana	'apple'	/manˈθana/	[pɑˈsanɑ]	María	(1;10,17)
			[paˈθanɑ]		(1;10,17)
trompeta	'trumpet'	/tromˈpeta/	[haˈbadɑ]		(1;10,17)
			[bɔˈpitɑ]		(2;0,11)

bilinguals. Examples of such trisyllabic words as produced by monolingual Spanish-speaking children appear in Table 3.2. It has been argued (Lleó 2002) that unfooted syllables fill a prosodically weak and thus vulnerable position, and are often deleted. Figure 3.1a shows the prosodic structure of the Spanish word *pelota*, 'ball', comprised of the trochaic foot *lota* and the pretonic syllable *pe*, which is the unfooted syllable. German also has unfooted syllables, but they are far less numerous than in Spanish. The majority of trisyllabic words produced by the German-speaking children do not show the structure of Figure 3.1a, but that of Figure 3.1b, comprised of two feet with primary stress on the initial one.

Figure 3.2a shows percentages of unfooted syllable truncation in German (higher curve) and Spanish (lower curve) monolinguals. The curves clearly show that the percentages of truncation in German are much higher than those of Spanish. Figure 3.2b shows the percentages of truncation by the three bilingual children, Jens, Nils and Simon (higher curves) in Spanish, in comparison to truncation by the group of Spanish monolinguals (lower curve). Two of the bilinguals of Figure 3.2b show percentages of truncation as high as those produced by the German monolinguals in Figure 3.2a. Thus, the similarity of truncation percentages shown in Figure 3.2b between the bilinguals in Spanish and the German monolinguals suggests that the Spanish of bilinguals is being influenced by German.

Vowel length in German

German has 15 vowels in its inventory (including *schwa*), out of which eight are short and seven are long (Wiese 1996: 19–20). There is a clear contrast between short and long vowels, the latter being about twice as long (Delattre 1965). Spanish has only five vowels in its inventory and there is no significant duration difference between them. According to the study by Kehoe and Lleó (2003), German monolinguals (Bernd, Marion and Thomas) already at age 1;10–2;0 produce a statistically significant difference between long and short vowels, although the distance between the two sets is shorter than in the case of adults. At 2;3–2;6 the difference in duration between long and short vowels is the same as in the adult language, reaching over 100 ms. Kehoe (2002) examined the length of vowels produced by the bilinguals growing up in Hamburg (Jens, Nils and Simon). According to the results of that study, bilinguals do not produce any significant difference between long and short vowels until almost 3;0, and the difference in duration has not reached the standard values yet. Thus, these bilingual children acquire long vowels (and the concomitant contrast between short and long vowels) with some months of delay, when compared to monolinguals.

VOT in German/VOT in Spanish

German distinguishes voiced and voiceless stops by means of short lag (voiced) and long lag (voiceless), whereas Spanish distinguishes them by means of short lag (voiceless) and lead voicing (voiced). In a study with three German monolingual children and four German-Spanish bilinguals (Kehoe, Lleó and Rakow 2004), the German monolinguals generally produced the contrast between long lag and short lag at age 2;0. Most bilingual children differentiated voicing in the two languages. However, Spanish lead voicing is delayed in the bilingual context. Whereas all Spanish monolinguals acquired lead voicing at 5;0, only one of the bilinguals did. Long lag is slightly delayed, as well: Two out of the four bilingual children produced the contrast towards age 2;6 and a third child produced it at age 3;0. Difficult features, like lead voicing (Davis 1995), when not supported by the linguistic community, tend to be substituted by more frequent ones, or values may be reduced or increased towards the values they have in the other language, reaching so-called 'compromise' values.

Rising pitch accent in Spanish prefinal phrases

Utterances produced by two monolingual German-speaking children (Marion and Thomas), one monolingual Spanish child (Miguel) and two German-Spanish bilingual children (Jens and Simon) between 2;10 and 3;1 were selected for the study of prefinal phrases and their contours. The focus was on the production of prefinally stressed broad focus declarative sentences, which do not contain a focused word. The main findings of our study are in Lleó, Rakow and Kehoe (2004):

(a) The German monolinguals produce H*L as a nuclear and prenuclear accent in broad focus declaratives before 3;0.
(b) The Spanish monolingual produces[2] L*H or L>H* as a prenuclear accent in broad focus declaratives before 3;0.
(c) One German-Spanish bilingual produces both H*L and L>H* as a prefinal accent before 3;0 with frequencies equivalent to those of monolinguals.
(d) Another German-Spanish bilingual also produces both H*L and L>H* as a prefinal accent, but he substitutes many of them, especially Spanish patterns being replaced with German ones.

Given the substitution patterns we have found in our data, we hypothesize that L>H* is more marked than H*L. Markedness can explain the higher frequency of substitution of H*L for L>H* in Spanish, but it cannot explain the reverse substitution of L>H* for H*L which was occasionally found in German. We assume that the latter substitution is due to Spanish influence.

Rhythm

The study of rhythm comprised utterances by three monolingual Spanish, three monolingual German, and six German-Spanish bilingual children, three living in Hamburg (Germany) and three in Madrid (Spain) at about 3 years of age. Spanish is considered to be syllable-timed and German stress-timed (Kehoe, Lleó and Rakow 2011). Spanish and German 3-year-old monolingual children produce different rhythmic patterns based on the Pairwise Variability Index of vowels (PVI-V) and on the Pairwise Variability Index of consonants (PVI-C), showing a higher degree of variability in German than in Spanish. See Figure 3.3, where the PVIs of Spanish child

2 The standard contour of this pitch accent is described as rising with delayed peak, which used to be represented as L*H. Nowadays L>H* is the preferred representation.

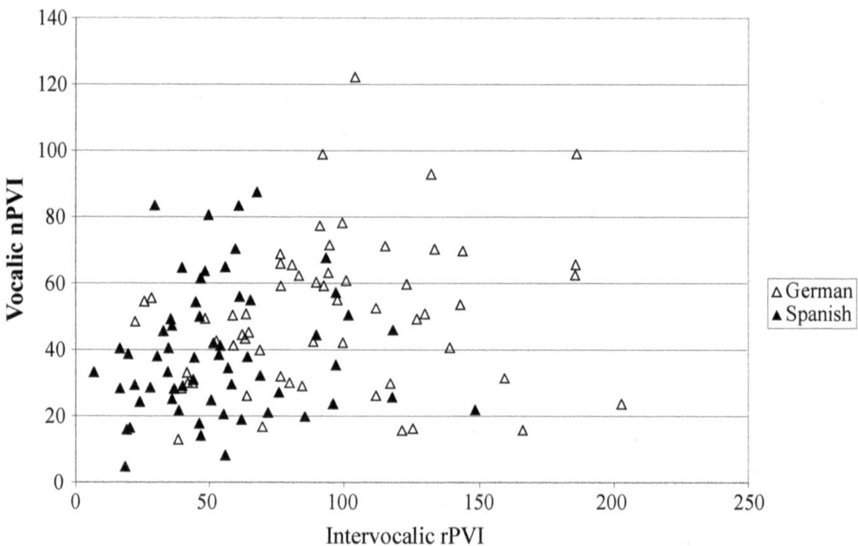

Figure 3.3. Pairwise Variability Index of consonants (x axis) and vowels (y axis) for 3-year-old German and Spanish monolingual children. (Adapted from Kehoe, Lleó and Rakow 2011: 339, Fig. 3.)

utterances appear closely grouped, while the PVIs of German child utterances occupy a larger extension in the diagram. However, bilingual children displayed similar rhythmic patterns in both languages. In general, there were no statistically significant differences between the PVIs of the Spanish and German of bilinguals, according to *t*-tests. The PVI-Cs were generally higher in the Spanish of the bilinguals than in monolingual Spanish, i.e. the Spanish syllable-timed pattern of bilinguals had become more stress-timed. Influence of Spanish on German was found to be greater in Spain (based on the Pairwise Variability Index of vowels) than the influence of German on Spanish in Germany (only Pairwise Variability Index of consonants). The explanation proposed for the different degrees of influence is based on the unmarkedness of Spanish syllable timing being resilient to becoming stress-timed (Bunta and Ingram 2007).

Summarizing, our study showed a tendency for stress timing to become closer to syllable timing and vice versa, for syllable timing to become closer to stress timing. This phenomenon has been encountered in other contexts and has been called bidirectional transfer (Olson 2013), compromise values in relation to VOT and rhythm (Kehoe, Lleó and Rakow 2004, 2011), fusion (Queen 2001) and merger (Bullock, Dalola and Gerfen 2006).

Order of acquisition

According to Lleó (2006), trisyllables of the type as in Figure 3.1a (with a pretonic or unfooted syllable) are produced before monosyllables by Spanish monolinguals, but monosyllables in Spanish are produced by German-Spanish bilinguals before trisyllables. The latter order coincides with that in which German monolinguals acquire Prosodic Word structures: i.e. monosyllables before trisyllables. This means that the interaction between the two languages leads to producing monosyllabic words before trisyllabic ones in bilingual Spanish. That is, the influence of German becomes clear in the order adopted in the Spanish of bilinguals.

One more aspect to note in relation to this form of interaction is that order of acquisition seems to be, in principle, a quantitative relation which is, in fact, reducible to delay and acceleration: if monolinguals produce first A and then B, whereas bilinguals produce first B and then A, this could also mean that bilinguals show acceleration of B and delay of A. However, it may be useful to maintain the distinction between delay and acceleration on the one hand and order of acquisition on the other, because delay and acceleration are temporal relations that are mutually exclusive; if the acquisition of a certain phenomenon is delayed, it cannot be accelerated, and vice versa: if it is accelerated it cannot at the same time be delayed. But order of acquisition, if analysed by means of delay and acceleration, could not be characterized in a differentiating manner, as it would be taking place with simultaneous activation of both, delay and acceleration.

Table 3.3 shows the development of Prosodic Word structures in Spanish by monolinguals and bilinguals, and in German by monolinguals, with indication of age at each different step. Feet are represented as sequences of syllables or as a single syllable (if heavy, i.e. if the rhyme is comprised of a

Table 3.3. Developmental order of word types in monolingual Spanish, monolingual German and bilingual Spanish.

Spanish monolinguals

1;2–1;3 $[{}'(\sigma\sigma)_{Ft}]_{PW\rightarrow}$ 1;3–1;6 $[\sigma{}'(\sigma)_{Ft}]_{PW}\,[{}'(\sigma\sigma)_{Ft}]_{PW\rightarrow}$ 1;7 $[{}'(\sigma)]_{PW}$

German monolinguals

1;0–1;6 $[{}'(\sigma\sigma)_{Ft}]_{PW}[{}'(\sigma)_{Ft}]_{PW\rightarrow}$ 1;8–1;10 $[[{}'(\sigma)_{Ft}]_{PW}[{}'(\sigma)_{Ft}]_{PWPW\rightarrow}$ 1;11–2;2 $[\sigma{}'(\sigma)_{Ft}]_{PW}[\sigma{}'(\sigma\sigma)_{Ft}]_{PW}$

Spanish bilinguals

1;2–1;4 $[{}'(\sigma\sigma)_{Ft}]_{PW\rightarrow}$ 1;5–1;6 $[{}'(\sigma)]_{PW\rightarrow}$ 1;8–1;10 $[\sigma{}'(\sigma)_{FtPW}[\sigma{}'(\sigma)_{Ft}]_{PW}$

σ = syllable; Ft = Foot; PW = Prosodic Word; Trochaic Ft = 'sw; Iambic Ft = w's; Amphybrachic Ft = w'sw; s = prosodically strong; w = prosodically weak.

long vowel or a vowel followed by a coda). In the case of Spanish monolinguals, the evolution of word structures goes from disyllables to trisyllables, to monosyllables, whereas bilinguals in Spanish also begin with disyllables, and from there they go to monosyllables and later on to trisyllables. In the second stage, monolingual German-speaking children produce words comprised of two feet, coinciding with the prosodic structure of *zumachen* in Figure 3.1b above, whereas monolingual Spanish-speaking children produce words comprised of a single foot, often preceded by an unfooted syllable. In fact, the order followed by the bilinguals in Spanish is comparable to the one followed by the German monolinguals (Lleó 2006), who begin producing monosyllables and disyllables.

No effect

Inventory of vowels in Spanish

Spanish has a very simple vocalic system, comprised of the five cardinal vowels: /i e a o u/. We observed the vowel system of two monolingual Spanish-speaking children from PAIDUS and of three bilingual children from PhonBLA (Kehoe 2002). Results show that monolingual Spanish-speaking children acquire vowels very soon: at 1;6 they already produce 80% of the Spanish vowels target-like, and at 2;3–2;6 they almost produce 95% target-like. Bilinguals acquire the Spanish vowels in a comparable manner: at 1;6 they already produce more than 80% target-like, and at 2;3–2;6 one child produces 83% and the other children 92% and 100% target-like, that is, the bilinguals even reach slightly higher percentages than the monolinguals. Spanish vowels are very frequent because of the syllable timing status of Spanish (Ramus, Nespor and Mehler 1999), and because they can be considered a subset of the cardinal vowels, which implies that they are unmarked and simple. Moreover, they are rather similar to the German short ones, and are simple, in the sense of practically not having allophones.[3]

3 Spanish vowels do not exhibit significant duration differences, which does not preclude the presence of very small differences of duration and quality that depend on the surrounding context. For instance, vowels may be slightly longer if stressed, and the vowels /e/ and /o/ may have a higher degree of openness when they appear in the context of /r/ or /x/ (see Kehoe and Lleó 2017; Navarro Tomás 1916, 1917, 1918).

Acceleration

Bilinguals in Spanish acquire syllable codas faster, compared to Spanish monolinguals (Lleó, Kuchenbrandt, Kehoe and Trujillo 2003). German has about 67% of closed syllables, whereas Spanish has less than 30%. The reason for this difference is that in German, many of the early words are monosyllabic, but prosodic constituents must be binary. This entails that the coda of monosyllables is often required to fulfil binarity at the syllabic level. Since closed syllables are marked (Jakobson 1941), the two factors, markedness and frequency, appear to be in contradiction to one another in German closed syllables, given that markedness is expected to cause delay, whereas highly frequent production (e.g. of codas) may lead to their enhancement. Two outcomes of crosslanguage interaction in relation to codas are possible: either (a) more codas are produced by the bilinguals in Spanish as compared to those produced by monolinguals, or (b) bilinguals produce fewer codas in German than monolinguals. The first hypothesis turned out to be correct. A look to the percentages of coda production brings the following results: monolingual German-speaking children produce more than 80% of codas after 1;11, but monolingual Spanish do not yet produce 50% of codas at 2;4. Bilinguals produce more than 50% of codas in Spanish after 1;9. Because both languages have codas, an additive effect takes place too. It is also important to note that coda production by bilinguals in German does not differ from that of German monolinguals.

Transfer: Spirants

Spanish has an obligatory process of spirantization by which the voiced stops /b, d, g/ are produced as such in absolute initial position, after nasal consonants, and after other non-continuant consonants; but after vowel or continuant consonants, they are produced as continuants or spirants: [β, ð, ɣ] (Lleó and Rakow 2005). Bilinguals substitute voiced stops for spirants in Spanish, following a period in which both monolinguals and bilinguals produced many spirants. Figure 3.4 shows the percentages of target-like spirantization by monolinguals and bilinguals. Percentages by three monolinguals of the database PAIDUS (Jose, Maria and Miguel) are presented as a group, while bilingual values are shown individually for three children: Jens, Nils and Simon. Monolinguals produce high percentages of spirants at the earliest stage, whereas bilinguals have high percentages of continuants at first, but after 2;6 they mainly produce stops. Replacement of stops for spirants could be due to markedness (stops are unmarked) or

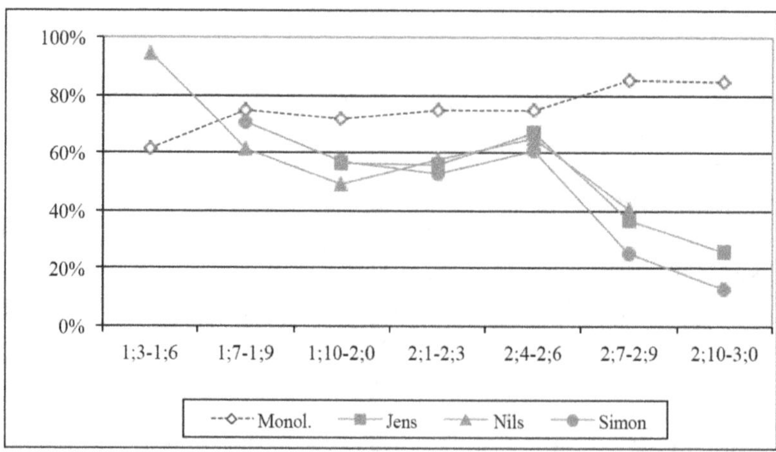

Figure 3.4. Percentages of target-like spirantization in Spanish by three monolingual Spanish children as a group, and three German Spanish bilinguals, individually. (Adapted from Lleó and Rakow 2005, Fig. 6.)

to transfer (from German) which lacks spirantization.[4] Given the regression that begins at about 2;6 in the case of bilinguals, the avoidance of spirants in Spanish is rather interpretable as due to transfer from German into Spanish. The question then arises as to what is being transferred.

The most straightforward answer to this question has been based on the classical proposal that considers phonological segments as the target for transfer. Obviously, segments are not transferred here, because Spanish already has voiced stops in its inventory. Is it then the occurrence of a certain type of segment (here, voiceless stops) in a certain type of environment (here, following a continuant segment, as e.g. a vowel, /s/, /ɾ/, etc.) that is being transferred? Some clarification about my use of the notion transfer may be needed here. Any category or phenomenon going from language A to language B constitutes transfer, if it fills an empty space in language B. The notion of transfer was born and was maximally used in the era of structuralism, which mainly dealt with tangible categories. That is the reason why *segments* were the targets of transfer (Gass and Selinker 1983). Later on, with the advent of Generative Phonology, *rules* were transferred, e.g. the rule of Glottal Stop Insertion (GSI, Wiese 1996: 173; see also Lleó

4 German has some spirantization, limited to fast and informal registers. See Kohler (1995: 210, 212). Wiese (1996: 206–07) also refers to a different type of spirantization in German.

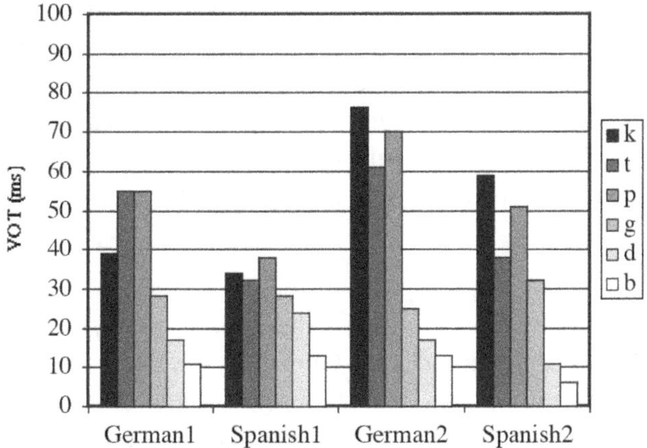

Figure 3.5. VOT values for the German and Spanish voiceless and voiced stops produced by the German-Spanish bilingual child Nils, during two time spans (Nils 1 = 2;0–2;3, Nils 2 = 2;3–2;6). (Adopted from Kehoe, Lleó and Rakow 2004, Fig. 8, p. 80.)

and Vogel 2004: 82) in the L2 Spanish produced by L1 speakers of German, and this meant making a large step into abstraction. More recently, within Optimality Theory, abstraction is going even farther, and hierarchies of constraints, i.e. parts of grammar, can be targeted by transfer, as well.

Fusion

VOT

Figure 3.5 shows the VOT values for the bilingual child Nils at two different time points. At time 1 (2;0–2;3), the German voiceless stops have a mean value of 50 ms whereas the mean value of the Spanish voiceless stops amounts to 35 ms. German voiced stops have a mean of 19 ms and 31% of lead voicing (11/35). The mean of Spanish voiced stops amounts to 21 ms and 19% of lead voicing (5/26). At time 2 (2;3–2;6), the VOT of German voiceless stops has notably increased to a mean of 70 ms, and the VOT of Spanish voiceless reaches a mean of 50 ms. German voiced stops have a mean of 18 ms and 10% of lead voicing (3/30). The mean of Spanish voiced stops is similar: 16 ms with 44% of lead voicing (4/9) (Kehoe, Lleó and Rakow 2004).

These results show an interesting phenomenon, namely the creation of a new category, a sort of 'shortish' long lag, which in Spanish has a mean of 50 ms, and in German a mean of 70 ms. Thus, it is a bit too long in Spanish, and it falls in the short range in German. The values at time 2 show that short lag is used to produce both the German and Spanish voiced stops. This illustrates that fusion involves bidirectional transfer, plus some new category emerging from the joining or merging of two categories, one from each language. The child differentiates voiceless and voiced in both languages, with values approaching the German adult ones, but not totally.

Rhythm

Something comparable was found in the domain of rhythm, in relation to Spanish being syllable-timed and German being stress-timed. Findings from a study with monolinguals and bilinguals (see above) showed that the stress timing of bilingual German was less variable, and the syllable timing of bilingual Spanish was more variable than in the case of monolinguals. Both phenomena are due to the influence of the other language of the bilingual learner.

Acquisition of grammar in Optimality Theory

Back in 1993, the birth of Optimality Theory (OT) introduced a new perspective into the acquisition of phonology. Instead of looking at processes from input to output, as theories based on standard generative phonology used to do, the proposal in OT was to tackle the output directly by means of constraints that are in a hierarchical relation, from outranking to dominated ones. Constraints that are not outranking can be violated in order to fulfil a more dominant constraint. The procedure for acquisition in OT is constraint demotion. It is well known and generally accepted that there are two types of constraints: markedness and faithfulness, and that in early child language, markedness outranks faithfulness (Gnanadesikan 1995, among others). In this context, if the target language requires it, markedness constraints lose force and find their way down, interspersed among faithfulness constraints in agreement with the Error Driven Constraint Demotion (EDCD) and Recursive Constraint Demotion (RCD) Algorithm of Tesar and Smolensky (1993). According to them, a constraint that is often violated must be demoted. For example, CVC syllables are marked compared to CV syllables, because each coda production violates the No Coda constraint. Thus, the many violations of the No Coda constraint lead soon to its demotion in German, and in bilingual Spanish, as well, when it is under pressure from German. That is, the No Coda constraint is violated very often, especially in bilingualism, and such frequent violations lead to the result that German-Spanish bilinguals produce more codas than Spanish-speaking monolinguals. (Recall the discussion in the section above.)

Demotion of constraints and bilingual child language

Bilingual crosslanguage interaction may lead to the demotion of certain constraints, which in the bilingual condition will be accelerated, delayed or not affected. In what follows, demotion of particular constraints will be discussed.

Delayed demotion of alignment constraints

Pretonic (unfooted) syllables in the Spanish of bilinguals are produced with some delay. One might want to compare this with the production of codas, which led to acceleration. However, codas occur in both languages and are very frequent in one of the languages, but unfooted syllables are not numerous in either of the two languages, being especially scarce in German. In order to produce one of these unfooted syllables a constraint disallowing them must be violated. Such a constraint is Align Left.

(1) Align (PW, L, Ft, L): All PWs must have their left edge aligned with a Ft.

Constraint (1) requires that PWs begin with a foot and, thus, disallows the presence of material (e.g. the underscored syllable in [pe'lota] 'ball') between the left edge of the PW and the left edge of the foot (Figure 3.1a). On the other hand, in order to produce more than one foot (as the German-speaking children begin to do before producing unfooted syllables), a constraint requiring that all feet be aligned to the right-hand side with a PW (disallowing prosodic structures with more feet than one) must be violated. This constraint is Align Right.

(2) Align (Ft, R, PW, R): The right edge of all Ft must be aligned with the right edge of a PW.

Taking into consideration that align constraints are markedness constraints, they should be outranking at the initial stages of acquisition. In the following stages, these align constraints will be demoted: in Spanish which has many unfooted syllables, the demoted constraint is Align Left and in German, where PW structures are mainly comprised of two feet, it is Align Right. Both will be positioned below the faithfulness constraint, MaxIO (banning deletions), but with a certain delay in comparison with monolinguals.

Order of acquisition

For the child to produce unfooted syllables, Align Left is relevant, but bilinguals do not reach the threshold to demote Align Left as soon as the monolinguals, given the reduced number of amphibrachs (word structures comprised of an unfooted syllable followed by a disyllabic foot) in child German. In Lleó (2006) it was shown that the order of acquisition in Spanish is related to the need to produce unfooted syllables, which leads to early demotion of Left Alignment. See Table 3.3 above.

Demotion of markedness constraints

There is another class of constraints that ban specific marked segments, like German long vowels, long lag stops, Spanish prevoiced stops or /r/. In order for the child to produce such marked segments, violation of the relevant constraint must be allowed by demotion. These are some of the constraints: No Long Vowels (Ge), No Fricatives (Ge/Sp), No Long Lag Stops (Ge), No Prevoiced Stops (Sp), No /r/ (Sp). Such marked segments are produced by the monolingual child sooner or later depending on frequency and on the degree of difficulty. For instance, it is well known that the Spanish /r/ is a difficult segment, being one of the last to be acquired (not before 3 years of age), followed by prevoiced stops, which are not generally mastered before the child is 4 or 5 years old (Davis 1995). Such marked segments are replaced by less marked ones, for example [d] or [ð] generally replace /r/ in child Spanish. In the case of bilinguals, on the one hand, replacements have a larger choice given the presence of the other language, which in the case of German offers /R/ as a choice (also sporadically produced by Spanish monolinguals as a substitute for /r/, but not as often as by bilinguals). Notice that constraints constitute groups, whose members are ordered at some levels of the hierarchy. Thus, for instance, in the following hierarchy:

(3) No Prevoiced Stops >> No Long Lag Stops >> No Short Lag Stops

demotion has already taken place following the hierarchy of markedness. As the resulting order suggests, Short Lag Stops, being the least marked stops, are the first to be produced, and this agrees with their position at the right-hand side of the hierarchy. Their production will be followed by the production of Long Lag Stops and prevoiced or lead voice stops in that order, from right to left, which again shows that the order in which they will be produced converges with the degree of markedness.

Accelerated demotion of the No Coda constraint

A good case for acceleration has been presented in the section above, involving the No Coda constraint. Bilinguals in Spanish produce more closed syllables and sooner than monolinguals, which suggests that the No Coda constraint is demoted in the bilingual grammar earlier than in the monolingual grammar. This phenomenon is better explained by OT than by any other theory, given that multiple violations of a constraint accelerate its demotion. Violations of the No Coda constraint are very frequent, given the presence of codas in both languages (additiveness), and especially given their function in German, codas being often required by the stress system of the language (Féry and Herbst 2004). Whereas from the point of view of universals, marked categories are expected to be acquired later than unmarked ones, from the perspective of OT it is frequency (i.e. repeated violations of a constraint) that will cause its demotion. Thus, assuming that at the initial state of acquisition markedness outranks faithfulness, the markedness No Coda constraint banning codas and the faithfulness MaxIO constraint banning deletions are related as shown in (4).

(4) Initial hierarchy: No Coda >> MaxIO

At the next stage faithfulness outranks markedness, leading to the hierarchy (5).

(5) Hierarchy at the next stage: MaxIO >> No Coda

Each coda production by the child presupposes a violation of No Coda, and the numerous violations of No Coda end up with a rapid demotion of this constraint in German as well as in bilingual Spanish. According to OT tenets, we can say that the more marked and frequent an entity is, the faster it will be acquired.

Intonation: Delay of another type of alignment constraint

In an earlier section it has been shown that Spanish prefinal or prenuclear phrases may be delayed in the production of bilinguals in comparison to monolinguals, which means that the alignment of the pitch accent L>H* with delayed peak is generally acquired later by bilinguals in Spanish than by Spanish monolinguals. This can be expressed as delay of Align L>H*. German prefers a H*L pitch accent both in prefinal as well as final phrases. Thus, Align L>H* may be violated later by bilinguals, because it is not very frequent given that its occurrence in prefinal phrases is limited to Spanish.

No effect

Spanish vowels are unmarked (Jakobson 1941 and above). Their production implies that a constraint of type No Canonical Vowels has been systematically demoted, and this has happened at a very early age. Early demotion is most appropriate here, given the universal validity of these vowels. No difference from their acquisition in the Spanish monolingual condition could be observed. Another candidate for no effect are branching onsets. Given the combination of obstruent plus liquid in both languages, which is not very frequent in either language, no bilingual effect is expected.

Demotion of constraints as transfer: Voiced stops vs. spirants in Spanish

The bilingual child is capable of comparing the segments belonging to each language, and of choosing one for reasons that appear to be guided by simplicity. For instance, avoidance of spirantization in Spanish leads to uniform production of morphemes, e.g. the child may not apply spirantization and produce /b/ invariably as [b]. Assuming that constraints (6) and (7) are involved in spirantization (see below), if the constraint (7) Agree outranks (6) UE, there will be a lot of form variability, which in German is usually dispreferred. An outranking Agree corresponds rather to the grammar of Spanish. Thus, OT explicitly shows that in the present case *Transfer*, understood as transfer of (part of) the hierarchy of constraints, maintains the uniformity of lexical forms.

(6) Uniform Exponence (UE): A lexical item is invariable for property P (from Kenstowicz 1996).

(7) $\text{Agree}_{[\text{cont}]}$: After a vowel (or a [+cont] segment), voiced obstruents are [+cont].

Constraint (7) adapts Autosegmental phonology to the present analysis, and predicts assimilation. Both constraints are present in both languages, but whereas Spanish abides by the constraint $\text{Agree}_{[\text{cont}]}$, German does not and keeps the voiced stops, generally, without modifying them. This means that the two languages have different hierarchies of constraints. The Spanish hierarchy has an outranking Agree which favours assimilation, thus spirantization, whereas the German one has an outranking UE, which keeps the underlying form unchanged.

(8) Spanish hierarchy: $\text{Agree}_{[\text{cont}]}$ >> UE

(9) German hierarchy: UE >> $\text{Agree}_{[\text{cont}]}$

Bilinguals in Germany at about 2;6 adopt the German grammar for Spanish, i.e. the German hierarchy without assimilation. Note that the notion of transfer is adaptable to different theories. Nowadays, within OT, constraints are the building blocks of grammar, and they build a hierarchy in each language. Thus, it is this order of constraints, alias Grammar, that is being transferred, bringing with it an ever greater degree of abstraction to the concept of transfer. In this particular case, transfer has been referred to as *empty transfer*, because it results in segments (voiced stops) already present in the language, i.e. Spanish (Lleó in press).

Fusion (or merger): VOT and rhythm

The bilingual child Nils produces what have been dubbed 'compromise' values, in the sense that the VOT of his voiceless stops in German is not as long as the long lag VOT produced by German monolinguals, and the VOT of short lag stops in Spanish is longer than the VOT of Spanish monolinguals (see above). Such compromise values correspond to fusion or merger: New categories are produced, which are influenced by the categories of monolinguals (Kehoe 2013). That is, the German long lag of bilinguals (corresponding to German voiceless) is influenced by Spanish short lag (corresponding to Spanish voiceless), and the Spanish short lag of voiceless stops is influenced by the German long lag of voiceless stops.

Findings from the study on rhythm with monolinguals and bilinguals discussed above showed that the stress timing of bilingual German was less variable compared to monolinguals, and the syllable timing of bilingual Spanish was more variable. Both phenomena are due to the influence of the other language of the bilingual child, i.e. to bidirectional transfer.

Summary of OT grammars

Although labels like Heritage Language, Majority Language, Additiveness, Markedness, Uniformity etc. are useful, and contribute to the understanding of some of the outcomes of crosslanguage interaction, they are only labels, and are not explanatory enough. We need some mechanism that explains when and why in the process of acquiring two languages simultaneously, language contact will lead to a certain type of influence, or to no influence. The procedure involved is based on stochastic learning, as proposed in OT (Boersma and Hayes 2001; Boersma and Levelt 2000; Prince and Smolensky 2004). Stochastic processes are random processes evolving with time. More specifically, in probability theory stochastic processes are time sequences showing the evolution of some system represented by a variable whose change is subject to random variation (Lawler 2006).

A good example for the way OT contributes to learning has been given in relation to the No Coda constraint. It is violated both in Spanish (not too often) and very often in German, which means that additiveness (occurrence of codas in both languages) and frequency (in at least one of the languages) play an important role. Both factors, additiveness and frequency, accelerate the demotion of No Coda in the bilingual Grammar of Spanish. No Coda and also Align, being markedness constraints, are outranking at first, and must be demoted in order for the child to produce codas and pretonic syllables, respectively (Tesar and Smolensky 1993). Although there are unfooted syllables in both languages, and thus Align Left appears to be additive, frequency is not high: in German child language unfooted syllables occur seldom, and in Spanish they appear more often but their frequency is not comparable with the frequency of codas in German. Thus, both languages, Spanish and German, together have an enhancing effect on codas (which leads to acceleration), but they need time to reach the threshold to produce unfooted syllables and to demote Align Left, which brings some delay, when bilinguals are compared to monolinguals.[5] Both types of constraints regulate prosodic structure, and should be demoted during the first months or initial stage, in order for the child to advance in the mastery of his/her phonological modules.

5 The existence of a threshold motivating the relevance of a certain constraint is predicted by the theory of constraints, although this is mute as to the number of violations required for the activation of a constraint.

Discussion: Effects of the various forms of interaction

According to the various results of our analyses, delay is soon overcome, and acquisition takes place in the bilinguals as in the case of monolinguals. Acceleration is a temporary advantage, which at the end is counterbalanced, and acquisition takes place as in the case of monolinguals. While these two manifestations of interaction are temporary effects, without long-lasting consequences, transfer may have long-lasting or even permanent effects. Order of acquisition is also compensated in the long run, so that acquisition is achieved as in the case of monolinguals. Fusion, as proposed by Queen (2001), is comparable to transfer, as it introduces new categories that emerge under contact.

We can, thus, say that crosslanguage interaction shows quantitative and qualitative differences. Quantitative differences are: delay, acceleration, and variation in the acquisition order. Qualitative differences are: transfer and fusion. Interaction is not a discrete category in a binary sense (of just being yes/no), but a gradient category which may have a short (Align Left in Spanish) or a long-lasting (Spanish UE >> $\text{Agree}_{[\text{cont}]}$) effect. Figure 3.6 just mentions the six cases of crosslanguage interaction discussed in this chapter. They show that the bilingual grammar is at the same time permeable and resilient to the influence of the other language of the bilingual child. Table 3.4 offers examples resulting from the crosslanguage interaction and corresponding factors.

Table 3.4. Effects of crosslanguage interaction, constraints and relevant phenomena.

Acceleration ←	Delay ←	Order ←	No effect →	Transfer →	Fusion
Max>>No Coda	Align Left	Align Left	No c. vowels	UE>>Agree	x+y
Codas	Unfooted σ	Mono-syllables	Sp vowels	Spirants	Short Lag
	No /r/	Trisyllables	Sp clusters	Long Lag	Long Lag
	No prevoice			Short Lag	Rhythm
	No Long Lag				Intonation

Is phonology different?

According to our findings, on the one hand, there is much crosslanguage interaction in the phonology, but apparently not in other domains, and on the other hand, interaction varies a lot as far as its outcome is concerned. Both issues raise the question: 'Why is Phonology different?' as Bromberger and Halle (1989) asked on *derivational* grounds. We can try to introduce some rationale to order the effects of interaction (see Table 3.4). The table can be assumed to begin with no effect, and then go into both directions: on the left-hand side, we find order, delay and acceleration; on the right-hand side, transfer and fusion. Most positions are filled by more than one phenomenon, depending on what we encountered as we were looking for various types of bilingual acquisition outcomes. We refer to them in a succinct way, considering that this has already been discussed all through the chapter. Here, the decisive criterion is the constraint(s) involved in each case. In the first place, no effect occurs only in case the relevant constraint is a No X constraint, banning unmarked or canonical segments, like the Spanish vowels, which are acquired fast, independently of the vowels of the other language. Another case without apparent effect is the acquisition of consonant clusters in Spanish, which in the bilingual condition are produced in a manner comparable to the monolingual condition (see Kehoe, Hilaire-Debove, Demuth and Lleó 2008).

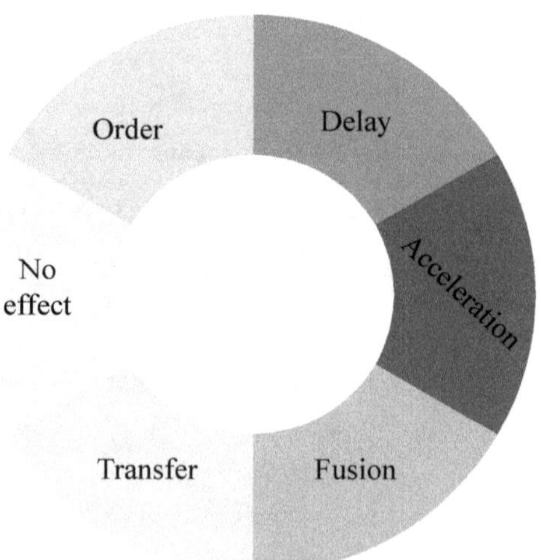

Figure 3.6. Outcomes of the simultaneous acquisition of two languages.

Order of acquisition has been dealt with in a section above. The production of trisyllables in Spanish (with a pretonic unfooted syllable) presupposes the demotion of Align Left. This gets demoted soon in the case of monolinguals. However, bilinguals need some more time to demote it, because such unfooted syllables are very scarce in German, and not too frequent in Spanish.

Delay will take place in case constraints banning marked segments are active, like No /r/, No Long Lag, which are demoted once a certain threshold is reached, and demotion finally makes the production of such segments possible. Acceleration is best exemplified by closed syllables, and their No Coda constraint, which is soon demoted underneath the faithfulness Max constraint against deletions. Note that the difference between the No Coda constraint and, for example, constraints like No /r/ is the great frequency with which German codas are produced, whereas /r/ occurs only in Spanish, and it is infrequent. Transfer is best exemplified by lack of spirantization among German-Spanish bilinguals. As we have shown above, Agree is the relevant constraint, outranking in monolingual Spanish, whereas in the case of bilinguals, assimilation (with concomitant variation of form) is not favoured, and this results in UE (Uniform Exposure) outranking Agree.

Other cases of transfer have been reported in the literature regarding VOT, as for example the production of Long Lag in Spanish instead of Short Lag (see Jakovljevic 2012, Olson 2013). It is common to find fusion instead of transfer in relation to phenomena that are continuous instead of categorical, e.g. Long Lag may not be replaced by another category, but rather, instead of being produced with mean values of +70 ms of VOT, it may use mean values of +50 ms. And at the same time that Long Lag is produced with lower values by the bilinguals, Short Lag may be produced with values that are higher than the monolingual ones.

Towards a classification of constraints

Different types of constraints lead to different outcomes which, in conjunction with the relevant constraints of the other language of the bilingual, end up with one of the six types of interaction discussed here, and summarized in Figure 3.6.

(1) The lack of an interaction effect in the Spanish vowels is based on constraints like No Canonical Vowels, which should be soon demoted,

since such vowels are the first to be produced, which implies that the constraint involved is violated from the very beginning.[6]

(2) Comparable constraints referring to individual segments, like No Long Vowels, No Long Lag Stops, No Lead Voice, need more time and more input to be demoted, given their presence only in one of the languages. They lead to a certain delay, because they do not occur so often as to enhance early demotion.

(3) Complex segments depend on constraints that by means of assimilation organize segments into allophonic entities. This leads to much delay and to transfer that can last long. Assimilation here is controlled by Agree constraints.

(4) A very interesting finding is the outcome of codas (i.e. closed syllables) in the bilingual condition. Spanish monolinguals produce few codas, whereas German monolinguals produce many codas. And the interesting fact is that bilinguals produce many more codas in Spanish than monolinguals. This result has been cited often in the literature, because it seemed unexpected since codas are marked. However, OT explains this elegantly: A markedness constraint just needs frequent violations to give way to demotion.

(5) Besides segmental constraints, there are constraints with the role of organizing prosody, e.g. the production of unfooted syllables. These are governed by Align constraints, in Spanish Align Left, which must be demoted soon, as Spanish-speaking children produce unfooted syllables sooner than German-speaking children. German-Spanish bilinguals need more time than monolinguals to demote Align Left, because such syllables are less frequent in German and lack of frequency delays demotion. The variegated results of bilingualism in this situation can be accounted for by observing the different development of word types in the grammar of monolinguals and bilinguals.

(6) VOT is governed by constraints that control single segments, but it may also lead to transfer, and/or fusion. Long Lag is borrowed by Spanish bilinguals in order to distinguish voiceless from voiced, since Spanish uses Lead Voice, which is a feature learned very late by Spanish-speaking children.

6 The OT analysis of unmarked entities like the canonical vowels of Spanish by means of constraints like No X, where X is the canonical entity, is ad hoc and thus not satisfactory. However, discussion of possible alternatives is not feasible here, for lack of space, and must be postponed.

(7) Moreover, we found fusion, which consisted in producing Long Lag, but shorter than the German one. That is, on the basis of the two categories of the two languages, Short Lag and Long Lag, a new category of 'Medium Lag' was created. This analysis implies that single segment constraints must be ordered, as the segments have various degrees of markedness: Short Lag is the least marked, and markedness increases from right to left. See hierarchy (3) on page 94 above.

(8) In the prosodic domain, Rising Pitch is often considered more marked than Falling Pitch, and thus more substitutions of Falling Pitch replacing Rising Pitch are expected.

(9) Stress is also governed by constraints, e.g. Trochees outrank Iambs, both in German and Spanish. These constraints governing prosody are as important as constraints related to segments. But, whereas segmental and structural constraints are easy to relate to, prosodic constraints are complex and more difficult to account for.

Not all constraints related to segments have the same explanatory adequacy. Those involving markedness are straightforward, and their formulation is intuitively acceptable. But even those related to markedness may leave some difficulties open (see footnote 4 above).

The present chapter and the notion of a Protolanguage

In this chapter we have inspected several bilingual child studies of utterances related to various language segmental and suprasegmental domains. According to the definitions of the book's prologue, all these utterances belong to a Protolanguage. A child will progressively abandon the Protolanguage and enter the adult Language. Our focus has been on the protolanguages of bilingual children, each one of which will end up going into Language. Moreover, one of the languages, Spanish, is the heritage language, which develops as the weaker language of the two (Montrul 2008). If this language does not develop totally to the adult stage, can it still be considered a Language or does it maintain its status as a Protolanguage? The main characteristic of a Protolanguage is that it has not yet arrived at its final stage. Once the Protolanguage reaches a stage that can be considered final, independently of whether it converges to the adult Language fully or only partially, it reaches a steady state with the potential of being modified and of showing variation.

Conclusion

Studies of phonological acquisition have come to the conclusion that child grammar is characterized by markedness constraints outranking faithfulness constraints. If the child is exposed to two languages simultaneously, crosslanguage interaction is not only possible, but also probable. However, the outcome of bilingual acquisition is difficult to predict, because it depends on various factors. Moreover, grammars may be more permeable or resilient to the influence of the other language of the bilingual child, depending on the domain under study. In our research we have found six different types of outcomes: no effect, order, delay, acceleration, transfer and fusion. Finding the nature of factors leading to one type or other of bilingual outcome is the main goal of the studies brought up in this chapter. In these studies we found grammars that after the initial time span of strong restrictions, based on markedness outranking faithfulness, markedness must be demoted in order for the grammar to converge with the target language. In general, markedness must be demoted, and so must be all constraints that, compared to the initial stage, imply a higher degree of complexity. We have argued in favour of OT as a theory of acquisition. That is, OT has proposed an Error Driven Constraint Demotion Algorithm, which can nicely provide an explanation for some of the outcomes of bilingual acquisition. We have also tried to provide one constraint relevant for each outcome type, but this one-to-one correspondence still remains a *desideratum*.

Acknowledgements

I would like to thank the Research Center for Multilingualism (SFB 538), German Research Foundation (DFG) and University of Hamburg for their support of my projects on phonological acquisition. I thank the research assistants of the projects along the last several years, especially Dr Margaret Kehoe, and the student assistants, for their work, as well as the children of the projects from Hamburg and Madrid, and their parents.

References

Almeida, L., Rose, Y. and Freitas, J., 2012, 'Prosodic influence in bilingual phonological development: Evidence from a Portuguese French first language learner', in A. Biller, E. Chung and A. Kimball (eds.), *Proceedings of the 36th Annual Boston University Conference on Language Development*, pp. 42–52, Somerville, MA: Cascadilla Press.

Babatsouli, E. and Ingram, D., 2015, 'What bilingualism tells us about phonological acquisition', in R.H. Bahr and E.R. Silliman (eds.), *Routledge Handbook of Communication Disorders*, pp. 173–82, Routledge: Taylor & Francis.

Boersma, P. and Hayes, B., 2001, 'Empirical tests of the gradual learning algorithm', *Linguistic Inquiry* 32, 45–86.

Boersma, P. and Levelt, C., 2000, 'Gradual constraint-ranking learning algorithm predicts acquisition order', *Proceedings of the Child Language Research Forum* 30, 229–37. https://doi.org/10.1162/002438901554586

Bromberger, S. and Halle, M., 1989, 'Why phonology is different', *Linguistic Inquiry* 20, 51–70.

Bullock, B., Dalola, A. and Gerfen, C., 2006, 'Mapping the patterns of maintenance versus merger in bilingual phonology: The preservation of [a] vs. [ɑ] in Frenchville French', in J.Y. Montreuil (ed.), *New perspectives on Romance linguistics*, pp. 15–29, Amsterdam/Philadelphia: John Benjamins.

Bunta, F. and Ingram, D., 2007, 'The acquisition of speech rhythm by bilingual Spanish- and English-speaking 4- and 5-year-old children', *Journal of Speech, Language and Hearing Research* 50, 999–1014. https://doi.org/10.1044/1092-4388(2007/070)

Davis, K., 1995, 'Phonetic and phonological contrasts in the acquisition of voicing: Voice onset time production in the acquisition of Hindi and English', *Journal of Child Language* 22, 275–305. https://doi.org/10.1017/S030500090000979X

Delattre, P., 1965, *Comparing the phonetic features of English, German, Spanish and French*, Heidelberg: Julius Groos Verlag.

Fabiano, L. and Goldstein, B.A., 2005, 'Phonological cross-linguistic influence in bilingual Spanish-English speaking children', *Journal of Multilingual Communication Disorders* 3, 56–63. https://doi.org/10.1080/14769670400027316

Fabiano-Smith, L. and Goldstein, B.A., 2010, 'Phonological acquisition in bilingual Spanish-English speaking children', *Journal of Speech, Language, and Hearing Research* 53, 160–78. https://doi.org/10.1044/1092-4388(2009/07-0064)

Féry, C. and Herbst, L., 2004, 'German sentence accent revisited', in S. Ishihara, M. Schmitz and A. Schwarz (eds.), *Interdisciplinary studies on information structure (ISIS)* 1, Liasion and syllable structure in French prenominal adjectives, Ms.

Gass, S.M. and Selinker, L. (eds.), 1983, *Language transfer in language learning*, Cambridge, MA: Newbury House.

Gnanadesikan, A.E., 1995, *Markedness and faithfulness constraints in child phonology*, University of Massachusetts at Amherst: Ms, ROA-67.

Jakobson, R., 1941, *Kindersprache, aphasie und allgemeine lautgesetze*, Uppsala: Almqvist & Wiksell.

Jakovljevic, B., 2012, 'VOT transfer in the production of English stops by Serbian native speakers', in T. Paunovic and B. Cubrovic (eds.), *Exploring English Phonetics*, pp. 31–47, Newcastle, UK: Cambridge Scholars Publishing.

Kehoe, M., 2002, 'Developing vowel systems as a window to bilingual phonology', *International Journal of Bilingualism* 6, 315–34. https://doi.org/10.1177/13670069020060030601

Kehoe, M., 2013, *The development of prosody and prosodic structure*, New York, NY: Nova Publishers.

Kehoe, M., 2015, 'Cross-linguistic interaction: A retrospective and prospective view', in E. Babatsouli and D. Ingram (eds.), *Proceedings of the International Symposium on Monolingual and Bilingual Speech 2015*, pp. 141–67, ISBN: 978-618-82351-0-6, retrieved from http://ismbs.eu/publications.

Kehoe, M., Hilaire-Debove, G., Demuth, K. and Lleó, C., 2008, 'The structure of branching onsets and rising diphthongs: Evidence from the acquisition of French and Spanish', *Language Acquisition* 15, 5–57. https://doi.org/10.1080/10489220701774229

Kehoe, M. and Lleó, C., 2003, 'The acquisition of nuclei: A longitudinal analysis of phonological vowel length in three German-speaking children', *Journal of Child Language* 30, 527–56. https://doi.org/10.1017/S030500090300566X

Kehoe, M. and Lleó, C., 2017, 'Vowel reduction in German-Spanish bilinguals', in M. Yavaş, M. Kehoe and W. Cardoso (eds.), *Romance-Germanic bilingual phonology*, pp. 14–37, Sheffield, UK: Equinox Publishing Ltd.

Kehoe, M., Lleó, C. and Rakow, M., 2004, 'Voice onset time in bilingual German-Spanish children', *Bilingualism: Language & Cognition* 7, 71–88. https://doi.org/10.1017/S1366728904001282

Kehoe, M., Lleó, C. and Rakow, M., 2011, 'Speech rhythm in the pronunciation of German and Spanish monolingual and German-Spanish bilingual 3 year olds', *Linguistische Berichte* 227, 323–51.

Kenstowicz, M., 1996, 'Base identity and uniform exponence: Alternatives to cyclicity', in J. Durand and B. Laks (eds.), *Current trends in phonology: Models and methods*, vol. 1, pp. 363–93, University of Salford.

Kohler, K.J., 1995, 'The realization of plosives in nasal/lateral environments in spontaneous speech in German', in *Proceedings of the XIIIth International Conference on Phonetic Studies*, Vol. 2, pp. 210–13, Stockholm.

Lawler, G., 2006, *Introduction to stochastic processes*, Boca Raton, FL: Chapman & Hall/CRC Press.

Lleó, C., 2002, 'The role of markedness in the acquisition of complex prosodic structures by German-Spanish bilinguals', *International Journal of Bilingualism* 6, 291–313. https://doi.org/10.1177/13670069020060030501

Lleó, C., 2006, 'The acquisition of prosodic word structures in Spanish by monolingual and Spanish-German bilingual children', *Language and Speech* 49, 207–31. https://doi.org/10.1177/00238309060490020401

Lleó, C., 2012, 'Monolingual and bilingual phonoprosodic corpora of child German and child Spanish', in T. Schmidt and K. Wörner (eds.), *Multilingual corpora and multilingual corpus analysis. Hamburger Studies on Multilingualism*, pp. 107–22, Amsterdam/Philadelphia: John Benjamins. https://doi.org/10.1075/hsm.14.08lle

Lleó, C., in press, 'Aspects of the phonology of Spanish as a heritage language: From incomplete acquisition to transfer', *Bilingualism, Language and Cognition.*

Lleó, C. and Cortés, S., 2013, 'Modelling the outcome of language contact in the speech of Spanish-German and Spanish-Catalan bilingual children', in J. Kabatek and L. Loureido (eds.), [Special Issue on 'Language competition and linguistic diffusion: Interdisciplinary models and case studies'], *International Journal of the Sociology of Language* 221, 101–25.

Lleó, C., Kuchenbrandt, I., Kehoe, M. and Trujillo, C., 2003, 'Syllable final consonants in Spanish and German monolingual and bilingual acquisition', in N. Müller (ed.), *(In)vulnerable domains in multilingualism*, pp. 191–220, Amsterdam/Philadelphia: John Benjamins. https://doi.org/10.1075/hsm.1.08lle

Lleó, C. and Rakow, M. 2005, 'Markedness effects in voiced stop spirantization in bilingual German-Spanish children', in J. Cohen, K.T. McAlister, K. Rolstad and J. MacSwan (eds.), *Proceedings of the 4th International Symposium on Bilingualism (ISB4)*, pp. 1353–71, CD ROM, Somerville, MA: Cascadilla Press.

Lleó, C., Rakow, M. and Kehoe, M., 2004, 'Acquisition of language-specific pitch accent by Spanish and German monolingual and bilingual children', in T. Face (ed.), *Laboratory Approaches to Spanish Phonology*, pp. 3–27, Berlin/New York: Mouton.

Lleó, C. and Vogel, I., 2004, 'Learning new segments and reducing domains in German L2 Phonology: The role of the prosodic hierarchy', *International Journal of Bilingualism* 8, 79–104. https://doi.org/10.1177/13670069040080010601

Montrul, S., 2008, *Incomplete acquisition in bilingualism: Re-examining the age factor* [Series on Studies in Bilingualism], Amsterdam: John Benjamins. https://doi.org/10.1177/13670069040080010601

Navarro Tomás, T., 1916, Cantidad de las vocales acentuadas, *Revista de Filología Española* 3: 387–408.

Navarro Tomás, T., 1917, Cantidad de las vocales inacentuadas, *Revista de Filología Española* 4: 371–88.

Navarro Tomás, T., 1918, *Manual de pronunciación española*, Madrid: Imprenta de los sucesores de Hernando.

Olson, D.J., 2013, 'Bilingual language switching and selection at the phonetic level: Asymmetrical transfer in VOT production', *Journal of Phonetics* 41, 407–20. https://doi.org/10.1016/j.wocn.2013.07.005

Paradis, J. and Genesee, F., 1996, 'Syntactic acquisition in bilingual children: Autonomous or interdependent?', *Studies in Second Language Acquisition* 18, 1–25. https://doi.org/10.1017/S0272263100014662

Prince, A. and Smolensky, P., 2004, *Optimality theory: Constraint interaction in generative grammar*, Malden, MA/Oxford, UK/Victoria, Australia: Blackwell Publishing. https://doi.org/10.1002/9780470759400

Queen, R.M., 2001, 'Bilingual intonation patterns: Evidence of language change from Turkish-German bilingual children', *Language in Society* 30, 55–80. https://doi.org/10.1017/S0047404501001038

Ramus, F., Nespor, M. and Mehler, J., 1999, 'Correlates of linguistic rhythm in the speech signal', *Cognition* 73, 265–92. https://doi.org/10.1016/S0010-0277(99)00058-X

Schmidt, T. and Wörner, K. (eds.), 2012, *Multilingual corpora and multilingual corpus analysis, Hamburger studies on multilingualism* Vol. 14, Amsterdam/Philadelphia: John Benjamins.

Tesar, B. and Smolensky, P., 1993, *The learnability of optimality theory: An algorithm and some basic complexity results*, Rutgers Optimality Archive ROA-2, http://ruccs.rutgers. edu/roa.html.

Thomason, S.G. and Kaufman, T., 1988, *Language contact, criolization and genetic linguistics*, University of California Press.

Wiese, R., 1996, *The phonology of German*, Oxford, UK: Clarendon Press.

Conxita Lleó, now retired, was Professor of Romance Linguistics at the University of Hamburg, Germany. She studied Romance Languages at the University of Barcelona and General Linguistics at the University of Washington (Seattle), and received two PhD degrees, one from each university. Her focus of research lies in bilingualism, child language, phonological acquisition and sound change, where she has published about 100 studies and several books. Over a period of about two decades she obtained research grants from the German Science Foundation.

4

Acquired singleton fricatives and lateral in cluster development: A bilingual child case

Elena Babatsouli

Introduction

This chapter is concerned with the development of CC clusters, where C_1 is a labial fricative and C_2 is a lateral ($F_{LAB}L$), longitudinally in child speech. The acquisition of consonant clusters by children is of particular interest in phonological acquisition research because clusters, being a marked construct, are difficult to master. Markedness (Jakobson 1941/1968) underpins ease or difficulty of phonological learning, it determines acquisition paths, and is subject to universal, language-specific and learner-specific tendencies. Research on consonant cluster acquisition crosslinguistically attempts to account for this interplay of factors. A longitudinal case study in child bilingual acquisition is a small-scale mirror of such research that adds to the crosslinguistic data pool and may inform typical and atypical language acquisition. Thus, the present study focuses on a bilingual child's simultaneous acquisition of $F_{LAB}L$ in English and standard Modern Greek in a span of 17 months of phonological development. This investigation differs from previous ones in the literature in at least three respects. Firstly, it addresses two-member cluster development in child speech based on longitudinal, quantifiable data providing further insights into the presence of developmental stages. Secondly, it investigates cluster acquisition in a single bilingual child whose two languages, Greek and English, exhibit different phonotactic distribution for the consonantal sequences involved in $F_{LAB}L$. Lastly, it examines how a CC cluster develops, given that the child has already acquired each member of the cluster in singleton contexts. There is no study in Greek, English or other bilingual pairs addressing these questions. The perspective taken here is new to the literature on CC cluster acquisition by either monolingual or bilingual children.

$F_{LAB}L$ clusters in Greek and English

A description of the basic phonological and phonetic properties of $F_{LAB}L$ clusters follows with a focus on English and Greek. The acoustic characteristics of Greek consonants (Botinis 2011; Nirgianaki 2014) largely match those of English (Ladefoged 2006). The labial fricatives present in the phonemic and phonetic inventory of these two languages, *f* and *v*, belong in the larger sound class of obstruents which includes both continuant (fricatives) and non-continuant (stops) consonants. The clear lateral [l] (found in these cluster contexts) belongs to the class of liquids (laterals and rhotics). The production of fricative obstruents impedes the flow of air in the oral cavity to the point of creating indefinite turbulence. On the other hand, no or little constriction is involved in the articulation of lateral sounds, which allows for continuous non-turbulent airflow in the vocal tract. The extent of opening of the articulators relates to sonority, and decides how prominent one sound class is over another. As a result, according to the sonority scale in increasing values: *stops, fricatives, nasals, liquids, glides, vowels* (Selkirk 1984), a fricative is a less sonorant sound than a lateral.

Due to sonority, the distinction between obstruent and liquid becomes a fundamental one, having an impact on the way that CC sequences, like /f, v/ + /l/, are acquired in typical and atypical contexts of language acquisition. An obstruent-liquid cluster is the optimal branching CC onset under standard phonological theory, though a distinction is regularly made between 'true' clusters and /sC/ clusters. The latter are named 'adjuncts' because /s/ is not part of the syllable onset but is syllabified independently. Due to this special status and because /sC/ clusters commonly violate the homorganic rule and sonority (e.g. Gierut 1999; Kenstowicz 1994), they are often singled out in investigations (Barlow 2001; Ben-David 2006; Yavaş 2010; Yavaş and Babatsouli 2016) on cluster acquisition. It is also known that a minimal sonority distance (SD) between cluster members leads to markedness in acquisition (Clements 1990).

Markedness in this chapter refers to two things: complexity as specification for a phonological distinction and production difficulty caused by articulatory and perceptual factors; markedness may also imply the scarcity of a sound in terms of typological implication hierarchies and distributional frequencies in a language and across languages. Given these, rising sonority clusters (such as *pl* in Greek ˈple.no 'wash') are less marked than level-sonority clusters (such as *pt* in Greek pti.ˈno 'fowl'), while falling sonority clusters (like *ft* in Greek ˈfta.no 'I reach') are the most marked of all. The Greek data presented in IPA throughout the chapter show adult surface forms (for a key to Greek orthography see Table 4.3 in the Appendix).

A rising sonority from onset C_1 to C_2 at a maximal sonority distance is the least marked option in child developmental productions (Clements 1990; Gierut 1999). In other words, the requirements for the ultimately unmarked onset-cluster, excluding the glides (*j*, *w*) as C_2, should have the following profile: a low sonority stop followed by a highly sonorant liquid. Despite the central role sonority plays in explaining cluster acquisition, a consonantal segment's melodic structure in terms of binary features is often more influential than sonority (Stemberger and Chavez-Peón 2015; Yavaş 2013).

The production of CC sequences also relates to gestural combinations affecting the speed at which articulators (lips, tongue tip and tongue dorsum) move and the degree to which they influence cluster production. There are three phonetic factors involved in the gestural coordination and timing patterns of the C_1C_2 overlap: the position in the word, the order of C_1C_2 place of articulation and the manner of articulation of C_1 and C_2. It is known that there is less overlap in CC production in the following circumstances: word-initially rather than word-medially; in a dorsal-coronal sequence than in a labial-coronal sequence; in $C_{1[\text{STOP}]}$ than in $C_{1[\text{FRICATIVE}]}$; and in $C_{2[\text{STOP}]}$ than in $C_{2[\text{LIQUID}]}$ (see Yip 2013 and references therein). The presence or lack of voicing in C_1 does not emerge as a decisive factor in the gestural production of consonant clusters. Overall, it is sensible to conclude that because of these stipulations in phonological and phonetic theory, the production of a fricative-lateral sequence is not among the least marked options in cluster production; indeed, children acquire fricative-liquid clusters after stop-liquid clusters (Ingram 1976).

Comparing English and Greek, /fl/ and /vl/ are similar with regard to their syllabification occurring at syllable onsets word-initially and -medially, e.g. *fly*, ˈflu.ði 'fruit skin'; pa.ˈdo.fles 'slippers'; ˈvle.po 'see'. This does not hold true for the phonotactic distribution of the clusters in the two languages. Thus, while */fl/* occurs in both English and Greek, English phonotactics do not permit /vl/ (Kenstonwicz 1994; PAL 1995; Setatos 1974). This phonotactic difference between English and Greek may reflect a more general tendency among languages to lack the voiced alternative of $F_{\text{LAB}}L$. Though Russian also permits /#vl/, to my knowledge, there are no studies assessing the developmental path of /vl/ in child speech.

Labial fricative clusters are quite frequent in the Greek language (Yip 2013) which features a sum of nine word-initial obstruent-lateral clusters (PAL 1995), *pl, bl, fl, vl, θl, kl, gl, γl, xl*. Excluding *sl, ðl, #zl* in coronal place, Greek permits all permutations of obstruent manner, place and voicing. The distribution of *fl* in English is also quite high (Saporta 1955). There are fewer /#fl/ words in Greek than in English: a simple dictionary search on words starting with /fl/ produces some 1,223 types in English and some 100 types in Greek. There are also fewer Greek /#vl/ than /#fl/ words. The simple search gives a total of 74 words, of which only about 29 are likely to be in the input directed to a child: one of these is ˈvle.po 'see'. The frequency of *fl* in the vocabulary is further attested by commonly recurring words in child speech in English – words like *flower* and *fly* in studies of monolingual and bilingual development (Kirk 2008; Leopold 1949; Smith 1973). Such words are also common in the data elicitation designs of studies (e.g. Anthony, Bogle, Ingram and McIsaac 1971) and in picture/word worksheets intended for use in speech-language pathology intervention (e.g. Bowen 1995–2016). The emphasis on children's lexical repertoire here serves to stress the known lexical dependency of phonological patterns in development (Kehoe 2011, 2015; Stoel-Gammon 2011).

On the acquisition of $F_{LAB}L$ clusters in child speech

Relating existing studies

There is an abundance of studies reporting on the typical development of CC clusters in monolingual speech crosslinguistically, as in Dutch (Fikkert 1994; Gerrits and Zumach 2006), French (Demuth and McCullough 2008; Kehoe and Hilaire-Debove 2004; Rose 2000), German (Lleó and Prinz 1996), Hebrew (Ben-David 2006), Norwegian (Kristoffersen and Simonsen 2006), Polish (Szreder 2011), Spanish (Barlow 2005) etc. Alongside these, research has also tackled cluster development in studies of typically developing bilingual children (Goldstein and Swasey Washington 2001; Holm and Dodd 1999; Yavaş 2010; Yavaş and Babatsouli 2016). Moreover, there is an array of studies that examine the acquisition of consonant clusters in child disordered speech (Barlow 2001; Chin and Dinnsen 1992; Ingram 1976; Klopfenstein and Ball 2010). Only a few studies trace cluster development longitudinally in case studies of individual children (Demuth and McCullough 2008; Dyson 1988; Holm and Dodd 1999; Yavaş and Babatsouli, 2016; Watson and Scukanec 1997a, 1997b). Detailed and longitudinal accounts of consonantal segment acquisition in child case studies (Leopold 1949; Schnitzer and Krasinski 1994; Smith 1973; etc.), on the other hand, do not focus on cluster development and the data provided are not quantifiable in nature to allow direct comparisons with studies on cluster development.

Large cross-sectional studies on the acquisition of word-initial CC sequences in English assess monolingual children that mostly speak General American English (GAE). The majority of these studies investigate clusters in *single word productions*: e.g. Templin (1957) in 480 children aged 3;0–8;0; Smit (1993) in 1,049 children aged 2;0–9;0; and Smit et al. (1990) in 997 children aged 3;0–9;0. Two other cross-sectional studies also report on cluster production in *the connected* English *speech* of 204 children aged 2;0–6;0 (Wellman, Case, Mengert and Bradbury 1931), and in 100 children aged 1;3–4;6 (Olmsted 1971). The Edinburgh Articulation Test (EAT) (Anthony et al. 1971) assessed the developing speech of 510 Scottish children aged between 2;6 and 6;0 to provide information on the acquisition of /fl/ based on data elicitation using the word *flower*. McLeod, Doorn and Reed (2002) have also investigated normative cluster development for Australian English with similar results. With regard to the Greek language, PAL (1995) is the only large cross-sectional study on the acquisition of consonant singletons that evaluated the speech of 300 children aged 2;6–6;0 and elicited data through the picture naming of 101 words. PAL (1995) also reports on the acquisition of Greek CCs by relating the proportion of children within an age group (like 3;6–4;0, 4;0–4;6) that has acquired a specific consonant cluster; there is, however, no definition of the criterion of acquisition used.

Developmental aspects: Acquisition level

First instances of CC cluster productions crosslinguistically (as in German and Spanish) have been reported to appear as early as age 1;10 word-initially and 1;5 word-medially (Lleó and Prinz 1996). Studies on CC clusters in GAE mention adult-like productions as early as ages 2;0–2;6 (Dyson 1988; Preisser, Hodson and Paden 1988; Stoel-Gammon 1987; Watson and Scukanec 1997a, 1997b). By age 3;0, there is more variety in the production of both true and adjunct clusters. Also, word-initial clusters appear later than word-final ones crosslinguistically (Macken 1977; Watson and Scukanec 1997a, 1997b). Smit et al. (1990) found that 75% of children produce obstruent-lateral clusters between ages 4;6 and 5;6. The acquisition level of /fl/ in GAE is reported to be 75% at age 5;0 (Templin 1957), and 90% (Smit et al. 1990) at ages 5;6 (girls) and 6;0 (boys). Scottish children acquire /fl/ at 50% correctness by age 3;0, 74% by age 4;0 and 87% by 5;6 (Anthony et al. 1971). Dutch children show /fl/ correctness at 61.2% by age 3;4 (Jongstra 2003). Earlier acquisition of CC in Spanish than in English is reported by Goldstein (2007) and references therein.

Greek /fl/ is reported to be in the productions of 75% of the children in the age group 4;0–4;6, while Greek /vl/ appears to be present in 75% of the children earlier (age group 3;6–4;0, PAL 1995). It is worth noting, however, that the information on Greek cluster acquisition reported in PAL (1995) is limited to a single table (without a corresponding discussion to rule out errors) that shows targeted clusters and respective age groups in which adult-like productions are in the phonetic inventory of 75% of the children in each age group. The word types used in the test are: fli.ˈdza.ni 'cup' for /fl/, and vi.ˈvli.o 'book' for /vl/. Given the phonotactic differences of the two clusters in the word types used, the finding that /fl/ is acquired after /vl/ in Greek (PAL 1995) may be misleading. Nevertheless, an immediate comparison indicates that Greek monolinguals acquire $F_{LAB}L$ earlier than GAE-speaking monolinguals.

It is worth mentioning the acquisition patterns found for /fl/ in the two monumental case studies undertaken by Leopold (1949) and Smith (1973) of their own children acquiring English. Amahl's attempts at /fl/ (Smith 1973) are reported as follows in: *fly* → [w] (2;4, 2;5); [βʷ] (2;4); [ʋ], [v], [l], [w], [ʋl] [vl] (2;6); *flower* → [w] (2;2); [l] (2;6, 2;8); [ɫ] (2;8, 2;9); and *flowers* → [ɫ] (2;10, 3;0, 3;1). Adult-like productions are reported in *flower* and *flowers* at 3;3 and 3;1, respectively, though a couple of instances of voiced two-member production, [vl], occur sporadically at the early age of 2;6. Though these data are not evidence of acquisition level, it is clear that /fl/ establishes itself in the phonetic inventory of the child after age 3;0. Hildegard's productions of attempted /fl/ in her English (Leopold 1949) also show a preference for [w] in e.g. *fly* and *flower* (1;11), *Florence* (1;11–2;0), though initial combinations are treated as [f], with [v] becoming more frequent after 2;0. There is no mention of adult-like cluster productions in Hildegard's speech, since the study only addresses her sound learning in the first two years.

Typically, developmental studies on clusters do not directly assess the acquisition level of their members in singleton context in relation to their acquisition level in the cluster context. It is common in studies of obstruent-lateral acquisition in English that children have not acquired both cluster members as singletons, especially the lateral. In this line of thought, it is worth giving an account of the normative acquisition levels of singleton /f, v, l/ in English and Greek. With regard to /f/ in GAE, it is found acquired at syllable onset: at 78% (age 2;8) in Olmsted (1971) and 78% (age 2;10) in Ingram, Christensen, Veach and Webster (1980); and at 86% (age 3;0) and 90% (age 3;6) in Smit et al. (1990). On the other hand, /v/ is acquired at syllable onset at 10% (age 2;10) in Ingram et al. (1980), at 41% (3;0), and 90% by age 5;6 in Smit et al. (1990). The clear lateral is reported acquired at 77% (age 3;0) and at 90% by age 5;0 in Smit et al. (1990). Greek /f, v, l/ are reported acquired by 50–75% of the children in the age group 2;6–3;0 (PAL 1995). Based on these findings, singletons /f/ and /l/ appear acquired somewhat earlier by monolingual Greek than monolingual GAE children, though Greek monolinguals acquire singleton /v/ much earlier than GAE monolinguals. Ingram (1992) and references therein have reported earlier acquisition of fricatives in Greek. Hence, the studies addressing acquisition of /fl/ in English base their evaluations on children whose acquisition of singleton /f/ and /l/ is partial during the course of $F_{LAB}L$ development. The same holds for the cross-sectional study in Greek.

Developmental aspects: Production patterns

The production patterns for attempted clusters among 2;0–3;0-year-olds are reported to be, early on, inconsistent with the phonotactics of the language acquired, so that in English they are [fw] or stop-[w], and only later become legal, as in the case of sC productions (Dyson 1988; Smit et al. 1990; Templin 1957). In the course of development, however, as exemplified by Amahl's productions of *fly* → [ʋaɪ, vaɪ, laɪ, waɪ, ʋlaɪ, vlaɪ] at age 2;6 (Smith 1973), two-member cluster production involves variable phonological processes. Among the most common ones are: cluster reduction, substitutions as in respective singletons, voice/place/manner assimilations, coalescence and vowel epenthesis (Grunwell 1987; Ingram 1981; Smit 1993), or combinations of these.

On the prosodic level, children tend to produce the universally unmarked syllable, CV, (Clements and Keyser 1983) in place of the more complex CCV. This is the most common simplification pattern in cluster development (Preisser et al. 1988) that is attested to be universally present cross-linguistically (see review in McLeod et al. 2001). Studies as early as 1899 mention CC cluster reduction retaining C_2 (Greenlee 1974 and references therein). Ever since, the reverse is argued to be the case: a C_1[obstruent]-C_2[lateral] cluster has been found to typically reduce to C_1, i.e. /fl/→[f], /vl/→[v] (e.g. Smit 1993 for English; Kappa 2002 and PAL 1995 for Greek). This is because children's CV productions need to conform to a requirement for the largest rise in sonority values from syllable onset to nucleus (Ohala 1999). Pater and Barlow (2003) have abridged reduction patterns evidenced in cluster development by proposing the following implicational prediction: if a segment of a given sonority is retained instead of the fricative, then all segments of lesser sonority will also be retained instead of the fricative.

Cluster simplification is further evidenced in the substitutions of cluster members that are concomitant with the substitutions of the respective sounds in singleton contexts (Smit 1993), thus relating to the acquisition level of singletons. Regarding substitution patterns, C_1 is substituted if C_1[fricative] and C_2 is substituted if C_1[stop] (Kirk 2008). Some feature of the reduced C_2 may also assimilate in the C_1 production, such as the voice assimilation evidenced in *fly*→[vaɪ] (Smith 1973). Mostly assimilations and fewer dissimilations guide the substitution processes (Kirk 2008). Clusters may further be simplified in development by coalescing (mixing) some features of its members, as in /fl/→[w] (Leopold 1949; Smith 1973) that retains the [labial] of C_1 in its secondary place of articulation, as well as the voiced and approximant nature of C_2. Interestingly, singleton *w* is non-marked in monolingual English development (Smit et al. 1990). Another simplification process in children's cluster productions is the epenthesis of /ə/ or another vowel (Olmsted 1971) that increases the articulatory distance between C_1 and C_2 and facilitates production of the unmarked core syllable, i.e. /CCV/→[CV.CV]. Lastly, metathesis, which involves the switching of two adjacent consonants, is found to occur infrequently in cluster development.

Developmental aspects: Acquisition stages

Studies that investigate the speech performance of their participants longitudinally can portray linguistic performance at several points in time, analysing and accounting for changes between successive time points. The first study suggesting stages in the development of cluster production is Greenlee (1974). Greenlee investigated the acquisition of stop-liquid clusters from the published developmental data of ten children aged between 0;10–4;0 in Czech, English, Estonian, French, Serbian and Slovenian. She found that similar temporal and phonological processes control cluster production, proposing that cluster production in children progresses through three main stages:

Stage I: reduction to a single element,
Stage II: two-element production involving assimilatory substitutions,
Stage III: correct productions.

Despite considerable overlapping between stages, there is evident cohesiveness across languages and children. Reductions to [stop] dominate *Stage I*, and intermittent reductions to [liquid] are rare. Two-element clusters occur from 10 months to age 4;0. Idiosyncratic variation characterizes cluster production across children and languages: (i) not all phonological processes apply to all clusters, nor are all stages evidenced in all produced words; (ii) the length of overlapping between stages varies; (iii) the effect of phonological processes varies; and (iv) element substitutions vary even in individual children. Following up this line of work, Elbert and McReynolds (1979) found that the development of all two-member clusters follow Greenlee's stages: deletion of CC (*Non-production*), C_1 or C_2 is deleted

(*Stage I*), CC is produced with at least one member substituted (*Stage II*), C_1C_2 is produced as targeted (*Stage III*). Despite these observations, it is known that cluster types follow individual developmental paths, and that they are at different stages even within a single child (Ingram 1976).

Subsequent investigations on several English-speaking children have provided further evidence of Greenlee's stages. The largest cross-sectional study is Smit (1993) that investigated word-initial two-member clusters in 1,049 GAE-speaking children, aged 2;0–9;0. Smit's results validate the following: negligible whole-cluster deletion, reduction to a single element, and two-element production substituting either both elements or one. The last three processes are present in all ages. The substitutions of cluster members are predicted based on the substitutions of consonants in singleton contexts. Smit (1993) also found that reduction patterns are not necessarily bound to feature markedness in the acquisition of consonants. That is, attempted /tw/ is reduced to the stop though /w/ is also unmarked in children's early productions in English. In their overwhelming majority, obstruent-lateral clusters reduce to the targeted obstruent or an obstruent substitution. A single exception to this pattern seems to be intermittent instances of reduction of the $F_{LAB}L$: /fl/→[l]~[w], also attested in the longitudinal data of the children in Leopold (1949) and Smith (1973). The single stimulus word in Smit's study for targeted *fl* is *flag* that is produced at 13% correctness by age 3;0 and at 80% after 4;6. As mentioned earlier, the /fl/→[w] production pattern may be a result of coalescence or simply a reduction to C_2[lateral] where [w] is a common developmental mismatch for /l/. The aforementioned simplification pattern is not surprising given that the acquisition of /l/ is delayed in monolingual English-speaking children.

Because children delay in acquiring consonant clusters, cluster acquisition research provides important insights on developmental phonology, which in turn puts in perspective patterns found in children's disordered speech, and may guide remediation practices. For instance, Babatsouli (2016) showed that consonant clusters by excrescence (CCEs), i.e. /CV/→[CCV] in child speech appear to be an inherent articulatory and phonological mechanism that facilitates singleton and CC acquisition. Hodson (1989), among others, proposes that clusters are priority targets in speech intervention. This being the broader framework intended here, the present study focuses on a bilingual child's acquisition of /fl/ (English, Greek) and /vl/ (Greek) from age 2;7 to 4;0. Specific research questions steering this study are:

(i) Does a complete acquisition level (90%) of cluster members in singleton contexts challenge known facts in cluster development?
(ii) Are developmental stages and processes in the acquisition of fricative-lateral validated in bilingual Greek/English?
(iii) What is the effect of phonotactic differences across the languages?

The remaining sections address pertinent issues in the methodology of the study, present the data on the child's acquisition of $F_{LAB}L$, discuss results and repercussions, and finally present a summary and conclusions.

The study method

This is a single-subject case study of a female bilingual child's naturalistic speech in Greek and English that was recorded longitudinally from ages 2;7–4;0. Case study methodology is commonly employed in developmental linguistics (e.g. Brown 1973; Nice 1925), and their usual longitudinal time span helps account for changes diachronically. The author took audio recordings of regular interactions with the child, using a hand-held Olympus WS11-311M. Data collection, averaging an hour daily, four days a week, began at 2;7 to better document the child's speech production in her weaker English that was increasing at the time. The author transcribed the child's utterances orthographically and phonetically (IPA) in a CLAN (MacWhinney 2000) database of 511 chat-files, totaling 45,624 utterances in both languages.

Simultaneous consultation of waveform and wideband spectrograms in Praat (Boersma and Weenink 2016) verifies transcription reliability. The frequency range in the software was set between 0 Hz and 10 kHz to capture frication and the pitch range between 200 and 600 Hz, as per child norms (e.g. Kent and Read 1992). The spectrograms (see Figures 4.1–4.9 in the Appendix) of the child's following erroneous and adult-like productions were examined that include lateral deletion, voice assimilation and an instance of consonant epenthesis: *flat* →[fat, sfat, flat] (3;0.24); *fly*→[flaɪ, vlaɪ] (3;5); ˈflu.ði→[ˈflu.ði] 'fruit skin' (3;4.24); ˈvle.po→[ˈve.po] (2;7.19)~[ˈle.po] (2;8.08)~[ˈvle.po] 'see' (3;5.21). Results show that: (i) the acoustic characteristics of the child's consonant productions correspond to expected standards, and (ii) there is direct transition from C_1 to C_2 in two-member productions, which is counter-evidence of vowel epenthesis in this child's speech at ages 2;7 to 4;0.

On the child's acquisition of $F_{LAB}L$

The child's /fl/ in English and Greek

Between ages 2;7 and 3;5, the child targeted /fl/ 124 times in 14 words in English and 3 words in Greek. English words are provided next in italics, while Greek words are provided in IPA as per adult surface production (see Table 4.3 in the Appendix for orthography). The words in English are: *butterfly(ies), flag, flash(ed), flat, flip, flippers, floor, flower(s), flush, fly(ies).* The words in Greek are: ˈflu.ði 'fruit skin'; ˈflu.ðʝa 'fruit skins'; pa.ˈdo.fles 'slippers'. The realizations of /fl/ are shown monthly in Table 4.1 together with non-contextual [fl] productions, meaning [fl] productions in words not targeting /fl/.

Ages 2;7 and 2;8 are evidence of Greenlee's (1974) cluster reduction stage, where /fl/ is reduced to [f]. The lateral is deleted following the 'sonority-based onset selection' (Pater and Barlow 2003), whereby the least sonorant element is retained. The child remains faithful to this reduction pattern even after 2;8, whenever there is a reduction. It is noted that the child has fully acquired (> 90%) singletons /f/ and /l/ by 2;7 which explains why these are rarely substituted when targeting /fl/. In fact, only /f/ is substituted in 5 out 124 /fl/ attempts, in all of which /l/ is deleted. It is observed that Greenlee's reported *Stage II,* where there is substitution of cluster element(s), is basically *absent* in this child's acquisition of /fl/, and this is not due to sampling deficiencies. There is a single occurrence at age 3 where the child deletes /l/ and produces /fl/→[sf], [s] being a substitution of singleton /f/. It may be that the child realized her error in producing /f/→[s] and immediately corrected herself producing [sf]. This, however, happened while repeating *flat* three times consecutively in the same utterance in the form of practice. This is an instance of CCE production: it facilitates acquisition of the complex onset, CCV, on both the articulatory and abstract level (Babatsouli 2016) during phonological development.

At 2;9, [fl] occurs for the first time in 1 out of 4 attempts in *flower(s),* though /fl/ is reduced to [f] at all other times. Also in all other words, /fl/ reduces to [f]. During this month, there is evidence of instantaneous overlapping of Greenlee's reduction stage with the final stage of correct realizations of the targeted cluster, skipping the substitution stage. Until age 3;1, the only correct instance of /fl/ occurs at 3;0 in *flat* in 1 out 3 consecutive attempts in the same utterance. Repetition is known to generally increase variability in productions (e.g. Ingram 1989).

Table 4.1. The child's realizations of /fl/.

		Age										
		2;7	2;8	2;9	2;10	2;11	3;0	3;1	3;2	3;3	3;4	3;5
	butterfly			3f	3f				f	2f	2f	f
	butteflies									f		
	flag							f				
	flash			f					fl			
	flashed						f					
	flat						f, sf, fl					
	flip		f			s						
	flippers					s						
	floor	f	4f	5f	5f, s	2f	6f	11f	f			3fl
	flower	f	f	f, ʃ	4f		4f	3f		2fl	fl	2fl
	flowers		f	f, fl	f				fl	fl	9fl, f	
words	flúði						2f				fl	
	flúðja						f					
	flush			2f			f					
	flies					f						
	fly		f	6f	f	3f				3fl	fl	vl, fl
	paˈdofles									fl		
	non-contextual [fl]											
	dolphin											fl
	fráula									fl		
	fresh										fl	
	Friday											fl
	friendly										fl	
	fruit								fl			
	further										fl	
	pretty											fl
	swap										fl	

Greek /fl/ words are targeted for the first time at age 3;0, which is rather expected as there are fewer /fl/ words in Greek than in English. At age 3;0, /fl/ was reduced to [f] all three times in ˈflu.ði, ˈflu.ðja 'fruit-skin(s)', as was also the case for *flashed, floor, flower, flush*. As mentioned earlier, the only exception is *flat* where realizations varied because of repetition.

At age 3;1, there is evidence of a continued reduction stage, as /fl/ reduces to [f] in every attempted *flag, floor* and *flower.* At 3;2, there is evidence of substantial overlapping between the first and final stages in the acquisition of /fl/. Adult-like [fl] occurs in *flash, flowers,* and reductions to [f] in *butterfly, floor.* It is interesting that non-contextual [fl] also starts appearing at this age, overgeneralizing the cluster in the wrong context. This happened in ***fr**uit* →[fl], possibly because [l] is the child's substitution of the Greek rhotic, [ɾ], which interferes in the child's productions of the rhotic in English, [ɹ].

Age 3;3 shows clear evidence of the final stage of adult-like cluster production. The only reductions to [f] occur in the compound *butterfly(ies)* that persist until age 4;0. It is noted, however, that *dragonfly* was produced correctly at age 3;6, the first time it was targeted. This suggests that the child's difficulty comes from the rhotic preceding /fl/, whose main substitution is [l]. Correct productions of /fl/ occur in English *flower(s), fly* and in tri-syllabic Greek pa.dó.flɛs 'slippers' that was targeted for the first time. Here, there is another non-contextual [fl] in Greek ˈ**fr**a.u.la 'strawberry'.

At ages 3;4–3;5, the patterns are reminiscent of age 3;3. /fl/ is reduced to [f] in the compound word *butterfly,* though preserved in all the other words: *floor, flower, fly.* At 3;5, however, an exception is found to the child's realization patterns longitudinally. In one out of two times, /fl/ is produced as [vl] in *fly.* The child voices /f/ by assimilation to the following lateral and overgeneralizes acquired [vl] in the context of /fl/.

During this same period, non-contextual [fl] is produced at an increasing rate in *dolphin, fresh, Friday, friendly, further, pretty* and *swap.* When targeting *dolphin,* metathesis of /l/ and /f/ occurs, producing the heterosyllabic cluster /lf/ as a tautosyllabic cluster [fl]; this repeats at age 3;8. In *pretty,* both cluster members are substituted: /p/ becomes [f] and /ɹ/ is substituted by [l], the child's substitution for the Greek rhotic, [ɾ]. Lastly, /sw/ in *swap* becomes [sl] through lateralization of /w/. Notably, this is the reverse phonological process observed in monolingual English children (Smit 1993), where unmarked [w] substitutes the later-acquired /l/. Babatsouli (2015) showed late acquisition of /w/ in this same bilingual child's English, though /l/ was acquired early in both languages, as a result of the quality and quantity of input to the languages in this child's bilingualism.

The child's /vl/ in Greek

Target /vl/ is permitted in Greek but not in English. From age 2;7 to 3;6, the child targeted /vl/ 155 times in the following 15 words: a.ˈvli, a.ˈvles 'yard(s)'; ˈe.vle.pa 'I was seeing'; su.ˈvla.ci 'skewer'; tu.ˈvla.ca 'small bricks';

vi.ˈvli.o, vi.ˈvli.a ‘book(s)’; vi.ˈvli.a.ˈɾa.ci ‘small book’; vi.vlio.θí.ci ‘bookcase’; ˈvle.pe ‘see!’; ˈvle.po ‘I see’; ˈvle.pis ‘you see’; ˈvle.pi ‘he sees’; ˈvle.pu.me ‘we see’; ˈvle.pe.te ‘you (plural) see.’ The realizations of /vl/ are presented monthly in Table 4.2, where non-contextual [vl] productions and their corresponding targeted words are also shown.

Table 4.2. The child’s realizations of /vl/.

words	Age											
	2;7	2;8	2;9	2;10	2;11	3;0	3;1	3;2	3;3	3;4	3;5	3;6
aˈvli		v	vl	3v,vl		3vl	vl					
aˈvles						vl						
ˈevlepa								l		l		
suˈvlaci				2v,l								
tuˈvlaca	3v		v	5v			v	3vl				
viˈvlia				3v		4v	v			3v,3vl		
viˈvliaˈɾaci								v				
viˈvlio	v					2v	v	v		4v 3vl, vɾ	2v	
vivlioˈθici											vl	
ˈvlepe										vl		
ˈvlepo	v				2l,2vl	3l	l	4l	2l,vl	2l, ð	2vl	8vl,m
ˈvlepis		2l	4l,vl		2l	6l,t	l	l	5l,ɾ	2ð,ɸ,ɾ	l,ð	4vl,l
ˈvlepi			3l		l	2l			ð		vl,ð	vl
ˈvlepume			2l						2l	2l	l	
ˈvlepete		4l 2tl,vl		l		v				3l		
non-contextual [vl]												
every				vl								
ble											vl	
fly											vl	
let											vl	
solve										2vl		
the								vl				
this				vl								
ɾavˈðí									vl			
ˈvapso												vl
ˈvɣali												vl
ˈvɣalis											2vl	
ˈvɣalo											vl	
ˈvɾaci				vl								
ˈvɾika										vl		
ˈvɾo												vl

As was also the case in /fl/, 2;7 clearly marks the reduction stage in /vl/ becoming [v] both word-initially and word-medially; this supports previous findings in the literature (Kappa 2002; PAL 1995). An exception to this pattern is a striking reduction pattern to [l] from age 2;8 until full acquisition at 3;6 in a single word, ˈvle.po, its conjugations ˈvle.pis, ˈvle.pi, ˈvle.pu.me, ˈvle.pe.te, and its past progressive tense ˈe.vle.pa. Greenlee (1974) and Smit (1993) report obstruent-lateral reduction to [l] as exceptional, only occurring for short spells. Here, /vl/ consistently reduces to [l] for ten months! A possible explanation is that the child anticipates [labial] in /p/, which inhibits her production of labiodental /v/ in the cluster.

Reductions dominate the child's /vl/ realizations until 3;3, showing some overlapping with the final stage of correct production between 2;8 and 3;3. The second stage is evidenced to be instantaneous and very weak, appearing at 2;8 (also overlapping with correct productions), with only 3 occurrences out of 155 targeted /vl/ longitudinally: /vl/ becomes [tl] twice at 2;8 and [vɾ] once at 3;4 (a time when both first and third stage dominate). /l/ is substituted by a rhotic that is overgeneralized in the wrong context; note that [l] is the substitution of the targeted rhotic all along. This overgeneralization also occurs in /vl/ reduction at 3;3–3;4. Similarly, [ð] is overgeneralized substituting /l/ during the development of /vl/. [tl] occurs twice in ˈvle.pe.te stopping /v/ to [t], even though reduction to [t] at 3;0 is also evidenced in ˈvle.pis; in both cases assimilation to the coronal place of /l/ dominates.

Further, there are non-contextual [vl] productions starting at 2;10. These appear in three occurrences of epenthetic [v] either next to a targeted /l/ in *let*→[vlet] or next to a targeted /ð/ in *the*→[vlə] and *this*→[vlɪs], leading to CCE production (Babatsouli 2016). There is also an instance of epenthetic [l] next to a targeted /v/ in Greek ˈva.pso 'to paint.' Other occurrences involve Greek /vɾ, vɣ, vð/, where [l] substitutes the second member, as also in singleton contexts. Lastly, /b/ in Greek ˈble 'blue' is fricated, and heterosyllabic members [ɫ], [v] in *solve* are shifted in metathesis producing [vl].

Discussion

The discussion will address the research questions set at the end of the introductory section, comparing the child's performance of $F_{LAB}L$ in English and Greek, and with known patterns in other children's speech in the respective languages.

Stages in the child's acquisition of $F_{LAB}L$

Detailed and quantifiable data on the child's production of $F_{LAB}L$ longitudinally provide evidence for the presence of stages as outlined by Greenlee (1974). A comparison of English /fl/ and Greek /vl/ in development shows that both clusters show evidence of reduction to a single member (*Stage I*) from the beginning, at 2;7, all the way to ages 3;3 and 3;6, when adult-like /fl/ and /vl/ respectively are acquired by the child. In just a couple of months from the point of 'reductions-only', Greek /#vl/ and /-vl-/ /enter the stage of adult-like production (*Stage III*) at 2;8 and English /fl/ at 2;9. Greek /fl/ is not targeted during these months. These results do not contradict the general statement that adult-like CC in English appears as early as 2;0–2;6 (Stoel-Gammon 1987), though Amahl's data (Smith 1973), that provide detail on /fl-/, show first adult-like instances in *flower/flowers* much later (ages: 3;1, 3;3). During the period between 2;9 and 3;0, this child's data for English /fl/ show evidence of the substitution stage (*Stage II*). There is, however, no evidence of this stage in Greek /fl/ that is not due to sampling deficiencies. The reason may be that Greek /fl/ is not targeted before 3;0 and it also shows lexical dependence effects. On the other hand, Greek /vl/ provides intermittent evidence of *Stage II* substitutions during the entire time it is targeted (2;7–3;6).

With regard to the overlapping of stages, the following are observed. For /fl/, there is *no* stage-overlapping at 2;7–2;8, there *is* regular overlapping of all three stages at 2;9–3;0, which fades in subsequent months till 3;6. Greek /vl/ also shows *no* stage-overlapping at 2;7, though regular overlapping of *Stages I-II-III* occur throughout, with *Stage II*-substitutions overlapping more forcefully in the months following 3;2. In short, while both clusters start off early on with both reductions and adult-like productions, their *Stage II*-substitutions are weaker and occur earlier in /fl/ than in /vl/. Interestingly, the child produces adult-like $F_{LAB}L$ in both languages after age 3;2, though /vl/ is *fully* acquired three months after /fl/, at age 3;6. The child's articulatory skill is nevertheless evidenced earlier, at 2;10 for [vl] and 3;2 for [fl], in non-contextual productions where $F_{LAB}L$ is not targeted, e.g. in CCE *this*→[**vl**ɪs], where [v] is added before /ð/→[l], and in ˈvɣalis→[ˈ**vl**alis] 'remove clothing', where the lateral substitutes fricative /ɣ/. These results indicate that the child has acquired $F_{LAB}L$ earlier than monolinguals in the respective languages (PAL 1995; Smit 1993).

This may be because she had already acquired (90%) singleton *f, v, l,* when data collection started at 2;7. Her singleton acquisition preceded the monolingual norms for singletons (PAL 1995; Smit et al. 1990) which facilitated earlier cluster acquisition than the norms for clusters. Another explanation for the early $F_{LAB}L$ acquisition in this child may be acceleration as a positive manifestation of crosslinguistic interaction (Kehoe in this volume and references therein). As we have seen, $F_{LAB}L$ is quite frequent in both English and Greek (Saporta 1955; Yip 2013) and, despite the discrepancies between the languages (e.g. fewer /fl/ words in Greek; no /vl/ in English), the bilingual child here was exposed to a wider variety of $F_{LAB}L$ than a monolingual in one of the languages would normally be. Unsurprisingly then, the smaller distribution of /vl/ in Greek may possibly be a contributing factor for the child's delay in acquiring /vl/ when compared to /fl/. Though PAL (1995) reports that Greek monolinguals acquire /vl/ faster than /fl/, it is not relevant to compare this finding with the results here, since PAL (1995) only investigated word-medial /vl/ in a single word. The child's data here, by and large, provide evidence in favour of universals that even includes specific words in the usual vocabulary of children, like *flower/flowers, fly, flag, floor,* ˈvlepo, viˈvlio, etc.

Despite the facilitatory effect of singleton mastery on the acquisition level of clusters, the same does not hold true for the developmental path: the child's acquired status of singleton *f, v, l,* does not challenge the theoretical framework on developmental stages. The acquisition of $F_{LAB}L$ here showed cohesiveness with all aspects involved in normative cluster development, i.e. evidence of stages, and their overlapping, idiosyncratic tendencies (differentiating productions of /fl/ and /vl/ in the words that carried them) with regard to the length and nature of stages, as well as stage-overlapping. I have not come across a study on cluster acquisition in childhood that begins on the grounds of fully acquired cluster members in singleton contexts. The single-subject results presented here are new and, as such, are therefore neither conclusive nor generalizable.

In spite of this, there are two reasons that make these results valid. First, there is further evidence in this child's CC development that supports the claim made here, this time with respect to /sl/. Like /f, v, l/, singleton /s/ is acquired (> 90%) in both languages at 2;7. Though /sl/ is acquired after 2;10 (Yavaş and Babatsouli 2016), the developmental path to adult-like *sl* involves all three *Stages I-II-III* and their overlapping from 2;7 to 2;10: /sl/→[s] (2;7–2;10), /sl/→[t, sl] (2;9), /sl/→[z, l, ʦ, pl, sl] (2;10). Interestingly, the adjunct cluster is acquired by English monolinguals after age 6;0 (Smit 1993), reflecting difficulties in the acquisition of singleton /s/ in English (Templin 1957; Smit et al. 1990). The development of fricative-lateral in /fl/, /vl/ and /sl/ involves, therefore, singletons that the child in this study has acquired. This is not true for the child's other targeted fricative-lateral clusters: *θl* (English and Greek) and *ɣl, xl* (Greek). Because she has not acquired marked fricatives, *θ, ɣ, x* at 2;7, these clusters are excluded from the investigation here. The second and more important reason validating the results discussed above is that the transition from [C] to [CC] is known to signify a key departure in the child's developmental phonotactics from simple to complex onset (e.g. Ingram 1976). That is, as developmental stages in cluster production are assigned to a higher prosodic level (the syllable), the acquisition of feature contrasts needed for adult-like singleton production is not enough and becomes redundant.

The effect of phonotactic differences

When we look at the acquisition level of clusters in terms of the phonotactic differences in the child's languages, we observe the following: (i) The child's /fl/ is more commonly targeted word-initially in her English and it is acquired faster than word-initial and -medial /fl/ in Greek. This may relate to the fact that English /fl/ is more commonly targeted word-initially in English than in Greek. Further, all of the non-contextual [fl] instances are also word-initial. (ii) By contrast, Greek /vl/ shows no preference for either word-initial or -medial positions, though some of the targeted words are quite complex having more than two syllables, e.g. tu.ˈvla.ca 'blocks'. With respect to non-targeted contexts, the majority of productions involve word-initial [vl], e.g. ˈvɣalis→[ˈvlalis], though not singly, e.g. ɾavˈðí→[ɾavˈli] 'a stick'. Noting that these clusters are all onsets rather than codas, the results do not support evidence favouring the word-medial over the word-initial position (Lleó and Prinz 1996) at a later age in development, as in this child. Nevertheless, word-initial success here may be explained by the fact that there is less overlap in CC production word-initially rather than word-medially (Yip 2013).

Lastly, the delayed acquisition rate of Greek /vl/ may relate to its less frequent distribution in the child's languages (as noted above) and to the voicing contrast in $F_{LAB}L$ that differentiates the two languages phonotactically. This argument is supported by the fact that the only instance of /fl/ being voiced to [vl] in the monosyllabic *fly*, occurs after the child has acquired /fl/ in both languages, and as late as 3;5. Also, there is negligible evidence of /v/ in /vl/ devoicing to the coronal stop [t] (2;8 and 3;0) and to [ɸ] (3;4). The child has a clear representation of the voicing contrast of $F_{LAB}L$ in the two languages, but has difficulty mastering it in [vl] because the two consonants in the pair are by default voiced, and the contiguousness of voice in them is problematic for the acquisition of CC.

Variability in the production of $F_{LAB}L$

Reductions

As related above, both /fl/ and /vl/ in the child's speech reduce to the obstruent at age 2;7, thus simplifying the targeted CC. This supports the 'sonority-based onset selection' (Pater and Barlow 2003), whereby the least sonorant element is retained. The child stays faithful to this reduction pattern whenever there is a reduction in /fl/, even after 2;7 and all the way to consistent adult-like productions of /fl/ at age 3;5. However, the child's /#vl/ and /-vl-/ reductions to [v], that support previous findings on Greek cluster reductions (PAL 1995; Kappa 2002) intermingle with reductions to [l] after 2;7. This reduction pattern, /vl/→[l], only occurs in the word ˈvlepo, its conjugations ˈvle.pis, ˈvle.pi, ˈvle.pu.me, ˈvle.pe.te and past progressive tense ˈe.vle.pa, which is the only word type targeted by the child with /vl/ in word-initial position.

Though intermittent reduction to the sonorant is known to occur (Greenlee 1974; Smit 1993) – also compare Amahl's *fly*→[laɪ] (2;9) (Smith 1973), the persisting duration of this pattern for 10 months in a single word suggests an idiosyncratic pattern. It is known that individual words play a critical role in the acquisition of phonology (Kehoe 2011; Stoel-Gammon 2011). Thus, at 2;8, the child's reductions to [l] shift away from the overwhelming norm, /vl/→[v], showing lexical dependence. This reduction pattern freezes there, possibly becoming an archaism, even until age 3;6 after [vl] reaches an acceptable acquisition level. An explanation taking into consideration the phonological context in the word may be that anticipation to [labial] in the following /p/ inhibits production of labiodental /v/ in the cluster. The verb ˈvlepo and its grammatical forms is the only word type in the child's targeted /vl/ vocabulary that involves another labial that is not /v/. The idiosyncratic and intermittent nature of this pattern is further supported by evidence on the acquisition of /vɾ/ in this child's Greek that also reduces to the obstruent, e.g. vɾoˈçi→[voˈsi] 'rain'; ˈmavɾo→[ˈmavo] 'black' (3;0).

Variants

Cluster simplification is further evidenced in the substitutions of cluster members that are concomitant with the substitutions of the respective sounds in singleton contexts (e.g. Smit 1993), thus relating to the acquisition level of singletons. With regard to $F_{LAB}L$, both fricatives get substituted though at low rates: /fl/→[s] also less commonly →[ʃ]; and /vl/→[tl]~[ɸ]. The sibilant variants for /f/ are common in this child's speech, though not so in respective monolinguals who resort to labial stops (PAL 1995; Smit et al. 1990). The stopping and devoicing of /v/ is no surprise. What comes as a surprise is the production of /fl/→[sf] that reduces the sonorant but retains the CC onset by adding [s] (a substitution of /f/) before [f] itself; this is an instance of consonant epenthesis since /s/ is not targeted here. Babatsouli (2016) argues that adding a non-targeted consonant next to a targeted one is an infrequent practice that serves to facilitate acquisition of the complex onset, CCV, on both the articulatory and abstract levels. The consonantal epenthesis here seems to serve a similar purpose: it enables the onset complexity the child is trying to master. Though this is a single occurrence, thus negligible, it is a pattern used during practice. It is not coincidental that the error appears in an utterance with multiple repetitions of *flat* (3;0). Lastly, as also argued in the section on methodology, the child shows no patterns of vocalic epenthesis to simplify CC.

These C_1-substitution patterns support the claim that C_1 is substituted if C_1[fricative] (Kirk 2008), though the child's substitutions of C_2 do not support Kirk's claim that C_2 is substituted if C_1[stop]. We see that the lateral is never substituted in /fl/, though regularly substituted in /vl/ becoming [ɾ] (3;3) and [ð] (3;4) as overgeneralizations of /ɾ/, /ð/ in the context of the lateral. The lateral happens to be the child's regular substitution for both /ɾ, ð/. Given that the lateral is acquired by the child early on (2;7), the substitutions found here do not serve to simplify the targeted sound, since a typical substitution of /l/ in monolingual English children would be [w] (Leopold 1949; Smit et al. 1990; Smith 1973). By contrast, the substitutions employed are more marked than the sound targeted, as the child overgeneralizes [ɾ, ð] in the wrong context. She reduces CC but, at the same time, practices other sounds not targeted in the CC. This is a kind of overgeneralization where sounds /l, ɾ, ð/ swap place though locked together on the phonological and phonetic levels. Lastly, an instance of coalescence is evidenced in /vl/→[m] (3;6) where [m] combines /labial/, /voice/ and [sonorant] targeted in the cluster.

What springs from the observations on the child's substitutions is the following. When cluster members are acquired in singleton contexts, the substitution patterns of the members cannot just be viewed as 'simplification' processes (McLeod et al. 2001). In both cases, i.e. that of /l/→[ɾ, ð] and of the epenthetic [s], the resulting realization is not necessarily simpler than the one targeted. Also, while consonant epenthesis occurs minimally, there is no evidence in this child's production of $F_{LAB}L$ of vocalic epenthesis. It is notable that extended variability in substitutions occurs in /vl/, which is the targeted $F_{LAB}L$ that is less frequent in Greek, less common in the child's bilingualism, more marked than /fl/ in terms of its melody, and involves members that are both voiced by default. In sum, the data here show that there are more processes involved in the variability of cluster production during development, that favour a penchant for complexity, than just the known tendency to simplify.

Summary and conclusions

In spite of the limitations involved in a single-subject case study, this chapter has given insights into the development of fricative-lateral clusters in child developmental speech by investigating a bilingual child's English and Greek longitudinally (2;7–4;0). The emphasis is on the acquisition of labial fricatives pairing in two-member onsets with the alveolar lateral, i.e. $F_{LAB}L$, in the child's languages, though the comparison also includes aspects in the acquisition of English /sl/. These fricative-lateral combinations are singled out from other targeted ones in the child's speech because it is only in these that the child enters the developmental path of cluster acquisition having already acquired the respective cluster members in singleton contexts. The study enriches the crosslinguistic data pool in monolingual and bilingual child speech, and builds on existing gaps.

Detailed and longitudinal data substantiate existing knowledge on developmental stages and related phonological processes in cluster acquisition, also making novel contributions. Known facts on developing complex onsets are not challenged by the new perspective adopted here, though cluster development is shown to be both independent and associated with the acquisition level of singletons, including those that are part of the cluster and those linked to cluster members via substitution processes. The development of two similar clusters /fl, vl/ with different phonotactic distribution in a single person's bilingualism show different acquisition levels and developmental paths, though still within a larger framework of typical behaviour that outperforms the monolingual norms. Lastly, the child's data indicate that it is not only the known tendency in child speech to simplify that is implicated in the developmental processes involved in cluster acquisition, but also complexity on both articulatory and abstract levels.

Results here are of interest in the acquisition of C-lateral clusters, as most children acquire /l/ much later than the consonant in first-member position. This study informs research in the acquisition of clusters in childhood, where detailed longitudinal data are infrequent. Zooming in on minute details in the developmental aspects of phonology may prove useful in understanding speech delay or disorder in children, and in guiding intervention techniques. More such data are needed for comparisons between children, and crosslinguistically.

Appendix

Figures 4.1–4.9. Spectrograms of example /fl/, /vl/ realizations by the child.

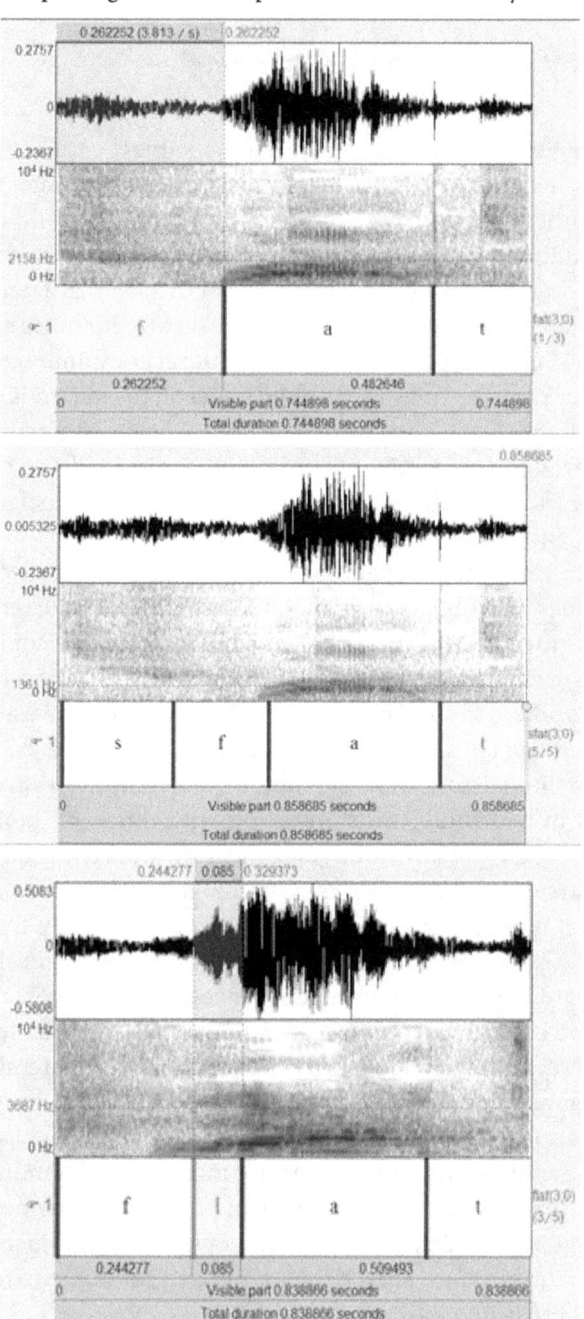

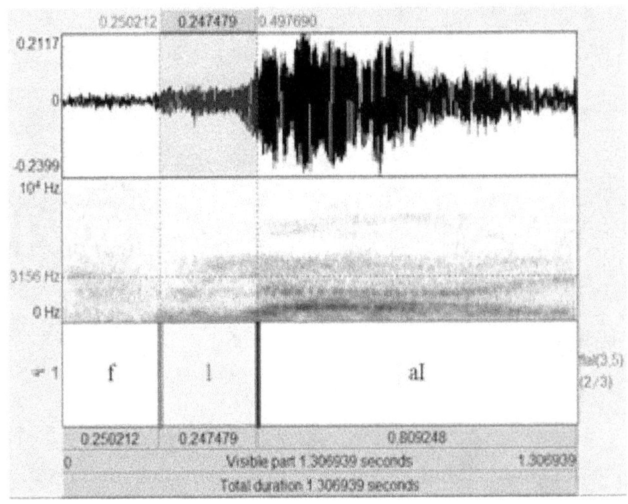
0.250212
0.247479
0.497690
0.2117
0
-0.2399
3156 Hz
0 Hz
f
l
aI
0.250212
0.247479
0.809248
0
Visible part 1.306939 seconds
1.306939
Total duration 1.306939 seconds

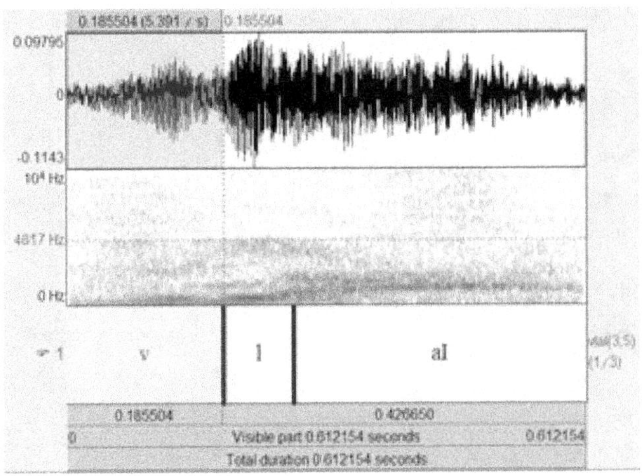
0.185504 (5.391 / s)
0.185504
0.09796
0
-0.1143
4817 Hz
0 Hz
v
l
aI
0.185504
0.426650
0
Visible part 0.612154 seconds
0.612154
Total duration 0.612154 seconds

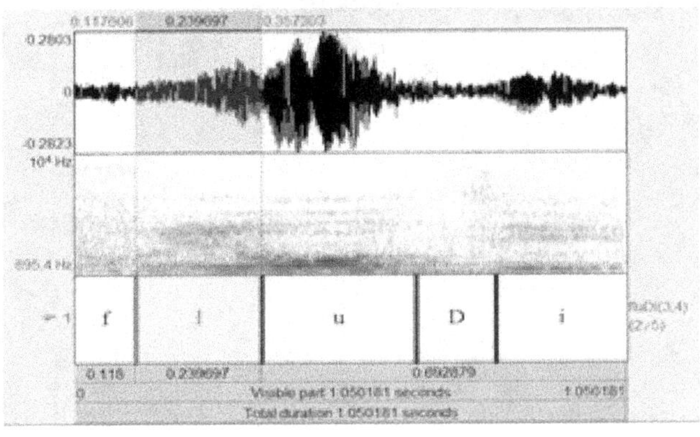
0
f
l
u
D
i
0.118
0.692879
Visible part 1.050181 seconds
Total duration 1.050181 seconds

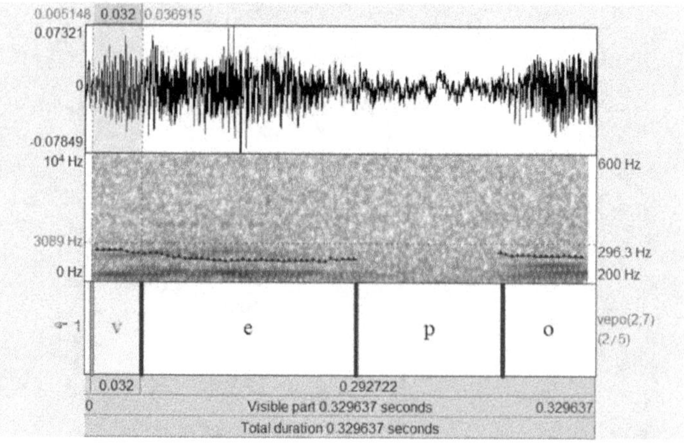
0.005148
0.032
0.036915
0.07321
0
-0.07849
10⁴ Hz
3089 Hz
0 Hz
600 Hz
296.3 Hz
200 Hz
v
e
p
o
vepo(2,7)
(2/5)
0.032
0.292722
0
Visible part 0.329637 seconds
0.329637
Total duration 0.329637 seconds

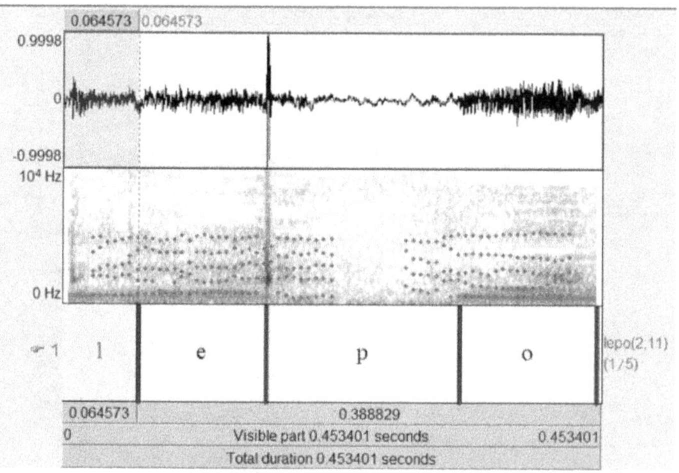
0.064573
0.064573
0.9998
0
-0.9998
10⁴ Hz
0 Hz
l
e
p
o
lepo(2,11)
(1/5)
0.064573
0.388829
0
Visible part 0.453401 seconds
0.453401
Total duration 0.453401 seconds

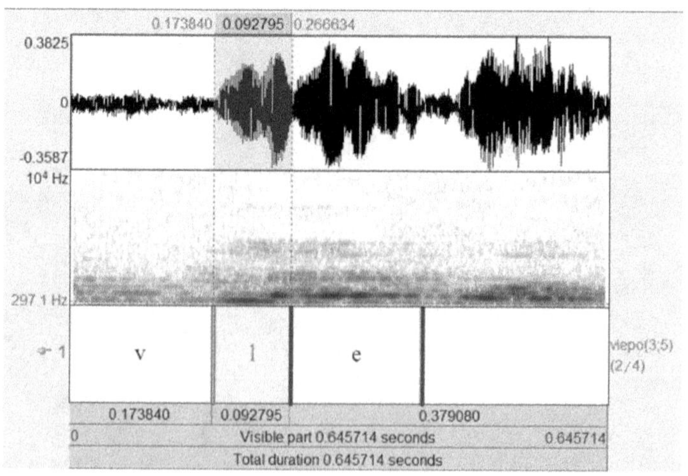
0.173840
0.092795
0.266634
0.3825
0
-0.3587
10⁴ Hz
297.1 Hz
v
l
e
vlepo(3;5)
(2/4)
0.173840
0.092795
0.379080
0
Visible part 0.645714 seconds
0.645714
Total duration 0.645714 seconds

Table 4.3. The child's /fl, vl/ words in Greek: IPA, orthography and English translation.

IPA (adult surface form)	**Orthography** (Greek)	**Translation** (English)
aˈvli	*αυλή*	yard
aˈvles	*αυλές*	yards
ˈble	*μπλέ*	blue
ˈevlepa	*έβλεπα*	I was seeing
fliˈdzani	*φλυτζάνι*	cup
ˈfluði	*φλούδι*	fruit peel
ˈfluðja	*φλούδια*	fruit peels
ˈfɾaula	*φράουλα*	strawberry
ˈmavɾo	*μαύρο*	black
paˈdofles	*παντόφλες*	slippers
ɾavˈði	*ραβδί*	stick
suˈvlaci	*σουβλάκι*	skewer
tuˈvlaca	*τουβλάκια*	blocks
ˈvapso	*βάψω*	to paint
viˈvlia	*βιβλία*	books
ˈvɣali	*βγάλει*	take off (he/she/it)
ˈvɣalis	*βγάλεις*	take off (you)
ˈvɣalo	*βγάλω*	take off (I)
vivliaˈɾaci	*βιβλιαράκι*	small book
viˈvlio	*βιβλίο*	book
vivlioˈθici	*βιβλιοθήκη*	bookcase
ˈvlepe	*βλέπε*	see!
ˈvlepo	*βλέπω*	I see
ˈvlepis	*βλέπεις*	you see
ˈvlepi	*βλέπε*	he/she/it sees
ˈvlepume	*βλέπουμε*	we see
ˈvlepete	*βλέπετε*	you see (plural)
vɾaˈci	*βρακί*	underwear
ˈvɾika	*βρήκα*	I found
ˈvɾo	*βρώ*	to find (I)
vɾoˈçí	*βροχή*	rain

References

Anthony, A., Bogle, D., Ingram, T.T.S. and McIsaac, M.W., 1971, *The Edinburgh articulation test*, Edinburgh: E. & S. Livingston.

Babatsouli, E., 2015, 'Technologies for the study of speech: Review and an application', *Themes in Science and Technology Education* 8(1), 17–32.

Babatsouli, E., 2016, 'Added syllable complexity in a child's developmental speech and clinical implications', *Clinical Linguistics and Phonetics*, 1464–5076. doi/f10.3109/02699206.2016.1162200

Barlow, J.A., 2001, 'The structure of /s/-sequences: Evidence from a disordered system', *Journal of Child Language* 28(2), 291–324. https://doi.org/10.1017/S0305000901004652

Barlow, J.A., 2005, 'Sonority effects in the production of consonant clusters by Spanish-speaking children', in D. Eddington (ed.), *Selected proceedings of the sixth conference on the acquisition of Spanish and Portuguese as a first and second language*, pp. 1–14, Somerville, MA: Cascadilla.

Ben-David, A., 2006, 'On the acquisition of Hebrew #sC onsets', *Journal of Multilingual Communication Disorders* 4, 205–17. https://doi.org/10.1080/14769670601110531

Boersma, P. and Weenink, D., 2016, *Praat: Doing phonetics by computer* [Computer program], Version 6.0.20, from http://www.praat.org/ retrieved September 3, 2016.

Botinis, A., 2011, *The phonetics of Greek*, Athens: ISEL Editions (in Greek).

Bowen, C., 1995–2016, Online worksheets from speech-language-therapy.com.

Brown, R., 1973, *A first language: The early stages*, Cambridge, MA: Harvard University Press. https://doi.org/10.4159/harvard.9780674732469

Chin, S.B. and Dinnsen, D.A., 1992, 'Consonant clusters in disordered speech: Constraints and correspondence patterns', *Journal of Child Language* 19(2), 259–85. https://doi.org/10.1017/S0305000900011417

Clements, G.N., 1990, 'The role of sonority cycle in core syllabification', in J. Kingston and M.E. Beckman (eds.), *Papers in laboratory phonology 1: Between the grammar and physics of speech*, pp. 283–333, Cambridge: Cambridge University Press. https://doi.org/10.1017/CBO9780511627736.017

Clements, G.N. and Keyser, J., 1983, *CV phonology*, Cambridge, MA: MIT Press.

Demuth, K. and McCullough, E., 2008, 'The longitudinal development of clusters in French', *Journal of Child Language* 36, 425–48.

Dyson, A.T., 1988, 'Phonetic inventories of 2- and 3-year old children', *Journal of Speech and Hearing Disorders* 53, 89–93. https://doi.org/10.1044/jshd.5301.89

Elbert, M. and McReynolds, L.V., 1979, 'Aspects of phonological acquisition during articulation training', *Journal of Speech and Hearing Disorders* 64, 459–71. https://doi.org/10.1044/jshd.4404.459

Fikkert, P., 1994, *On the acquisition of prosodic structure*, PhD dissertation, Leiden University/HIL, The Hague: Holland Academic Graphics.

Gerrits, E. and Zumach, A., 2006, 'The acquisition of #sC clusters in Dutch', *Journal of Multilingual Communication Disorders* 4, 218–30. https://doi.org/10.1080/14769670601110549

Gierut, J., 1999, 'Syllable onsets: Clusters and adjuncts in acquisition', *Journal of Speech, Language and Hearing Research* 42, 708–26. https://doi.org/10.1044/jslhr.4203.708

Goldstein, B.A., 2007, 'Spanish speech acquisition', in S. McLeod, S. (ed.), *The international guide to speech acquisition*, pp. 540–53, Clifton Park, NY: Thomson Delmar Learning.

Goldstein, B. and Swasey Washington, P., 2001, 'An initial investigation of phonological patterns in typically developing 4-year-old Spanish-English bilingual children', *Language, Speech and Hearing Services in School* 32, 153–64. https://doi.org/10.1044/0161-1461(2001/014)

Greenlee, M., 1974, 'Interacting processes in the child's acquisition of stop-liquid clusters', *Papers and Reports on Child Language Development* (Stanford University) 7, 85–100.

Grunwell, P., 1987, *Clinical phonology*, London: Croom Helm.

Hodson, B., 1989, 'Phonological remediation: The cycles approach', in N. Creaghead, W. Second and P. Newman (eds.), *Assessment and remediation of articulatory and phonological disorders*, pp. 323–33, Englewood Cliffs, NJ: Paramount.

Holm, A. and Dodd, B., 1999, 'A longitudinal study of the phonological development of two Cantonese-English bilingual children', *Applied Psycholinguistics* 20(3), 349–76. https://doi.org/10.1017/S0142716499003021

Ingram, D., 1976, *Phonological disability in children*, New York: Elsevier.

Ingram, D., 1981, *Procedures for the phonological analysis of children's language*, Baltimore, MD: University Park Press.

Ingram, D., 1989, *Phonological disability in children* (2nd edn.), London: Cole and Whurr Limited.

Ingram, D., 1992, 'Early phonological acquisition: A crosslinguistic perspective', in C.A. Ferguson, L. Menn and C. Stoel-Gammon (eds.), *Phonological development: Models, research, implications*, pp. 147–58, Timonium, MD: York Press.

Ingram, D., Christensen, L., Veach, S. and Webster, B., 1980, 'The acquisition of word-initial fricatives and affricates in English by children between 2 and 6 years', in G.H. Yeni-Komshian, J.F. Kavanaugh and C.A. Ferguson (eds.), *Child phonology, Vol. I: Production*, pp. 169–92, New York: Academic Press. https://doi.org/10.1016/b978-0-12-770601-6.50014-0

Jakobson, R., 1941/1968, *Child language, aphasia and phonological universals* (trans. A. Keiler), The Hague: Mouton, original work published in 1941 as *Kindersprache, aphasie und allgemeine Lautgesetze.*

Jongstra, W., 2003, *Variation in reduction strategies of Dutch word-initial consonant clusters*, PhD dissertation, University of Toronto, Canada.

Kappa, I., 2002, 'On the acquisition of syllabic structure in Greek', *Journal of Greek Linguistics* 3, 1–52. https://doi.org/10.1075/jgl.3.03kap

Kehoe, M., 2011, 'Relationships between lexical and phonological development: A look at bilingual children – A commentary on Stoel-Gammon's "Relationships between lexical and phonological development in young children'", *Journal of Child Language* 38, 75–81. https://doi.org/10.1017/S0305000910000474

Kehoe, M., 2015, 'Cross-linguistic interaction: A retrospective and prospective view', in E. Babatsouli and D. Ingram (eds.), *Proceedings of the International Symposium on Monolingual and Bilingual Speech 2015*, pp. 141–67, Chania, Greece (ISBN: 978-618-82351-0-6).

Kehoe, M. and Hilaire-Debove, G., 2004, 'The structure of branching onsets and rising diphthongs: Evidence from the acquisition of French', paper presented at the *28th Annual Boston University Conference on Language Development*, Somerville, MA.

Kenstowicz, M., 1994, *Phonology in generative grammar*, Cambridge, MA: Blackwell.

Kent, R.D. and Read, C., 1992, *The acoustic analysis of speech*, London/San Diego: Whurr Publishers, Singular Publishing Group.

Kirk, C., 2008, 'Substitution errors in the production of word-initial and word-final consonant clusters', *Journal of Speech, Language, and Hearing Research*, 51, 35–48. https://doi.org/10.1044/1092-4388(2008/003)

Klopfenstein, M. and Ball, M.J., 2010, 'An analysis of the sonority hypothesis and cluster realization in a child with phonological disorder', *Clinical Linguistics and Phonetics* 24(4–5), 261–70. https://doi.org/10.3109/02699201003587012

Kristoffersen, K. and Simonsen, H., 2006, 'The acquisition of #sC clusters in Norwegian', *Journal of Multilingual Communication Disorders* 4, 231–41. https://doi.org/10.1080/14769670601110556

Ladefoged, P., 2006, *A course in phonetics*, Boston: Thompson/Wadsworth.

Leopold, W.F., 1949, *Speech development of a bilingual child: A linguist's record*, Evanston, IL: Northwestern University Press.

Lleó, C. and Prinz, M., 1996, 'Consonant clusters in child phonology and the directionality of syllable structure assignment', *Journal of Child Language* 23, 31–56. https://doi.org/10.1017/S0305000900010084

Macken, M.A., 1977, 'Developmental re-organization of phonology: A hierarchy of basic units of acquisition', *Papers and Reports in Child Language* 4, 1–36.

MacWhinney, B., 2000, *The CHILDES project: Tools for analyzing talk*. Mahwah, NJ: Lawrence Erlbaum.

McLeod, S., van Doorn, J. and Reed, V.A., 2001, 'Normal acquisition of consonant clusters', *American Journal of Speech-Language Pathology* 10, 99–110.

McLeod, S., van Doorn, J. and Reed, V.A., 2002, 'Typological description of the normal acquisition of consonant clusters', in F. Windsor, L. Kelly and N. Hewlett (eds.), *Themes in Clinical Phonetics and Linguistics*, pp. 185–200, Hillsdale, NJ: Lawrence Erlbaum. https://doi.org/10.1044/1058-0360(2001/011)

Nice, M., 1925, 'Length of sentence as a criterion of child progress in speech', *Journal of Educational Psychology* 16, 370–79. https://doi.org/10.1037/h0073259

Nirgianaki, E., 2014, 'Acoustic characteristics of Greek fricatives', *Journal of the Acoustical Society of America* 135(5), 2964–76. https://doi.org/10.1121/1.4870487

Ohala, D., 1999, 'The influence of sonority on children's cluster reductions', *Journal of Communication Disorders* 32, 397–421. https://doi.org/10.1016/S0021-9924(99)00018-0

Olmsted, D., 1971, *Out of the mouth of babes*, The Hague: Mouton.

PAL (Panhellenic Association of Logopaedics), 1995, *Assessment of phonetic and phonological development*, Athens: PAL (in Greek).

Pater, J. and Barlow, J., 2003, 'Constraint conflict in cluster reduction', *Journal of Child Language* 30, 487–526. https://doi.org/10.1017/S0305000903005658

Preisser, D.A., Hodson, B.W. and Paden E.P., 1988, 'Developmental phonology: 18–29 months', *Journal of Speech and Hearing disorders*, 53, 125–30. https://doi.org/10.1044/jshd.5302.125

Rose, Y., 2000, *Headedness and prosodic licensing in the L1 acquisition of phonology*, PhD dissertation, McGill University, Montreal.

Saporta, S., 1955, 'Frequency of consonant clusters', *Language* 31(1), 25–30. https://doi.org/10.2307/410889

Schnitzer, M.L. and Krasinski, E., 1994, 'The development of segmental phonological production in a bilingual child', *Journal of Child Language* 21, 585–622. https://doi.org/10.1017/S0305000900009478

Selkirk, E., 1984, 'On the major class features and syllable theory', in M. Aronoff and R.T. Oehrle (eds.), *Language sound structure: Studies in phonology presented to Morris Halle by his teacher and students*, pp. 107–36, Cambridge, MA: MIT Press.

Setatos, M. 1974, *Phonology of Modern Greek*, Athens: Papazisis Publications (in Greek).

Smit, A.B., 1993, 'Phonological error distributions in the Iowa-Nebraska Articulation Norms Project: Word-initial consonant clusters', *Journal of Speech and Hearing Research* 36, 931–947. https://doi.org/10.1044/jshr.3605.931

Smit, A.B., Hand, L., Freilinger, J.J., Bernthal, J.E. and Bird, A., 1990, 'The Iowa Articulation Norms Project and its Nebraska replication', *Joumal of Speech and Hearing Disorders* 55, 779–98. https://doi.org/10.1044/jshd.5504.779

Smith, N.V., 1973, *The acquisition of phonology: A case study, Cambridge Studies in Linguistics 25*, Cambridge: Cambridge University Press.

Stemberger, J.P. and Chavez-Peón, M.E., 2015, 'Development of word-initial consonant clusters in Valley Zapotec: Universals vs. language-specific effects of sonority', in M. Yavaş (ed.), *Unusual productions in phonology: Universals and language-specific considerations*, pp. 49–69, New York, NY: Psychology Press.

Stoel-Gammon, C., 1987, 'Phonological skills of two-year-olds', *Language, Speech and Hearing Services in Schools* 18, 323–29. https://doi.org/10.1044/0161-1461.1804.323

Stoel-Gammon, C., 2011, 'Relationships between lexical and phonological development in young children', *Journal of Child Language* 38, 1–34. https://doi.org/10.1017/S0305000910000425

Szreder, M., 2011, 'The acquisition of consonant clusters in Polish', *York Papers in Linguistics* 2(1), 88–102.

Templin, M., 1957, *Certain language skills in children: Their development and interrelationships*, Institute of Child Welfare Monograph 26, Minneapolis: The University of Minnesota Press.

Watson, M.M. and Scukanec, G.P., 1997a, 'Phonological changes in the speech of two-year olds: A longitudinal investigation', *Infant-Toddler Intervention* 7, 67–77.

Watson, M.M. and Scukanec, G.P., 1997b, 'Profiling the phonological abilities of 2-year-olds: A longitudinal investigation', *Child Language Teaching and Therapy* 13, 3–14. https://doi.org/10.1177/026565909701300102

Wellman, B.L., Case, I.M., Mengert, I.G. and Bradbury, D.E., 1931, 'Speech sounds of young children', *University of Iowa Studies in Child Welfare* 2(5).

Yavaş, M., 2010, 'Acquisition of #sC clusters in Haitian Creole-English bilingual children', *Journal of Multilingual Communication Disorders* 4(1), 194–204.

Yavaş, M., 2013, 'What explains the reduction of /s/-clusters: Sonority or [continuant]?', *Clinical Linguistics and Phonetics* 27(6), 394–403. https://doi.org/10.3109/02699206.2013.767378

Yavaş, M. and Babatsouli, E., 2016, 'Acquisition of /s/-clusters in a Greek-English bilingual child: Sonority or OCP?', in M.J. Ball and N. Müller (eds.), *Challenging sonority: Cross-linguistic evidence*, pp. 337–54, Sheffield, UK: Equinox Publishing.

Yip, J., 2013, *Phonetic effects on the timing of gestural coordination in Modern Greek consonant clusters*, PhD dissertation, University of Michigan, Ann Arbor.

Elena Babatsouli is the Director of the Institute of Monolingual and Bilingual Speech in Greece, whose purpose is the advancement and dissemination of scientific knowledge in monolingual and bilingual acquisition and use, typical and atypical. She has a BA in English from the University of London, an MA in Languages and Business from London South Bank University, and a PhD in Linguistics from the University of Crete. Her publications and research interests are in language acquisition and use by children and adults, with a focus on phonology and morphology. She co-chaired the organization of the *International Symposium of Monolingual and Bilingual Speech 2015* and is co-editor of its *Proceedings* and of *Crosslinguistic encounters in language acquisition: Typical and atypical development* (Multilingual Matters, 2017).

5
The production of selected phonemically short versus long Hungarian vowel pairs by 5-, 6- and 7-year-olds

Ferenc Bunta, Tilda Neuberger, Judit Bóna, Alexandra Markó and Ágnes Jordanidisz

Introduction

The present study is an extension of research by Neuberger et al. (2015), including more participants (42 versus 27), balancing the number of participants in each age group by gender (7 male and 7 female participants per age group), and providing more in-depth analyses of the extended data than we did in our previous study. In this chapter, we focus on the production of vowels; specifically, the differentiation of vowel quantity[1] in phonemically short versus long vowel pairs in Hungarian using quasi-naturalistic conversational speech samples collected from 5-, 6- and 7-year-old children with typical speech and language development. Moreover, in keeping with the theme of this volume we also discuss our findings in the context of how phonological systems may function in the protolanguages of children acquiring Hungarian as their native language.

1 Throughout this chapter, we will refer to vowel quantity as the feature that differentiates phonemically short from long vowels in Hungarian. In the relevant literature, the terms 'vowel quantity', 'vowel length' and 'vowel duration' are used when referencing the phonemic differentiation of vowels based on duration. We are making a conscious effort to use the term 'vowel quantity' to refer to the phonological feature, but we also use the terms 'phonemically short' versus 'phonemically long' vowels when referring to the underlying phonemes themselves. We use the term 'vowel duration' to denote the actual physical property of the allophones of the vowels in production.

Languages vary in their use of segmental duration in the temporal domain to differentiate vowels. As Neuberger et al. (2015) discuss, three types of languages can be identified based on the role vowel quantity (as a phonemic feature) and duration (as an acoustic cue) play in the vowel system. First, there are languages such as Spanish that do not differentiate vowel phonemes based on quantity and that, also, do not use relative vowel duration as an acoustic cue to vowel identification (cf. Malmberg 1971). The second 'type' includes languages such as English that do not have vowel quantity as a distinctive phonological feature, but that do use relative vowel duration as a fairly reliable cue to differentiating vowels. Languages of the third type (such as Hungarian or German) have phonemic differentiation based on vowel quantity (i.e. phonemically short versus long vowels) relying on vowel duration as a cue to systematically differentiate vowels. This issue will be revisited and expanded below for more clarity. Moreover, segmental duration itself is affected by a variety of factors from phonemic function to vowel quality, stress patterns, adjacent segments and position in the word, to name a few issues (cf. Santen 1992). Some factors (such as utterance-final vowel duration extension) appear to be less language-specific and may be due to the limitations imposed by physical reality, while other factors may be more linguistic in nature (e.g. the use of vowel quantity differentiation to discriminate phonemically short versus long vowels).

Buder and Stoel-Gammon (2002: 1854) discuss vowel length variations in terms of 'extrinsic variations' that are dependent on the context of the vowel as opposed to 'intrinsic variations' that are related to the identity of the vowel itself, that can be further sub-categorized as variations attributable to non-linguistic factors (such as articulatory differences) versus intrinsic variations due to phonological factors. In our chapter, we are more concerned with the latter: vowel quantity differentiation from a phonological perspective, and its acquisition by Hungarian-speaking children. As such, it is important to differentiate what constitutes linguistically meaningful vowel quantity differentiation versus vowel duration differences due to phonologically less (or even non-)relevant factors.

As Neuberger et al. (2015) point out, from a linguistic perspective, the reliance on vowel quantity as a meaningful phonological feature, as opposed to an environmentally conditioned phonemically non-contrastive durational difference, varies from one language to another. As previously noted, there are languages that have no phonologically meaningful vowel quantity differentiation, such as Spanish (cf. Malmberg 1971). In Spanish, environmentally conditioned extrinsic variation of vowel duration (such as phrase-final lengthening) may exist to some degree, but vowel duration is neither a reliable acoustic cue to distinguishing vowels nor is there phonemic vowel quantity discrimination in the language.

On the other hand, there are languages that rely on duration as a perceptual cue for distinguishing different vowels but do not have a phonological system in which phonemically short versus phonemically long vowels would be differentiated as pairs of vowels that vary solely along a vowel quantity dimension. That is to say, in these languages, durational aspects are relevant for distinguishing various vowels, but vowel quantity does not function as a systematic distinctive phonological feature. For example, in English vowel duration is an acoustic cue that helps differentiate various vowels (e.g. /æ/ as in *bat* tends to be relatively longer than /ɛ/ as in *bet*), but vowel quantity is not a phonological feature (cf. Kassai 1979). In fact, the vowel feature often loosely associated with duration in English may be tenseness (or advanced tongue root), but tenseness and vowel quantity are not interchangeable, because the English low front vowel is a lax one, but it also tends to be long, unlike the rest of the English lax vowels. Furthermore, the primary cue to differentiating lax versus tense vowels in English is one of quality and linguistic function rather than quantity. As Giegerich (1992) noted, when English listeners were faced with contradictory acoustic cues in listening to [i] as in *heat* versus [ɪ] as in *hit*, and vowel duration was reduced, native speakers of English still made perceptual judgements based on vowel quality rather than quantity. Specifically, if a vowel whose quality corresponds to an /i/ is shortened to match the duration of a typical /ɪ/, listeners still perceive the former, suggesting that vowel quality supersedes vowel quantity perception in English, at least for this tense and lax pair of vowels. Thus, with respect to vowel duration, languages like English may rely on relative vowel duration as a perceptual cue, but do not have a systematic phonemically long versus short contrast that would be based primarily on vowel quantity in the phonological system.

Finally, as previously noted, there are languages that rely on duration as an acoustic cue for differentiating pairs of vowels that also have vowel quantity as a distinctive phonological feature (e.g. Hungarian, Estonian or Swedish, cf. Lehiste 1965). In these languages, vowels are produced and perceived differentially depending on the quantity of the vowel, and vowels are treated as phonemically short or phonemically long. Buder and Stoel-Gammon (2002) found evidence that children acquiring languages with phonemic vowel quantity differentiation (such as Swedish) showed more sensitivity to differences in vowel duration at earlier ages than their age-matched peers acquiring languages that did not rely on vowel quantity as a distinctive phonological feature (such as English). It is important to note that having a contrastive phonological feature of vowel quantity based on which phonemically short versus long vowels are differentiated as part of the linguistic system is not necessarily the same as what Buder and Stoel-Gammon (2002) refer to as 'intrinsic vowel length.' Rather, as Buder and Stoel-Gammon suggest, phonemic vowel quantity differentiation is an intrinsic feature that is also an inherent part of the phonological system in some languages that may carry linguistic function in the phonological systems of languages such as Swedish or Hungarian.

In Hungarian, there are seven phonemically short versus long pairs of vowels that are primarily differentiated based on vowel quantity: /i – iː, y – yː, ø – øː, ɛ – eː, u – uː, o – oː, ɒ – aː/ (Nádasdy and Siptár 2001; Neuberger et al. 2015). Thus, vowel quantity is a distinctive phonological feature in Hungarian despite the fact that only 5 of the 7 vowel pairs (/i – iː, y – yː, ø – øː, u – uː, o – oː/) are solely reliant on differences based on relative vowel duration (cf. Gósy 2004). The remaining Hungarian phonemically short versus long vowel pairs (/ɛ – eː/ and /ɒ – aː/) are also distinguished based on the quality of the vowel in addition to differences based on quantity (Szende 1994). Vowel quantity is so engrained in Hungarian – a language with a relatively transparent orthography – that it is even reflected in the writing system of the language, marked by accent (typical spelling of phonemically short vowels: *i* /i/, *ü* /y/, *ö* /ø/, *e* /ɛ/, *u* /u/, *o* /o/, *a* /ɒ/; typical spelling of phonemically long vowels: *í* /iː/, *ű* /yː/, *ő* /øː/, *é* /eː/, *ú* /uː/, *ó* /oː/, *á* /aː/). In fact, vowels are often taught as 'short' (= *rövid*) versus 'long' (= *hosszú*) pairs in educational settings, reflecting the significance of the vowel quantity for the phonological system of Hungarian.

The process of acquisition of vowel quantity as a distinctive phonological feature in children's speech tends to be protracted, and it is one of the relatively later developing vowel features (Zajdó and Powell 2008). Moreover, the development of the vowel quantity contrast can vary based on the specific vowel pair, and it follows a relatively gradual, piecemeal trajectory starting with certain vowel pairs such as /i/ versus /iː/ and spreading to other phonemically short versus long pairs. Awareness of the relevance of vowel quantity as a significant contrastive feature may be established earlier in children learning languages that use phonemic vowel length (such as Swedish or Hungarian) than in the speech of their peers whose languages do not use vowel quantity as a distinctive phonological feature (such as English). This was illustrated by the findings of Buder and Stoel-Gammon (2002) in that children acquiring Swedish as their native language displayed more sensitivity to vowel quantity than children acquiring English. Along these lines, Zajdó (2002) found that Hungarian 3-year-olds demonstrated high levels of accuracy (about 90%) when imitating their caregivers' speech patterns involving disyllabic CVCV items in which vowel duration was varied. There was also a tendency in the Hungarian children's speech toward more accurate production of unrounded vowels as compared to rounded ones, as perceived by adult Hungarian-speaking judges. Expanding on her 2002 work, Zajdó (2015) investigated Hungarian-speaking children's ability to adjust vowel duration based on an adult model. The results indicated that children between the ages of 2 and 5 years acquiring Hungarian were able to change the durations of the vowels produced to match the adult target.

In an earlier version of the present study, Neuberger et al. (2015) investigated vowel quantity differentiation in three pairs of vowels that differed only in duration (/i, iː, o, oː, u, uː/) and found that by 5 years of age, Hungarian-speaking children did produce the phonemically short versus long contrast on the basis of vowel quantity in a reliable fashion. The authors focused on the above vowels to minimize potential vowel quality effects, considering that these pairs of vowels were qualitatively non-distinct from each other, allowing for focusing on the vowel quantity difference. Aside from the robust overall vowel quantity effect, there was neither a main effect for age nor an interaction effect for age by vowel quantity, indicating that by 5 years of age, vowel quantity had reached a stable and significant level of differentiation, and no evidence was found of more pronounced vowel quantity discrimination at later ages. However, displaying a vowel quantity contrast does not necessarily imply completely adult-like productions. It is still unclear as to when vowel quantity discrimination reaches fully developed, mature levels.

There are studies that suggest that while vowel quantity differentiation may manifest itself in children's productions even before 3 years of age (cf. Zajdó 2002, 2015), that does not necessarily mean that the productions are adult-like or mature in the productions of young Hungarian-speaking children (cf. Bóna and Imre 2010). Using conversational speech production samples, Bóna and Imre (2010) found that only around 5 to 6 years of age did Hungarian-speaking children demonstrate separation of phonemically short versus long vowels along a vowel duration dimension. In fact, even at 6 years the contrast had not reached full maturity. Vowel quantity contrasts were also uneven across phonemically short versus long vowel pairs in that the /u/ versus /uː/ and /o/ versus /oː/ pairs did display durational differences in the productions of the children. The contrast did not manifest itself to the same extent in other vowel pairs. Deme (2012) later replicated these results with 6- to 7-year-olds, finding significant differential patterns akin to the ones found by Bóna and Imre (2010), displaying further evidence of vowel quantity discrimination in /u/ versus /uː/ and /o/ versus /oː/ but not in other phonemically short versus long Hungarian vowel pairs.

As for perceptual differentiation of vowels based on their duration, Gósy (2006) found that at 5 years of age, children display accurate vowel discrimination only about 28% of the time with respect to phonemically short versus long Hungarian vowels. At 7 years of age, the accuracy of perceptual discrimination of phonemically short versus long vowels based on duration increases to 65–70%, and it reaches a level of accuracy of 75–80% in 8- and 9-year-olds. Gósy's (2006) results indicate that the differentiation of phonemically short versus long vowels from a perceptual perspective undergoes considerable development between the ages of 5 and 7 years in Hungarian-speaking children, and their development continues even at later ages. Based on these findings, Neuberger et al. (2015) predicted that vowel quantity contrasts in production would show similar developmental patterns; however, the authors did not find statistically significant differences in three Hungarian vowel pairs that differed based on vowel quantity when produced by 5-, 6- and 7-year-old children. It is possible that the divergent findings of these studies were due to methodological differences, but it is equally possible that albeit the contrasts are not completely stabilized or adult-like by 5 to 7 years of age, the level of differentiation may be sufficient even as early as 5 years of age, at least for vowel pairs that only differ based on vowel quantity (such as /i/ – /iː/, /o/ – /oː/, or /u/ – /uː/).

It is important to note that even in languages in which vowel duration is a perceptually relevant acoustic cue, vowel quantity is susceptible to phonologically non-relevant durational variation due to a number of factors that could be both vowel-internal (such as vowel quality) and vowel-external (such as the phonetic environment), as previously noted. Consequently, while the phonemic vowel quantity contrast may be categorical (such as in Hungarian where they are binary), the actual durational differences between phonemically short versus long vowels may overlap to some extent. The amount of overlap in terms of duration between phonemically short versus long vowels can also vary by language. For example, German was found to have a relatively high degree of durational overlap between phonemically short versus long vowels (about 90%) as compared to Thai that also displayed overlap but to a lesser degree (28%; Lehiste 1970). In Hungarian, the duration of the vowel is dependent on its quantity (phonemically short versus long), but other factors that affect vowel duration may include speaking rate, the quality of the vowel, its position in the word, word length and others (Gósy and Beke 2010). Nonetheless, as Neuberger et al. (2015) pointed out, irrespective of and sometimes despite non-phonological factors, vowel quantity differences persist so that the duration of a phonemically long vowel tends to exceed that of its phonemically short counterpart in Hungarian (cf. Gósy and Beke 2010). Phonologically driven vowel quantity differences between pairs of phonemically short versus long pairs of Hungarian vowels are even retained in the duration domain in both conversational speech samples and more formal settings, such as reading out loud, with limited categorical overlap (Bóna 2012; Gósy and Beke 2010). The prevalence of vowel quantity differentiation in Hungarian is more notable in young adults and middle-aged individuals than older adults, but maintenance of the vowel quantity contrast as measured by duration can even be found in speech samples provided by adults over 70 years of age despite a reduction of vowel quality differences with advancing age (Bóna 2012).

All of these findings point to the significance and resilience of vowel duration when it comes to discriminating phonemically short from phonemically long vowels in Hungarian, so the acquisition of this robust phonological feature is essential for the development of the Hungarian vowel system. Consequently, it is important to have a more complete understanding of how vowel quantity is acquired by Hungarian-speaking children, and more specifically, how this phonological contrast manifests itself in the protolanguage of children at various developmental stages. The research questions of the present study are the same as the ones posited by Neuberger et al. (2015) with special attention to how the phonological contrast based on vowel quantity manifests itself in the protolanguage of children acquiring Hungarian as their native language. These questions are:

(i) How does vowel quantity differentiation manifest itself in the speech production patterns of 5-, 6- and 7-year-old children acquiring Hungarian as their native language?
(ii) Would there be differences in vowel quantity discrimination depending on the children's ages? More specifically, would there be age effects when comparing each individual age group to the other, in pairs?
(iii) Related to the above issues, does the quality of the vowel pair affect the vowel quantity contrast?

The research questions above and the existing research literature on the topic prompted us to formulate the following three hypotheses:

(1) We hypothesize that there will be differences between phonemically long and short vowels at each age group in that the duration of phonemically long vowels will exceed that of their phonemically short counterparts considering each vowel pair (/i/ versus / iː/, /o/ versus /oː/, and /u/ versus /uː/).
(2) We also predict that as vowel quantity contrasts develop over time, the productions of older groups will differ from the productions of

their younger peers. Consequently, we expect there to be differences in vowel quantity productions at different ages.

(3) We expect that there will be an effect of vowel quality on the duration of the vowels produced in each phonemically long versus short pair. We further hypothesize the existence of a differential vowel quality effect on duration, so that we predict that vowel quality and vowel quantity will display an interaction effect, because we expect vowel duration to depend on the qualitative differences between vowel pairs defined by their places of articulation.

Method

The general method (participant recruitment, data collection procedure, materials and analyses) in the present study was consistent with the one used by Neuberger et al. (2015). The study also adheres to the guidelines for ethical treatment of human subjects set forth by the Hungarian scientific review board overseeing research involving human participants. Before participating in the study, parents or legal guardians provided written consent and the child participants gave assent to taking part in the research.

Participants

Three groups of monolingual Hungarian-speaking children participated in the present study: 5-year-olds (n = 14), 6-year-olds (n = 14) and 7-year-olds (n = 14), who were recruited from Hungarian public schools in the Budapest metropolitan area. Each group had an equal number of male and female participants (7 in each group; 21 boys and 21 girls in total). Parent and teacher reports were also administered to inquire about the participants' background and relevant information that may affect the speech, language or hearing of the children who participated in our study. Based on these reports, the participants of the present study had typical speech, language and hearing. Parents also reported no concerns regarding the cognitive skills of their children. The socio-economic status of the participants and their families was not specifically controlled; however, the children recruited for the present study constituted a fairly homogeneous group, because they were from the same geographical region and attended public school in typical middle-class neighbourhoods in Budapest, Hungary. Hungary has a population of approximately 9.5 million people with a low Gini coefficient (Gini 1921), indicating relatively low income-inequality. Public education in Hungary is fairly uniform with a standard curriculum, so while the home and – to some extent – children's educational backgrounds in Hungary may vary, that level of variability is considerably less than in some other countries with more income-inequality that also lack a national curriculum.

Materials and Procedure

Audio recordings were collected via conversational speech samples as the children interacted with an experimenter, discussing their favourite pastimes, everyday lives or favourite stories. This method of collecting the data was chosen because it promotes quasi-naturalistic conversational interactions between the child and the experimenter, and it also tends to elicit connected speech samples while having control over the choice of topics, providing a certain level of consistency across the different participants. More spontaneous interactions between interlocutors than the ones employed in our research tend to yield relatively less predictable and more variable language samples that may make acoustic analyses of vowels less consistent. On the other hand, single-word elicitation tasks tend to prompt more formal productions from the participants, yielding less naturalistic speech samples than the ones obtained via our sampling technique. Choosing our method of elicitation was a reasonable compromise for the purposes of our study, while we acknowledge the limitations that may exist due to our sampling method (see also the Discussion section of our chapter).

The data were collected at the participants' schools (either kindergarten or elementary) in a quiet room with the experimenter and the child present. Audio recordings were conducted using a Zoom H4n portable recorder. A session included at least a 5-minute conversation between the child participant and the adult experimenter. Vowels produced by the child during the conversation were analysed later using acoustic measurements of vowel duration. When selecting vowels for analysis from the connected speech sample, we controlled for a number of factors to ensure consistency across the measurements and to be certain that the vowel produced was the intended target. The following criteria were established for vowel selection:

(1) In order to control for vowel quality, pairs of phonemically short versus long vowels that were most alike in terms of their place of

articulation or quality were selected for analysis. Specifically, only allophones of /i/, /iː/, /o/, /oː/, /u/ and /uː/ were analysed. This measure was taken in order to ensure that the phoneme pairs were qualitatively as similar as possible, and that the durational differences were not attributable to different tongue placement or other aspects of vowel articulation. Furthermore, these particular vowel pairs are among the most frequent ones in spoken Hungarian (Gósy 2004).

(2) Only target-like productions of the vowels were analysed. That is to say, substitutions and distorted exemplars (such as ones involving hesitation) were not included in the analyses. This criterion was set to eliminate variations due to atypical productions.

(3) Vowels in absolute final word position were excluded from the analyses. This measure was introduced to avoid the potential effects of terminal lengthening that may characterize vowels in final position.

After controlling for the factors noted above, the final set of vowels that were measured acoustically consisted of a total of 3,296 vowel tokens whose durations were analysed with Praat (Boersma and Weenink 2015). The number of vowel tokens analysed for each phoneme category are listed in Table 5.1. It is important to note that due to the variations in vowel frequency in naturally occurring (and also in quasi-naturalistic) speech samples, the range of vowel tokens also varied from 159 (/uː/) to 1,179 (/o/). This variation is expected in natural or quasi-naturalistic samples. Vowel duration was measured based on established criteria, using markers typically used in this type of research (cf. Ladefoged 2003; Peterson and Lehiste 1960; Shah 2002). Specifically, for the purpose of determining vowel boundaries, we used a combination of a waveform display and wide-band spectrogram with the latter showing formants, relying primarily on identifiable second formants to assist in the location of segmental boundaries. The measurements of vowel durations were verified independently by two of the authors of the present chapter. Both individuals who conducted the measurements were trained in linguistics and acoustic analyses of speech, and they also conduct research in the field of speech and language analysis. Duration measurements were considered to be in agreement within 10 ms of each other (cf. Peterson and Lehiste 1960). Inter-rater reliability was over 90%, and the items that were in disagreement were not used for our analyses. Consequently, the data used for this study represent a sample that had 100% inter-rater agreement after discarding items that were not agreed upon. Figure 5.1 illustrates a sample of a Praat analysis window with the vowel boundaries noted on the phonetic transcription line.

Table 5.1. Number of vowel tokens analysed per phoneme category.

Vowel Pair	*Phonemically Short*	*Phonemically Long*
/i/ versus /iː/	1,011	221
/o/ versus /oː/	1,179	355
/u/ versus /uː/	371	159
Totals	2,561	735

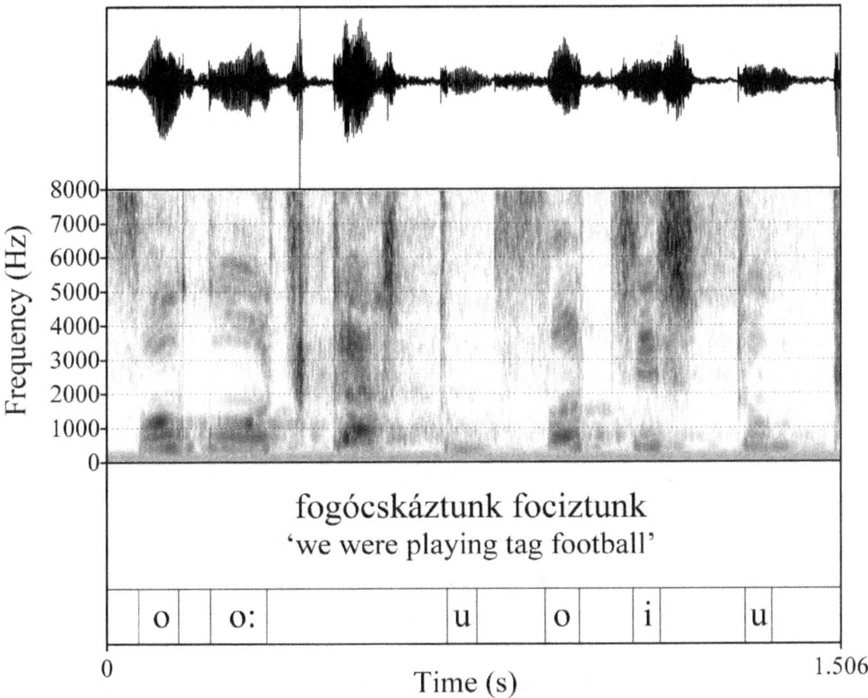

Figure 5.1. Sample of a Praat analysis window.

Statistical Analyses

We conducted a repeated measures analysis of variance (ANOVA) using the General Linear Model function available via the Statistical Package for the Social Sciences (SPSS, version 23). The analyses were similar to the ones conducted by Neuberger et al. (2015) with the addition of more participants and the added independent variable of gender. Specifically, regarding the independent variables, there were two within-subjects factors (vowel quantity and vowel quality) and two between-subjects factors (age and gender). Vowel quantity had two levels (phonemically short versus long) and vowel quality had three levels (/i/ versus /iː/, /o/ versus /oː/, and /u/ versus /uː/). Age had three levels (5-, 6- and 7-year-olds) and gender had two (male and female). The dependent variable was the duration of the vowel measured in milliseconds.

Having a within-subjects factor with three levels (i.e. vowel quality) means that there is a possibility that the variances of the differences between possible pairs of conditions (the different levels of vowel quality) would be unequal, which would violate sphericity (i.e. that those variances would be equal). Because violations of sphericity are potential causes for concern in repeated measures designs, Mauchly's test of sphericity was also conducted involving the within-subjects independent variable of quality (/i, iː/, /o, oː/ and /u, uː/). This measure was taken to ensure that if violation of sphericity were to be found, the statistical tests would be adjusted to limit the possibility of alpha error inflation. No such measure was needed for the within-subjects variable of quantity, because it had only two levels.

Results

Before discussing the effects of the independent variables and their interactions on vowel duration, it must be noted that Mauchly's test of sphericity was statistically significant for vowel quality [$\chi^2(2) = 14.72$, $p = 0.001$]. Consequently, the assumption of sphericity for vowel quality had been violated, and therefore, the degrees of freedom were corrected using Greenhouse-Geisser estimates of sphericity to limit the possibility of making a type I error. The statistical tests reported involving the independent variable vowel quality will reflect this correction in our results.

Vowel quantity

As discussed in the introduction to this chapter, vowel quantity is a phonemically distinctive feature in Hungarian in that there are seven phonemically long versus short pairs of vowels in the language. Consequently, we hypothesized that children learning Hungarian would differentiate vowels along the dimension of vowel quantity that would manifest itself in producing phonemically long vowels with relatively more extended duration than their phonemically short counterparts. This hypothesis was supported by our data via a main effect for vowel quantity on the duration of vowels produced [$F(1,36) = 92.82$, $p < 0.001$, partial $\eta^2 = 0.721$], indicating that phonemically long versus short vowel pairs were realized differently based on vowel quantity. Our data indicate that the duration of phonemically long vowels exceeded those of their phonemically short counterparts. Furthermore, there was no statistically significant vowel quantity by age interaction, suggesting that differentiation of phonemically long versus short vowels did not depend on the participant's age. In other words, irrespective of the child's age, phonemically long versus short vowels were produced differentially as measured by vowel duration. Figure 5.2 illustrates the average duration of each vowel at different ages, and Table 5.2 includes the means and standard deviations for each vowel per group as well as the totals for each vowel category. We provide additional details regarding the findings related to age in the subsequent section.

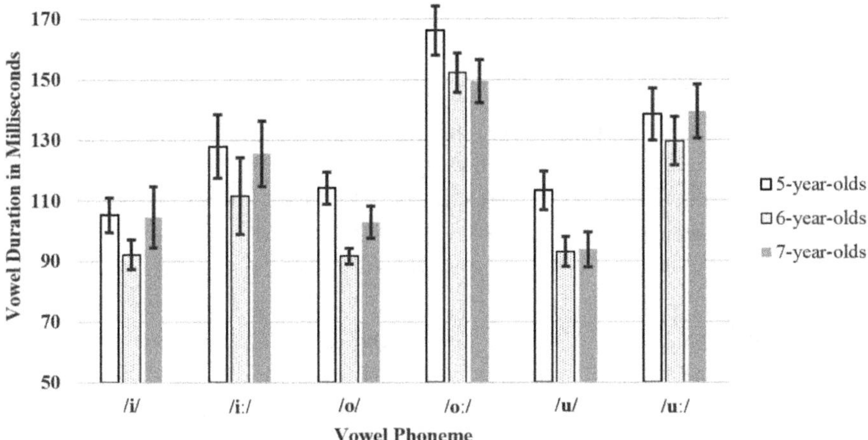

Figure 5.2. Vowel duration by age group.

Table 5.2. Means and standard deviations of vowel duration in milliseconds for each category per age group.

	Vowel Category Mean Duration (standard deviations)					
Age Group	/i/	/i:/	/o/	/o:/	/u/	/u:/
5-year-olds	105 (21)	128 (39)	114 (20)	166 (30)	113 (24)	138 (32)
6-year-olds	92 (19)	112 (47)	92 (10)	152 (24)	93 (19)	130 (30)
7-year-olds	105 (38)	126 (41)	103 (20)	150 (27)	94 (22)	139 (33)
Totals	101 (27)	122 (42)	103 (20)	156 (27)	100 (23)	136 (31)

Age

We also hypothesized that vowel quantity differentiation would show differences across the various age groups, but this hypothesis was not supported by the data. There was no statistically significant main effect for age [$F(2,36) = 2.92, p = 0.067$, partial $\eta^2 = 0.140$]. Furthermore none of the post-hoc tests comparing the specific groups (5-year-olds versus 6-year-olds, 5-year-olds versus 7-year-olds, and 6-year-olds versus 7-year-olds) were statistically significant using Tukey's pairwise contrasts. Therefore, we conclude that by 5 years of age, the phonemic differentiation between the pairs of vowels we analysed (/i/ versus /iː/, /o/ versus /oː/, and /u/ versus /uː/) display sufficient differentiation and that vowel quantity discrimination becomes stable and does not change statistically significantly from 5 to 7 years of age. This and related issues are further explored in the discussion.

Vowel quality

As previously disclosed, Mauchly's test of sphericity indicated potential violation of this assumption for vowel quality, and therefore the Greenhouse-Geisser correction was applied to our statistical tests involving this variable. There was a statistically significant effect for vowel quality on vowel duration [$F(1.5,53.6) = 13.76$, $p < 0.001$, partial $\eta^2 = 0.277$]. Furthermore, specific analysis revealed a quadratic trend for vowel quantity [$F(1,36) = 37.00, p < 0.001$, partial $\eta^2 = 0.507$], suggesting that the vowel pair /o/ and /oː/ differed from the other two pairs at a statistically significant level. More detailed statistical analyses confirmed these differences by finding that /o/ and /oː/, as a pair, differed statistically significantly from /i/ and /iː/ (mean difference = 18.266, $p < 0.001$) and the mid-back phonemically long-short vowel pair also differed from their higher back neighbours, /u/ and /uː/ (mean difference = 11.533, $p < 0.001$).

There was also an interaction effect for vowel quantity by quality [$F(1.9,69.7) = 8.45$, $p = 0.001$, partial $\eta^2 = 0.190$], indicating that vowel quantity depended on the quality of the phonemically long versus short vowel pairs. Together, the results for vowel quality indicate that phonemically long versus short pairs of Hungarian vowels are differentiated by children and that these contrasts also vary depending on the place of articulation for the vowel pairs. Consequently, our third hypothesis that posited an overall vowel quality effect as well as an interaction between vowel quality and vowel quantity was supported by our data. Figure 5.3 illustrates the differences between the phonemically long versus short vowel pairs

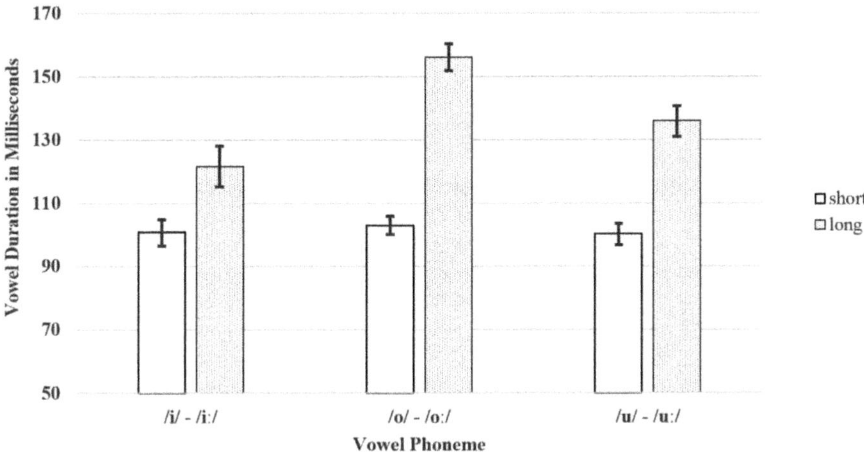

Figure 5.3. Vowel duration by quality.

and that the distinction between /o/ and /o:/ is more substantial than the difference between the other two pairs (/i/ versus /i:/ and /u/ versus /u:/).

Gender

Despite the fact that we had no predictions regarding the effects of gender on the production of phonemically long versus short Hungarian vowel

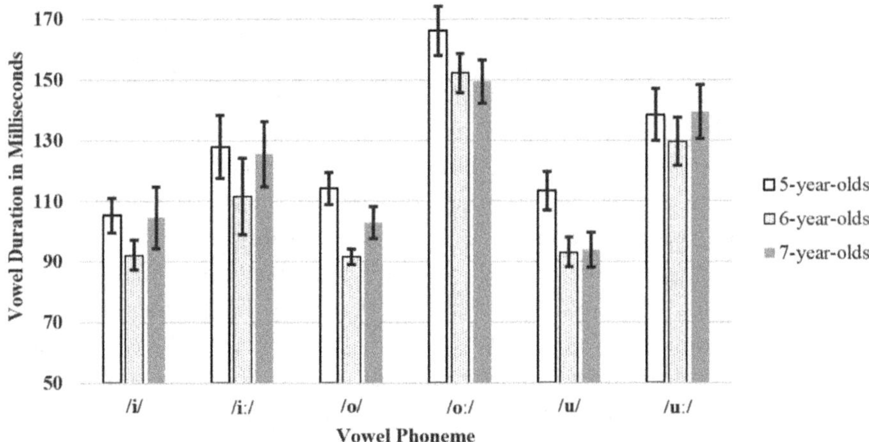

Figure 5.4. Vowel duration by gender.

pairs, since our data contained an equal number of female and male participants in each group, we provide an analysis of the effects of this variable on vowel duration. No statistically significant differences were found in the productions of our participants based on gender [$F(1,36) = 1.57$, $p = 0.218$, partial $\eta^2 = 0.042$], and there is no clearly identifiable pattern based on gender differences in the productions of our participants (see Figure 5.4).

Discussion

The findings presented in this chapter represent an expanded version of the results of our previous study (Neuberger et al. 2015) – both in terms of an increased number of participants, as well as via additional analyses that allowed us to elaborate on the results of our previous work. There is evidence for phonemic vowel quantity differentiation of the three vowel pairs we tested (i.e. /i/ versus /iː/, /o/ versus /oː/, and /u/ versus /uː/) in the productions of Hungarian-speaking children between the ages of 5 and 7 years as measured by the duration of the vowels. Also, vowel quantity is differentiated in each age group, including 5-year-olds, and there were no statistically significant differences based on the ages of the participants or any interaction effects that would have indicated ongoing development of the phonemic vowel quantity contrast from 5 to 7 years of age, at least for the vowel pairs we tested. The results reinforce the idea that by age 5 monolingual Hungarian-speaking children produce the phonemic vowel quantity differences reliably as measured by vowel duration. Our findings are also consistent with Zajdó and Powell's results (Zajdó 2002, 2015; Zajdó and Powell 2008) in that children acquiring Hungarian may display differentiation based on vowel quantity at a relatively early age, because the durational contrast between phonemically short versus long pairs is evident in the productions of 5-year-olds, and possibly even at younger ages that were not systematically tested in the present study.

In addition to the analyses conducted in our previous study, in the present study we expanded them to include comparisions of each age group to the other groups, in pairs, to investigate potential differences between the age groups. Our analyses yielded no statistically significant differences between 5- and 6-year-olds, 6- and 7-year-olds, and even 5- and 7-year-olds. These results diverge from the findings reported in other studies such as the ones presented in Bóna and Imre (2010) and Deme (2012). The differences in findings could be due to methodological discrepancies. In fact, both the Bóna and Imre (2010) and Deme (2012) studies found the same results we did with respect to the /o/ versus /oː/ and the /u/ versus /uː/ vowel pairs. It is reasonable to assume that phonemically short versus long vowel pairs that were not included in the current study may undergo a developmental trajectory different from the one found in our study. Had our research included those pairs, they may have shown ongoing development in the age range we studied. Nevertheless, more research is needed to investigate those issues further. Moreover, longitudinal data collection may offer a more sensitive means of capturing phonological development, so future studies should include data from the same participants followed over time.

As in Neuberger et al. (2015), it is further corroborated here that vowel quality has an effect on vowel duration. We also found a vowel quality by quantity interaction, suggesting that the way in which phonemically short versus long vowel pairs were differentiated also depended on the vowel pair. Specific analyses revealed that the phonemically short versus long /o/ – /oː/ pair was different from both the /i/ versus /iː/ pair and the /u/ versus /uː/ pair. The latter two (high front and high back) phonemically short versus phonemically long pairs, on the other hand, did not differ from each other at a statistically significant level. This specific finding is novel to our present study, and upon closer investigation of the data, it seems that the /o/ versus /oː/ pair displays more marked differences than the other two pairs (see Figure 5.3 for a display of the three vowel quality pairs). In general, these findings are consistent with the results of previous studies on the acquisition of the vowel quantity contrast in Hungarian, because existing studies focusing on the acquisition of vowel quantity in production (e.g. Bóna and Imre 2010; Deme 2012; Zajdó 2002) claim differences based on the quality of the vowel pair. Moreover, even in speech perception, it appears that the development of vowel quantity discrimination is gradual and may be affected by the vowel pair being acquired (cf. Gósy 2006). Taken together, the cumulative findings of various research studies on the topic indicate that the appearance of the contrastive feature of vowel quantity is both gradual and dependent on various factors, such as the quantity of the phonemically short versus long vowel pairs. These issues need further investigation and they also have implications for phonology in protolanguages (see the final section).

Unlike in the Neuberger et al. (2015) study, we managed to include an equal number of male and female participants (7 males and 7 females in each age group) that allowed us to examine the effects of gender on the production of vowel duration, as well as possible interactions between gender and the other independent variables (vowel quantity, vowel quality and age). Our results indicated no main effect and no interaction effects in any combination between gender and the other variables. Therefore, we concluded that the production of the phonemic vowel quantity contrast in the vowel pairs /i/ versus /i:/, /o/ versus /o/, and /u/ versus /u:/ was not affected by the gender of the participants, as illustrated in Figure 5.4. In fact, it appears that no clear pattern emerges that could be attributed to the gender of the participants of our study.

Limitations

With the addition of more participants and more in-depth analyses, our present study reinforces the findings of our earlier work, and it further elaborates and clarifies those results, as noted above. Nonetheless, as we conducted more in-depth analyses, it became clear that there are still some limitations that we have not been able to overcome, and our results also highlight future directions for research in the area of phonological development in Hungarian-speaking children. Despite the fact that we succeeded in increasing the number of our participants from 27 to 42, the numbers per cell were still relatively small, so future research should include a larger number of participants to verify our findings. Furthermore, it became abundantly clear that investigating the development of phonemic vowel quantity differentiation requires a longitudinal approach that starts at an earlier age. Specifically, scientific inquiry into the acquisition of the vowel quantity contrast should begin at an age when such contrasts have not been developed. By 5 years of age, Hungarian-speaking children appear to be able to differentiate phonemically short versus long vowels based on vowel duration. In addition, having an adult control group is also desirable to have a basis of comparison to a fully developed target.

It is also clear that investigating the full range of vowels (all 7 phonemically short versus long vowel pairs) is necessary, because in the three pairs examined in the current study, we found differences based on vowel quality, as well as interactions between vowel quality and quantity. If the phonological feature of vowel quantity in Hungarian develops in a gradual, piecemeal fashion, it is conceivable that while the contrasts on which our study has focused display durational differences, other phonemically short versus long vowel pairs may still be undergoing development. In order to obtain a complete picture of how phonemic vowel quantity contrasts develop over time, a longitudinal approach starting at the first signs of differentiation and following the contrast until it matures to a stable and adult-like level would be necessary, including all 7 pairs of phonemically short versus long Hungarian vowels.

Another limitation that we noted with respect to our previous work is that all of the samples used for the present and the previous study were based on conversational, quasi-naturalistic speech samples. While our methodology created a quasi-naturalistic conversational sample, it also limited the topics of choice to favourite stories or pastimes and discussion regarding the everyday lives of the participants. Furthermore, as the uneven numbers of tokens per vowel demonstrated, a conversational sample may yield uneven representation of target items, so more controlled data – such as elicited word lists – could be used to supplement a quasi-naturalistic sample that would also provide more control for the phonetic environment. Future studies should incorporate a variety of speech samples ranging from spontaneous to more structured data.

Irrespective of the limitations of our study, the findings are promising and advance our understanding of Hungarian phonological development. Our work has also produced more questions for further research into how phonology in general, and vowels in particular, are acquired by Hungarian-speaking children. In that sense, this chapter contributes novel information to how phonological development occurs in protolanguages. Being consistent with the use of the term in this volume, we define protolanguage broadly to refer to a developing linguistic system at any given stage from the first meaningful forms to complete language acquisition. In the spirit of this volume, in the final section below, we elaborate on what our data may mean for phonological systems in protolanguages and reflect on what protolanguages themselves may be.

Implications for Phonology in Protolanguage

As part of a volume on phonology in protolanguage and in interlanguage, our paper has implications for the former, because it presents data on the production of the vowel quantity contrast from monolingual Hungarian-speaking children in three cross-sectional age groups (5-, 6- and 7-year-olds). The patterns of production of phonemically short versus long Hungarian vowels offer a window on how phonological contrasts manifest themselves in the protolanguage of Hungarian-speaking 5- to 7-year-olds.

An issue we noted previously in the discussion is that vowel quality has a differential effect on the production of phonemically short versus long vowel pairs in Hungarian and their manifestations in the participants' speech productions. Specifically, /o/ versus /oː/ displayed a different (more distinct) pattern than the other two pairs of vowels (i.e. /i/ versus /iː/ and /u/ versus /uː/). It appears that phonological contrasts – in our case the quantitative difference between phonemically short versus long Hungarian vowels – in protolanguages may develop gradually rather than instantaneously, as previously noted. At the very least, evidence from our study suggests that even when a contrast is used consistently, the degree to which the categorical difference manifests itself can vary. As Buder and Stoel-Gammon (2002) point out, the properties of the language being acquired – and specifically its phonological system – seem to drive the acquisition of its phonological features, and the development of those features may be further guided by both factors that are intrinsic to the vowel as well as those that are vowel-extrinsic. In fact, vowel characteristics that are linguistically relevant for the distinctive phonological feature of vowel quantity, namely intrinsic vowel duration, can and do interact with vowel features that are not necessarily relevant for the given contrast, such as intrinsic vowel quality, as demonstrated by an interaction of vowel quantity with quality in phonemically short versus long vowel pairs in our study.

Naturally, before drawing any definitive conclusions, it is necessary to (i) collect longitudinal data from the same participants over time starting at younger ages to full maturity, or at least until the contrasts stabilize for all the vowel pairs tested (we suggest at least from 3 years of age to 7 years of age), (ii) have an adult control group and (iii) include all the Hungarian phonemically short versus long pairs. Nonetheless our data suggest a somewhat piecemeal *burgeoning* of a phonological contrast in protolanguage and not an all-or-nothing, sudden emergence of vowel quantity discrimination. It is important to note, however, that while some phonological features may develop gradually over time other contrasts and features may appear more abruptly, which is why more comprehensive analyses of phonological development in protolanguages is recommended.

Finally, adopting the definition of protolanguage (a developing linguistic system at a given stage before it reaches full maturity) presented in this volume, we would like to comment on – and wonder about – what it means for linguistic systems to reach a fully developed stage and whether or not that also implies an end-state of such systems. As an individual's linguistic system – including phonology – matures, its components become more stable and less variable, especially as the developmental trajectory becomes more asymptotic. Nonetheless, even after reaching a relatively stable level, linguistic systems continue to change, modified by experience, use, the lack of use, aging and other factors. Consequently, in a sense, one may argue that linguistic systems never reach an end-state, but rather one's language continues to evolve and/or devolve during one's lifetime. We leave the reader with the following question: Is there ever such a thing as a completely and fully stable final state of a phonological system?

References

Boersma, P. and Weenink, D., 2015, *Praat (Version 5.4.08)*, computer software from http://www.praat.org/ viewed May 23, 2015.

Bóna, J., 2012, 'A rövid-hosszú magánhangzók realizációi idősek spontán beszédében' [The production of long and short vowels in the spontaneous speech of the elderly], *Beszédkutatás* 20, 43–57.

Bóna, J. and Imre, A., 2010, 'A rövid/hosszú magánhangzók óvodás és kisiskolás gyermekek beszédprodukciójában' [Long/short vowels in preschool- and school-age children's speech], in J. Navracsics (ed.), *Nyelv – beszéd – írás*, pp. 49–56, Budapest: Tinta Kiadó.

Buder, E.H. and Stoel-Gammon, C., 2002, 'American and Swedish children's acquisition of vowel duration: Effects of vowel identity and final stop voicing', *Journal of the Acoustical Society of America* 111(4), 1854–64. https://doi.org/10.1121/1.1463448

Deme, A., 2012, 'Óvodások magánhangzóinak akusztikai jellemzői' [Acoustic properties of vowels produced by preschoolers], in A. Markó (ed.), *Beszédtudomány. Az anyanyelv-elsajátítástól a zöngekezdési időig*, pp. 77–99, Budapest: ELTE – MTA Nyelvtudományi Intézet.

Gini, C., 1921, 'Measurement of inequality of incomes', *The Economic Journal* 31(121), 124–26. https://doi.org/10.2307/2223319

Giegerich, H., 1992, *English phonology: An introduction*, Cambridge, UK: Cambridge University Press. https://doi.org/10.1017/CBO9781139166126

Gósy, M., 2004, *Fonetika, a beszéd tudománya* [Phonetics: The science of speech], Budapest: Osiris Kiadó.

Gósy, M., 2006, 'A beszédhangok megkülönböztetésének fejlődése' [The development of phonemic differentiation], *Beszédkutatás* 14, 147–59.

Gósy, M. and Beke, A., 2010, 'Magánhangzó-időtartamok a spontán beszédben' [Vowel duration in spontaneous speech], *Magyar Nyelvőr* 134, 140–65.

Kassai, I., 1979, *Időtartam és kvantitás a magyar nyelvben* [Duration and quantity in Hungarian], *Nyelvtudományi Értekezések* 102, Budapest: Akadémiai Kiadó.

Ladefoged, P., 2003, *Phonetic data analysis: An introduction to fieldwork and instrumental techniques*, Oxford, UK: Blackwell.

Lehiste, I., 1965, 'The function of quantity in Finnish and Estonian', *Language* 41(3), 447–56. https://doi.org/10.2307/411787

Lehiste, I., 1970, *Suprasegmentals*, Cambridge, MA: Cambridge University Press.

Malmberg, B., 1971, *Svensk fonetik* [Swedish phonetics], Lund: Gleerups.

Nádasdy, Á. and Siptár, P., 2001, 'A magánhangzók' [Vowels], in F. Kiefer (ed.), *Strukturális magyar nyelvtan 2: Fonológia* [Sturctural Hungarian grammar 2: Phonology], pp. 42–94, Budapest: Akadémiai Kiadó.

Neuberger, T., Bóna, J., Markó, A., Jordanidisz, Á. and Bunta, F., 2015, 'Vowel duration contrast in three long-short pairs by Hungarian 5-, 6-, and 7-year-olds', in E. Babatsouli and D. Ingram (eds.), *The Proceedings of the International Symposium on Monolingual and Bilingual Speech*, pp. 246–51, Chania, Greece, September 7–10, 2015, ISBN: 978-618-82351-0-6, http://ismbs.eu/publications.

Peterson, G.E. and Lehiste, I., 1960, 'Duration of syllable nuclei in English', *Journal of the Acoustical Society of America* 32, 693–703. https://doi.org/10.1121/1.1908183

Santen, J.P.H. van, 1992, 'Contextual effects on vowel duration', *Speech Communication* 11, 513–46. https://doi.org/10.1016/0167-6393(92)90027-5

Shah, A., 2002, *Temporal characteristics of Spanish-accented English: Acoustic measures and their correlation with accentedness ratings*, PhD thesis, The City University of New York.

Szende, T., 1994, 'Illustrations of the IPA: Hungarian', *Journal of the International Phonetic Alphabet* 24(2), 91–94. https://doi.org/10.1017/S0025100300005090

Zajdó, K., 2002, *The acquisition of vowels by Hungarian-speaking children aged two to four years: A cross-sectional study*, PhD thesis, University of Washington.

Zajdó, K., 2015, 'Can caregivers facilitate the acquisition of language-specific segment-duration patterns in children's speech?', paper presented at the International Symposium on Monolingual and Bilingual Speech 2015 (ISMBS), Chania, Greece, September 7–10.

Zajdó, K. and Powell, S., 2008, 'The acquisition of phonological vowel length in children acquiring Hungarian', in R. Sock, S. Fuchs and Y. Laprie (eds.), *Proceedings of the 8th International Seminar on Speech Production*, pp. 173–76, December 8–12, 2008, Strasbourg, France.

Ferenc Bunta is an Associate Professor in the Department of Communication Sciences and Disorders at the University of Houston. His research focuses primarily on bilingual and crosslinguistic phonological acquisition in both typical populations and individuals with communication disorders (such as children with hearing loss). His work has included both children and adults, ranging from children undergoing bilingual as first-language acquisition to later second-language learners.

Tilda Neuberger is a research fellow in the Department of Phonetics at the Research Institute for Linguistics of the Hungarian Academy of Sciences. She received her PhD in Hungarian linguistics from Eötvös Loránd University, Budapest in 2013. Her research interests include speech and language development of 5–14-year-old children. Her current research focuses on the phonetic and phonological aspects of gemination in Hungarian.

Judit Bóna is an Associate Professor in the Department of Phonetics at Eötvös Loránd University in Budapest, Hungary. Since 2002 she has been teaching courses in Phonetics and Psycholinguistics. Her research focuses primarily on phonetic and psycholinguistic characteristics of speech in individuals of different ages, from children to older adults, including populations who are typical and who have communication disorders (such as speakers with fluency disorders).

Alexandra Markó is an Associate Professor at the Department of Phonetics at Eötvös Loránd University, Budapest, Hungary. Her research focuses primarily on spontaneous speech with special regard to intonation, temporal characteristics and voice quality (especially irregular phonation) both in typical and pathological speech. The subjects' ages range from the age of 5 to adulthood. The pragmatic functions of prosody were also included in her studies, principally the suprasegmental characteristics of discourse markers. Her research has involved mainly acoustic analysis but recently it has been extended to articulatory investigations.

Agnes Jordanidisz is the Chair of the Association for Educational Needs since 2004 and as the representative of NILD Educational Therapy® in Central and Eastern Europe, she works in post-graduate teacher training. Her main research interest is child language development. Her PhD research disclosed Hungarian children's phonological awareness development between ages 4 and 10. She also works in research application.

6
Phonological development and language proficiency of bilingual children who learn Greek as a second language

Eleni Morfidi and Eleni Samsari

Introduction

Greek is an alphabetic language with transparent orthography meaning that there is a high degree of letter to sound correspondence. However, preserving elements of historic orthography and older forms of language, Greek is, in fact, easier to read than write (Seymour, Aro and Erskine 2003). Spoken Greek involves a range of consonantal sounds which amount to 21, if one takes into account allophones and affricates. There are five vowel sounds and combinations of them entail short diphthongs (Arvaniti 1999). The syllable structure of Greek has been described as $C_{0\text{-}3}VC_{0\text{-}1}$, with /s/ and /n/ being the only consonantal sounds allowed in word-final position, making vowels common at the end of Greek words (Kappa 2002). Phenomena such as juncture (e.g. /n/ deletion) and assimilation do occur but vary according to dialect, speed and formality of speech. Consonant clusters consisting of two or three consonants appear at word-initial and word-medial position. For instance, the word *εκστρατεία* /ekstratía/ 'crusade' comprises a sequence of four consonants in the middle of the word that are, however, syllabified as /ek.stra.tia/. Greek words may take one stress in one of the last three syllables. The first sounds produced by Greek children are plosives, nasals and glides, whereas first word productions are usually bisyllabic (CVCV) words with reduplicated syllables. Studies on Greek language acquisition report universal patterns of development. Between ages 3;6 and 4;0 most sounds appear in children's phonetic repertoire and consonant clusters are established between 4;0 to 4;6 (see Mennen and Okalidou 2007, for a review).

Bilingual acquisition of Greek has received limited attention in research (e.g. Babatsouli to appear, and in this volume; Chionidou and Nicolaidis 2015; Haritos and Nelson 2001). Morfidi and Samsari (2015) provide an account of Greek bilinguals' speech errors and derive percentages of vowels (PVC), consonants (PCC) and phonemes correct (PPC). The phonologies of children in that study indicate L1 interference and a complex developmental process. In addition, the study reported a link between linguistic, metalinguistic and literacy skills within and across languages. The interdependence and transfer in languages learnt simultaneously is well documented (e.g. Genesee, Paradis and Crago 2004; Kehoe 2015). Despite the consensus there is in the literature on the presence of interaction in bilingual phonological acquisition (e.g. Babatsouli and Ingram 2015; Fabiano-Smith and Barlow 2010; Kehoe, Lleó in this volume), the configuration of the exact nature and degree of interaction still remains elusive.

The most common approach to the investigation of speech production has been the use of phonetic inventories and consonant correctness. An insightful approach to phonological assessment employing whole-word measures has been proposed by Ingram (2002). The whole-word approach builds on the assumption that children's productions are word-oriented, not segment-oriented, and assessment is framed around the idea that the child is an active learner attempting compensatory patterns to overcome problems and match the adult target. The rationale for adopting a broader phonological assessment stems from the fact that children's words get longer and more complex as their vocabulary increases. Complexity and accuracy influence each other due to trade-off effects. Whole-word measures can be used to compare the complexity of the child's words to the complexity of the target words being attempted. A simple, yet easy to use, and potentially highly reliable measure of whole-word complexity is the Phonological Mean Length of Utterance (pMLU). The term approximates that of the Mean Length of Utterance (MLU) that is utilized in language assessment to measure the increase in the length of an utterance. MLU applies to sentences, whereas pMLU applies to words. A child's pMLU or word complexity increases with age. Thus, pMLU can be used to identify a child's stage of phonological acquisition, assess proximity to target words, and evaluate the complexity of words (Ingram and Ingram 2001).

Phonological whole-word measures are adaptable in various settings, can be applied to a variety of languages, and may be used in studies comparing monolingual speech perfomance to bilingual speech performance (Saaristo-Helin, Savinainen-Makkonen and Kunnari 2006). The measures that have been used in the present study are: Phonological Mean Length of Utterance (pMLU) in conjunction with Percentage of Consonant

Correctness (PCC), used to assess accuracy; Proportion of Whole-Word Proximity (PWP), used to assess proximity of productions to the adult target; and Proportion of Whole-Word Variation (PWV), used to indicate variability in children's productions. The main purpose of whole-word measurement is to assess word complexity both in terms of the complexity of the target words and that of the child's productions. Target word pMLU and child pMLU scores provide an account of what the child is actually producing and the level of complexity of the words produced. The actual calculation includes vowels and it is, therefore, recommended that they are used in conjunction with a score of consonant correctness (Ingram 2015). The Proportion of Whole-Word Proximity (PWP) shows how well the phonological target is approximated and captures the relationship between the child pMLU and the target word pMLU. A discrepancy between the two may serve as an indicator of the intelligibility of the child's productions. The last measure used in the present study is the Proportion of Whole-Word Variability (PWV), which describes the consistency of children's productions and may be an important window into children's representations and phonological processing (Ingram 2002; Ingram and Dubasic, 2011; Ingram and Ingram 2001). Details and examples are provided in the section on Method.

Phonological development is a driving force in language acquisition, though aspects such as lexical and semantic knowledge cannot be overlooked. The investigation of monolingual and bilingual phonological and broader language skills may shed light on patterns in development, and inform research and practice on individual differences with respect to phonological and other language disorders. Recent research emphasizes the interactions between domains (i.e. phonological/lexical), since they mutually facilitate each other. Phonological ability has been shown to influence lexical acquisition (e.g. Beckman, Munson and Edwards 2007). Their relationship is bidirectional, that is, the nature and structure of the lexicon may also influence phonological knowledge. This is evident in the relationship between the acquisition of phonology and that of new words. Children's early words tend to be short and contain consonants that are acquired early in the course of language acquisition. Lexical acquisition and development are commensurate with children's phonological abilities, and the underlying phonological representations change as vocabulary increases (Stoel-Gammon 2011, for a review). However, to what extent phonological influences apply more to the development of expressive or receptive vocabulary is still an issue to be explored further (Hoff and Parra 2011).

Phonological awareness is the ability to detect and manipulate the sound structure of spoken words (Wagner et al. 1993). Phonological awareness and vocabulary knowledge share a bidirectional relationship. The Lexical Restructuring Model (LPM; Metsala and Walley 1998) predicts that, as children's vocabularies increase, children become more sensitive to the detection of specific phonemes. In turn, this fine-grained restructuring is an important precursor to the explicit segmentation of phoneme awareness of spoken words which is strongly related to early reading. Age of acquisition and lexical characteristics (word frequency, neighbourhood density and phonotactic probability) may interfere with subsequent skills (Goodrich and Lonigan 2015). However, evidence is needed in order to refine our understanding of the co-developing relations between spoken word recognition, speech and reading-related abilities (Sosa and Stoel-Gammon 2012; Walley, Metsala and Garlock 2003).

The properties of oral language are not limited to speech production processes. Areas of narrative production, such as the macrostructure referring to the global scheme of a produced story structure and the microstructure representing linguistic features, i.e. the vocabulary and grammar used to express the narrative content, must also be considered. A strong relationship between these distinct levels of observation is assumed (Licandro 2016). Oral narratives provide a useful source of information for children's language and story retelling. It is a preferred method of assessing language skills in diverse populations (Reese, Sparks and Suggate 2012). An additional reason to implement a narrative task in language assessment is the relationship of children's narratives with literacy acquisition. Such a relationship has been evidenced among monolingual (Reese, Suggate, Long and Schaughency 2010; Suggate, Schaughency and Reese 2011) and bilingual populations (Miller et al. 2006; Tsimpli, Peristeri and Andreou 2016).

In the present study, the relationship between speech production, oral narrative production and other linguistic and metalinguistic abilities is examined in order to investigate whether these aspects of oral language differentiate between monolingual and bilingual users of Greek, as well as the extent of association between these abilities and literacy skills in each group. The major goal here is to investigate children's phonological and overall language abilities when Greek is either a first or a second language. Differences in reading are expected to occur since related abilities develop across the continuum of oral-written language.

The research questions are as follows:

(1) Do English/Greek bilingual 10-year-old children differ from their monolingual peers on phonological whole-word measures of complexity (as measured by pMLU), consonant accuracy (as measured

by PCC), phonological target approximations (as measured by PWP) and variability (PWV) of Greek?

(2) Do English/Greek bilingual 10-year-old children differ from their monolingual peers on measures of phonological awareness, vocabulary knowledge, syntactic development (MLU), expressive vocabulary (NDW), verbal fluency (WPM) and narrative structure (NSS) of Greek?

(3) What is the pattern of relationships between phonological whole-word measures (PCC, pMLU, PWP, PWV), phonological awareness, vocabulary knowledge, syntactic development (MLU), expressive vocabulary (NDW), verbal fluency (WPM), narrative structure (NSS) and literacy in the bilinguals' first language (English, L1) and second language (Greek, L2)?

(4) What is the level of association between phonological, language and literacy measures of Greek in the monolinguals?

Whole-word measures have largely been used to explore children's phonologies at the early stages of acquisition. Previous research has shown that bilinguals may differ from their monolingual peers on phonological performance at least when the target language involves the bilinguals' L2 (see for example, Gildersleeve-Neumann, Kester, Davis and Peña 2008; Bunta, Fabiano-Smith, Goldstein and Ingram 2009). Because of their age, the level of linguistic development of the children/participants in the current study is no longer representative of the early stages of a developing linguistic system, the protolanguage, which studies on child language acquisition usually employ. The linguistic system of these children belongs to an early transitional system, which is different from both the learner's native language and the targeted second language. However, it is expected that there will still be differences between the two groups of bilinguals and monolingual controls regarding phonological whole-word measures since phonological, morphological and semantic aspects of the target language are still developing.

These differences may be revealed in the full range of language proficiency measures addressing vocabulary, fluency, syntax and narrative structure. Monolinguals outperform bilingual children in language proficiency and reading skills. Lexical-semantic aspects of language interfere with the comprehension and production of oral language as well as its processing in written forms (Cremer and Schoonen 2013; Friesen, Luo, Luk and Bialystok 2015). Narrative macrostructure follows the same course of development in monolingual and bilingual children. It is influenced by both age and schooling (i.e. language exposure) (Roch, Florit and Levorato 2016) whilst, from a crosslinguistic perspective, it is moderately associated with L2 equivalents (Ucceli and Paez 2007). Microstructure skills such as vocabulary knowledge are important in bilingual acquisition, determining both the perception and the production of the L2. It is well established that bilinguals know fewer words in each language than their monolingual counterparts and have slower lexical access (Bialystock, Luk, Peets and Yang 2010; Simos et al. 2014).

Phonological awareness taps on the quality of phonological representations at a metalinguistic level and relates to reading acquisition (Wagner et al. 1993). Early phonemic awareness, in particular, is an indicator of future reading abilities and it develops rapidly during the first stages of acquisition in languages with transparent orthographies, such as Greek (Papadopoulos, Kendeou and Spanoudis 2012). It has been found that bilingual learners, who are exposed to both English and Greek from a young age, outperform their monolingual counterparts on phonological awareness tasks. Loizou and Stuart (2003), who compared four samples of five-year-old English and Greek monolinguals, and English-Greek and Greek-English bilinguals, described a 'bilingual enhancement effect', which they observed when children are exposed to a second language that is phonologically simpler than their first language. However, the children in the present study are much older than those in early developmental stages, and phonological awareness tasks are expected to show low discriminant validity in comparisons with normally developing children of that age.

There is evidence suggesting relationships across measures of phonological performance (i.e. PCC, pMLU, PWP), since they relate to underlying phonological representations (Bunta et al. 2009). However, to what extent this may be evident in the two groups of the present study remains to be seen. One more measure, PWV, has also been included in the study because bilingual children may vary in their efforts to produce novel items and syllabic structures that are less familiar. PWV provides an insight into the processes of a mechanism to stabilize the categorization and phonological representation of L2 sounds. The bilinguals' comparison on this measure reveals differences with monolinguals which persist until adulthood (Borsch and Ramon-Casas 2011; Diaz et al. 2016).

Method

Participants

The present study included 22 children: 11 monolingual Greek children (mean age = 10.18, sd = 1.41, range = 8.80–12.10) and 11 bilingual children with English (L1) and Greek (L2) (mean age = 10.73, sd = 1.06, range = 8.12–11.84). There were no significant age differences between the two groups [$F(1,20) = 1.06, p = 0.31$]. Seven males and four females participated in each group. All participants attended local state-run schools. They were typically developing children without a diagnosis of any speech and/or language disorder. The bilingual sample was recruited from the community schools of Houston, Texas US and the monolingual sample from inner-city schools in Ioannina, Greece. The community school in the Houston area requires instruction in Greek twice a week for 3 hours each afternoon and participation in extra-curricular activities in the weekend. An extensive parent questionnaire was used to collect information on the language background of the bilingual group. It was confirmed that the dominant language was English and at least one of the parents was of Greek origin. The children had 3 to 6 years of Greek schooling and all of them had been speaking and studying Greek at home with at least one of the parents and/or relatives.

Materials and procedure

The whole-word measures

PCC: the percentage of correct consonants is commonly used in speech assessment. It has been selected in the present study to supplement phonological information on accuracy by whole-word measures. The simple formula is provided by Ingram (2015).

pMLU: The phonological mean length of utterance is a measure of phonological complexity both in terms of the complexity of the target words and the child productions. The target word pMLU formula allocates two points to each consonant and one to each vowel. The child pMLU formula gives two points to each correct consonant and one to each vowel and consonant substitution. For a full list of calculation rules, see Ingram (2002). For example, the word pMLU of *βάτραχος* /ˈvatraxos/ 'frog' has 5 consonants and 3 vowels and a value of 13. A child substituting the original word with *βάταχος* [ˈvataxos] gets a value of 11.

PWP: The proportion of whole-word proximity captures how well the phonological target is approximated by dividing the child pMLU by the target pMLU. For example, considering the word *βάτραχος* /ˈvatɾaxos/ 'frog' and the child's production, the value of 11 is divided by 13 to get the PWP score of 0.85. It is considered suggestive of the intelligibility of a child's speech. Typically developing children already show a PWP above 0.50 from early childhood.

PWV: The proportion of whole-word variation is an index of children's inconsistencies in their productions. The number of different forms the child produced is divided by the number of productions. The values range from 0.00 to 1.00. For example, if a child produces the word *βάτραχος* /ˈvatɾaxos/ 'frog' 7 times using 3 different forms: [ˈvatɾakos] (4 times), [ˈvataxos] (twice) and [ˈvɾataxos] (once), the PWV score is 3/7= 0.42.

Phonological awareness

The Comprehensive Test of Phonological Processing (Wagner, Torgesen and Rashotte 1999) was used for the English language and an adaptation for the Greek language was developed by the first author (see Appendix I). The Elision, Word Blending, Word Segmenting, Non-Word Blending and Non-Word Segmenting subtests were employed to measure the ability to process sounds at the phoneme level in both languages.

Vocabulary

The Woodcock Picture Vocabulary test (Woodcock 1991) was used in both languages to assess vocabulary knowledge in both L1 and L2. It includes 58 picture items of increasing difficulty.

Oral narratives

Lexical, syntactic, fluency and discourse measures of oral language were assessed using the children's retelling of the 'Frog where are you?' story (Mayer 1969) in Greek (see Appendix II). Specifically, the four measures used are the following: mean length of utterance (MLU), calculated by the number of words in each utterance; number of different words (NDW), calculated by counting the number of different lexemes; the words per minute (WPM), calculated by dividing the total number of words in the transcript by the time taken to retell the story; and finally the children's ability to produce a coherent narrative, assessed by a total score on the seven categories comprising the narrative structure scheme (NSS). The systematic analysis of language transcripts (SALT) (Miller and Iglesias 2003–04) is used for analysing children's narratives.

Reading

The sight word efficiency subtest of the Test of Word Reading Efficiency (TOWRE, Torgesen, Wagner and Rashotte 1999) was used to measure word reading fluency. The test contains 104 words of increasing difficulty. This was also the model for the Greek Word Reading Test, as developed with Greek words and lemmas by the Hellenic National Corpus (HNC) (Hatzigeorgiu et al. 2000) (see Appendix III). The Woodcock Passage Comprehension from the Woodcock Language Proficiency Battery – Revised (Woodcock 1991) was administered to examine reading comprehension using a cloze task. The children read a sentence or short passage where individual words had been omitted. In order to develop a parallel Greek version, the original items were translated by the first author, while for a few items adaptations were necessary.

Procedure

All children were tested in their school setting. Sessions for monolinguals lasted around 45 minutes, whereas the bilingual assessment took double the time (i.e. 90 minutes). Their oral narratives were recorded, transcribed and analysed using SALT. All words produced in the children's retellings were used to derive the full set of oral language measures.

Results

The first research question seeks to investigate whether the whole-word measures differentiate the two groups. In the following section results for each one of the four measures are presented.

PCC. Figure 6.1 presents the means and standard deviations for each group of child participants. The mean differences were statistically significant [Bilinguals: mean = 90.96, sd = 4.15; Monolinguals: mean = 99.45, sd = 0.68, $F(1,20) = 44.61$, $p \leq 0.001$].

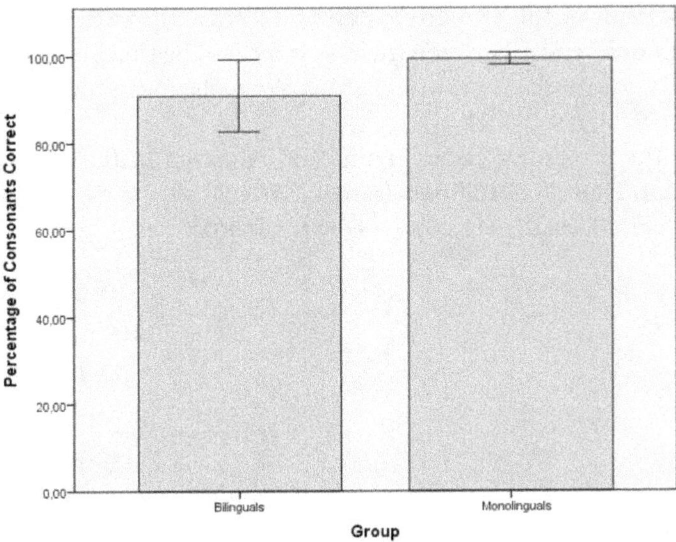

Figure 6.1. Percentage of Consonants Correct.

pMLU. The targeted word pMLU score was calculated and showed that the two groups use words of similar complexity. There are no significant mean differences between them [Bilinguals: mean = 5.95, sd = 0.27; Monolinguals: mean = 6.11, sd = 0.15, $F(1{,}20) = 3.31$, $p = 0.08$]. Figure 6.2 displays the results of child pMLU.

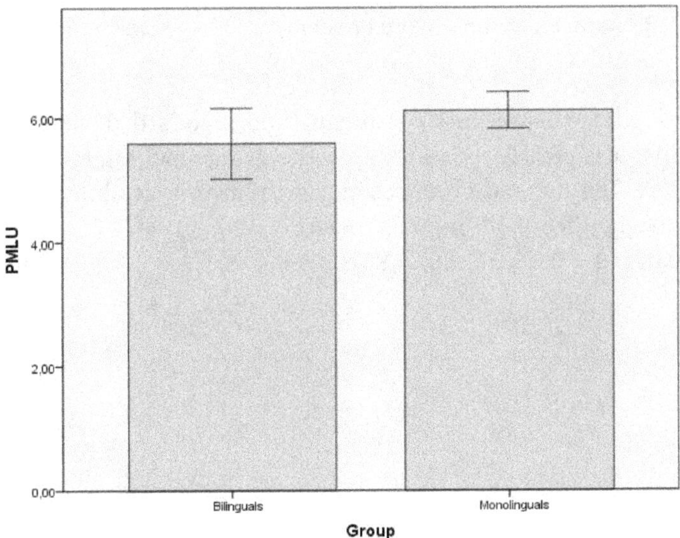

Figure 6.2. Phonological Mean Length of Utterance.

Comparison of the two groups on child pMLU reveals that there are significant differences between them as indicated by the one-way ANOVA [Bilinguals: mean = 5.59, sd = 0.28; Monolinguals: mean = 6.11, sd = 0.15, $F(1,20) = 29.96, p \leq 0.001$].

PWP. The proximity values significantly differed in the two groups as displayed in Figure 6.3 [Bilinguals: mean = 0.94, sd = 0.03; Monolinguals: mean = 0.99, sd = 0.01, $F(1,20) = 48.68, p \leq 0.001$].

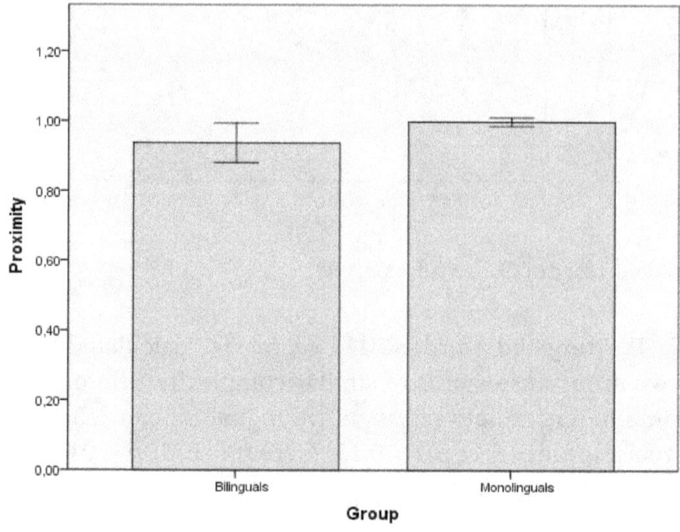

Figure 6.3. Proportion of Whole-Word Proximity.

PWV. Figure 6.4 presents the means and standard deviations for the two groups. It is clearly indicated that the groups belong to two different populations. The mean differences of the children's variability scores were statistically significant [Bilinguals: mean = 0.50, sd = 0.17; Monolinguals: mean = 0.02, sd = 0.05, $F(1,20) = 80.32, p \leq 0.001$].

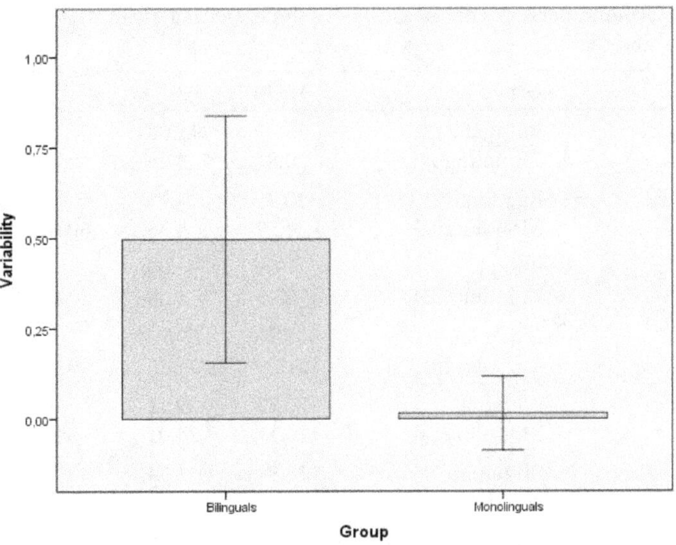

Figure 6.4. Proportion of Whole-Word Variation.

Furthermore, the variability of the children's productions and the word variability in their retellings were calculated. The results indicated no significant differences across monosyllabic [Bilinguals: mean = 40.91, sd = 3.27; Monolinguals: mean = 39.18, sd = 2.32, $F(1,20) = 2.55, p = 0.13$], bisyllabic [Bilinguals: mean = 33.09, sd = 3.30; Monolinguals: mean = 33.18, sd = 3.32, $F(1,20) = 0.01$, $p = 0.94$], trisyllabic [Bilinguals: mean = 21.27, sd = 3.13; Monolinguals: mean = 21.91, sd = 1.76, $F(1,20) = 0.35$, $p = 0.56$] and multisyllabic words [Bilinguals: mean = 4.54, sd = 2.87; Monolinguals: mean = 5.72, sd = 1.10, $F(1,20) = 1.62, p = 0.22$].

Our second research question inquired about group differences in the following variables: phonological awareness, vocabulary knowledge, oral language (MLU, NDW, WPM, NSS) and reading. The results are presented in Table 6.1.

Table 6.1. Group differences on measures of phonological awareness, oral language proficiency and reading.

Variable	*Group*	*Mean*	*sd*	*F*	*p*
Phonological Awareness	Bilingual	65.00	11.08		
	Monolingual	70.81	3.48	2.76	0.110
Vocabulary	Bilingual	20.91	3.70		
	Monolingual	34.27	4.36	60.06	0.001
MLU	Bilingual	7.09	1.00		
	Monolingual	8.68	1.09	12.60	0.002
NDW	Bilingual	114.36	30.75		
	Monolingual	161.09	41.46	9.01	0.007
WPM	Bilingual	70.53	29.92		
	Monolingual	116.17	24.01	15.56	0.035
NSS	Bilingual	18.81	2.44		
	Monolingual	20.18	1.88	6.45	0.020
Word Reading	Bilingual	59.81	27.90		
	Monolingual	80.27	10.95	5.12	0.035
Reading Comprehension	Bilingual	23.00	5.14		
	Monolingual	28.36	3.90	7.60	0.012

The findings support predictions regarding performance in the above variables. Significant differences are found across all measures with one exception, i.e. phonological awareness, which is not expected to discriminate between linguistic groups at late stages of schooling unless the children encounter language and learning difficulties.

In order to investigate the relationship between phonological, language proficiency and literacy variables across groups, a series of Pearson product moment correlations were calculated and are presented in Table 6.2. Inter-correlations for the bilinguals are presented above the diagonal and for the monolinguals below the diagonal.

Table 6.2. Inter-correlations of the target variables in the two groups.

	1	2	3	4	5	6	7	8	9	10	11	12	13	14	15	16	17	18	19	20
PCC		.38	**.96**	.46	.02	.52	.10	.49	.47	.29	−.03	−.09	.38	.05	−.22	−.25	−.33	−.33	−.03	−.01
PLMU	.11		.52	.06	.37	.50	−.07	.53	.28	.45	.38	.29	.37	.15	−.13	.01	.19	−.12	.51	.16
PWP	**.70**	.49		.34	.10	.58	.21	.54	.50	.40	.03	.09	.40	.13	−.22	−.11	−.21	−.26	.09	.11
PWV	.26	−.04	.10		−.11	.23	−.47	.04	.34	.05	.02	.30	.06	.07	−.15	**−.61**	.07	−.33	−.16	.02
G. Phon. Awareness	.08	−.23	−.02	**−.74**		.57	.32	**.60**	.49	**.59**	**.66**	.58	**.81**	**.86**	.51	.42	**.61**	.50	**.84**	**.73**
G. Vocabulary	.26	−.45	.17	−.33	**.69**		.38	**.87**	**.89**	**.77**	**.80**	**.80**	.51	.58	.37	.16	.51	.27	**.76**	**.59**
G. MLU	−.01	.02	.14	.45	−.26	−.03		.51	.33	**.61**	.15	.25	.27	.44	**.61**	**.63**	.13	.35	.36	.28
G. NDW	.09	.20	.26	.33	−.32	−.12	**.84**		**.80**	**.70**	**.67**	**.76**	**.64**	.58	.46	.25	.31	.29	**.72**	**.60**
G. WPM	.13	.07	.34	−.11	.15	.07	**.67**	**.70**		.56	**.67**	**.84**	.54	.53	.26	−.09	.51	.13	**.61**	**.84**
G. NSS	.01	.35	.03	−.21	.29	.01	.51	.54	.44		**.60**	**.65**	.47	**.64**	**.61**	.44	.47	.40	**.70**	.39
G. Word Reading	.48	.06	.49	−.25	**.60**	.55	.17	.08	.52	.21		**.84**	.36	**.59**	.47	.29	**.75**	.57	**.88**	**.67**
G.R. Comprehension	−.03	−.14	.03	**−.63**	**.81**	.47	−.04	−.04	.24	.49	.51		.46	**.63**	.54	.06	**.69**	.38	**.75**	**.70**
E. Phon. Awareness														.57	.21	.01	.15	.13	.55	.48
E. Vocabulary															**.69**	.56	**.70**	**.60**	**.71**	**.83**
E. MLU																**.63**	.47	.56	.58	.40
E. NDW																	.31	**.75**	.41	.38
E. WPM																		.45	**.75**	**.73**
E. NSS																			.44	**.61**
E. Word Reading																				**.66**
E.R. Comprehension																				

Note. Significant correlations above 0.59 (in bold).
Bilinguals above the diagonal, Monolinguals below.
G = Greek (L2); E = English (L1).

Whole-word measures

There was a strong, consistent and statistically significant correlation in the two groups of children between PCC and PWP ($r_{bilinguals} = 0.96$, $p \leq 0.001$; $r_{monolinguals} = 0.70$, $p \leq 0.05$), since both measures show how well the child's production approximates a target, with PCC focusing on consonant accuracy, and proximity on segmental structure as well as accuracy. Two moderate correlations between pMLU and PWP emerged consistently in the two groups ($r_{bilinguals} = 0.52$, $r_{monolinguals} = 0.49$) but did not reach significance due to the small sample size. Similarly, the three moderate correlations of the bilinguals between PCC and pMLU ($r = 0.38$), PCC and PWV ($r = 0.46$), PWV and PWP ($r = 0.34$) did not reach the 0.05 significance level but they, still, are indicators of the validity of the measures. Furthermore, the correlation between word pMLU and child pMLU is strong ($r = 0.84$, $p \leq 0.001$) among the bilinguals, whereas it reaches the value of 1.00, $p \leq 0.001$ among the monolinguals (word pMLU results are not presented in Table 6.2).

There are a couple of more significant results to be noted. First, the negative correlations between PWV, phonological awareness ($r = -0.74$, $p \leq 0.01$) and reading comprehension ($r = -0.63$, $p \leq 0.05$) in the monolinguals. The lower the variability score, meaning greater consistency of production, the higher the phonological awareness and reading comprehension score respectively in the native Greek-speaking children. Moreover, the negative correlation between PWV and English NDW ($r = -0.61$, $p \leq 0.05$) in the bilingual group indicates the level of proficiency in the two languages, i.e. low variability of Greek word productions and advanced English vocabulary imply good linguistic abilities in both languages. Several moderate inter-correlations portray the relationship between the whole-word measures and overall language proficiency, as well as their relation to reading, particularly in the bilingual group. The small sample size, however, does not allow the significance level to be reached.

Linguistic, metalinguistic and reading abilities

The relationship between phonological awareness and vocabulary, and that of both with reading is evident in the two groups. There are significant correlations between phonological awareness and vocabulary ($r = 0.69$, $p \leq 0.05$), word reading ($r = 0.60$, $p \leq 0.05$) and reading comprehension ($r = 0.81$, $p \leq 0.01$) among the monolinguals. A greater number of sizable correlations is found in the bilingual group. Phonological awareness relates to the expressive vocabulary used in narrating a story (NDW) ($r = 0.60$, $p \leq 0.05$), marginally to narrative structure (NSS) ($r = 0.59$, $p = 0.052$) and word reading ($r = 0.66, p \leq 0.05$). Vocabulary knowledge highly correlates with other oral language measures, i.e. NDW ($r = 0.87, p \leq 0.001$), WPM ($r = 0.89, p \leq 0.001$), NSS ($r = 0.77, p \leq 0.01$) and both reading measures ($r = 0.80, p \leq 0.01$, respectively).

Three significant correlations in each group interrelate the language measures. In the monolingual sample, MLU significantly relates to NDW ($r = 0.84, p \leq 0.001$), WPM ($r = 0.67, p \leq 0.05$) and WPM to NDW ($r = 0.70, p \leq 0.05$). In the bilingual sample, the three significant correlations that emerged are between NSS and MLU ($r = 0.61, p \leq 0.05$), NDW with WPM ($r = 0.80, p \leq 0.01$) and NDW with NSS ($r = 0.70, p \leq 0.05$). Apart from the relationships contributing to the construct validity of the measures, the oral language measures, NDW, WPM and NSS, exhibit strong correlations with both reading measures. The significant correlations ranged from 0.60 to 0.84, whereas the two reading measures were highly interrelated ($r = 0.84, p \leq 0.001$).

Transfer

Three moderate and five strong correlations was the account of relationships of L2 phonological awareness with L1 phonological awareness ($r = 0.81, p \leq 0.01$), vocabulary ($r = 0.86, p \leq 0.001$), MLU ($r = 0.51$), NDW ($r = 0.42$), WPM ($r = 0.61, p \leq 0.05$), NSS ($r = 0.50$), word reading ($r = 0.84, p \leq 0.001$) and reading comprehension ($r = 0.73, p \leq 0.05$). L2 vocabulary showed a significant correlation with L1 word reading ($r = 0.76, p \leq 0.01$) and a marginally significant correlation with reading comprehension ($r = 0.59, p = 0.052$).

The four Greek oral language measures, MLU, NDW, WPM, NSS, exhibit four moderate significant correlations with the English equivalents ranging from 0.61 to 0.64, and five with English reading ranging from $r = 0.61, p \leq 0.05$ (L1 word reading and L2 WPM) to $r = 0.84, p \leq 0.001$ (L1 reading comprehension and L2 WPM), and a moderate one of L2 NDW with L1 phonological awareness ($r = 0.64, p \leq 0.05$).

The English oral language measures yielded three significant correlations with the Greek reading measures ranging from $r = 0.63, p \leq 0.05$ (L1 vocabulary and L2 reading comprehension) to $r = 0.75, p \leq 0.01$ (L1 WPM and L2 word reading), whereas there was a marginally significant correlation between L1 vocabulary and L2 word reading ($r = 0.59, p = 0.052$). Four more significant ones were found among the reading measures ranging from $r = 0.67, p \leq 0.05$ (L1 reading comprehension and L2 word reading) to $r = 0.88, p \leq 0.001$ (L1 and L2 word reading).

L1 Relationships

Eleven significant correlations were found between the English language and literacy measures, ranging from $r = 0.60$, $p \leq 0.05$ (L1 vocabulary and NSS) to $r = 0.83$, $p \leq 0.01$ (L1 vocabulary and reading comprehension).

Discussion

The present study compares monolingual and bilingual Greek-speaking children on whole-word measures that assess phonological production in order to examine phonological skills among 10-year-olds. It was evident that the bilinguals are doing relatively well in keeping their productions close to the targets, as indicated by the high levels of PCC accuracy, predictable pMLU, proximity above 0.50 and low variability scores. Furthermore, the two groups did not differ in word pMLU or the number of monosyllabic, bisyllabic, trisyllabic and multisyllabic words they use. Thus, the evidence in our study validates the fact that speech production is affected by word complexity and the ongoing relationship between what is targeted and what is produced. The observed differences between the two groups, however, also indicate that the language of the bilingual speaker may never be identical to that of the monolingual speaker (Grosjean 1989, 2013). Although the two groups were not selected to be matched on word pMLU, it turned out to be so. This provides a greater degree of certainty that the results between monolinguals and bilinguals reflect true differences and provide an accurate description of their phonological skill, uninfluenced by methodological discrepancies.

Two findings are worth special attention. Firstly, the strong, consistent correlation between PCC and PWP in the two groups is in line with results in Bunta et al. (2009). The proximity score is influenced by the complexity of words and, since longer words involve more consonants, consonant segmental accuracy may influence and get influenced by the level of target approximations in a communicative context and form the respective PWP values. We can assume that the level of accuracy regardless of linguistic group determines the level of intelligibility, and vice versa. If there is a threshold of phonological acquisition that is needed in order to maintain a level of accuracy and intelligibility even in complex words, it is evident that the children in the current study have accomplished that level. To add to that, correlations of the monolingual children (not presented in the Results section) between word/child pMLU and multisyllabic words ($r = 0.65$,

$p = 0.05$), as well as the strong correlation between whole-word proximity (PWP) with the number of multisyllabic words used ($r = 0.82$, $p = 0.01$) indicates the greater skill of monolinguals in longer words and it is, in fact, a pattern found in typical phonological development (Ingram 2015).

Secondly, a negligible relationship between variability (PWV) and complexity (pMLU) was evident in both groups that may take different interpretations. Regarding the monolinguals, it ought to be noted that scores were almost uniformly at zero, because these typically developing monolingual children do not diverge from the targets. Therefore, the value of the correlation represents more of a statistical artifact than a true relationship. Regarding the bilinguals, it seems that variability is not related to complexity. In order to explain this, we need to look into the kind of words they used. The percentage of monosyllabic words used ranged from 35 to 48%, whereas the percentages of bisyllabic and trisyllabic words were 28 to 37% and 15 to 16% respectively. Therefore, it is more likely that their faulty attempts occurred while producing mostly low complexity words. In Greek, a trisyllabic word may contain just five phonemes provided that it contains three vowels. This finding should not therefore be considered as an indication of underdeveloped phonologies, but rather of inaccuracies, perhaps a result of restricted speed due to the lack of fluency.

Theory determining acquisition of phonological characteristics referred to as the 'constraint-driven model' which posits that phonological development follows universal constraints (e.g. simple sounds are acquired early, while complex sounds are acquired later) and the 'target-driven model' which proposes that the complexity of the target language is important because children attempt to approximate the targets (Bunta, Davidovich and Ingram 2006), is relevant to the findings. In the current study, significant differences across the whole-word measures were found. It points to the differentiation between bilingual and monolingual speech production, and implies that there are still constraints in the bilinguals' phonological skills, suggesting that they are still in development. However, the non-significant differences in the percentage of mono-, bi-, tri- and multisyllabic words they use denotes that the bilinguals have acquired structures of varying complexity. Relating this to the pattern of inter-correlations, it is suggested that there are really two characteristics in their productions, namely to stabilize a good level of complexity and to maintain a constant relationship with their targets.

Linguistic complexity, i.e. larger mean length of utterances (MLUs), may impose fluency restrictions to bilingual learners. The negative moderate correlation of PWV indicator of consistent/inconsistent and fluent/disfluent production with MLU (−0.47, not statistically significant though) indicates a high level of variability and low MLU values, and vice versa. The constraint-driven hypothesis is relevant and must be considered in order to improve understanding on universal patterns across aspects of phonological development. Moreover, the negative correlations of PWV with phonological awareness, reading comprehension and number of different words used to narrate a story in English, highlight the relationship between the quality of phonological representations and lexical development. This issue is further discussed below.

With regard to the utility of the measures, it is confirmed that pMLU in conjunction with PCC can be used for assigning children in specific stages along the path of acquiring phonology. PWP scores confirmed selection procedures for both groups, i.e. scores above 0.50 indicating typically developing children. PWV showed sizable relations with external criteria (e.g. phonological awareness, reading, expressive vocabulary) and could be used as a proxy measure for assessing phonological skill in children of this age. Further research should implement the PWV measure in different research contexts in order to obtain more information on its efficacy.

Turning to phonological awareness, language proficiency and reading measures, it is notable that these attributes influence and get influenced by reading, and transfer across languages (Melby-Lervag and Lervag 2011; Miller et al. 2006; Heilmann, Rojas, Iglesias and Miller 2016). Phonological awareness and reading involve highly transferable skills, also evident in the present study in the relationships they form with each other and other linguistic measures across languages.

More specifically, the children in the present sample have well-developed phonological skills, with the actual phonological features and syllabic segments of the two languages built on the same underlying construct, and language-specific phonotactic differences. Phonological, semantic and orthographic aspects of language develop both within and between languages influencing and facilitating each other. Such a pattern of associations was consistently found between phonological awareness, vocabulary (in the form of lexical diversity or word specific knowledge) and reading within the two groups, as well as across the two languages of the bilinguals. Exposure to reading carries significant gains for L2 learners since orthography can assist in clarifying L2 phonological distinctions. Orthographic information can instal knowledge of subtle word distinctions in lexical representations which can be particularly useful when complex words with difficult phonemes are to be learnt. Both phonological and semantic representations can more easily be mapped into the lexicon. The written forms of words may influence both linguistic and metalinguistic processing. Though it is less likely that orthography influences speech production, it is more likely that it influences phonological representations at a metalinguistic level (Saletta, Goffman and Brentari 2016). The very strong association between L1 and L2 word reading (0.88) suggests that children in the present sample have reached a good level in decoding ability and are able to process both small and large units of words in order to achieve their goals. The strong link with reading comprehension suggests that they have acquired both accuracy and speed, which allows them to comprehend.

Phonological and semantic information are essential components in the acquisition of language. In her review, Stoel-Gammon (2011) discussed the significance of interaction between phonological and lexical development. It has been shown that phonological ability has been influencing lexical acquisition and, in turn, the nature and structure of the lexicon has been influencing phonological knowledge. The evidence she is reviewing involves early language acquisition. At a pre-reading stage of development, phonological development determined by accuracy of production and error patterns coincide with the children's lexical development in the formation of underlying representations of words. During early and middle childhood the increase in vocabulary size results in fine-grained underlying representations and affects expressive phonology. As children learn new words, they get more sensitive to phonological forms and add sub-lexical information. Thus, vocabulary growth leads to changes in the phonological structure of the underlying representations (see Lexical Restructuring hypothesis; Metsala and Walley 1998).

Nevertheless, fluency is also crucial when the end state in the acquisition of speech is considered. The present study relates L2 verbal fluency (WPM), L2 word reading and reading comprehension, and L2 vocabulary (both in the form of lexical diversity and word-specific knowledge) to L1. These relationships reveal the interactions of a developing mechanism establishing connections between oral language proficiency and reading. The children's semantic knowledge has reached a threshold that permits their understanding and producing language. Also, the WPM measure in conjunction with the growth of the narrative schema, indicate oral language proficiency. The children's ability to narrate a story in an organized structure along with their overall sufficient linguistic and reading skills (see correlations with both lexical diversity and word-specific knowledge, word reading and reading comprehension) clearly depict their advancing oral language and literacy skills.

Based on the findings of previous research that examines the growth of macrostructure skills in minority language individuals (Gamez, Lesaux and Rizzo 2016), the relatively small mean difference found here between the two groups on the NSS measure is expected to be eventually eradicated, and it is thus evidence of learning in process. However, it is not only the interactions with regard to lexical diversity (NDW), verbal fluency (WPM) and narrative structure (NSS) in Greek alone that formulate a resourceful relationship with reading; there is also a similar pattern in reading in English – a pattern that links the two languages of the bilinguals in this study on the level of literacy, as well. Such transferability across language and literacy is well documented in the literature (e.g. Castro, Paez, Dickinson and Frede 2011; Miller et al. 2006).

Overall, the findings in this study can be interpreted within the connectionist framework of learning to read (Seidenberg and McClelland 1989) which predicts that word recognition processes are influenced by connections between the phonological, orthographic and semantic information of words. This is important because it suggests that the literacy skills of the bilinguals in the present sample are still developing and provides an insight into the developmental models of reading. Typical developmental models focus primarily on the importance of phonological skills and tend to overlook the role of semantic processing (see for example Frith 1985).

Conclusion

The present study contributes to the literature on whole-word measures as potential measures indicating the nature of phonological skill in the context of bilingual L2 Greek. Furthermore, regarding the education of children learning Greek as a second language, we highlight priority areas on which instruction should focus and where parental involvement should be directed. Furthermore, future research should look more closely into children's productions in order to examine whether phenomena reported in young bilinguals at the early stages of phonological acquisition (e.g. Babatsouli 2016) are still part of a varying repertoire at a late stage, when Greek is acquired in bilingualism as the second language.

Appendix I: Greek Phonological Awareness Test

1. Elision

Practice Items: *προχθές* – προ = χθες, *παλιόδρομος* – *δρόμος* = παλιό, κατάσταση – κατα = στάση

Test Items: 1. *καλότυχη* – τύχη = καλό, 2. *μεταφέρω* – φέρω = μετά, 3. *αποστολή* – στολή = από

Practice Items: *σαν* – σ = αν, *λαγός* – γ = λαός, *πόλη* – π = όλη

Test Items: 4. *δώρα* – δ = ώρα, 5. *πόσο* – π = όσο, 6. *φως* – φ = ως, 7. *θέμα* – μ = θέα, 8. *μήνα* – ν = μία, 9. *λέξη* – ξ = λέει, 10. *Κύπρος* – ρ = κήπος, 11. *λίμνη* – μ = λύνει, 12. *κλίμα* – λ = κύμα, 13. *πίκρα* – κ = πήρα, 14. *φρύδι* – ρ = φίδι, 15. *κλέβω* – β = κλαίω, 16. *όπλο* – π = όλο, 17. *στροφή* – σ = τροφή, 18. *στρώμα* – ρ = στόμα, 19. *πάλι* – λ = πάει, 20. *τάξη* – κ = τάση

2. Word Blending

Practice Items: /φί/ /λος/ – φίλος, /κρέ/ /ας/ – κρέας, /ό/ /λα/ – όλα, /ε/ /σύ/ – εσύ, /θ/ /α/ – θα, /μ/ /α/ /ς/ – μας

Test Items: 1. /γρα/ /μμή/ γραμμή, 2. /σπί/ /τι/ σπίτι, 3. /κύ//κλος/ κύκλος, 4. /α/ /ν/ αν, 5. /τ/ /ου/ του, 6. /ν/ /αι/ ναι, 7. /εί/ /μαι/ είμαι, 8. /ζ/ /ω/ ζω, 9. /έ/ /ξ/ /ω/ έξω, 10. /θ/ /ε/ /ό/ /ς/ θεός, 11. /υ/ /γ/ /εί/ /α/ υγεία, 12. /γ/ /λ/ /ώ/ /σσ/ /α/ γλώσσα, 13. /τ/ /ά/ /ξ/ /η/ τάξη, 14. /β/ /ι/ /β/ /λ/ /ί/ /ο/ βιβλίο, 15. /π/ /αι/ /δ/ /ι/ /ά/ παιδιά, 16. /β/ /ο/ /ή/ /θ/ /ει/ /α/ βοήθεια, 17. /π/ /ρ/ /ο/ /σ/ /π/ /α/ /θ/ /ώ/ προσπαθώ, 18. /ε/ /ρ/ /γ/ /α/ /σ/ /ί/ /α/ εργασία, 19. /π/ /λ/ /υ/ /ν/ /τ/ /ή/ /ρ/ /ι/ /ο/ πλυντήριο, 20. /μ/ /ε/ /γ/ /α/ /λ/ /ύ/ /τ/ /ε/ /ρ/ /ο/ μεγαλύτερο

3. Word Segmentation

Practice Items: δε /δ//ε/, το /τ//ο/, και /κ//ε/

Test Items: 1. να /ν//α/, 2. μη /μ//η/, 3. που /π//ου/, 4. σε /σ//ε/, 5. τι /τ//ι/

Practice Items: την /τ//η//ν/, ένα /έ//ν//α/

Test Items: 6. για /γ/ /ι/ /α/, 7. ζώα /ζ/ ώ/ /α/, 8. έξι /έ/ /ξ/ /ι/, 9. αίμα /αί/ /μ/ /α/, 10. πλοίο /π/ /λ/ /οί/ /ο/, 11. χθες /χ/ /θ/ /ε/ /ς/, 12. ακούω /α/ /κ/ /ού/ /ω/, 13. βαθμός /β/ /α/ /θ/ /μ/ /ό/ /ς/, 14. Πάσχα /Π/ /ά/ /σ/ /χ/ /α/, 15. άσπρος /ά/ /σ/ /π/ /ρ/ /ο/ /ς/, 16. δασκάλα /δ//α//σ//κ//ά//λ//α/, 17. φουστάνι /φ/ /ου/ /σ/ /τ/ /ά/ /ν/ /ι/, 18. κάπνισμα /κ/ /ά/ /π/ /ν/ /ι/ /σ/ /μ/ /α/, 19. πορτοκάλι /π/ /ο/ /ρ/ /τ/ /ο/ /κ/ /ά/ /λ/ /ι/, 20. τραγούδι /τ/ /ρ/ /α/ /γ/ /ού/ /δ/ /ι/

4. Non-Word Blending

Practice Items: /ρέ/ /γγι/ ρέγγι, /ξό/ /μπα/ ξόμπα, /ό/ /πι/ όπι, /έ/ /μω/ έμω, /ρ/ /υ/ ρυ, /ά/ /τ/ /ο/ άτο

Test Items: 1. /νί/ /ζα/ νίζα, 2. /μί/ /βη/ μίβη, 3. /ή/ /θω/ ήθω, 4. /ι/ /γγε/ ιγγε, 5. /έ/ /βου/ έβου, 6. /β/ /ί/ /ψ/ /ο/ βίψο, 7. /χ/ /ο/ /ε/ χόε, 8. /τ/ /ρ/ /ο/ /ν/ τρον, 9. /θ/ /ή/ /ρ/ /ου/ θήρου, 10. /ξ/ /ό/ /ζ/ /η/ ξόζη, 11. /φ/ /έ/ /ξ/ /ου/ /ς/ φέξους, 12. /έ/ /φ/ /ρ/ /ο/ /ν/ έφρον, 13. /κ/ /ί/ /φ/ /ο/ /μ/ /αι/ κίφομαι, 14. /ρ/ /ί/ /δ/ /α/ /ς/ ρίδας, 15. /α/ /σ/ /ά/ /ρ/ /ει/ ασάρει, 16. /σ/ /ο/ /λ/ /ι/ /ζ/ /ύ/ /φ/ /ει/ σολιζύφει, 17. /π/ /ρ/ /ό/ /σ/ /α/ /θ/ /η/ /ς/ πρόσαθης, 18. /λ/ /ου/ /κ/ /ρ/ /ά/ /μ/ /ι/ λουκράμι

5. Non-Word Segmentation

Practice Items: λα /λ/ /α/, ακ /α/ /κ/, οτ /ο/ /τ/

Test Items: 1. ρι /ρ/ /ι/, 2. μο /μ/ /ο/, 3. ιβ /ι/ /β/, 4. αφ /α/ /φ/, 5. εμ /ε/ /μ/

Practice Items: βες /β/ /ε/ /ς/, τίπι /τ/ /ί/ /π/ /ι/

Test Items: 6. φεν /φ/ /ε/ /ν/, 7. ρέμι /ρ/ /έ/ /μ/ /ι/, 8. ξόνε /ξ/ /ό/ /ν/ /ε/, 9. γδο /γ/ /δ/ /ο/, 10. θράπι /θ/ /ρ/ /ά/ /π/ /ι/, 11. φλην /φ/ /λ/ /η/ /ν/, 12. δρος /δ/ /ρ/ /ο/ /ς/, 13. βότην /β/ /ό/ /τ/ /η/ /ν/, 14. σούκρες /σ/ /ού/ /κ/ /ρ/ /ε/ /ς/, 15. λάζων /λ/ /ά/ /ζ/ /ω/ /ν/, 16. κέδης /κ/ /έ/ /δ/ /η/ /ς/, 17. πόβραμι /π/ /ό/ /β/ /ρ/ /α/ /μ/ /ι/, 18. τασέλου /τ/ /α/ /σ/ /έ/ /λ/ /ου/, 19. στομνάς /σ/ /τ/ /ο/ /μ/ /ν/ /ά/ /ς/, 20. δώχραμης /δ/ /ώ/ /χ/ /ρ/ /α/ /μ/ /η/ /ς/

Appendix II: Greek Narrative Script

Examiner: *Here is a book. I am going to tell you this story in Greek while we are looking at the book together. When we finish, I want you to tell the story back to me in Greek. Okay? The book tells a story about a boy [point to picture on the cover], dog [point] and a frog [point].*

'Μια φορά ήταν ένα αγόρι που είχε ένα σκύλο και ένα βάτραχο. Ο βάτραχος ήταν σ' ένα βάζο στο δωμάτιό του. Μια νύχτα, ενώ το αγόρι και ο σκύλος κοιμόνταν, ο βάτραχος βγήκε από το βάζο και έφυγε από το ανοιχτό παράθυρο. Όταν το αγόρι και ο σκύλος ξύπνησαν το πρωί, βρήκαν το βάζο άδειο. Που ήταν ο βάτραχος; Το αγόρι έψαξε παντού ακόμα και μέσα στις μπότες του. Και ο σκύλος έψαξε για τον βάτραχο. Όταν κοίταξε μέσα στο βάζο, το κεφάλι του κόλλησε μέσα! Το αγόρι φώναξε από το ανοιχτό παράθυρο: 'Που είσαι βάτραχε'; Ο σκύλος έσκυψε από το παράθυρο αλλά το βάζο ήταν βαρύ κι έπεσε με το κεφάλι έξω από το παράθυρο. Το αγόρι πήρε το σκύλο στην αγκαλιά του για να σιγουρευτεί ότι ήταν καλά. Ο σκύλος ήταν εντάξει αλλά το βάζο είχε σπάσει. Ο σκύλος έγλειψε το αγόρι για να ζητήσει συγνώμη που έσπασε το βάζο. Το αγόρι και ο σκύλος έψαξαν έξω για το βάτραχο. Το αγόρι τον φώναζε. Τον φώναζε σε μια τρύπα στο έδαφος ενώ ο σκύλος γάβγιζε σε κάτι μέλισσες μέσα σε μια κυψέλη. Ένας τυφλοπόντικας πετάχτηκε έξω από την τρύπα και δάγκωσε το αγόρι στη μύτη γιατί τον ενόχλησε. 'Άουτς, αυτό πόνεσε' φώναξε το αγόρι. Στο μεταξύ, ο σκύλος συνέχισε να ενοχλεί τις μέλισσες πηδώντας πάνω στο δέντρο και γαβγίζοντάς τους. Η κυψέλη έπεσε και οι μέλισσες θύμωσαν γιατί ο σκύλος κατέστρεψε το σπίτι τους. Το αγόρι δεν πρόσεχε τι έκανε ο σκύλος. Είχε βρει μια μεγάλη τρύπα σ' ένα δέντρο και ήθελε να δει αν ο βάτραχος κρυβόταν εκεί. Ανέβηκε στο δέντρο και φώναξε: 'Βάτραχε είσαι μέσα;' Ξαφνικά μια κουκουβάγια του επιτέθηκε από την τρύπα και τον έριξε στο έδαφος. Η κουκουβάγια ήταν θυμωμένη. Τον μάλωσε και τον έδιωξε. Ο σκύλος πέρασε τρέχοντας γρήγορα γιατί τον κυνηγούσαν οι μέλισσες. Φοβόταν ότι οι μέλισσες θα τον τσιμπούσαν. Η κουκουβάγια κυνήγησε το αγόρι μέχρι ένα μεγάλο βράχο. Το αγόρι σκαρφάλωσε στο βράχο και φώναζε το βάτραχο. Κρατήθηκε από κάτι κλαδιά για να μην πέσει. Αλλά τα κλαδιά δεν ήταν κλαδιά. Ήταν κέρατα ελαφιού! Το ελάφι τον σήκωσε κι άρχισε να τρέχει με το αγόρι πάνω στο κεφάλι του. Ο σκύλος έτρεχε μαζί του, γαβγίζοντας στο ελάφι να αφήσει κάτω το αγόρι. Πλησίαζαν στο γκρεμό. Το ελάφι σταμάτησε ξαφνικά και το αγόρι και ο σκύλος έπεσαν από την άκρη του γκρεμού. Προσγειώθηκαν σε μια λιμνούλα, ο ένας πάνω στον άλλο. Άκουσαν το γνωστό ήχο: 'Κουάξ, κουάξ'. Το αγόρι είπε στο σκύλο να σωπάσει. Αυτοί σύρθηκαν και κοίταξαν πίσω από ένα μεγάλο κούτσουρο. Εκεί βρήκαν τον αγαπημένο βάτραχο του αγοριού. Είχε και μια βατραχίνα κοντά του. Είχαν και μερικά μικρά βατραχάκια και ένα από αυτά πήδηξε προς το αγόρι. Του άρεσε το αγόρι και ήθελε να πάει μαζί του. Το αγόρι και ο σκύλος ήταν χαρούμενοι για το νέο αγαπημένο βατραχάκι τους. Φεύγοντας το αγόρι αποχαιρέτησε τον παλιό του βάτραχο και την οικογένειά του.'

Examiner's cue for the child to retell: *'Okay, now I would like you to tell me the story in Greek.'*

Appendix III: Greek Word Reading Test

ας	καλά	σχέση	δεύτερη
νέο	μένω	άλλοι	μπροστά
όσα	ποτέ	κέντρο	περιοχή
εγώ	νίκη	ανάγκη	γεγονός
όλη	αρχή	παιδιά	ανάμεσα
πως	ξέρω	σχεδόν	πρόταση
δε	πόλη	παλιός	ποσοστό
ώρα	χέρι	ύστερα	φαίνεται
ζω	γύρω	κανείς	συνέχεια
δύο	είμαι	βιβλίο	παιχνίδι
έξω	μόλις	γίνεται	εταιρεία
πια	αγορά	εκείνη	προσφέρω
σου	πλέον	ταινία	εβδομάδα
εάν	σπίτι	κύριος	διάρκεια
έχω	είδος	πράγμα	εφημερίδα
λέει	τρεις	αμέσως	πρόγραμμα
μαζί	βάρος	μεγάλο	ιδιαίτερα
πίσω	μήνες	πλευρά	συμμετοχή
έργα	αυτόν	καιρός	τελευταία
λύση	εμείς	βέβαια	ενδιαφέρον
ίσως	αφήνω	δρόμος	περισσότερο
πήρε	πολλά	εικόνα	παράδειγμα
κάτω	βράδυ	μπαίνω	ανακοινώνω
εκεί	ίδιος	γυναίκα	κοινωνικός
πάλι	ξένος	τράπεζα	λειτουργία
λίγο	κοντά	πρόσωπο	χρησιμοποιώ

References

Arvaniti, A., 1999, 'Standard Modern Greek', *Journal of the International Phonetic Association* 29(2), 167–72. https://doi.org/10.1017/S0025100300006538

Babatsouli, E., 2016, 'Added syllable complexity in a child's developmental speech and clinical implications', *Clinical Linguistics and Phonetics* 1464–5076. https://doi.org/f10.3109/02699206.2016.1162200

Babatsouli, E. (to appear). 'Bilingual development of theta in a child', *Poznan Studies in Contemporary Linguistics*.

Babatsouli, E. and Ingram, D., 2015, 'What bilingualism tells us about phonological acquisition', in R.H. Bahr and E.R. Silliman (eds.), *Routledge handbook of communication disorders*, pp. 173–82, Oxford, UK: Taylor & Francis.

Beckman, M., Munson, B. and Edwards, J., 2007, 'Vocabulary growth and the developmental expansion of types of phonological knowledge', in J. Cole and J. Hualde (eds.), *Laboratory phonology*, pp. 241–64, New York, NY: Mouton de Gruyter.

Bialystock, E., Luk, G., Peets, K. and Yang, S., 2010, 'Receptive vocabulary differences in monolingual and bilingual children', *Bilingualism: Language and Cognition* 13(4), 525–31. https://doi.org/10.1017/S1366728909990423

Borsch, L. and Ramon-Casas, M., 2011, 'Variability in vowel production by bilingual speakers: Can input properties hinder the early stabilization of contrastive categories?', *Journal of Phonetics* 39(4), 514–26. https://doi.org/10.1016/j.wocn.2011.02.001

Bunta, F., Davidovich, I. and Ingram, D., 2006, 'The relationship between phonological complexity of a bilingual child's words and those of the target languages', *International Journal of Bilingualism* 10(1), 71–88. https://doi.org/10.1177/13670069060100010401

Bunta, F., Fabiano-Smith, L., Goldstein, B. and Ingram, D., 2009, 'Phonological whole-word measures in 3-year old children and their age-matched monolingual peers', *Clinical Linguistics and Phonetics* 23(2), 156–75. https://doi.org/10.1080/02699200802603058

Castro, D., Paez, M., Dickinson, D. and Frede, E., 2011, 'Promoting language and literacy in young dual language learners: Research, practice and policy', *Child Development Perspectives* 5(1), 15–21. https://doi.org/10.1111/j.1750-8606.2010.00142.x

Chionidou, A. and Nicolaidis, K., 2015, 'Voice onset time in bilingual Greek-German children', *Proceedings of the 18th International Congress of Phonetic Sciences*, Glasgow.

Cremer, M. and Schoonen, R., 2013, 'The role of accessibility of semantic word knowledge in monolingual and bilingual fifth-grade reading', *Applied Psycholinguistics* 34, 1195–217. https://doi.org/10.1017/S0142716412000203

Diaz, B., Mitterer, H., Boersma, M., Escera, C. and Sebastian-Galles, N., 2016, 'Variability in L2 phonemic learning originates from speech-specific capabilities',

Bilingualism: Language and Cognition 19(5), 955–70. https://doi.org/10.1017/S1366728915000450

Fabiano-Smith, L. and Barlow, J., 2010, 'Interaction in bilingual phonological acquisition: Evidence from phonetic inventories', *International Journal of Bilingual Education and Bilingualism* 13(1), 81–97. https://doi.org/10.1080/13670050902783528

Friesen, D., Luo, L., Luk, G. and Bialystok, E., 2015, 'Proficiency and control in verbal fluency performance across the lifespan for monolinguals and bilinguals', *Language, Cognition and Neuroscience* 30(3), 238–50. https://doi.org/10.1080/23273798.2014.918630

Frith, U., 1985, 'Beneath the surface of developmental dyslexia', in K.E. Patterson, J.C. Marshall and M. Coltheart (eds.), *Surface dyslexia*, pp. 301–30, London, UK: Routledge & Kegan Paul.

Gamez, P., Lesaux, N. and Rizzo, A., 2016, 'Narrative production skills of language minority learners and their English-only classmates in early adolescence', *Applied Psycholinguistics* 37, 933–61. https://doi.org/10.1017/S0142716415000314

Genesee, F., Paradis, J. and Crago, M.B., 2004, *Dual language development and disorders: A handbook on bilingualism and second language learning*. Baltimore, MD: Paul H. Brookes Publishing Company.

Gildersleeve-Neumann, C., Kester, E., Davis, B. and Peña, E., 2008, 'English speech sound development in preschool-aged children from bilingual English-Spanish backgrounds', *Language, Speech and Hearing Services in Schools* 39, 314–28. https://doi.org/10.1044/0161-1461(2008/030)

Goodrich, J.M. and Lonigan, C.J., 2015, 'Lexical characteristics of words and phonological awareness skills of preschool children, *Applied Psycholinguistics* 36, 1509–31. https://doi.org/10.1017/S0142716414000526

Grosjean, F., 1989, 'Neurolinguists, beware! The bilingual is not two monolinguals in one person', *Brain and Language* 36, 3–15. https://doi.org/10.1016/0093-934X(89)90048-5

Grosjean, F., 2013, 'Bilingual and monolingual language modes', in C. Chapelle (ed.), *The encyclopedia of applied linguistics*, Hoboken, NJ: Blackwell Publishing.

Haritos, C. and Nelson, K., 2001, 'Bilingual memory: The interaction of language and thought', *Bilingual Research Journal* 25(4), 605–26. https://doi.org/10.1080/15235882.2001.11074469

Hatzigeorgiu, N., Gavrilidou, M., Piperidis, S., Carayanis, G., Papakostopoulou, A., Spiliotopoulou, A., Vacalopoulou, A., Labropoulou P., Mantzari, E., Papageorgiou, H. and Demiros, I., 2000, 'Design and implementation of the online ILSP Greek corpus', in M. Gavrilidou et al. (eds.), *Proceedings of the LREC 2000 Conference*, pp. 1737–42, Athens.

Heilmann, J., Rojas, R., Iglesias, A. and Miller, J., 2016, 'Clinical impact of wordless picture storybooks on bilingual narrative language production: A comparison of the "Frog" stories', *International Journal of Language and Communication Disorders* 51, 339–45. https://doi.org/10.1111/1460-6984.12201

Hoff, E. and Parra, M., 2011, 'Mechanisms linking phonological development to lexical development – A commentary on Stoel-Gammon's "Relationships between lexical and phonological development in young children"', *Journal of Child Language* 38, 46–50. https://doi.org/10.1017/S0305000910000462

Ingram, D., 2002, 'The measurement of whole-word productions', *Journal of Child Language* 29, 713–33. https://doi.org/10.1017/S0305000902005275

Ingram, D., 2015, 'Whole-word measures: Using the pCC-PWP intersect to distinguish speech delay from speech disorder', in C. Bowen (ed.), *Children's speech sound disorders* (2nd edn.), pp. 100–04, Oxford, UK: Wiley-Blackwell.

Ingram, D. and Dubasic, V., 2011, 'Multidimensional assessment of phonological similarity within and between children', *Clinical Linguistics and Phonetics* 25(11–12), 962–67. https://doi.org/10.3109/02699206.2011.617855

Ingram, D. and Ingram K., 2001, 'A whole-word approach to phonological analysis and intervention', *Language Speech and Hearing Services in Schools* 32, 271–83. https://doi.org/10.1044/0161-1461(2001/024)

Kappa, I., 2002, 'On the acquisition of syllabic structure in Greek', *Journal of Greek Linguistics* 3, 1–52. https://doi.org/10.1075/jgl.3.03kap

Kehoe, M., 2015, 'Cross-linguistic interaction: A retrospective and prospective view', in E. Babatsouli and D. Ingram (eds.), *Proceedings of the International Symposium on Monolingual and Bilingual Speech 2015*, pp. 141–67, ISBN: 978-618-82351-0-6, retrieved from http://ismbs.eu/publications.

Licandro, U., 2016, *Narrative skills of dual language learners*. Wiesbaden: Springer. https://doi.org/10.1007/978-3-658-14673-3

Loizou, M. and Stuart, M., 2003, 'Phonological awareness in monolingual and bilingual English and Greek five-year-olds', *Journal of Research in Reading* 26(1), 3–18. https://doi.org/10.1111/1467-9817.261002

Mayer, M., 1969, *Frog, where are you*? New York: Puffin Books.

Melby-Lervag, M. and Lervag, A., 2011, 'Cross-linguistic transfer of oral language, decoding, phonological awareness and reading comprehension: A meta-analysis of the correlational evidence', *Journal of Research in Reading* 34(1), 114–35. https://doi.org/10.1111/j.1467-9817.2010.01477.x

Mennen, I. and Okalidou, A., 2007, 'Acquisition of Greek phonology: An overview;, in S. McLeod (ed.), *The international guide to speech acquisition*, pp. 398–407, Clifton Park, NY: Thomson Delmar Learning.

Metsala, J.L. and Walley, A.C., 1998, 'Spoken vocabulary growth and the segmental restructuring of lexical representations: Precursors to phonemic awareness and early reading ability', in J.L. Metsala and L.C. Ehri (eds.), *Word recognition in beginning literacy*, pp. 89–120, Mahwah, NJ: Erlbaum.

Miller, J., Heilmann, J., Nockerts, A., Iglesias A., Fabiano, L. and Francis, D., 2006, 'Oral language and reading in bilingual children', *Learning Disabilities Research and Practice* 27(1), 30–43.

Miller, J. and Iglesias, A., 2003–04, *Systematic analysis of English and Spanish language transcripts*. Language Analysis laboratory, Waisman Center, University of Wisconsin-Madison, Madison, WI. https://doi.org/10.1111/j.1540-5826.2006.00205.x

Morfidi, E. and Samsari, E., 2015, 'Bilingual language and speech patterns: Evidence from English (L1) and Greek (L2)', in E. Babatsouli and D. Ingram (eds.),

Proceedings of the International Symposium on Monolingual and Bilingual Speech 2015, pp. 233–38, ISBN: 978-618-82351-0-6, retrieved from http://ismbs.eu/publications.

Papadopoulos, T., Kendeou, P. and Spanoudis, G., 2012, 'Investigating the factor structure and measurement invariance of phonological abilities in a sufficiently transparent language', *Journal of Educational Psychology* 104(2), 321–36. https://doi.org/10.1037/a0026446

Reese, E., Sparks, A. and Suggate, S., 2012, 'Assessing children's narratives', in E. Hoff (ed.), *Research methods in child language*, pp. 133–48, Oxford, UK: Blackwell Publishing. https://doi.org/10.1002/9781444344035.ch9

Reese, E., Suggate, S., Long, J. and Schaughency, E., 2010, 'Children's oral narrative and reading skills in the first 3 years of reading instruction', *Reading and Writing* 23, 627–44. https://doi.org/10.1007/s11145-009-9175-9

Roch, M., Florit, E. and Levorato, C., 2016, 'Narrative competence of Italian–English bilingual children between 5 and 7 years', *Applied Psycholinguistics* 37, 49–67. https://doi.org/10.1017/S0142716415000417

Saaristo-Helin, K., Savinainen-Makkonen, T. and Kunnari, S., 2006, 'The phonological mean length of utterance: Methodological challenges from a cross-linguistic perspective', *Journal of Child Language* 33, 179–90. https://doi.org/10.1017/S0305000905007294

Saletta, M., Goffman, L. and Brentari, D., 2016, 'Reading skill and exposure to orthography influence speech production', *Applied Psycholinguistics* 37, 411–34. https://doi.org/10.1017/S0142716415000053

Seidenberg, M.S. and McClelland, J.L., 1989, 'A distributed developmental model of word recognition and naming', *Psychological Review* 96, 523–68. https://doi.org/10.1037/0033-295X.96.4.523

Seymour, P., Aro, M. and Erskine, J., 2003, 'Foundation literacy acquisition in European orthographies', *British Journal of Psychology* 94, 143–74. https://doi.org/10.1348/000712603321661859

Simos, P., Sideridis, G., Mouzaki, A., Chatzidaki, A. and Tzevelekou, M., 2014, 'Vocabulary growth in second language among immigrant school-aged children in Greece', *Applied Psycholinguistics* 35, 621–47. https://doi.org/10.1017/S0142716412000525

Sosa, A. and Stoel-Gammon, C., 2012, 'Lexical and phonological effects in early word production', *Journal of Speech, Language, and Hearing Research* 55, 596–608. https://doi.org/10.1044/1092-4388(2011/10-0113)

Stoel-Gammon, C., 2011, 'Relationship between lexical and phonological development in young children', *Journal of Child Language* 38, 1–34. https://doi.org/10.1017/S0305000910000425

Suggate, E., Schaughency, E. and Reese, E., 2011, 'The contribution of age and reading instruction to oral narrative and pre-reading skills', *First language* 31(4), 379–403. https://doi.org/10.1177/0142723710395165

Torgesen, H.K., Wagner, R.K. and Rashotte, C.A., 1999, *Test of word reading efficiency*, Austin, TX: PRO-ED.

Tsimpli, I.M., Peristeri, E. and Andreou, M., 2016, 'Narrative production in monolingual and bilingual children with specific language impairment', *Applied Psycholinguistics* 37, 195–216. https://doi.org/10.1017/S0142716415000478

Ucceli, P. and Paez, M., 2007, 'Narrative and vocabulary development of bilingual children from kindergarten to first grade: Developmental changes and associations among English and Spanish skills', *Language, Speech and Hearing Services in Schools* 38, 225–36. https://doi.org/10.1044/0161-1461(2007/024)

Wagner, R., Torgesen, J., Laughon, P., Simmons, K. and Rashotte, C., 1993, 'The development of young readers' phonological processing abilities', *Journal of Educational Psychology* 85, 83–103. https://doi.org/10.1037/0022-0663.85.1.83

Wagner, R., Torgesen, J. and Rashotte, C., 1999, *Comprehensive test of phonological processing*, Austin, TX: PRO ED.

Walley, A.C., Metsala, J.L. and Garlock, V.M., 2003, 'Spoken vocabulary growth: Its role in the development of phoneme awareness and early reading ability', *Reading and Writing* 16, 5–20. https://doi.org/10.1023/A:1021789804977

Woodcock, R., 1991, *Woodcock language proficiency battery-revised*, Itasca. IL: Riverside Publishing Company.

Eleni Morfidi is an assistant professor at the University of Ioannina, Greece. She graduated from the University of Athens, Greece and followed postgraduate studies (MEd, MSc, PhD) at the University of Manchester, UK. Her work focused on literacy development, phonological abilities and related problems. She has been a researcher at the University of Leeds, UK, University of Amsterdam, The Netherlands and University of Houston, Texas, USA. She is currently working in the area of special education and language disorders at the Department of Primary Education, University of Ioannina, Greece. Her research interests include bilingual language and literacy development, phonological acquisition and development across languages.

Eleni Samsari holds a Master's Degree in Education (MEd) and she is a PhD student at the Department of Primary Education of the University of Patras in Greece. She has presented her work at several conferences on Educational Sciences worldwide. Her articles have been published in national and international refereed conference proceedings and journals. Her research interests include intercultural education, special education, inclusion, bilingualism and educational psychology.

Synopsis on Protolanguage

The Authors and Editors

This section presents a summary of each of the foregoing chapters on protolanguage, addressing how each has served the theme of the book; the section has been put together combining write-ups by the contributing authors and the editors of the volume. Six studies have appeared under the main section named *Protolanguage* (PL) in this book: one has addressed issues in atypical development, three have discussed issues in early bilingualism, and two have investigated near-end states in monolingual and bilingual PL. If we were to add two more example studies in the PL section that we feel would enhance its current scope, these would be representative of PL in sequential bilingualism and bi-dialectal phonology. The chapters on protolanguage contributed to this edited volume are briefly described below.

1 Are speech sound disorders phonological or articulatory? A spectrum approach

Chapter 1 introduces the spectrum approach to speech sound disorders. It is argued that speech sound disorders should not be viewed as either the result of an articulatory problem or a phonological problem, but a combination of both. Specifically, it is proposed that speech sound disorders are considered within a model that incorporates the interaction of articulation and phonology as a spectrum upon which both reside. The speech of children within the spectrum may clearly show a tendency for phonological and/or articulatory patterns or varying combinations of them, depending on where these productions are in the spectrum as well as along the children's development of phonological and articulatory skill. The investigation utilized both group and case study methodology providing evidence that supports the validity of the new perspective. In particular, the child case study showed that CS's errors were sometimes of an articulatory nature and sometimes of a phonological nature. The group study assessed the speech of children with clefts, that is children who were expected to show patterns of articulatory errors due to their clefts. In spite of this, a combination of articulatory and phonological patterns were evidenced in the speech productions of this group that were shown to improve longitudinally, suggesting that the children were acquiring a typically developing phonological system, albeit with some speech delay.

This chapter continues in the Jakobsonian tradition which views oral language as having an underlying phonological structure that is responsible for phonetic outcomes. The spectrum approach proposal advanced here enhances work on speech sound disorders; it suggests that speech assessment needs to identify the articulatory and phonological influences on a child's speech by recognizing that they fall along a spectrum from one to the other. This study on young children's speech sound disorders exemplifies how even children with atypical speech patterns and atypical articulator anatomy rely on an underlying phonological system that guides speech towards typical acquisition, though at a delayed pace. As such, the evidence supports the argument that children's speech sound disorders ought to fall within the premises of protolanguage. As the single representative of work on atypical acquisition of phonology within this volume, it is chosen to start off the section on protolanguage.

2 Crosslinguistic interaction in early bilingual phonology: A critical review

Chapter 2 provides a critical review of research on crosslinguistic interaction in the phonetic and phonological development of young bilingual children. The first part of the chapter presents examples of crosslinguistic interaction (e.g. acceleration, delay, transfer) based on Paradis and Genesee's (1996) framework using a database of German-Spanish bilingual children tested in Hamburg, Germany. It then goes on to examine whether other investigators have documented similar results to the Hamburg study by testing comparable contact situations (e.g. comparing languages with high vs. low percentages of codas). This survey indicates that few generalizations can be gleaned across studies. The second part of the chapter explores possible reasons for the lack of generalizations, which include methodological limitations and the lack of an appropriate research model. It is argued that by incorporating additional interaction patterns into the current framework (such as merging and deflecting patterns) and by considering the developing speech-motor and lexical abilities of young children, a better explanatory model of phonological interaction in early bilingualism might be obtainable.

Just as protolanguage, the linguistic state of first-language acquisition (FLA), and interlanguage, the linguistic state of second-language acquisition (SLA), are set side by side in the current book, child and adult language are united in the current chapter as well. The chapter attempts to show that research on early child language acquisition and language acquisition in adulthood needs to be integrated in order to best understand the complexities of crosslinguistic interaction in child bilingual development. It is argued that research in bilingual phonology has not sufficiently linked findings in early bilingualism to those in SLA, nor have they sufficiently focused on important characteristics of FLA, such as developing lexical and motor-speech abilities when designing studies on young bilinguals. In sum, this chapter endorses the volume's aim to bring together the language acquisition sub-fields rather than studying them as separate entities.

3 German-Spanish bilinguals' phonological grammars: Permeable or resilient?

Chapter 3 focuses on the development of German-Spanish bilingual children's phonological grammars, which are compared to the grammars of two control groups: Spanish and German monolinguals. The bilingual children grew up in North Germany and were exposed to the two languages from birth. Data collection was done in the home of each child, while playing and conversing. The domains analysed are characterized by phonological differences between German and Spanish and cover segments as well as prosody. An interesting line of bilingual research began with the study by Paradis and Genesee (1996), where they asked about crosslanguage interaction between the languages of bilinguals. They did not find interaction in the morphosyntactic domains, but studies on phonological acquisition have found much interaction between the phonological components of bilingual grammars, which are permeable and resilient at the same time. The study presented in this chapter reports on the interaction between the phonology of simultaneous bilinguals and suggests that Optimality Theory, based on constraints and their demotion, is capable of carrying out the most explanatory analysis of the results on acquisition. Several studies of bilingual children producing utterances framed in various segmental and suprasegmental language domains are inspected here.

According to the definitions of the book's prologue, all these utterances belong to the protolanguage domain. Children will be progressively abandoning protolanguage and entering adult language. Our focus has been on the protolanguages of bilingual children who will end up producing two languages. Moreover, we have seen that one of the languages, Spanish, is the heritage language, which develops as the weaker language of the two. If this language does not develop totally to match the targeted adult language exactly, the argument is that it still reaches a certain adult status that is fairly fixed and stable, i.e. one which differs from the child's mutable developing system. Thus, assuming that the main characteristic of a protolanguage is that it has not yet reached its final stage, it is argued that, when it reaches a *final* stage, it becomes language. As is the case with results to be presented in Chapter 7, it is probable to expect, however, that languages developing in bilingualism may not be (and perhaps ought not to be) analogously comparable to adult monolingual standards. Adult bilinguals may be fluent in their languages, but their phonological systems may not be fully developed when compared to the phonological systems of those exposed to strictly monolingual input. In that case, adult bilinguals' productions are distinct instances of interlanguage. The concept of interlanguage incorporates both evolution (development) and stagnation (fossilization).

4 Acquired singleton fricatives and lateral in cluster development: A bilingual child case

Chapter 4 investigates the acquisition of fricative-lateral consonant clusters in child developmental speech longitudinally with a focus on clusters whose members have been acquired in singleton contexts. Specifically, the study investigates patterns in the acquisition of labial fricatives (C_1) clustering with the alveolar lateral (C_2), i.e. /fl, vl/, at syllable onsets in a bilingual child's speech in Greek and English across the span of 17 months of her phonological development, starting at age 2;7. Comparisons with the child's /sl/ in English are included where pertinent, since /sl/ is the only other targeted cluster in the child's bilingualism satisfying the research criterion. Dense, longitudinal data on the child's naturalistic cluster production were elicited during daily interaction with the author, who transcribed the child's full utterances orthographically and phonetically. The study provides a fresh insight into developmental speech by investigating cluster acquisition in detailed data longitudinally, re-examining developmental stages, paths and processes under the new perspective considered, and utilizing the single-subject methodology in bilingualism to investigate production disparity that emanates from differences in phonotactic distributions in the languages studied. The study reveals that known stages and processes in cluster development are not challenged by the new criterion, though still shown to be tempered by idiosyncratic tendencies. The acquisition level of singletons in the targeted contexts plays a role that is both facilitative and obsolete in the process of cluster acquisition. Furthermore, a propensity towards non-targeted complexity and markedness in the child's speech is evidenced alongside the known tendency towards simplified productions.

The theme that links protolanguage and interlanguage is *language in development*. When one speaks of development, however, progression from a given initial point *a* to a given final point *b* is, by default, the heart of the matter. Progression involves change and evolution. As stated in the prologue to the book, there have been a number of theoretical speculations and insights on the developmental nature of language acquisition. Nevertheless, due to the expansive nature of developmental paths over the span of many years in the acquisition of language, few studies in either protolanguage or interlanguage provide substantial evidence on the actual *course* of language acquisition. The present chapter is a study that investigates the acquisition of a specific phonological contrast without interruption over months of development in bilingual protolanguage. Though knowledge of the developmental path in PL will not directly illustrate the developmental path of IL, nor vice versa, eventual comparisons of developmental paths in the two will be very revealing for deciphering the course of language acquisition in general.

5 The production of selected phonemically short versus long Hungarian vowel pairs by 5-, 6- and 7-year-olds

Chapter 5 investigates the differences in duration of three pairs of phonemically short versus long Hungarian vowels reflecting a vowel quantity contrast, produced by monolingual children from 5 to 7 years of age. The study predicts differentiation between phonemically short and long vowels produced by Hungarian-speaking children based on quantity and quality, as well as more robust vowel differences over time that would become more pronounced in the productions of older children relative to their younger peers. Three groups of monolingual Hungarian-speaking children were selected based on age, and audio recorded samples were collected during interactions with an experimenter. Acoustic analyses of the target vowels (/i/, /iː/, /o/, /oː/, /u/ and /uː/) were performed measuring the duration of the sound segments. Statistically significant effects were found for vowel quality and vowel quantity, but no statistically significant main effects were found for age or for gender. There was also an interaction effect for vowel quantity by quality, suggesting that differences in vowel duration depended on the quality of the phonemically long versus short pairs. The results support the hypothesis that Hungarian 5- to 7-year-olds use vowel duration as an acoustic cue to differentiating phonemically short versus long vowel pairs, and the findings also support the hypothesis that this differentiation depends on the quality of the vowel pair. However, the authors' hypothesis that predicted age-related differences in discriminating vowel quantity was not proven, because no statistically significant age effects were found for any of the more specific, pairwise contrasts. By age 5, monolingual Hungarian-speaking children differentiate phonemic vowel quantity by producing phonemically long vowels with more extended duration than their phonemically short counterparts, and this contrast is also dependent on the quality of the vowel pair. However, no clear age or gender differences could be identified in the present sample. Future research should include longitudinal data, also incorporating younger participants, to allow for following the development of vowel quantity discrimination by Hungarian-speaking children over time.

The results of the study are discussed in the context of the current volume with special attention to phonology in protolanguage. Specifically, this chapter has implications for phonology in protolanguage, because it addresses the production of the vowel quantity contrast by monolingual Hungarian-speaking children in three cross-sectional age groups from 5 to 7 years of age. The patterns attested regarding the production of phonemically short versus long Hungarian vowels offer a glimpse into how the phonemic vowel quantity contrast manifests itself in the protolanguage of 5-, 6- and 7-year-olds. The chapter includes a more elaborate discussion of how phonological contrasts may manifest themselves at various stages of language development, interpreted in the context of protolanguages.

6 Phonological development and language proficiency of bilingual children who learn Greek as a second language

Chapter 6 investigates aspects of early L2 phonological acquisition in association with broader language skills in order to examine the development of bilingual phonology in English/Greek-speaking children, who acquired Greek as a second language. The study includes 11 bilingual English/Greek-speaking children from grades three to six, and 11 monolingual Greek-speaking peers as the control group. Phonological whole-word measures of accuracy (PCC), complexity (pMLU), proximity (PWP) and variability (PWV) were calculated from children's retelling of the Greek 'Frog where are you?' story. Measures of phonological awareness, vocabulary and reading in both languages have also been included. Results suggest that their level of phonological acquisition in their protolanguage exhibits a gradient mix of characteristics typical of both early bilingual and L2 acquisition of phonology. The research builds on the assumption that by identifying both similarities and differences between monolingual and bilingual acquisition, specific insights may be gained for phonological development and linguistic abilities across different modes and stages of language acquisition, which has significant implications for research and practice.

This study examines the language skills of children speaking Greek as a second language in the context of bilingual protolanguage. It explores aspects of phonology using a whole-word approach and their relations with language and literacy. The study contributes to the research areas of second-language phonological development, and the connections between oral language and literacy. Similarly to the results in Chapter 5, it was found that the threshold where protolanguage becomes language, that is when there is a guaranteed level of accuracy and intelligibility even in complex contexts, has already been reached by the children in the studies, as a result of their advanced age. Including studies like these in the volume highlights the need for being overly cautious with regard to ascertaining the extent of critical period effects in older children. A lot more research on various aspects of phonological skill needs to be carried out crosslinguistically in monolingual and multilingual children aged between 5 and 13 in order to tangibly determine actual critical period influences.

INTERLANGUAGE

7
Schwa productions in Spanish-English bilingual adults

Kelly Millard and Mehmet Yavaş

Introduction

It is a well-known fact that vowel reduction, which is one of the typical characteristics of stress-timed languages, is a commonly occurring phenomenon in Standard American English (SAE) (Flemming 2009). This vowel reduction is a result of contrasting vowel qualities becoming neutralized, and it occurs in unstressed syllables (Chomsky and Halle 1968). Spanish, as a typical syllable-timed language, does not have this feature. For example, if we consider the English word *probability* [prɑbəbɪləti] and its cognate in Spanish, *probabilidad* [pɾoβaβiliðað], we see the difference very clearly; the two words share sounds, the same meaning and the same number of syllables, but the similarities do not go beyond that. In Spanish, the stress is on the last syllable, and although the remaining syllables are unstressed, they all have full vowels. In English, on the other hand, the word reveals a rather different picture: the third syllable receives the primary stress, the first syllable has a secondary stress, and thus these two syllables have full vowels; the second and fourth syllables are unstressed and have reduced vowels (schwas). Consequently, such differences result in the different rhythms in the two languages.

Vowel reduction is very frequent in English; vowels can be reduced to a schwa /ə/ (an unstressed centralized mid vowel) when they are in an unstressed syllable. Unlike stressed vowels, reduced vowels in English are not produced with their full phonetic value (Chreist 1964). An example of this stress and reduction pattern can be seen in the English words *photograph* [f́otəgr̀æf] and *photography* [fətɑ́grəfi]; in the first word, the first syllable is stressed and it has a full vowel, and the second syllable is unstressed and squeezed between the syllables with primary and secondary stress, and thus it has a reduced vowel. In the second word, the primary stress shifts to the second syllable and the vowel becomes full. Since the first syllable is unstressed right before the primary stress, its vowel is reduced.

Previous studies have shown the average value of schwa duration by native English speakers to be around 55 to 64 ms, while full vowels, such as /i/ and /o/, in stressed syllables can reach up to 156 ms (Flemming 2009; Yavaş 2011). According to Chreist (1964), this vowel reduction rule is an important feature of American English which is not relevant in other languages, such as Spanish, and becomes important in L2 learning. Ignoring the rule of stress and vowel reduction will result in a foreign accent. Halle and Vergnaud (1987: 239) also describe this as a 'striking phonetic property of English'. Therefore, the differentiation between full vowels and reduced vowels in unstressed syllables is vital when learning English as a second language. Because vowels present more challenges than consonants in L2 acquisition, and because Spanish lacks the vowel reduction process altogether, it is reasonable to think that L1 Spanish speakers who learn English are likely to have difficulties in mastering the vowel reduction patterns of English.

Byers and Yavaş (2014) looked at the duration of schwa production in English with the expectation that the duration of schwa would be shorter for both monolingual English speakers and early Spanish-English bilingual speakers compared to late Spanish-English bilingual speakers. The study focused on words containing deletable and non-deletable schwas and was more concerned with the late Spanish-English bilingual group producing a significant difference in contrast to the monolingual and early bilingual groups. A deletable schwa appears in words which have two possible pronunciations; one in which the schwa is overtly pronounced and the other in which it undergoes deletion. An example can be seen in the English word *probably* → [prɑbəbli, prɑbli]. On the other hand, a non-deletable schwa is found in words which forbid this schwa deletion process. For example, in the word *probability* → [prɑbəbɪləti], the schwa cannot be deleted to form the word [prɑbɪləti]. As expected, the late bilinguals did produce a schwa that was much longer compared to the other two groups. However, in the non-deletable position, they also found that monolinguals produced a significantly shorter schwa than both early and late bilingual groups. In other words, even though the early bilinguals' productions were similar to those of the monolinguals, there was still a significant difference. From these results, we can infer that because the longer duration for the late Spanish-English bilingual group had a much larger significance, the difference would be audible; however, the early bilinguals produce a similar, yet still significantly longer, schwa than the monolinguals which may not be an audible difference. So, evidently, the age of acquisition (AOA) is critical in order to accurately acquire vowel reduction in English, but early bilinguals may still produce a significant difference when compared to monolinguals.

There have been a number of studies that support this assumption that non-native speakers of English do not exhibit vowel reduction in unstressed syllables to the same degree as native monolingual English speakers. According to Sanders and Neville (2008), accurately acquiring stress placement in stress-timed languages, such as English, is problematic for speakers whose first language is one that is syllable-timed, such as Spanish. However, Flege and Bohn (1989) found that it is the reduction of the vowels in the unstressed syllables that is problematic, rather than the stress placement. Flege and Bohn conducted a study in which they examined Spanish accented English by analysing the differences in stress and vowel quality caused by alternations between morphological word pairs. When examining the ability of English language learners to acquire the stress and reduction patterns of English, they found that vowel reduction proved to be more difficult for second-language learners to master rather than stress placement. Stress placement, on the other hand, was mastered by these speakers earlier than vowel reduction. Despite being able to master the stress placement and produce, to some extent, a difference in duration between stressed and unstressed vowels, they still could not fully reduce the vowel in unstressed syllables like that of a native English speaker, which is a necessary ability to have in order to be proficient in English and have a native or native-like accent. As previously discussed, different rhythmic patterns exist in English and Spanish, and this difference between the two languages lies in the amount of reduction in their vowels. Although Spanish vowels in unstressed syllables are shorter than those in stressed syllables, they still remain full vowels. In English, however, these unstressed syllables contain considerably shorter vowels compared to Spanish. Therefore, even though it is expected for Spanish speakers to be able to successfully alternate stress placement and produce a shortened vowel, the Spanish-English bilingual speakers may not reduce vowels as much as native English monolingual speakers.

Kehoe and Lleó (2017) conducted a study in which they analysed reduced vowel productions by Spanish-German bilinguals compared to those produced by German monolinguals. Like English, German is a stress-timed language in which vowels that occur in unstressed syllables undergo vowel reduction. Therefore, because Spanish is syllable-timed and does not undergo vowel reduction like German and English, Spanish speakers who have learned German as a second language may exhibit similar patterns in their ability to reduce unstressed vowels as those who have learned English as their second language. In addition, the English and German schwa is not only characterized by a shorter duration, but also a centralization of quality (Kehoe and Lleó 2017). Kehoe and Lleó concluded that although Spanish speakers do exhibit some degree of centralization of vowels that appear in unstressed syllables, it is not as extreme as the reduction and centralization of quality that is found in either English or German.

There are two major ways in which stressed and unstressed syllables contrast in English. These are: a shortened duration as previously discussed, and centralization of vowels in those syllables that are unstressed. The centralization of schwa has often been an area of focus in previous studies of vowel reduction. Therefore, in addition to duration, the formant frequencies of the reduced vowel may reveal contrasting patterns of vowel quality between the two groups, monolingual and early bilingual, when analysing languages with different rhythmic patterns. Schwa, being a weaker vowel than that of a full vowel, is characterized as having neutralized vowel qualities (Hillenbrand, Getty, Clark and Wheeler 1995). Due to this neutral position of the tongue in the oral cavity, an English reduced vowel is represented in the vowel quadrilateral as mid and central.

According to Olive, Greenwood and Coleman (1993), the F1 and F2 formant values for schwa generally occur around 500 Hz and 1,500 Hz, respectively. These values are very different compared to a full vowel in that they represent a more centralized location. For example, in a study on American English vowels, Hagiwara (1997) looked at the average formant frequencies of vowel production in men and women for the full vowel phonemes in English. For example, Hagiwara found that the average F1 and F2 values for women's production of the high front vowel, /i/, occurred around 362 Hz and 2,897 Hz, respectively; for men, the average values were 291 Hz and 2,338 Hz. The low value of F1 indicates a higher vowel while the high value of F2 indicates a more fronted location, therefore giving /i/ its high front characteristics. For /ɑ/, a low back vowel, the women produced the vowel with an F1 around 997 Hz and an F2 around 1,390 Hz. Men's production of /a/ revealed an F1 at 710 Hz and an F2 at 1,221 Hz. Contrastingly, the F1 vowels for /ɑ/ were not quite as low as they were for /i/ which gives /ɑ/ its low quality. Moreover, the F2 values for /ɑ/ were lower in value than they were for /i/, giving /ɑ/ a more backed location. Considering the average formant values of schwa, it was evident that these values fall in between those observed for /i/ and /ɑ/, therefore indicating a more mid central position.

In other words, there are three vowel features, duration, height and backness, that are affected by the destressing of vowels, and with which we are concerned for the purpose of this study. Given the differences between Spanish and English, it is possible that the bilingual group will produce a reduced vowel with formant frequencies that are not as centralized as those that are produced by the monolingual English group. Therefore, this study will analyse reduced vowels in English based on their duration as well as their formant frequency patterns.

In L2 phonological acquisition, it is a prevailing view that earlier acquisition is better for achieving native-like pronunciation. As a result, AOA has been treated as the most important variable with regard to native-like performance in bilingual speech. This is made evident by the adults in many immigrant families who may achieve L2 fluency with non-native phonology. Conversely, there is a large body of research which has shown that children with an early L2 AOA achieve native-like phonology. Researchers who support the Critical Age Hypothesis (Patkowski 1990; Scovel 1988) suggest that there is a sensitive period, starting at birth, during which it is possible to acquire second-language phonology in a native-like manner. This period is suggested to last until puberty after which the capacity to learn native-like phonology deteriorates. In other words, the L2 pronunciation of an individual with an AOA post-puberty will be accented.

There are, however, researchers who question the Critical Age Hypothesis with the claim that adults can in fact be successful in acquiring L2 phonology (Bongaerts 1999; Bongaerts, Mennen and Slik 2000). Moreover, it is suggested that there are a number of other factors, such as 'amount of L1 use', 'amount of native speaker input', 'length of residency', 'aptitude', 'motivation' and 'language dominance', that may have an impact on the performance of an L2 learner in addition to AOA (Flege 1987).

Regardless, there seems to be general agreement that earlier acquisition is better; however, there is still dispute about how early the acquisition needs to be. Although there are studies supporting the claim that people who learn a second language before the end of the critical period (puberty) have a much better chance of achieving native-like pronunciation as opposed to learners who learn a second language after the end of the critical period, several recent studies have shown that a lag of even a few years in acquiring an L2 tends to have dramatic consequences on both speech production and perception (Flege and MacKay 2004; Fowler et al. 2008; Sebastian-Galles and Soto-Faraco 1999). Also, recent comprehensive and detailed linguistic analyses of early learners have revealed that *even very low ages* of acquisition do not automatically result in completely native-like L2 proficiency (Abrahamsson 2012; Stolten, Abrahamsson and Hyltenstam 2014). To what extent Spanish English bilinguals' productions match the monolingual English patterns is the central question addressed in this chapter.

As previously mentioned, vowels in English can only be reduced to schwa when the syllable is unstressed. Although both syllables can be stressed in a disyllabic word, it is not typical for two consecutive stressed syllables to occur in words that have three syllables or more (Yavaş 2011). So, if a trisyllabic word has two stressed syllables, the unstressed syllable with the reduced vowel will be found between the two stressed syllables. Because Spanish does not have vowel reduction in unstressed syllables, a contrast in duration and overall intensity between syllables occurs, which results in the stressed vowel being produced longer or with more intensity than the norm (Ortega-Lebaria and Prieto 2009). Bearing in mind this relationship between stress and reduced vowels in English, it is relevant to consider the stress patterns when analysing reduced vowels between the two languages. Therefore, the vowels will also be analysed in two different stress environments for this study. These are: (a) post-secondary and pre-primary stress, (hereafter *Stress 1*), as in *constitution* [kànstətúʃən], and (b) post-primary and pre-secondary stress (hereafter *Stress 2*), as in *satisfied* [sǽtəsfaìd]. In both environments the vowel is located in between two stresses.

It is possible that the position of the vowel in reference to the primary stress may be a contributing factor to the reduction of the vowel with the expectation that the schwa, which occurs before primary stress (in the *Stress 1* position), will undergo more of a reduction since it is in a weaker position. By looking at the vowels in the two different stress environments, it can be determined whether or not the type of stress contributes to the length of the vowel.

Word frequency may also be a contributing factor in the accuracy of reduced vowel pronunciation. Frequency counts determine how frequently a word is said or used and, according to Fabiano-Smith and Goldstein (2010), a higher frequency is linked with a greater accuracy rate than a lower frequency. It may be possible that the production of reduced vowels by Spanish-English bilinguals in words with a higher frequency may be closer to the average norm of monolingual English speakers than the reduced vowel in words with a lower frequency.

The purpose of this research is to determine whether or not sequential Spanish-English bilinguals (having been exposed to English no later than age 9) do in fact produce an unstressed vowel with a duration and with formant frequency values that are measurably different than those of the average native monolingual English speaker, despite the fact that they have learned English during the critical period and appear to have fluency similar to that of a native speaker. This will be determined by acoustically analysing the phonetic and temporal qualities of the Spanish L2 productions of the unstressed vowel in the two stress environments, *Stress 1* and *Stress 2*.

Once the length of the vowel and the formant frequency values are measured, they will be compared to those of native English speakers.

Putting all the above together, we have the following main hypotheses:

H.1: Spanish-English bilingual adults (with English-dominant fluency) will produce English reduced vowels with longer durations than those of monolingual English speakers.

H.2: Spanish-English bilingual adults (with English-dominant fluency) will produce English reduced vowels with less centralized formant frequency values than those of monolingual English speakers.

These hypotheses will be supplemented with the following ancillary one:

H.3: Different stress environments and word frequency will be influential factors in the duration of the reduced vowels.

Method

Participants

The participants of this study include 40 Spanish-English sequential bilinguals and 40 monolingual English speakers. At the time of participation, the age of the sequential bilingual participants ranged from 18 to 62 years (M = 26.7, sd = 9.6). The age that these participants started learning English via formal instruction ranged from 1 to 9 years (M = 3.8, sd = 2.4). The large majority of bilinguals were female (34 females and 6 males). The majority of the participants were undergraduate students from Florida International University. Twenty-two of the bilingual participants were born in the United States. The other 18 participants who were not born in the US came from Cuba (8), Ecuador (3), Puerto Rico (2), Mexico (1), Colombia (1), Nicaragua (1), Argentina (1) and Panama (1). The non-US born bilingual participants arrived in the US no later than the age of 9;0. They belong to the very typical local pattern in Miami whereby the children are in a Spanish-speaking environment until they begin their education. Although their first language of acquisition is Spanish, the language dominance shifts to English through elementary education, and strengthens more thereafter. They completed a language history questionnaire prior to the study which confirmed that, at the time of data collection, their dominant language was English. However, the questionnaire also confirmed that Spanish was not neglected in their home environment where they continued to use Spanish with their parents and/or relatives. The majority of the participants also reported Spanish use and code switching among friends. The questionnaires indicated that the length of residence, the amount of L1 use and the amount of input are comparable among these participants. Therefore, individual differences could be due to the quality of input which is extremely difficult to quantify and not addressed in this study. The second group consisted of monolingual English speakers and ranged in age from 20 to 68 years (M = 40.7, sd = 17). All of the participants in the study were university-level students or adults living in the United States, and all were able to understand, speak, read and write English.

Stimuli

Each participant performed a reading task in which they were instructed to read 20 English sentences while being audio recorded. Each sentence contained a target word strategically placed in the middle of the sentence so as to avoid putting emphasis on that particular word. The target word contained a schwa in one of the two stress environments; 10 out of 20 words contained a schwa in *Stress 1* and the remaining 10 words contained a schwa in *Stress 2.* Words with sonorant consonants neighbouring the schwa were avoided to obtain a clearer reading and a more accurate measurement of the duration of the vowel. Table 7.1 displays examples of the stimuli used.

Participants were given a Language Background Questionnaire at the start of the procedure. They were then instructed to read the 20 English sentences which were presented individually on a computer screen via PowerPoint while being audio recorded. Recordings were saved at 44,100 Hz sampling rate and were segmented and analysed using Praat speech analysis software version 5.4.10 (Boersma and Weenink 2015).

Data yielded 800 tokens (20 targets x 40 participants). However, some of the data were unable to be used due to pronunciation errors. There were

Table 7.1. Examples of stimuli used from each stress environment.

Stress 1	*Stress 2*
The priest used an *invocation* to begin the service.	A library *database* is used to search for information.
We have called this *convocation* to discuss important issues.	The boy asked the man for his *autograph* after the game.
I try to avoid *repetition* in my day-to-day life.	He used a *megaphone* so that the crowd could hear him.

consistent pronunciation errors in the word *pedagogue* for both monolingual and bilingual groups. There were also some deletions among the monolinguals, particularly in the word *invocation* and *convocation,* due to the vowel production being longer than the normal range of schwa for monolingual English speakers. This may be a result of over pronunciation due to the spelling of those particular words. In general, monolingual schwa productions above 70 ms were not included as part of the control measurements because this does not represent a typical schwa duration by monolingual speakers; schwa productions of this length were due to mispronunciations, lack of familiarity of the word (e.g. *pedagogy*) or over-pronunciation. A small number of words also underwent schwa deletion and were therefore unusable. The final number of tokens used in the study was 765 (388 for bilinguals and 377 for monolinguals).

Analysis

The reduced vowel targets produced by the Spanish-English bilingual group were compared to those produced by the English monolingual group. *T*-tests were conducted in order to make comparisons of the length of the reduced vowel between the two groups and within each stress environment. In other words, *Stress 1* of the monolinguals was compared to *Stress 1* of the bilinguals and *Stress 2* of the monolinguals was compared to *Stress 2* of the bilinguals. A pairwise *t*-test was also conducted in order to compare the stress environments within each group; *Stress 1* was compared with *Stress 2* within the bilingual group and another pairwise *t*-test compared *Stress 1* with *Stress 2* within the monolingual group. The formant values for F1 and F2 were also measured and recorded for all target instances of schwa in order to analyse the vowel quality of the reduced vowels produced by each group. These values were taken at the midpoint of the formant frequencies. The mean values for each participant were calculated for each of the values: F1 and F2, for each language group and stress environment. *T*-tests were conducted to compare the F1 values between monolinguals and bilinguals within each stress environment. The same was done for F2 values.

The frequency of occurrence for each target word was recorded as well using the Corpus of Contemporary American English (COCA) (Davies 2008) word frequency database which is based on a 450 million word list. A *t*-test was conducted in order to compare the three most frequent words between the monolingual group and the bilingual group as well as the three least frequent words between the monolingual group and the bilingual group. Finally, the three most frequent words were compared with the three least frequent words for *Stress 1* within the bilingual group and also within the monolingual group, separately. The same was done for *Stress 2.*

Results and discussion

Item level averages

The mean duration of the schwa was first determined for each individual word for monolinguals and bilinguals, separately. In all words, the bilingual group resulted in a larger mean duration than the monolinguals with the largest difference being 18.3 ms in the word *pedagogue* and the smallest difference being 3.6 ms in the word *recognize.* Table 7.2 shows the mean durations for all of the target words for both the monolingual and bilingual groups.

Table 7.2. Mean duration of target words for both groups.

Words	*Monolingual Mean*	*Bilingual Mean*
invocation [ìnvəkéʃən]	40.25	58.21
avocado [æ̀vəkádo]	38.75	46.73
repetition [rɛpətíʃən]	28.58	34.78
constitution [kànstətúʃən]	31.15	37.35
preposition [prɛpəzíʃən]	40.8	49.25
photographic [fòtəgrǽfɪk]	45.14	63.1
academic [æ̀kədɛ́mɪk]	25.69	40.8
convocation [kànvəkéʃən]	38.23	42.76
epidemic [ɛpədɛmɪk]	31.53	38.4
visitation [vìzətéʃən]	40.59	47.57
satisfied [sǽtəsfaìd]	47.72	52.1
recognize [rɛ́kəgnaìz]	35.78	39.38
database [dǽɾəbès]	38	51.95
agitate [ǽʤətèt]	33.63	41.2
arbitrary [árbəʧræ̀ri]	37.33	54.25
appetizer [ǽpətaìzɚ]	24.7	32.3
autograph [áɾəgræ̀f]	46.67	61.23
megaphone [mɛ́gəfòn]	45.26	54.4
pedagogue [pɛ́dəgàg]	53.14	71.44
photograph [fóɾəgræ̀f]	44.29	59.88

Durational *t*-test results by stress environment

An independent sample *t*-test was conducted to compare the average time it took to produce a reduced vowel between bilinguals and monolinguals. This was done in both stress environments as shown in Table 7.3. In *Stress 1*, the results suggest that bilinguals take significantly longer (M = 46.01, sd = 6.27) than monolinguals (M = 36.02, sd = 5.07); $t(78) = 7.833, p < 0.05$. In *Stress 2*, the bilinguals again take significantly longer (M = 51.70, sd = 7.71) than monolinguals (M = 40.16, sd = 4.96); $t(78) = 7.833, p < 0.05$.

Figures 7.1 and 7.2 show the *Stress 1* and *Stress 2* results displayed in separate box plots. The graphs clearly show that the monolingual group

Table 7.3. Mean duration of reduced vowels produced by monolinguals and bilinguals in each stress environment.

	Monolinguals	*Bilinguals*	*p-value*
Stress 1	36.02	46.01	< 0.05
Stress 2	40.16	51.70	< 0.05

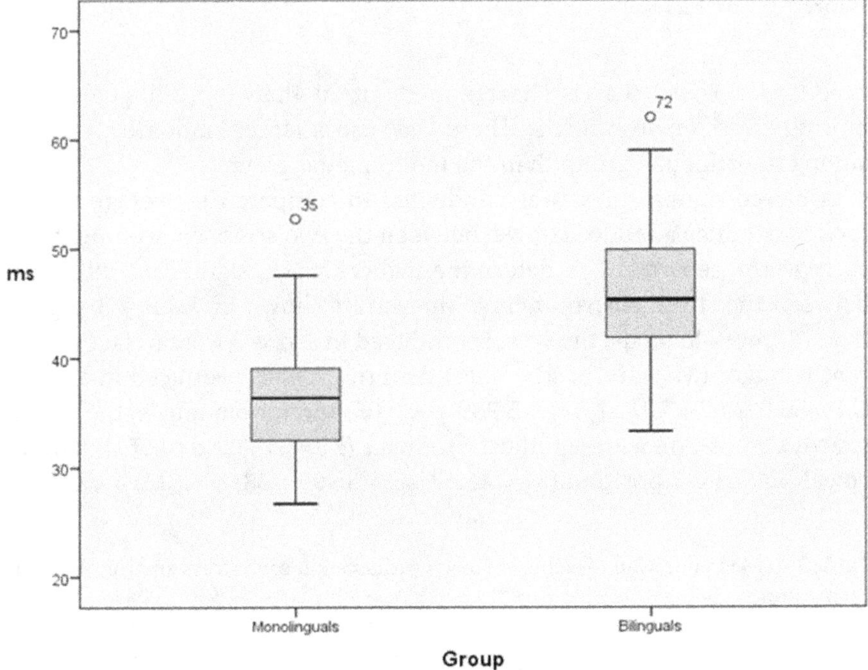

Figure 7.1. *Stress 1* results.

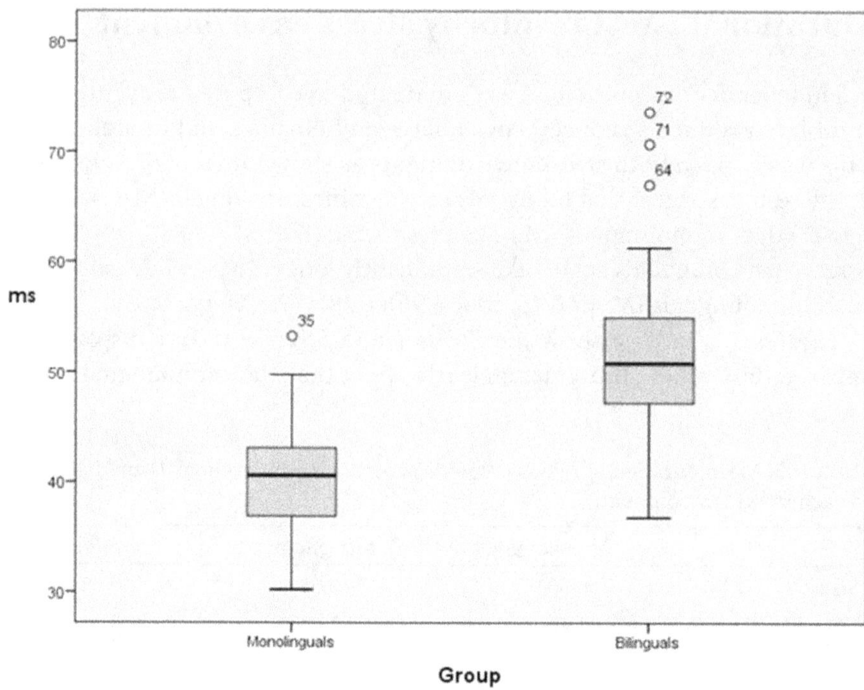

Figure 7.2. *Stress 2* results.

produced a vowel that is shorter in duration than the bilingual group in both stress environments. There was also a larger standard deviation among the bilingual group than the monolingual group.

A paired sample *t*-test was conducted to compare the average time it took to produce a reduced vowel between the two stress environments for each group, separately, to determine if there was a significant difference between the stress environments. The results shown in Table 7.4 suggest that, for monolinguals, the vowels produced in *Stress 2* were in fact significantly longer (M = 40.16, sd = 4.96) than the vowels produced in *Stress 1* (M = 36.02, sd = 5.07); $t(39) = 5.939, p < 0.05$; and for bilinguals, the vowels in *Stress 2* position were significantly longer (M = 51.70, sd = 7.71) than the vowels in *Stress 1* position (M = 46.68, sd = 5.99); $t(38) = 5.815, p < 0.05$.

Table 7.4. Mean duration of reduced vowels produced in each stress environment for each group.

	Stress 1	*Stress 2*	*p-value*
Monolinguals	36.02	40.16	< 0.05
Bilinguals	45.68	51.70	< 0.05

Table 7.5. The number of in-range productions for the bilingual group.

Bilingual Participant	*Stress 1*	*Stress 2*
1	4/10	1/10
2	1/10	1/10
3	3/10	1/10
4	3/10	4/10
5	4/10	1/10
6	3/10	4/10
7	5/10	1/10
8	5/10	0/10
9	4/10	2/10
10	5/10	1/10
11	3/10	1/10
12	2/10	3/10
13	1/10	1/10
14	1/10	3/10
15	1/10	0/10
16	3/10	2/10
17	8/10	3/10
18	4/10	5/10
19	2/10	3/10
20	3/10	2/10
21	1/10	4/10
22	5/10	3/10
23	3/10	1/10
24	3/10	0/10
25	3/10	3/10
26	5/10	2/10
27	2/10	2/10
28	4/10	0/10
29	4/10	1/10
30	2/10	2/10
31	2/10	1/10
32	1/10	0/10
33	2/10	3/10
34	2/10	1/10
35	3/10	2/10
36	2/10	1/10
37	2/10	2/10
38	2/10	2/10
39	2/10	2/10
40	5/10	1/10
Total	120/400	72/400

The difference in duration between the bilingual and monolingual groups is not a simple issue. There is varying difference between the two groups based on the participants. One bilingual participant may produce a reduced vowel that is closer to the target produced by a monolingual than another bilingual participant. Therefore, Table 7.5 displays the number of in-range productions for each individual bilingual participant. The number of in-range productions is out of target words for each stress environment. If the bilingual production was within 5 ms above or below the monolingual mean for that stress environment, it was counted as an 'in-range' production.

It is evident from the Table 7.5 that some participants produced a reduced vowel that was closer to the target than others. However, it is also evident that there were fewer in-range productions within the *Stress 2* environment than within the *Stress 1* environment. The total in range productions for stress was 120 out of 400 tokens whereas, for *Stress 2*, there were only 72 in-range productions out of 400 tokens. This provides further evidence to support the suggestion that stress environment is a contributing factor to the reduction of vowels by the Spanish-English bilinguals; although bilinguals produce vowels that are significantly longer in both stress environments, the significance is larger in the *Stress 2* environment.

Word frequency *t*-test results

A paired sample *t*-test was conducted in each stress environment for the monolingual and bilingual groups, separately, to compare the average duration of the vowel in the three most frequent words with the three least frequent words. The results are displayed in Table 7.6.

In *Stress 1*, there is a significant difference suggesting that the least frequent words (M = 40.08, sd = 9.17) produced by monolinguals are longer than the most frequent words (M = 29.45, sd = 6.54); $t(39) = 5.873$, $p < 0.05$.

Table 7.6. Mean vowel duration in the most and least frequent words for each group and stress environment.

	Stress 1: Most Frequent	*Stress 1: Least Frequent*	*p-value*	*Stress 2: Most Frequent*	*Stress 2: Least Frequent*	*p-value*
Monolingual	29.45	40.08	< 0.05	41.38	44.08	0.051
Bilingual	38.63	49.75	< 0.05	50.53	55.03	0.007

In bilingual production, the least frequent words (M = 49.75, sd = 11.96) are longer than the most frequent words (M = 38.63, sd = 9.61); $t(39) = 6.236$, $p < 0.05$.

In *Stress 2,* no significant difference in the monolingual comparison was found; however, longer vowels were observed in the most frequent words (M = 44.08, sd =7.27) than in the least frequent words (M = 41.38, sd = 7.20). It is expected that a larger sample size may produce significant results for this comparison. On the other hand, the vowels in the least frequent words produced by bilinguals (M = 55.03, sd = 9.24) were significantly longer than those in the most frequent words (M = 50.53, sd = 10.27); $t(39) = 2.861$, $p = 0.007$.

A *t*-test was then conducted to compare the duration of the reduced vowel between monolinguals and bilinguals in the frequent and infrequent words, separately, and within each stress environment, separately. In all comparisons, the bilinguals produced a longer reduced vowel. In *Stress 1,* bilingual production was significantly longer in frequent (M = 38.63, sd = 9.61) and infrequent words (M = 49.75, sd = 11.96) than that of the monolinguals (M = 29.45, sd = 6.54); $t(78) = 4.99$, $p < 0.05$, (M = 40.08, sd = 9.17); $t(78) = 4.06$, $p < 0.05$). In *Stress 2,* the bilingual production was significantly longer in frequent (M = 50.53, sd = 10.27) and infrequent (M = 55.03, sd = 9.24) words than that of monolinguals (M = 41.38, sd = 7.20); $t(78) = 4.61$, $p < 0.05$, (M = 44.08, sd = 7.27); $t(78) = 5.89$, $p < 0.05$. Table 7.7 displays these results of the comparisons of monolingual and bilingual productions of the reduced vowel in frequent and infrequent words in each stress environment.

Presented in Figures 7.3–7.6 are the box plots corresponding to the above findings.

Table 7.7. Mean monolingual and bilingual productions in frequent and infrequent words within each stress environment

	Monolingual	*Bilingual*	*p-value*
Most Frequent Stress 1	29.45	38.63	< 0.05
Most Infrequent Stress 1	40.08	49.75	< 0.05
Most Frequent Stress 2	41.38	50.53	< 0.05
Most Infrequent Stress 2	44.08	55.03	< 0.05

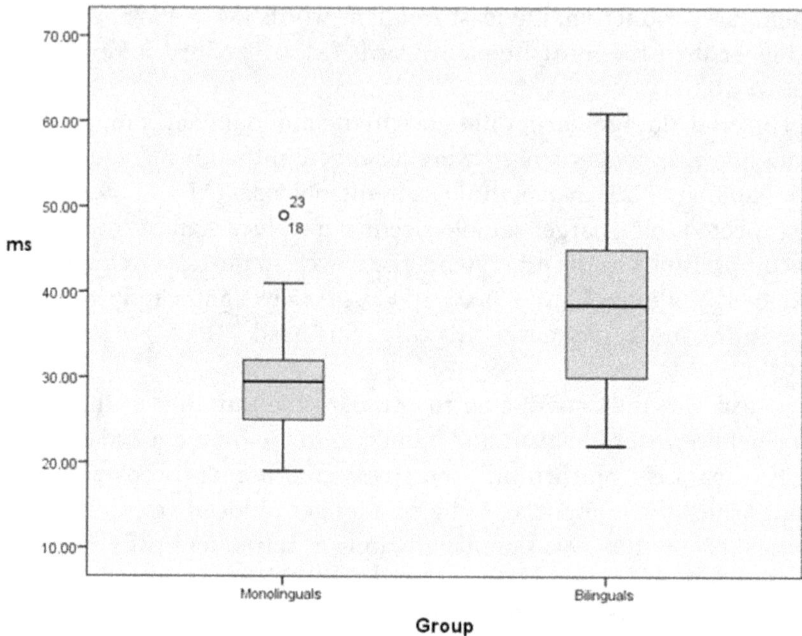

Figure 7.3. Most Frequent *Stress 1* results.

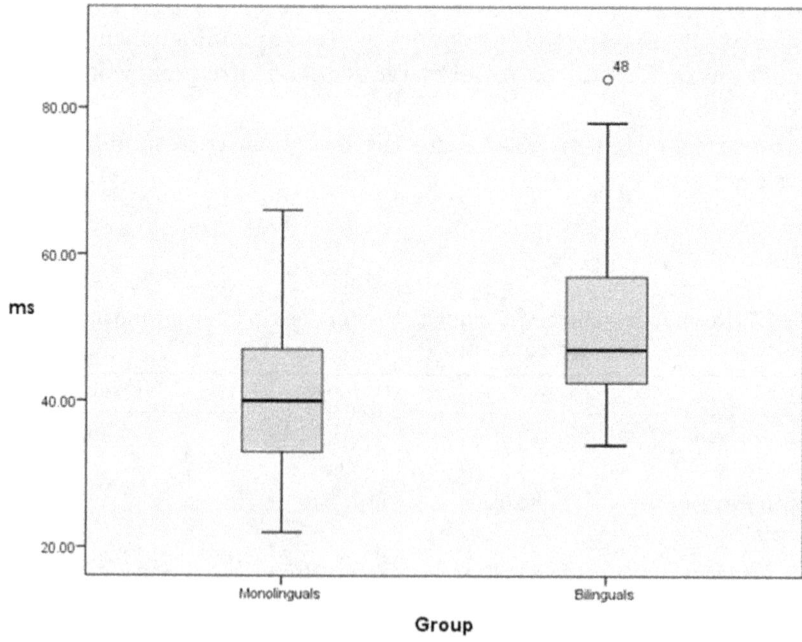

Figure 7.4. Most Infrequent *Stress 1* results.

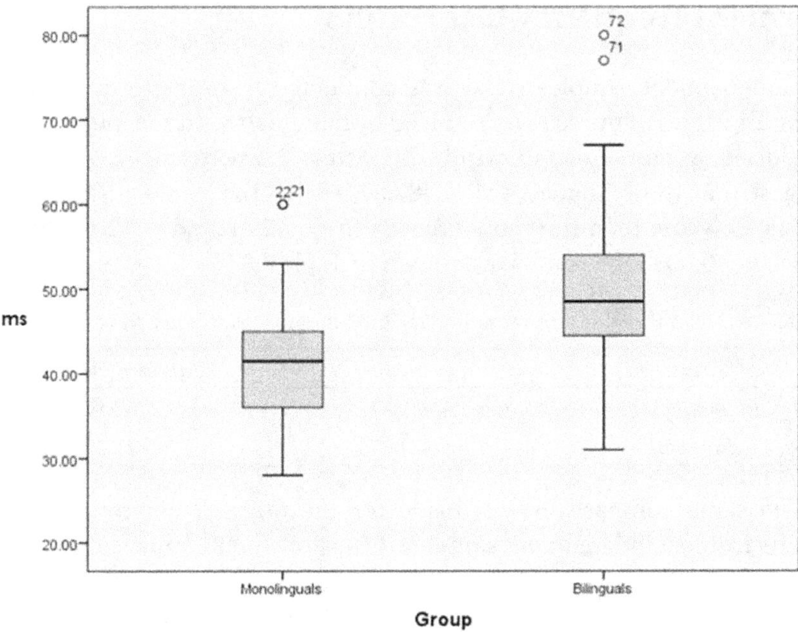

Figure 7.5. Most Frequent *Stress 2* results.

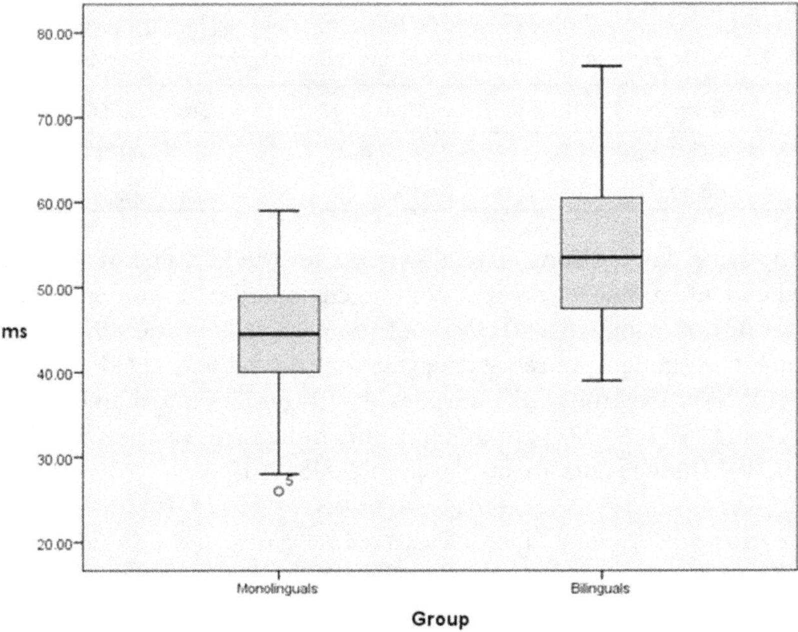

Figure 7.6. Most Infrequent *Stress 2* results.

Formant frequency test results

An independent-samples *t*-test was conducted in order to compare the mean F1 values of the schwa produced by bilinguals with the mean of those produced by monolinguals within the *Stress 1* environment. The results suggest that the bilinguals (M = 487.87, sd = 41.28) have a significantly higher F1 value than the monolinguals (M = 459.11, sd = 42.17); $t(77) = 3.063$, $p = 0.003$. The results are shown in Table 7.8.

Table 7.8. Mean F1 values for monolingual and bilingual groups in *Stress 1*.

Stress 1	*Mean*	*Standard Deviation*
Monolinguals	459.11	42.17
Bilinguals	487.87	41.28

The same comparison was made for the *Stress 2* environment. The results from an independent sample *t*-test show the F1 values of the schwa produced by bilinguals compared with monolinguals in the *Stress 2* environment. Table 7.9 displays these results which suggest that the bilinguals (M = 514.57, sd = 45.93) have a significantly higher F1 value than the monolinguals (M = 486.55, sd = 46.23); $t(78) = 2.720$, $p = 0.008$. In other words, these results suggest that the bilinguals produce a lower vowel than the monolinguals.

Table 7.9. Mean F1 values for monolingual and bilingual groups in *Stress 2*.

Stress 2	*Mean*	*Standard Deviation*
Monolinguals	486.55	46.23
Bilinguals	514.57	45.93

The same comparisons were also made for the F2 value of schwa. An independent sample *t*-test was conducted in order to compare the F2 values of the bilinguals with those of monolinguals in the *Stress 1* environment. Although the results suggest that the bilinguals (M = 1697.45, sd = 124.64) have produced a schwa with a larger F2 value than the monolinguals (M = 1664.28, sd = 165.32), this difference was not significant: $p = 0.314$. These results are displayed in Table 7.10.

Table 7.10. Mean F2 values for monolingual and bilingual groups in *Stress 1*.

Stress 1	*Mean*	*Standard Deviation*
Monolinguals	1664.28	165.32
Bilinguals	1697.45	124.64

For the *Stress 2* environment, another independent sample *t*-test compares the F2 values of the schwa produced by bilinguals compared with monolinguals. The results suggest that the bilinguals (M = 1793.49, sd = 122.47) have a significantly higher F2 value than the monolinguals (M = 1711.51, sd = 153.60); $t(78) = 2.639$, $p = 0.010$. Therefore, these results suggest that the bilinguals produce a more front vowel than the monolinguals. Table 7.11 displays these results.

Table 7.11. Mean F2 values for monolingual and bilingual groups in *Stress 2*.

Stress 2	*Mean*	*Standard Deviation*
Monolinguals	1711.51	153.60
Bilinguals	1793.49	122.47

Figures 7.7 and 7.8 display the box plots for the results of the F1 comparison between monolinguals and bilinguals in each stress environment, 1 and 2, respectively.

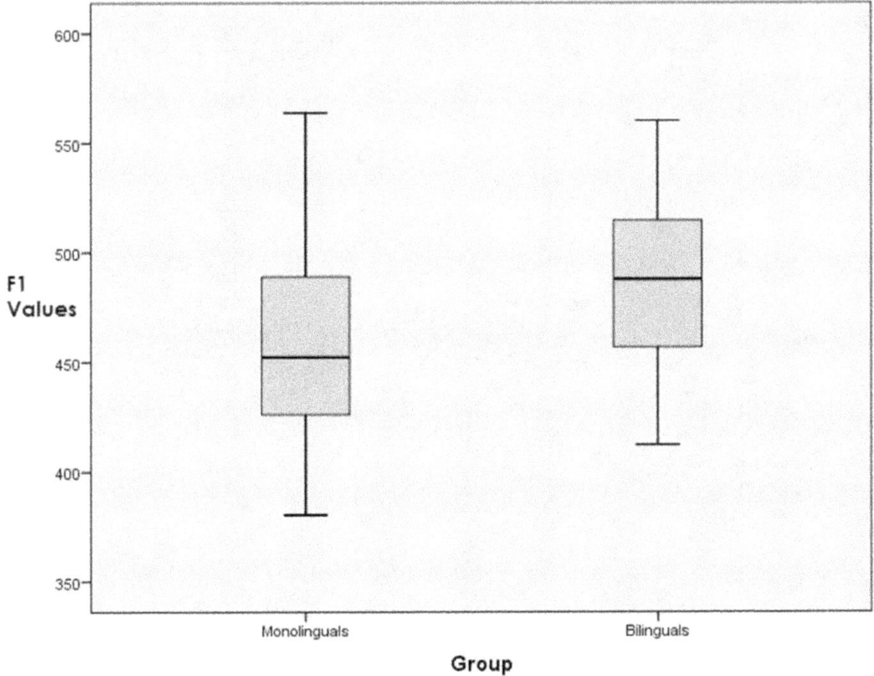

Figure 7.7. F1 *Stress 1* results.

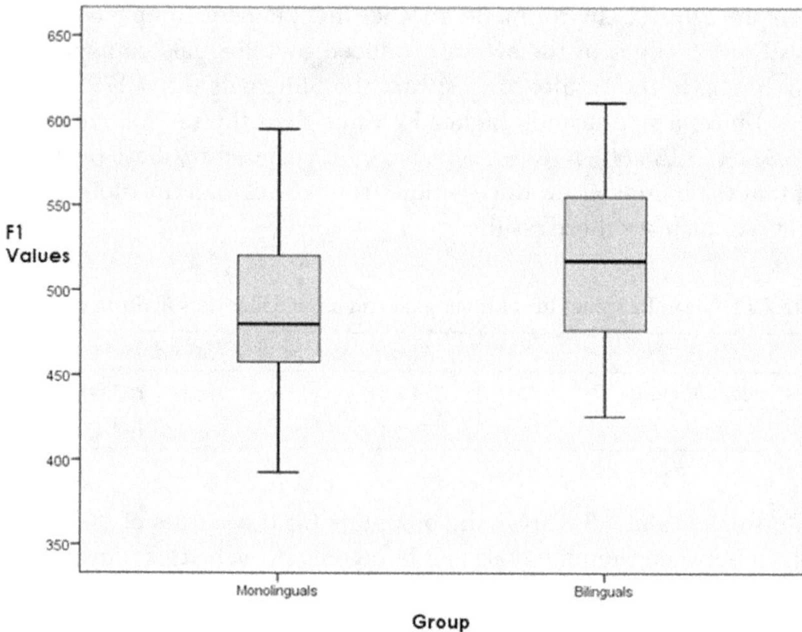

Figure 7.8. F1 *Stress 2* results.

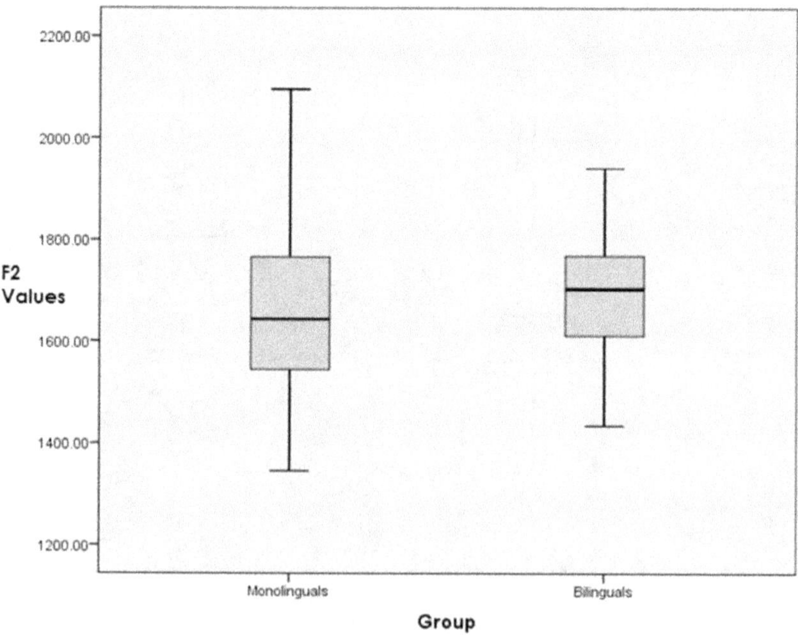

Figure 7.9. F2 *Stress 1* results.

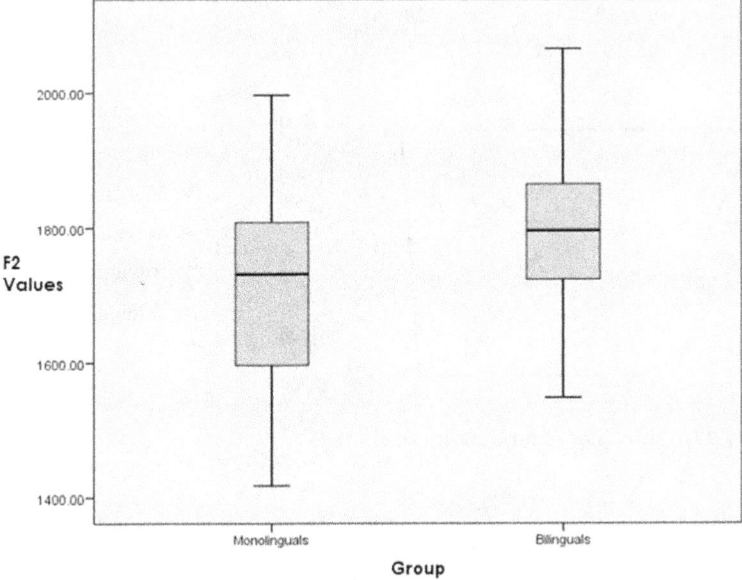

Figure 7.10. F2 *Stress 2* results.

Figures 7.9 and 7.10 display the box plots for the results of the F2 comparisons between monolinguals and bilinguals in each stress environment, 1 and 2, respectively.

To better show the variance in vowel qualities between monolinguals and bilinguals, the difference of the means of F1 and F2 for each group and stress environment was calculated. These values were then plotted on a vowel quadrilateral which shows the position of the vowel in relation to the oral cavity. Table 7.12 displays the values of F2 – F1; this is followed by the vowel plot representing these values in Figure 7.11.

Table 7.12. F2–F1 values for each group and stress environment.

Group/Environment	*F2 – F1*
Monolinguals, *Stress 1*	1205.17
Bilinguals, *Stress 1*	1187.15
Monolinguals, *Stress 2*	1224.96
Bilinguals, *Stress 2*	1278.89

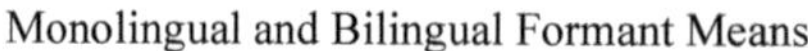

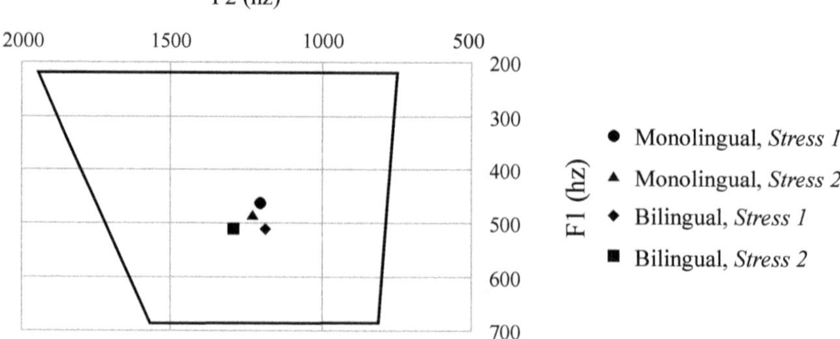

Figure 7.11. Vowel plot of formant means.

Overall, the vowel plot shows that, on average, the bilingual production of schwa is lower than the monolingual production. When comparing within each stress environment, the results suggest that the bilingual vowels are more front than the monolingual vowels only in the *Stress 2* environment.

Conclusion

The results confirm the hypotheses that, despite having been exposed to English before puberty and having become English-dominant regarding fluency, the Spanish-English bilingual adults in the study do not match the norms of the American English reduced vowels provided by monolingual speakers; the productions of the bilinguals were significantly longer than those produced by the monolingual English speakers. The findings are in agreement with other studies (Bosch, Costa and Sebastian-Galles 2000; Dupoux, Peperkamp and Sebastian-Galles 2010) in that even early exposure to L2 may not be enough for bilinguals to acquire native-like phonetic patterns in the L2.

It is very difficult at this point to explain the reasons for the non-nativeness of the productions by the bilinguals in the study. While one can advance the idea that the speech patterns attuned to the native language act as a filter that interferes with the way the L2 can be acquired (Flege 2007; Iverson et al. 2003; Kuhl et al. 2008), it is equally viable to point at the quality of input the subjects received in their early stages of English acquisition, which may have been predominantly by non-monolingual agents.

Additionally, similar to many other studies involving adult bilinguals, this study has limitations regarding the exact accounts of the quantity of monolingual English input during the sensitive period of acquisition and the amount of L1 use throughout. Information regarding the extent of how these variables factor in for each individual's performance is not recoverable at present.

The stress environment in which the schwa occurred also seems to be a contributing factor to the length of the vowel. There is a significant difference between monolinguals and bilinguals in both *Stress 1* and *Stress 2* environments, both of which resulted in the bilinguals producing a much longer vowel than monolinguals. Moreover, the vowels in the *Stress 2* environment appear to be longer than those in *Stress 1* when each group was looked at individually. In other words, these results suggest that, for both monolinguals and bilinguals, there is more of a reduction in the *Stress 1* environment. The number of in-range productions, depicted in Table 7.5, also provides further evidence to the argument that there is more reduction in the *Stress 1* environment by showing that the number of in-range productions was larger for *Stress 1* than for *Stress 2*. This is a logical outcome considering that the vowel that is positioned before primary stress, rather than secondary stress, is in weaker position and is, therefore, expected to undergo a more severe reduction.

The frequency tests for both stress environments were, as expected, in accordance with Fabiano-Smith and Goldstein (2010) in that the words of lower frequency had a significantly longer schwa duration than the most frequent words. In other words, the more frequent words were produced with a schwa that was closer to the native production. This was the pattern for both the monolingual group and the bilingual group confirming the hypothesis that accuracy is linked with word frequency.

The first formant values were found to be significantly different between the monolingual and bilingual groups in each stress environment with the bilinguals producing a larger F1 value. The significance was greater in the *Stress 1* environment ($p = 0.003$) than in the *Stress 2* environment ($p = 0.008$). Therefore, the vowels produced by the bilingual group appear to be lower than those produced by the monolingual group, as seen in the vowel plot diagram in Figure 7.11. The second formant values were found to be significantly different between the monolingual and bilingual groups only in the *Stress 2* environment; however, bilinguals still produced a larger F2 value in both stress environments than that of the monolinguals. As can be seen in Figure 7.11, it is not the case that reduced vowels produced by bilingual speakers are *always* more fronted. The results suggest that, only when comparing within each stress environment individually, the bilingual vowels are more front than monolingual vowels in the *Stress 2* environment, but not in the *Stress 1* environment.

Acknowledgements

We would like to thank the participants who generously shared their time for the purpose of this research. We would also like to thank Tyler Stout for his assistance with the statistical analyses used in this study.

Appendix I: Spanish Vowel Phonemes

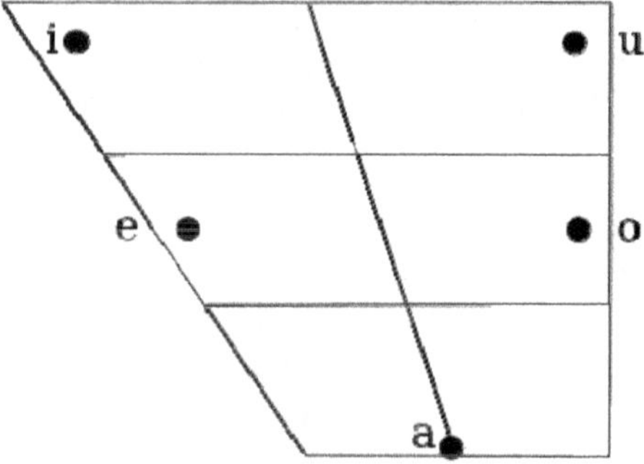

Appendix II: English Vowel Phonemes

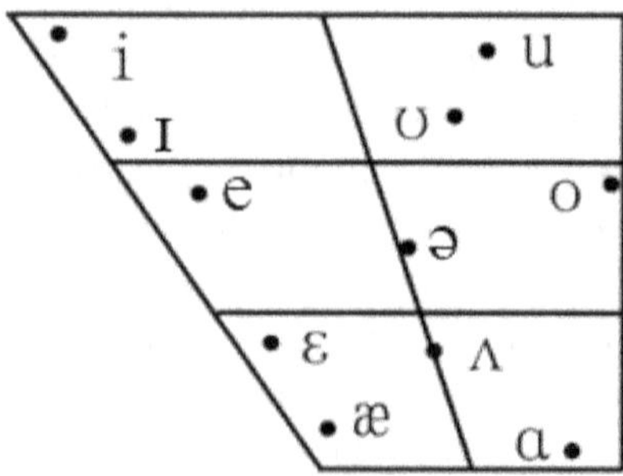

Appendix III: Instrument 1 – Target Words and Transcriptions

Stress Environment 1: Post-Secondary & Pre-Primary Stress	*Stress Environment 2: Post-Primary & Pre-Secondary Stress*
invocation [ìnvəkéʃən]	satisfied [sǽtəsfaìd]
avocado [æ̀vəkádo]	recognize [rɛ́kəgnaìz]
repetition [rɛpətíʃən]	database [dǽɾəbès]
constitution [kànstətúʃən]	agitate [ǽʤətèt]
preposition [prɛpəzíʃən]	arbitrary [árbəʧræ̀ri]
photographic [fòtəgrǽfɪk]	appetizer [ǽpətaìzɚ]
academic [æ̀kədɛ́mɪk]	autograph [áɾəgræ̀f]
convocation [kànvəkéʃən]	megaphone [mɛ́gəfòn]
epidemic [ɛpədɛmɪk]	pedagogue [pɛ́dəgàg]
visitation [vìzətéʃən]	photograph [fóɾəgræ̀f]

Appendix IV: Instrument 2 – Sentences

1. The priest used an invocation to begin the service.
2. I like to eat avocado in my salad.
3. I try to avoid repetition in my day to day life.
4. The United States Constitution was adopted in 1787.
5. English uses prepositions instead of postpositions.
6. There was no photographic evidence available.
7. To achieve academic success, you must study hard.
8. We have called this convocation to discuss important issues.
9. The town suffered an epidemic outbreak of influenza.
10. The regular visitation hours conflict with her schedule.
11. The guests were satisfied with the service.
12. I hope that I recognize everyone at the reunion.
13. A library database is used to search for information.
14. The news upsets and agitates my father.
15. Some rules are arbitrary and ridiculous.
16. The waiter serves the appetizer before the main dish.
17. The boy asked the man for his autograph after the game.
18. He used a megaphone so that the crowd could hear him.
19. In order to be a pedagogue you must complete a course in pedagogy.
20. This is an old photograph of my grandmother.

Appendix V: Demographic information for bilingual participants

Participant	*Gender*	*Age at Time of Study*	*Country of Origin*	*Age of Language Exposure*
B1	Male	28	Ecuador	4
B2	Male	31	Ecuador	7
B3	Male	54	Cuba	4
B4	Female	20	United States	2
B5	Female	54	Puerto Rico	5
B6	Female	26	Mexico	6
B7	Female	23	United States	4
B8	Female	21	United States	1
B9	Female	21	United States	1
B10	Female	27	United States	4
B11	Female	21	United States	5
B12	Male	18	Colombia	7
B13	Female	24	United States	1
B14	Female	24	United States	1
B15	Female	24	United States	3
B16	Female	21	United States	3
B17	Female	38	United States	4
B18	Female	20	Cuba	9
B19	Female	20	Nicaragua	7
B20	Male	26	United States	1
B21	Female	22	Cuba	1
B22	Female	25	Cuba	4
B23	Female	28	United States	1
B24	Female	38	Argentina	1
B25	Female	31	United States	1
B26	Female	24	Cuba	9
B27	Female	26	United States	5
B28	Female	22	United States	4
B29	Female	25	Cuba	7
B30	Female	62	Puerto Rico	2
B31	Female	24	Ecuador	1
B32	Female	22	United States	1
B33	Female	21	Cuba	2
B34	Male	22	United States	5
B35	Female	21	Cuba	8
B36	Female	20	United States	5
B37	Female	23	United States	1
B38	Female	21	Panama	4
B39	Female	23	United States	4
B40	Female	25	United States	5

Appendix VI: Complete list of frequency results

Words	*Frequency Value*
invocation	581
avocado	1,486
repetition	3,048
constitution	18,664
preposition	99
photographic	3,920
academic	33,547
convocation	216
epidemic	5,152
visitation	1,332
satisfied	10,162
recognize	25,027
database	7,199
agitate	197
arbitrary	2,894
appetizer	1,176
autograph	1,261
megaphone	288
pedagogue	57
photograph	67,963

Based on the Corpus of Contemporary American English (COCA) (Davies 2008)

References

Abrahamsson, N., 2012, 'Age of onset and ultimate attainment of L2 phonetic and grammatical intuition', *Studies in Second Language Acquisition* 34(2), 187–214. https://doi.org/10.1017/S0272263112000022

Boersma, P. and Weenink, D., 2015, *Praat: doing phonetics by computer [PRAAT]*. Version 6.0.04, viewed from http://www.praat.org/, November 1, 2015.

Bongaerts, T., 1999, 'Ultimate attainment in foreign language pronunciation: The case of very advanced late language learners', in D. Birdsong (ed.), *Second language acquisition and the critical period hypothesis*, pp. 133–59, Mahwah, NJ: Lawrence Erlbaum Associates. https://doi.org/10.1111/1467-9582.00069

Bongaerts, T., Mennen, S. and Slik, F.V., 2000, 'Authenticity of pronunciation in naturalistic second language acquisition: The case of very advanced late learners of Dutch as a second language', *Studia Linguistica* 54(2), 298–308.

Bosch, L., Costa, A. and Sebastian-Galles, N., 2000, 'First and second language vowel perception in early bilinguals', *European Journal of Cognitive Psychology* 12, 189–221. https://doi.org/10.1080/09541446.2000.10590222

Byers, E. and Yavaş, M., 2014, 'Durational variability of schwa in early and late Spanish-English bilinguals', *International Journal of Bilingualism* 20(2), 190–209. https://doi.org/10.1177/1367006914547936

Chomsky, N. and Halle, M., 1968, *The sound pattern of English*, New York, NY: Harper & Row.

Chreist, F.M., 1964, *Foreign accent*, Englewood Cliffs, NJ: Prentice-Hall.

Davies, M., 2008, *The corpus of contemporary American English: 450 million words, 1990 present*, retrieved from http://corpus.byu.edu/coca/, viewed November 1, 2015.

Dupoux, E., Peperkamp, S. and Sebastián-Gallés, N., 2010, 'Limits on bilingualism revisited: Stress "deafness" in simultaneous French–Spanish bilinguals', *Cognition* 114, 266–75. https://doi.org/10.1016/j.cognition.2009.10.001

Fabiano-Smith, L. and Goldstein, B.A., 2010, 'Phonological acquisition in bilingual Spanish-English speaking children', *Journal of Speech, Language, and Hearing Research* 53(1), 160–78. https://doi.org/10.1044/1092-4388(2009/07-0064)

Flege, J.E., 1987, 'A critical period for learning to pronounce foreign languages?' *Applied Linguistics* 8(2), 162–77. https://doi.org/10.1093/applin/8.2.162

Flege, J.E., 2007, 'Language contact in bilingualism: Phonetic system interactions', in J. Cole and J.I. Hualde (eds.), *Laboratory phonology 9*, pp. 353–82, Berlin, Germany: Mouton de Gruyter.

Flege, J.E. and Bohn, O., 1989, 'An instrumental study of vowel reduction and stress placement in Spanish-accented English', *Studies in Second Language Acquisition* 11(1), 35–62. https://doi.org/10.1017/S0272263100007828

Flege, J.E. and MacKay, I., 2004, 'Perceiving vowels in a second language', *Studies in Second Language Acquisition* 26, 1–34. https://doi.org/10.1017/S0272263104261010

Flemming, E., 2009, 'The phonetics of schwa vowels', in D. Minkova (ed.), *Phonological weakness in English*, Hampshire, UK: Palgrave Macmillan Publishing. https://doi.org/10.1007/978-0-230-29686-2_5

Fowler, C., Sramko, V., Ostry, D., Rowland, S. and Halle, P., 2008, 'Cross-language phonetic influences on the speech of French-English bilinguals', *Journal of Phonetics* 36, 649–63. https://doi.org/10.1016/j.wocn.2008.04.001

Hagiwara, R., 1997, 'Dialect variation and formant frequency: The American English vowels revisited', *The Journal of the Acoustical Society of America*, 102(1), 655. https://doi.org/10.1121/1.419712

Halle, M. and Vergnaud, J.R., 1987, *An essay on stress*, Cambridge, MA: MIT Press.

Hillenbrand, J., Getty, L.A., Clark, M.J. and Wheeler, K., 1995, 'Acoustic characteristics of American English vowels', *The Journal of the Acoustical Society of America* 97(5 I), 3099–111.
Iverson, P., Kuhl, P., Yamada, R., Diesch, E., Tohkura, Y. and Ketterman, A., 2003, 'A perceptual interference account of acquisition difficulties for non-native phonemes', *Cognition* 87, 47–57. https://doi.org/10.1016/S0010-0277(02)00198-1
Kehoe, M. and Lleó, C., 2017, 'Vowel reduction in German-Spanish bilinguals', in M. Yavaş, M. Kehoe and W. Cardoso (eds.), *Romance-Germanic bilingual phonology*, pp. 14–37, Sheffield, UK: Equinox Publishing.
Kuhl, P., Conboy, B., Coffey-Corina, S., Padden, D., Rivera-Gaxiola, M. and Nelson, T., 2008, 'Phonetic learning as a pathway to language; new data and native language magnet theory expanded', *Philosophical Transactions of the Royal Society* 636, 979–1000. https://doi.org/10.1098/rstb.2007.2154
Olive, J.P., Greenwood, A. and Coleman, J., 1993, *Acoustics of American English speech: A dynamic approach*, New York, NY: Springer Verlag.
Ortega-Llebaria, M. and Prieto, P., 2009, 'Perception of word stress in Castilian Spanish', in M. Vigário, S. Frota and M.J. Freitas (eds.), *Phonetics and Phonology Interactions and Interrelations Current Issues in Linguistic Theory*, pp. 35–50, Amsterdam: John Benjamins. https://doi.org/10.1075/cilt.306.02ort
Patkowski, M.S., 1990, 'Age and accent in a second language: A Reply to James Emil Flege', *Applied Linguistics* 11(1), 73–89. https://doi.org/10.1093/applin/11.1.73
Sanders, L. and Neville, H., 2008, 'Speech segmentation by native and non-native speakers: The use of lexical, syntactic, and stress-pattern cues', *Journal of Speech, Language, and Hearing Research* 45(30), 519–30.
Scovel, T., 1988, *A time to speak: A psycholinguistic inquiry into the critical period for human speech*, Cambridge, UK: Newbury House.
Sebastian-Galles, N. and Soto-Faraco, S., 1999, 'Online processing of native and non-native phonemic contrasts in early bilinguals', *Cognition* 72, 111–23. https://doi.org/10.1016/S0010-0277(99)00024-4
Stolten, K., Abrahamsson, N. and Hyltenstam, K., 2014, 'Effects of age of learning on voice onset time: Categorical perception of Swedish stops by near-native L2 speakers', *Language and Speech* 57(4), 425–50. https://doi.org/10.1177/0023830913508760
Yavaş, M., 2011, *Applied English phonology*, Oxford, UK: Wiley-Blackwell. https://doi.org/10.1002/9781444392623

Kelly Millard is from Miami, Florida and attended Florida State University where she received her Bachelor's degree in English and Spanish. In 2015, she received a Master's in Linguistics from Florida International University where she focused on acoustic phonetics. While at FIU, she was awarded the Truby Award for her outstanding achievements in the Linguistics programme. Currently, she is a PhD student in the Department of Communicative Disorders at the University of Louisiana at Lafayette where she studies Applied Language and Speech Sciences.

Mehmet Yavaş is a Professor of Linguistics at Florida International University, Miami. He has published numerous articles on applied phonology. His other publications include *Applied English phonology* (3rd edition 2016), *Unusual productions in phonology: Universals* and *language-specific considerations* (2015), *Phonology: Development and disorders* (1998), *First and second language phonology* (1994), *Phonological disorders in children* (1991) and *Avaliacao fonologica da crianca*, a phonological assessment procedure for Brazilian Portuguese. He is the lead editor of *Romance-Germanic bilingual phonology* (2017).

8
Identification and discrimination of initial voiceless stops by Catalan and Portuguese learners of English: The role of formal instruction and L2 exposure

Angélica Carlet and Anabela Rato

Introduction

It is notorious that non-native speech sound acquisition tends to be challenging for late L2 learners. It is so, due to perceptual and production difficulties which result from the interplay of different factors, such as L1 attunement and L2 experience (Flege, Munro and MacKay 1995). In fact, L1 attunement has been said to promote the creation of an *Interlanguage* (Selinker 1972), which is the language product resulting from learning and/or acquiring a target language (TL) following acquisition of the native language (L1). Interlanguage (IL) corresponds neither to the system of the native language, nor to that of the second language (L2). Instead, it is an intermediate system that falls between the two and often contains features of both (Selinker 1972). Attempting to perceive and/or produce the TL sounds, L2 learners identify and discriminate non-native speech sounds with reference to the linguistic categories of their L1 (Pisoni 1982). According to L2 speech learning models (Best and Tyler 2007; Flege 1995), degree of crosslanguage phonetic (dis)similarity tends to predict perceptual ease or difficulty. For instance, the *Speech Learning Model* (SLM, Flege 1995, 2003) predicts that L1 and L2 categories co-occur in a shared phonological space, unavoidably influencing each other and resulting in a bidirectional 'interlanguage interaction' (Flege 1995). More specifically, the model predicts that the more dissimilar a sound is in comparison to the learner's first language (L1), the easier the acquisition and category formation will be. Conversely, if the L2 sound is an allophone of an L1 sound (i.e. perceptually equivalent to an L1 sound) the less likely the establishment of a new category will occur. The *Perceptual Assimilation Model* (PAM, Best 1995; PAM-L2, Best and Tyler 2007) accounts for different patterns in the perceptual assimilation of non-native speech contrasts. If two non-native phones are perceived as exemplars of two different native phonemes (TC – 'two category'), discrimination is expected to be excellent; conversely, poor discrimination is predicted if two non-native sounds are perceived as equally good or poor instances of the same native phoneme (SG – 'single category'). Another case occurs when two non-native phones are heard as instances of the same native phoneme, but one fits the L1 category better than the other (CG –'category-goodness').

On the basis that perception precedes production, both linguistic models described above account for the intermediate linguistic properties (interlanguage) observed in L2 learners' speech. In the case of English initial voiceless stop consonants, several studies have previously reported that Romance language learners have difficulties when perceiving (e.g. Aliaga-Garcia and Mora 2009; Flege and Eefting 1988; Pisoni 1982) and producing (Flege and Eefting 1988; Mora 2008) these non-native categories. Other than L1 interference being the cause, another reason for such difficulty may lie in the fact that perception of an allophonic contrast in complementary distribution, such as that between English aspirated-unaspirated voiceless stops, tends to be more difficult, and thus less accurate than perception of a phonemic contrast (e.g. Boomershine, Currie Hall, Hume and Johnson 2008; Celata 2009; Whalen, Best and Irwin 1997).

The current study

This study investigated whether years of formal instruction (FI) and language exposure (i.e. outside classroom input) affect the non-native perception of the English voiceless stops /p, t, k/ by Romance language learners of English. Specifically, the study examined whether Catalan and Portuguese learners of English were able to identify and discriminate between aspirated and unaspirated English voiceless stop contrasts, which consist of two context-dependent phones of one and the same phonological category (Celata 2009). Since L2 learners have a fully developed L1 system and L2-L1 mapping is a common source of L2 errors, it becomes important to describe the differences and similarities between the stop consonant inventories of the L1 (Spanish/Catalan and Portuguese) and the TL (Standard Southern British English).

In Standard Southern British English (SSBE), which is the target language in the present study, the voiceless stops /p, t, k/ are allophones in complementary distribution, and are realized either as aspirated stops (in the onset of a stressed syllable) or as unaspirated stops (following the phoneme /s/, among other cases). The aspirated stops are produced with a long lag, in which the voicing onset occurs substantially after the release. This voicing delay results in a VOT (voice onset time) of 30 ms or longer, corresponding to the aspiration interval (Cho and Ladefoged 1999; Lisker and Abramson 1964). In Romance languages, on the other hand, the phonemes /p, t, k/ are always realized as unaspirated voiceless stops (Yavaş 2016). They are produced with a short lag, in which the onset of voicing coincides with the release of the stop closure resulting in VOT values that are nearly zero. According to Lisker and Abramson (1964), the voiceless stops in Spanish tend to be produced with VOTs between 0 and 10 ms. Similarly, Andrade (1980) reported VOTs ranging from 0 to 30 ms for Portuguese voiceless stops produced in isolated words. Moreover, aspiration is a non-existent phonetic property in their L1s (Ladefoged 1972) and learning the English long-lag VOT pattern is challenging for these learners (Alves and Zimmer 2015; Fullana and MacKay 2008). A few studies that investigated the perception and/or production of English initial stops by Spanish/Catalan and Portuguese learners of English are described next.

Flege and Eefting (1988) examined the perception and production of English L2 voiced and voiceless stops in word-initial position by two groups of Spanish learners of English. Perception was measured through the identification of a VOT continuum and revealed that the mean category boundaries of the L2 learners occurred at significantly lower mean values than those of native English speakers. Production was elicited by means of a reading-aloud task and the results showed that L2 learners realized English initial stops with significantly shorter VOT values than native English speakers did. The researchers concluded that although the Spanish learners of English were able to develop phonetic categories for English aspirated stops, they were not able to produce them accurately, since much of their L2 exposure involved Spanish-accented English rather than authentic input of native speakers.

Aliaga-García and Mora (2009) assessed the perception and production of English initial stop consonants (/b/-/p/, /t/-/d/) in a VOT continuum by Catalan learners of English, as well as the learners' ability to modify both domains through perceptual training. Perception results, both before and after training, revealed that the perceptual boundaries were located at shorter VOT values for the Catalan/Spanish learners than for native English speakers, suggesting that training was not effective in enhancing native-like VOT cue enhancement in a continuum. Results in production showed that, although the experimental group significantly improved their perception of the voiceless stop /p/ as a result of the perceptual training received, the mean VOT values obtained after training were still far from the native-like standard.

To the best of our knowledge, no experimental study has investigated the perception of English voiceless stops by European Portuguese speakers. However, several studies have examined the learning of English stops by Brazilian speakers (e.g. Alves and Zimmer 2015; Alves, Schwartzhaupt and Baratz 2011; Cohen 2004; Reis and Nobre-Oliveira 2007; Schwartzhaupt, Alves and Fontes 2015), and all of them reported difficulties in both the production and perception of English VOT stop patterns. Since positive VOT (aspiration) is not a relevant acoustic cue in their L1 sound system, learners do not distinguish aspirated from unaspirated plosives, and consequently do not produce the targeted aspiration. For instance, Schwartzhaupt, Alves and Fontes (2015) investigated how VOT patterns are categorized by Brazilian learners of English and native American English speakers. Specifically, the study examined how four VOT patterns (negative VOT, zero VOT, positive VOT and artificial zero VOT, a manipulated pattern) were categorized in two perceptual tasks (ABX discrimination and identification tasks). Results revealed that both native American English speakers and Brazilian learners perceived negative VOT and positive VOT as cues of voiced and voiceless stops, respectively. The zero VOT pattern was identified as a cue of voiced plosives by both groups, but Brazilian L2-English learners also associated it with voiceless consonants. With regard to artificial zero VOT, perception differed between the two groups of speakers. Native American English perceivers associated the manipulated zero VOT pattern with voiced stops due to the absence of the long lag of positive VOT, but Brazilian L2-English learners did not make this shift from voiceless to voiced stop. This means that both positive and artificial zero VOTs were perceived as acoustic cues of voiceless plosives. According to the authors, this finding suggests that there are other acoustic cues that are more relevant than positive VOT to the perception of voiceless plosives. In other words, Brazilian L2-English learners did not seem to perceive a positive VOT as a determinant cue to contrast the voiceless-voiced distinction.

In a similar study, Alves and Zimmer (2015) tested 34 Brazilian learners of English on the perception and production of VOT patterns of initial stops in English and hypothesized that VOT was not the main acoustic cue used in the perception of the voicing distinctions, particularly in learners with an elementary level of English proficiency. Their findings on perception showed that, regardless of the learners' proficiency level (elementary or advanced), VOT is not the main acoustic cue for the distinction between voiced and voiceless stops. The results of the production test revealed that the length of the target English VOT of both elementary and advanced learners was higher than the VOT values produced in their L1, but not as high as the VOT values found in the native English stop productions.

In a pilot study, Reis and Nobre-Oliveira (2007) investigated whether 11 adult Brazilian learners of English perceived the different phonetic realizations of English voiceless stops in word-initial position, and if perceptual training could modify both perception and production of /p/, /t/ and /k/. The battery of tests included two tasks of reading words aloud, and two perception tests: a discrimination task and an identification task. The results yielded a significantly positive effect of training on the production of both labial and coronal stops; however, the learners' VOT values did not reach native-like patterns. The results of the training effects on the learners' perceptual performance were to some extent conflicting, since along with a positive effect on the identification of English voiceless stops, a significantly negative effect on the discrimination of the target sounds was also reported (see Reis and Nobre-Oliveira 2007, for a detailed discussion). Similarly to Aliaga-García and Mora's (2009) participants, the Brazilian L2-English learners were still not able to produce the target voiceless stops with native-like VOT values following perceptual training.

Another important factor in the acquisition of speech in a non-native language is L2 experience, which usually refers to the amount of use and/or exposure to the second language. Acording to Flege (1991), target language experience is essential in order to improve one's ability to differentiate native from non-native sounds, and the greater the amount of exposure to the target language, the more target-like its acquisition will be. The participants of the present study were immersed in an English as a Foreign Language (EFL) context, which is characterized by limited target language exposure (Murcia, Brinton and Goodwin 1996; Muñoz 2008; Saito 2015). The predominant source of L2 experience for EFL learners is found in formal instruction (FI). In fact, according to Perez-Vidal (2014), FI tends to be the only or main provider of opportunities to practice the TL for these learners. Moreover, even though FI settings might provide researchers with consistent measures of the quantity of input in the L2 (Aliaga-García and Mora 2009), formal instruction can be carried out in different ways and, according to Muñoz (2008), it can vary with regard to the length of the instruction period and/or the frequency of L2 conversation opportunities.

Furthermore, literature on formal instruction reports little success in L2 phonological attainment as a consequence of the lack of systematic attention paid to the oral dimension of language (Saito 2012). In a study assessing the impact of formal instruction on the perception and production of English final stops by Spanish/Catalan learners of English in a foreign language context, Fullana and Mora (2009) failed to find a significant improvement. Along the same lines, García Lecumberri and Gallardo del Puerto (2003) have reported pronunciation attainment in a FI setting to be weak. Conversely, Pérez-Vidal, Juan-Garau and Mora (2011) found a significant improvement in the perception and production of English consonant minimal pairs after three months of FI; and Saito and Hanzawa (2015) found that large amounts of FL instruction (> 875 hours) resulted in improved L2 oral ability by Japanese learners of English. However, the large inter-subject variability found in their data suggests that the success was somewhat dependent on the language exposure that some learners were receiving outside the classroom.

In fact, another important consideration in the present study is language exposure, understood as language input received outside the classroom. While it has been argued that these opportunities are usually scarce in the foreign language (FL) context, and that the quantity and quality of input received is highly dependent on learner motivation and individual differences (Saito and Hanzawa 2015), previous research seems to indicate that learning English as an L2 in some countries may slightly differ from that in other countries. To exemplify, according to Rubio and Lirola (2010: 32), Denmark, Finland and Portugal are among the European countries that do not dub television programmes and, thus, 'television broadcasting of films in the original version can be considered a major facilitator for FL learning' in these countries. The authors add that learners who watch television programmes in the original version, captioned or subtitled, should be more successful in FL learning than learners who are exposed to dubbed versions in other countries, such as Spain, Italy, Germany and France. More specifically relating to Portugal, where two of our groups of participants come from, Tonoian (2014) mentions that exposure to English outside the classroom is very high in this country. Consequently, the author argues that learning English as an L2 in Portugal significantly differs from learning it in countries where only classroom input is available.

Taking into account these issues discussed above and the differences between the consonant inventories of the participants' L1 and the target language, this study sought to answer the following research questions and to attest the corresponding hypotheses:

RQ1. Does **amount of formal instruction (FI)** influence the perception of non-native English voiceless stops /p, t, k/?

H1. **Amount of formal instruction (FI)** will play a role in the perception of the allophonic contrast (aspirated-unaspirated voiceless stops). Advanced learners of L2 English will discriminate and identify the target sounds better than upper-intermediate learners.

RQ2. Does the **first language (L1)** affect the perception of non-native English voiceless stops /p, t, k/?

H2. The **L1** will not significantly affect the perception of the non-native voiceless stops due to the high degree of similarity between the consonant sound systems of the learners' L1s, European Portuguese (EP) and Catalan (Cat). Due to the fact that the allophonic contrast between aspirated and unaspirated voiceless stops does not exist in the learners' L1s, both EP and Cat perceivers will have difficulty distinguishing the target sounds.

RQ3. Does **language exposure** influence the perception of non-native English voiceless stops /p, t, k/?

H3. **Language exposure** will play a role in the perception of the target language allophonic contrast. Learners who are exposed to native input outside the classroom will outperform the learners who do not. Moreover, despite the comparable L1 systems and the comparable amount of FI, the Portuguese learners of L2 English will perceive the target sounds better than the Catalan learners due to the greater quality of daily exposure to the TL.

Method

Participants

Sixty-three (63) learners of English as a FL took part in the present study and were divided into three experimental groups: (i) 22 native speakers of Catalan at an upper-intermediate level in English; (ii) 19 native speakers of European Portuguese at an upper-intermediate level in English; and (iii) 22 native speakers of European Portuguese at an advanced level in English. The upper-intermediate Catalan and upper-intermediate Portuguese subjects were first-year English majors at the Universitat Autònoma de Barcelona and at the Universidade do Minho, respectively. The advanced Portuguese L2-English learners were second-year English majors at the

Table 8.1. Participant characteristics by group.

Group	*Catalan (Upper-int.)*	*Portuguese (Upper-int.)*	*Portuguese (Advanced)*
Age Mean (sd)	20.1 yrs. (4.03)	19.1 yrs. (1.04)	21.9 yrs. (5.75)
Sex (F = female, M = male)	16F, 6M	15F, 4M	14F, 8M
Self-reported daily amount of use of English Mean % (sd)	23.8 (8.93)	14.2 (10.17)	27.7 (11.52)
Exposure to English outside the classroom* Mean %	94.1%	94.7%	90.9%

* The figures illustrate the percentage of students of each group who reported to be exposed to English outside the classroom either by watching TV, playing online games or interacting with peers.

latter institution. In both institutions, students were majoring in English philology, and these degree courses were taught entirely in English. In both cases, L2 input was delivered by native or near-native English teachers. Even though the academic curricula differed slightly in the two institutions, the amount of formal instruction, measured by hours of instruction, was comparable.

Moreover, three native speakers took part in the study by validating the stimuli and providing baseline data. The characteristics of the participants of each group can be seen in Table 8.1.

Stimuli

The audio stimuli were natural recordings of (C)CVC words with word-initial voiceless aspirated stops, [p^h, t^h, k^h], and word-initial consonant clusters, /sp, st, sk/, embedded in the carrier phrase *This* (*target word*), so that the aspirated and unaspirated stop allophones would be aurally presented in similar contexts. The target stimuli included nine paired noun-phrases contrasting the aspirated-unaspirated English voiceless stop /p/ (e.g. *This pan – This span; This pot – This spot*), nine paired noun-phrases contrasting /t/ (e.g. *This tool – This stool; This table – This stable*), and six paired noun-phrases contrasting /k/ (e.g. *This can – This scan; This key – This ski).* Testing stimuli were elicited from three native British English speakers by means of a phrase-reading task recorded with a Sony PCM-D50 portable digital recorder in a quiet room. Each speaker read each phrase twice, so that the best tokens could be chosen for the perception test. All instances were closely monitored by one of the researchers.

Procedure and tasks

The perception tests were administered in quiet computer laboratory rooms with individual computers and headphones. The L1-Catalan participants were tested at the Universitat Autònoma de Barcelona and the L1-Portuguese participants were tested at the Universidade do Minho. It is important to note that the learners received formal instruction in different institutions, and thus, such formal instruction was delivered through different curricula and by different teachers. However, for this study we consider the quantity of input received by the groups to be similar and comparable, due to the similar amount of hours of class exposure to the L2 received by the students. The exact same procedure was followed for each of the three experimental groups. After completing a language background questionnaire, the participants performed two perception tasks which are described in detail below. The overall duration of the testing session was approximately 25–30 minutes, and the learners were given course credit for their participation.

Three native English speakers performed both tasks and obtained very high percentages of correct identification and discrimination (> 95%), indicating that the testing stimuli were appropriately representative of each category tested. Each participant performed two different tests, namely a categorical AX discrimination task and a 2AFC (alternative forced-choice) identification task. The perception tasks were set up in *TP* v. 3.1. (Rato, Rauber, Kluge and Santos 2015) and the order of both task and stimulus presentation was randomized. The categorical discrimination task (CDT, Flege, Munro and Fox 1994) adopted in the present study was an AX type, having *same* and *different* trials and two different talkers within each trial. Subjects were presented with two subsequent stimuli (e.g. *This pot – This spot)* and had to decide whether they were being presented with two different allophonic realizations of the voiceless stop consonant or if the two stimuli consisted of the same allophonic realization of the stop consonant sound. Participants responded by clicking on the answers *same* or *different* (and they were allowed to listen to the same trial twice). There were a total of 108 trials, of which 54 were *same* trials and 54 were *different* trials, counterbalanced for each target allophonic contrast. Figure 8.1 exemplifies the AX discrimination task.

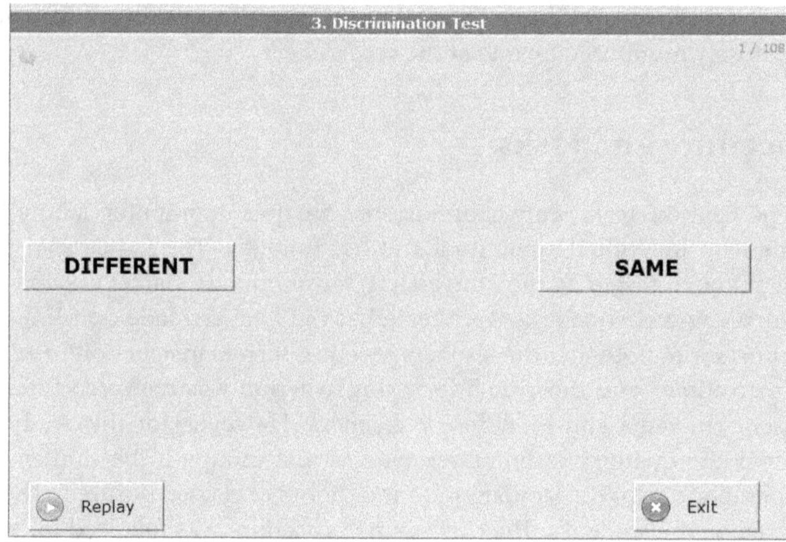

Figure 8.1. The AX discrimination task screen.

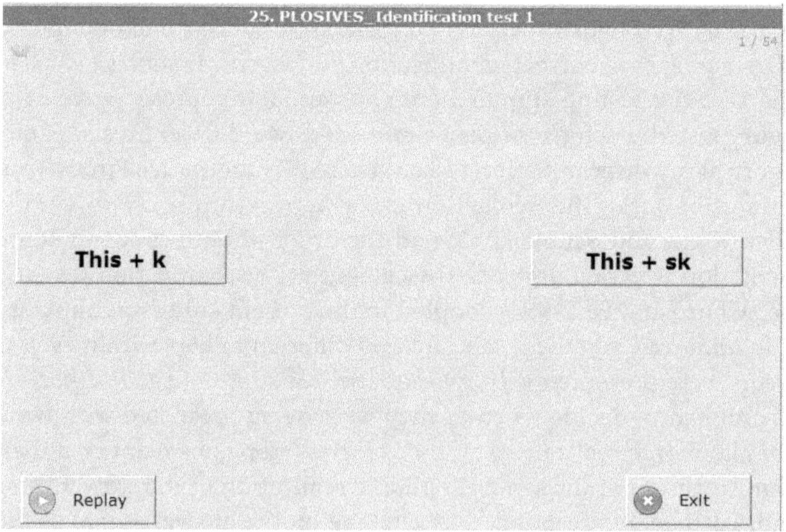

Figure 8.2. The 2AFC identification task screen.

In the two alternative forced-choice identification tasks, subjects heard one single stimulus (e.g. *This pot*) and were asked to answer by labelling the noun-phrase they heard. The response options were *This* + *k* and *This* + *sk* for the stimuli containing the velar voiceless stops; *This* + *t* and *This* + *st* for the stimuli containing the alveolar voiceless stops; and *This* + *p* and *This* + *sp* for the stimuli containing the bilabial voiceless stops. There were a total of 162 trials, 54 per each voiceless stop consonant contrast (aspirated-unaspirated). Figure 8.2 exemplifies the 2 AFC identification task.

Results and discussion

The participants' perception of the target stop consonant sounds was assessed by calculating the correct percentage obtained in the two perception tests, namely the identification task (ID) and the categorical discrimination task (CDT). The results concerning the effect of formal instruction in consonant perception will be presented first, followed by the results on the influence of the L1 and the exposure outside the classroom.

Formal instruction

The effect of formal instruction was examined by comparing the two groups of Portuguese L2-English learners studying in the same university: first- and second-year undergraduate students. These two groups were expected to differ solely in the amount of exposure, since they were all trained in the same institution and, thus, received input in the L2 input based on the exact same curricula, that was also delivered by either the same teachers or by educators with a similar profile. For the sake of clarity, we will refer to them as advanced (Adv) and intermediate (Interm) learners of English, the former being the second-year students and the latter, first-year students. We hypothesized that a greater number of years of FI would have a positive effect on the perception of the English allophonic contrast, due to the larger amount of L2 exposure that it entails. The second-year learners of English (Adv learners) were expected to both discriminate and identify the target sounds better than the first-year students (Interm learners).

A mixed-design 2×2 ANOVA exploring the effect of group, as a between-subject factor, and task, as a within-subject factor, yielded a significant effect of task, $F(1,39) = 131.878$, $p < 0.001$, no group per task interaction, $F(1,39) = 0.288$, $p > 0.05$, and a significant main effect of group,

F(1,39) = 6.900, $p < 0.05$. The interaction of group per task revealed no significant effect due to higher identification scores in comparison with the discrimination scores for both groups. The main effect of group is explained by the outperformance of the more advanced learners in both tasks. Follow-up one-way ANOVAs revealed a significant effect of formal instruction on the discrimination [$F(1,39) = 5.650$, $p < 0.05$] and identification of the target sounds [$F(1,39) = 5.687$, $p < 0.05$]. Figure 8.3 shows the learners' performance in each task.

In order to further assess the effect of formal instruction on the identification of the stop consonants, follow-up one-way ANOVAs were

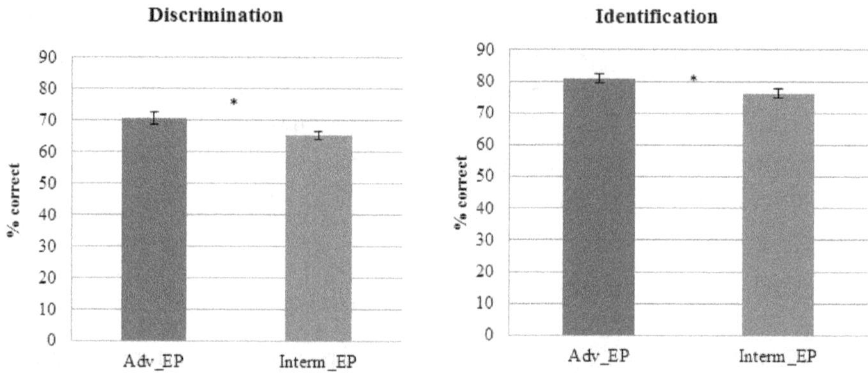

Figure 8.3. Learners' performance in discrimination and identification.

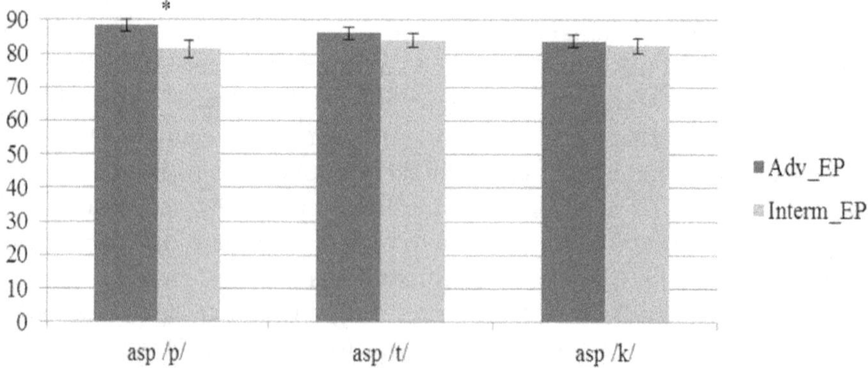

Figure 8.4. Learners' performance in identification of the aspirated voiceless bilabial stop.

conducted, having *segment* as the within variable and *group* as the between variable. The results yielded a significant effect of group on the identification of the aspirated voiceless bilabial stop only [$F(1,39) = 4.923, p < 0.05$], as presented in Figure 8.4.

Although the group of advanced learners obtained slightly higher numerical scores (M = 88.39, sd = 8.65 for [p^h], M = 86.21, sd = 8.78 for [t^h], M = 83.86, sd = 8.81 for [k^h]) than the upper-intermediate group (M = 81.48, sd = 11.25 for [p^h], M = 84.02, sd = 8.91 for [t^h], M = 82.46, sd = 9.06 for [k^h]) in the identification of the three target allophonic consonants, a significant difference was only found in the identification of the bilabial L2 allophone, with the more advanced group outperforming the less advanced group of learners. Thus, formal instruction positively affected the perceptual performance of the Portuguese learners at a more advanced proficiency level in English, which suggests that quantity of L2 input and possibly L2 use are factors that facilitate improvement in L2 speech learning, as shown in previous studies (Flege, Munro and MacKay 1995; Flege, Munro and Skelton 1992). However, since these two groups only differed with regard to a single year of L2 experience, the advanced learners' outperformance was not pervasive. Nonetheless, the high scores for accurate identification reported for the L2 allophones (ranging from 84 to 88%) seem to suggest that the group with more language experience was able to successfully perceive the English allophonic contrast (aspirated-unaspirated) leading to the establishment of new phonetic categories, according to the PAM-L2 (Best and Tyler 2007).

Finally, in order to verify whether there was a relation between the performance of the three experimental groups in the identification and discrimination tasks, a Pearson correlation test was run. The result revealed a significant positive correlation between the perceptual performance of the three groups in both the AX discrimination task and the 2AFC identification task ($r = 0.706, p < 0.01$). This indicates that the ability to both identify and discriminate stop consonant sounds were positively correlated, as can be observed in Figure 8.5. Moreover, the correlation became stronger as the number of years of instruction increased. The data of the two less experienced groups (i.e. upper-intermediate Portuguese and Catalan learners of L2-English) resulted in moderate r values ($r = 0.430, p < 0.05$; $r = 0.513, p < 0.01$, respectively) while the data of the more experienced group (i.e. advanced Portuguese learners) showed a stronger r value ($r = 0.741, p < 0.01$).

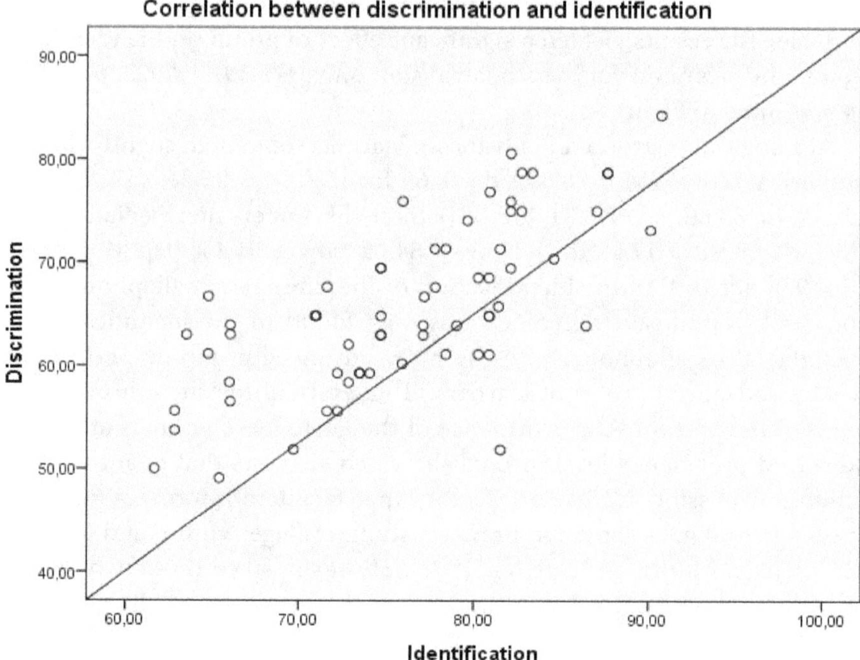

Figure 8.5. Correlation between identification and discrimination of stop consonant sounds.

First language (L1)

First-language effect was assessed by comparing the two intermediate groups, European Portuguese (EP) and Catalan (Cat). We had initially hypothesized that L1 would not be a significant predictor affecting the perception of the non-native voiceless stops due to the high degree of similarity between the consonant sound systems of the participants' L1s. Thus, both EP and Cat perceivers were expected to have similar difficulties distinguishing the target allophonic sounds.

The identification and discrimination percentage scores obtained by both groups of learners were submitted to a mixed-design 2×2 ANOVA, in which the effect of group was explored as the between-subject factor and task as a within-subject factor. The results yielded a significant effect of task, $F(1,39) = 134.061$, $p < 0.001$, no group per task interaction, $F(1, 39) = 0.054$, $p > 0.05$, and a significant main effect of group, $F(1,39) = 8.050$, $p < 0.01$. The effect of task and no interaction can be explained by the fact that the scores in the identification test were higher than the discrimination

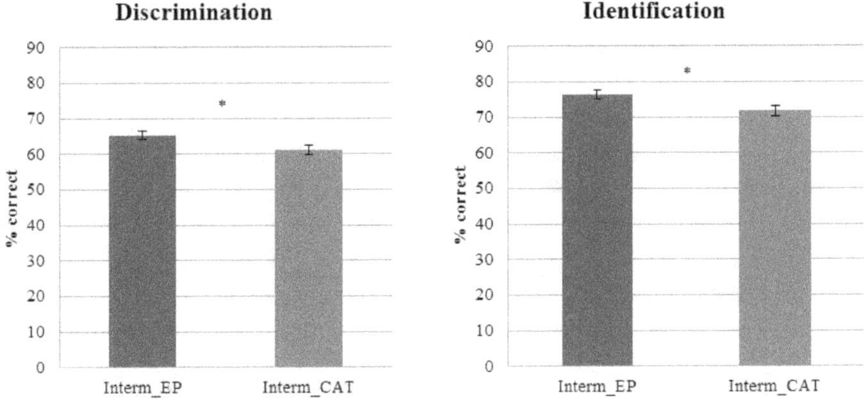

Figure 8.6. Performance in discrimination and identification tasks.

scores for both groups. The effect of group corresponds to the fact that the EP learners outperformed the Cat learners in both tasks.

A follow-up one-way ANOVA revealed a significant effect of group on the discrimination [$F(1,39) = 5.642$, $p < 0.05$] and identification of the target sounds [$F(1,39) = 6.276$, $p < 0.05$]. The EP L2-English learners had significantly better perceptual performance than the Cat group in the discrimination (M = 65.25, sd = 5.06; M = 60.99; sd = 6.26) and identification (M = 73.32, sd = 5.56; M = 71.61, sd = 6.34) of the voiceless stop contrasts. Figure 8.6 shows the participants' performance in each task.

Overall, as observed in Figure 8.6, identifying the target sounds was less difficult than discriminating between them for both groups of L2 learners. This may be explained by the fact that different tasks involve different mechanisms of short-term memory. In the categorical discrimination task, which allows listeners to compare two stimuli in the auditory sensory memory, allophones were more difficult to distinguish than in the identification task, in which perceivers can rely on pre-existing mental representations of the target sounds (Beddor and Gottfried 1995; Jamieson and Morosan 1986). Contrary to Celata (2009), the allophonic effect seemed to emerge only in the discrimination paradigm impeding L2 listeners from successfully distinguishing the two phones of the English allophonic contrasts. One of the reasons that may explain this difficulty is the fact that the target stimuli were presented in noun-phrase tokens whose length may have negatively interfered with listeners' attention to focus in the between-category acoustic differences.

To further examine the learners' perceptual performance in the identification of both aspirated and unaspirated voiceless stops, a one-way

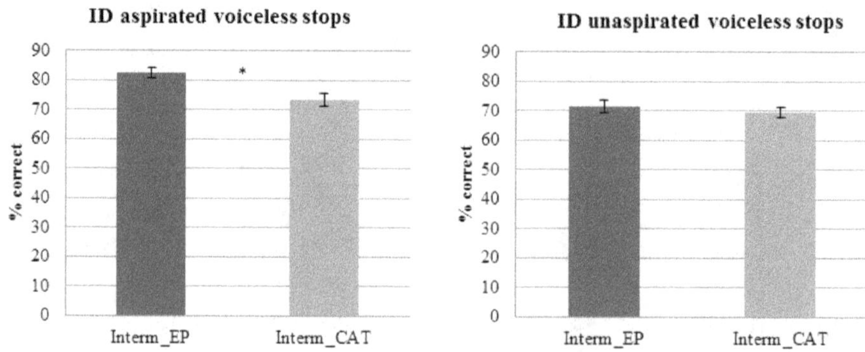

Figure 8.7. Effect of learners' L1 on identification of voiceless stops.

ANOVA was run with a between-subjects design. The results showed a significant effect of the learners' L1 on the identification of the target aspirated voiceless stops [$F(1,39) = 11.090, p < 0.01$], and no effect on the unaspirated voiceless stops [$F(1,39) = 0.424, p > 0.05$], as presented in Figure 8.7.

Although both groups had higher correct scores on the identification of the non-existent (in their L1s) aspirated allophones [pʰ, tʰ, kʰ] than on the identification of the existent L1 unaspirated phonemes [p, t, k], the Portuguese learners performed significantly better (M = 82.65, sd = 1.88) than the Catalan learners (M = 73.51, sd = 1.75). The intergroup difference arose in the case of the aspirated L2 allophones, because both Portuguese and Catalan phonological systems only include the unaspirated voiceless stops and, thus, no differences were expected to be found for this group of L1 consonants. Taking into account the PAM-L2, the aspirated allophones may be considered the deviant phones, for which new L2 categories were predicted to be established. The better performance on the deviant phones suggests that these allophonic variants already coexist in the learners' phonological system.

Further follow-up statistical analysis of the performance in the categorization of each aspirated stop revealed a significant group effect on the identification of two aspirated voiceless stops: [tʰ], $F(1,39) = 7.227$, $p < 0.05$; and [kʰ], $F(1,39) = 10.504, p < 0.01$. Portuguese learners identified the alveolar aspirated voiceless stop (M = 84.02, sd = 8.91) and the velar aspirated voiceless stop (M = 82.46, sd = 9.06) significantly better than the Catalan speakers did (M = 74.24, sd = 13.50; M = 71.21, sd = 12.47, respectively). Regarding the bilabial aspirated stop, the perceptual performance of Catalan L2-English learners (M = 75.08, sd = 12.27) did not differ significantly from the performance of the Portuguese participants (M = 81.48,

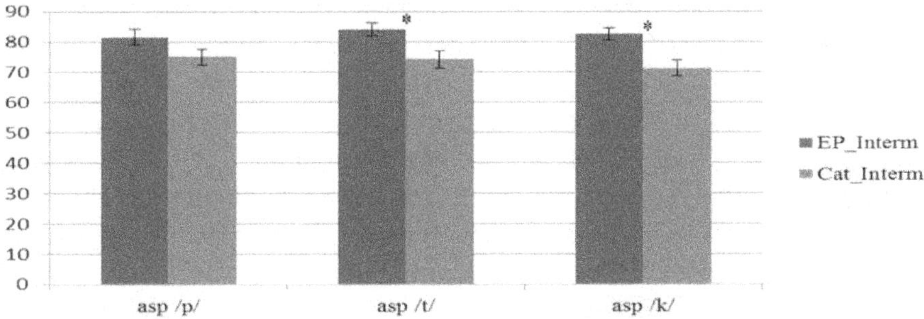

Figure 8.8. Effect of learners' L1 on identification of allophones.

sd = 11.25). This may be due to the fact that the perceptual scores obtained on the identification of the bilabial voiceless stop were higher than the ones obtained for the other two target sounds, which made the intergroup difference smaller.

As observed in Figure 8.8, Portuguese L2-English learners outperformed Catalan L2-English learners in the identification of the target allophones. Since the number of years of formal instruction were comparable between the two groups, and since both the L1 Catalan and Portuguese systems are similar as regards to the initial consonant stops inventory, these findings may be explained by the fact that other variables, such as language exposure, may have also played a role. Language exposure is further investigated next in order to answer research question 3 (RQ3).

Language exposure

The effect of TL exposure was assessed by comparing the qualitative data obtained from the two groups with a similar amount of years of formal instruction, i.e. Portuguese and Catalan Intermediate L2-English learners. The amount of language exposure was self-reported through the linguistic background questionnaires, in which students described the daily amount of usage of the target language and whether they used English outside the university setting (see Table 8.1 for more details). It was originally hypothesized that language exposure would be a significant predictor affecting the perception of the non-native voiceless stops, since learners that exposed themselves to the TL outside the classroom would obtain better results than the learners who did not. The qualitative results obtained from the language background questionnaires for the two intermediate groups of learners will be reported next.

The results for the intermediate L2-English Catalan group revealed that only one participant (representing 5.9% of the learners) reported not to be exposed to English outside the classroom, whereas 94.1% of the participants claimed to use it outside the classroom (20% talking to native English-speaking friends, 73.3% watching TV/reading and 13.3% through videogames). The qualitative results from the intermediate L2-English Portuguese group revealed a similar scenario, since only one participant (representing 5.3% of the learners) reported not to use English outside the university setting. From the 94.7% who reported to be exposed to English during their extra-curricular time, 94.4% reported that their exposure to the TL included native input received through TV programmes and online gaming. The 5.6% remaining (one participant) reported to be exposed to English only when talking to native English-speaking friends.

The results presented here indicate that both groups seem to be homogeneous, as over 94% of the participants in both groups reported to be exposed to English during extra-curricular hours. Thus, according to the initial predictions of the study, both groups of learners should perform similarly in both the identification and discrimination of English initial stops. However, as previously described, the Portuguese intermediate learners of English outperformed the Catalan intermediate learners of English.

Since the quantity of reported language exposure did not diverge between the groups of learners, these findings might be explained by the fact that other variables, such as quality of language exposure, may have also played a role. The Portuguese L2-English learners had daily exposure to the target language outside the classroom, since non-dubbing on television allows Portuguese EFL learners to watch films and programmes in the original version, which, according to Rubio and Lirola (2010), enhances success in foreign language learning.

Discussion and conclusion

The findings of this experimental study shed some light on the effect of the three investigated variables – years of formal instruction, L1 influence and language exposure – on L2 speech perception. More specifically, and as hypothesized, the results have shown that the more advanced learners obtained significantly higher scores than the intermediate learners, which seems to indicate an effect of years of formal instruction (FI), in line with previous studies (Flege, Munro and Skelton 1992; Pérez-Vidal, Juan-Garau and Mora 2011; Saito and Hanzawa 2015). Moreover, despite the comparable VOT patterns in their L1s and the similar amount of exposure to the target language, the intermediate L2-English Portuguese group outperformed the intermediate L2-English Catalan group in both tasks, as predicted, and particularly in the identification of two new allophones, aspirated /t/ and /k/. These results are explained in light of the greater quality exposure to English that the Portuguese learners receive on a daily basis through television broadcasting. According to Tonoian (2014), the outside-classroom exposure to English is very high in Portugal, and Rubio and Lirola (2010) emphasize that this exposure entails positive effect for FL learning. Therefore, the differences found in the perceptual performance of Portuguese and Catalan intermediate learners of English seem to be explained mostly by differences in the quality of input.

These results taken together confirm that formal instruction (FI) plays a significant role in L2 speech perception. Moreover, the findings seem to indicate that not only quantity but also quality of L2 input in different L1 linguistic environments might influence non-native speech perception, and that L2 language experience promotes accurate L2 allophonic speech perception. According to the SLM (Flege 1995), the establishment of a new category is less likely to occur if the L2 sound is perceptually equivalent to an L1 sound, which we could argue is the case of the allophonic realization of the English voiceless plosives. Moreover, as previous studies have shown, the perception of an allophonic contrast tends to be more difficult than a phonemic contrast (e.g. Celata 2009). Therefore, the results of the present study revealed that the allophonic aspirated realizations of English /p, t, k/ seem to be, to some extent, difficult to distinguish perceptually from their unaspirated counterparts, particularly by the less advanced learners. However, in light of the results of the present study, we also suggest that the aspirated allophones were perceived as deviant phones by the advanced learners. Although both aspirated and unaspirated allophones may have been heard as exemplars of the same L1 category (/p, t, k/), the aspirated variants were perceived as different instances of the same L1 phonemes. This explains the overall better performance in the identification of the aspirated allophones. Furthermore, according to the predictions of the PAM-L2 (Best and Tyler 2007), new L2 categories are likely to be formed for the deviant phones. As shown by the better results of the advanced learners, it seems that the allophonic variants already coexisted in their interlanguage phonological system.

In sum, although L2 allophonic contrasts may pose some difficulty for L2 learners, our findings suggest that, given increased quantity and better quality of input, new categories are likely to be established for the non-native phones that are perceived as deviant realizations of L1 categories.

Limitations and future directions of study

The current study is not without limitations and these limitations suggest interesting directions for future research. Firstly, formal instruction was assessed by comparing a group of first-year majors and a group of second-year majors. Further investigation should be carried out with groups at more variable proficiency levels in order to provide a complete picture regarding the effect of formal instruction on the perception of non-native stop consonants.

Secondly, despite the similarities of the stop consonant inventories of the two populations tested, a difference in the quality of target language input seems to have arisen between the two groups, which influenced the outcome of the present study. Therefore, more controlled assessment of language proficiency (e.g. a vocabulary size test) and more extensive qualitative analysis on the type of input the learners are exposed to outside the classroom would be ideally administered in a future study. Having more fine-grained measures for each group could shed some light on some of the questions that remain unanswered. According to Aliaga-García and Mora (2009), formal instructional settings offer reliable measures of the quantity of input in the L2; however, controlling for input quality effects would require assessing qualitative speech data that is not normally available for analysis. The better results obtained by the Portuguese learners of English, when compared to the Catalan learners of English with the same amount of years of formal instruction and self-reported quantity of outside classroom exposure, should encourage further investigation on the quality of exposure to L2 linguistic input outside the classroom.

References

Aliaga-García, C. and Mora, J.C., 2009, 'Assessing the effects of phonetic training on L2 sound perception and production', in A.M.A. Watkins, A.S. Rauber and B.O. Baptista (eds.), *Recent research in second language phonetics/phonology: Perception and production*, pp. 2–31, Newcastle upon Tyne, UK: Cambridge Scholars Publishing.

Alves, U., Schwartzhaupt, B.M. and Baratz, A.H., 2011, 'Percepção e produção dos padrões de VOT do inglês (L2) por aprendizes brasileiros', *Estudos em Aquisição Fonológica* 4, 179–90.

Alves, U. and Zimmer, M., 2015, 'Perception and production of English VOT patterns by Brazilian learners – The role of multiple acoustic cues in a DST perspective', *Alfa* 59, 155–75.

Andrade, A., 1980, *Estudos experimentais aerodinâmicos, acústicos e palatográficos do vozeamento nas consoantes*, Lisbon: CLUL.

Beddor, P.S. and Gottfried, T.L., 1995, 'Methodological issues in cross-language speech perception research with adults', in W. Strange (ed.), *Speech perception and linguistic experience: Theoretical and methodological issues in cross-language speech research*, pp. 207–32, Timonium, MD: York Press.

Best, C., 1995, 'A direct realist view of cross-language speech perception', in W. Strange (ed.), *Speech perception and linguistic experience: Issues in cross-language research*, pp. 171–204, Timonium, MD: York Press.

Best, C.T. and Tyler, M.D., 2007, 'Nonnative and second-language speech perception: Commonalities and complementarities', in O.S. Bohn and M.J. Munro (eds.), *Language experience in second language speech learning: In honour of James Emil Flege*, pp. 13–34, Amsterdam: John Benjamins. https://doi.org/10.1075/lllt.17.07bes

Boomershine, A., Currie Hall, K., Hume, E. and Johnson, K., 2008, 'The influence of allophony vs. contrast on perception: The case of Spanish and English', in P. Avery, B. Dresher and K. Rice (eds.), *Contrast in phonology: Perception and acquisition*, pp. 145–71, Berlin: Mouton.

Celata, C., 2009, 'The impact of allophonic variation on L2 speech perception', in A.M.A. Watkins, A.S. Rauber and B.O. Baptista (eds.), *Recent research in second language phonetics/phonology: Perception and production*, pp. 64–80, Newcastle upon Tyne, UK: Cambridge Scholars Publishing.

Cho, T. and Ladefoged, P., 1999, 'Variation and universals in VOT: Evidence from 18 languages', *Journal of Phonetics* 27(2), 207–29. https://doi.org/10.1006/jpho.1999.0094

Cohen, G.V., 2004, *The VOT Dimension: a bi-directional experiment with English Brazilian Portuguese stops*, Master's thesis, Department of Languages, Federal University of Santa Catarina.

Flege, J.E., 1991, 'Age of learning affects the authenticity of voice-onset time (VOT) in stop consonants produced in a second language', *Journal of the Acoustical Society of America* 89(1), 395–411. https://doi.org/10.1121/1.400473

Flege, J.E., 1995, 'Second language speech learning: Theory, findings and problems', in W. Strange (ed.), *Speech perception and linguistic experience: Theoretical and methodological issues in cross-language speech research*, pp. 233–77, Timonium, MD: York Press.

Flege, J.E., 2003, 'Assessing constraints on second-language segmental production and perception', in A. Meyer and N. Schiller (eds.), *Phonetics and phonology in language comprehension and production: Differences and similarities*, pp. 319–55, Berlin: Mouton de Gruyter. https://doi.org/10.1515/9783110895094.319

Flege, J.E. and Eefting, W., 1988, 'Imitation of a VOT continuum by native speakers of English and Spanish: Evidence for phonetic category formation',

The Journal of the Acoustical Society of America 83(2), 729–40. https://doi.org/10.1121/1.396115

Flege, J.E., Munro, M.J. and Fox, R.A., 1994, 'Auditory and categorical effects on cross-language vowel perception', *The Journal of the Acoustical Society of America* 95(6), 3623–41. https://doi.org/10.1121/1.409931

Flege, J.E., Munro, M. and MacKay, I., 1995, 'Factors affecting strength of perceived foreign accent in a second language', *The Journal of the Acoustical Society of America* 97(5), 3125–34. https://doi.org/10.1121/1.413041

Flege, J.E., Munro, M.J. and Skelton, L., 1992, 'Production of the word-final English /t/–/d/ contrast by native speakers of English, Mandarin, and Spanish', *The Journal of the Acoustical Society of America* 92(1), 128–43. https://doi.org/10.1121/1.404278

Fullana, N. and MacKay, I.R., 2008, 'I said made (mate?): Catalan/Spanish bilinguals' production of English word-final obstruents', *Canadian Acoustics* 36(3), 118–19.

Fullana, N. and Mora, J.C., 2009, 'Production and perception of voicing contrasts in English word-final obstruents: Assessing the effects of experience and starting age', In M.A. Watkins, A.S. Rauber, and B.O. Baptista (eds.), *Recent research in second language phonetics/phonology: Perception and production*, pp. 97–117, Newcastle upon Tyne, UK: Cambridge Scholars Publishing.

García Lecumberri, M.L. and Gallardo del Puerto, F., 2003, 'English FL sounds in school learners of different ages', in M.P. García Mayo and M.L. García Lecumberri (eds.), *Age and the acquisition of English as a foreign language*, pp. 115–35, Clevedon, UK: Multilingual Matters.

Jamieson, D. and Morosan, D., 1986, 'Training non-native speech contrasts in adults: Acquisition of the English /ð/-/θ/contrast by francophones', *Perception and Psychophysics* 40(4), 205–15. https://doi.org/10.3758/BF03211500

Ladefoged, P., 1972, 'Phonological features and their phonetic correlates', *Journal of the International Phonetic Association* 2(01), 2–12. https://doi.org/10.1017/S0025100300000384

Lisker, L. and Abramson, A.S., 1964, 'A cross-language study of voicing in initial stops: Acoustical measurements', *Word* 20, 384–422. https://doi.org/10.1080/00437956.1964.11659830

Mora, J.C., 2008, 'Learning context effects on the acquisition of a second language phonology', in C. Pérez-Vidal, M. Juan-Garau and A. Bel (eds.), *A portrait of the young in the new multilingual Spain*, pp. 241–73, Clevedon, UK: Multilingual Matters.

Muñoz, C., 2008, 'Age-related differences in foreign language learning, Revisiting the empirical evidence', *IRAL-International Review of Applied Linguistics in Language Teaching* 46(3), 197–220.

Murcia, M.C., Brinton, D. and Goodwin, J., 1996, *Teaching pronunciation: A reference for teachers of English to speakers of other languages*, New York, NY: Cambridge University Press.

Pérez-Vidal, C. (ed.), 2014, *Language acquisition in study abroad and formal instruction contexts*, Amsterdam/Philadelphia: John Benjamins.

Pérez-Vidal, C., Juan-Garau, M. and Mora, J.C., 2011, 'The effects of formal instruction and study abroad contexts on foreign language development: The SALA project', In C. Sanz, and R.P. Leow (eds.), *Implicit and explicit conditions, processes and knowledge in SLA and bilingualism*, pp. 115–38, Washington, DC: Georgetown University Press.

Pisoni, D.B., 1982, 'Perception of speech: The human listener as a cognitive interface', *Speech Technology* 1(2), 10–23.

Rato, A., Rauber, A.S., Kluge, D.C. and Santos, G.R., 2015, 'Designing speech perception tasks with TP', in J.A. Mompean and J. Fouz-González (eds.), *Investigating English pronunciation: Trends and directions*, pp. 295–313, Basingstoke, UK/New York: Palgrave Macmillan. https://doi.org/10.1057/9781137509437_13

Reis, M. and Nobre-Oliveira, D., 2007. 'Effects of perceptual training on the identification and production of English voiceless plosives aspiration by Brazilian EFL learners', in A.S. Rauber, M.A. Watkins and B.O. Baptista (eds.), *Proceedings of the Fifth International Symposium on the Acquisition of Second Language Speech*, pp. 398–407, Florianópolis, Brazil: Federal University of Santa California, 2528, November 2007.

Rubio, F. and Lirola, M.M., 2010, 'English as a foreign language in the EU: Preliminary analysis of the difference in proficiency levels among the member states'. *European Journal of Language Policy* 2(1), 23–39. https://doi.org/10.3828/ejlp.2010.4

Saito, K., 2012, 'Effects of instruction on L2 pronunciation development: A synthesis of 15 quasi-experimental intervention studies', *TESOL Quarterly* 46, 842–54. https://doi.org/10.1002/tesq.67

Saito, K., 2015, 'Communicative focus on second language phonetic form: Teaching Japanese learners to perceive and produce English without explicit instruction', *Applied Psycholinguistics* 36(2), 377–409. https://doi.org/10.1017/S0142716413000271

Saito, K. and Hanzawa, K., 2015, 'Developing second language oral ability in foreign language classrooms: The role of the length and focus of instruction and individual differences', *Applied Psycholinguistics* 1(28), 1–28.

Schwartzhaupt, B., Alves, U. and Fontes, A., 2015, 'The role of L1 knowledge on L2 speech perception: Investigating how native speakers and Brazilian learners categorize different VOT patterns in English', *Revista de Estudos da Linguagem*, 311–34.

Selinker, L., 1972, 'Interlanguage', *IRAL-International Review of Applied Linguistics in Language Teaching* 10(1/4), 209–32. https://doi.org/10.1515/iral.1972.10.1-4.209

Tonoian, L., 2014, *English language learning inside and outside the classroom in Portugal*, PhD thesis, Department of Human Sciences, Nova Lisboa University.

Whalen, D.H., Best, C.T. and Irwin, J.R., 1997, 'Lexical effects in the perception and production of American English /p/ allophones', *Journal of Phonetics* 25(4), 501–28. https://doi.org/10.1006/jpho.1997.0058

Yavaş, M., 2016, *Applied English Phonology*, West Sussex, UK: Wiley-Blackwell.

Angélica Carlet holds a PhD in English philology, a Master's degree in second-language acquisition from the Universitat Autònoma de Barcelona (UAB) and a BA in English and Brazilian Portuguese studies from UNISINOS, Brazil. The influence of one's native language phonology in the acquisition of a second language constitutes the main area of her interest along with the effect of phonetic training for non-native speakers of English. She is currently lecturing and coordinating the English Minor degree at the faculty of Education at Universitat Internacional de Catalunya (UIC) in Barcelona, Spain.

Anabela Rato graduated in Portuguese and English Teaching (2004) at the University of Minho, Portugal. She also holds an MA in English Language, Literature and Culture (2009) and a PhD in Language Sciences (2014) from the University of Minho. She is currently an assistant professor at the Department of Spanish and Portuguese, University of Toronto, Canada. Her research interests include non-native speech perception and production, second-language acquisition, foreign language learning and applied phonetics.

9
The impact of production complexity in German L2 by French native speakers: Focus on /h/ and vowel duration contrast

Jane Wottawa, Martine Adda-Decker and Frédéric Isel

Introduction

Second-language learning represents a big part of education nowadays. In Europe, secondary school students have to clear at least one foreign language exam in order to get a high-school diploma. Learning two foreign languages is also common in continental Europe. Empowering young adults to express themselves in different languages encourages international exchanges and mobility. Moreover, today's affordable digital technologies such as smart phones and the internet enable easy instantaneous communication with remote partners all over the world. New opportunities continuously arise to practice our command of a foreign language not only on a written level, but more and more so in oral form.

In line with this observation, we decided to investigate production difficulties for German second-language (L2) learners with French as a first language (L1). We were interested in common production difficulties L1 French speakers have in German as a second language on a segmental level (e.g. vowel and consonant production) and on a supra-segmental level (e.g. lexical stress realization). In the following study, we focus on word-initial /h/ productions as well as on the vowel duration contrast. The German vowel duration contrast, often described as lax and tense vowel contrast on the phonological level, translates in differences of acoustic-phonetic properties (segment durations and vowel timbre) of the uttered vowels. Some of the German phonological vowels find a counterpart in the French language. For instance, /œ/-/ø/ – French: *neuf* /nœf/ 'nine' or *nœud* /nø/

'knot'; German: *können* /ˈkœnən/ 'to be able to' or *Söhne* /ˈzøːnə/ 'sons'; and /ɔ/-/o/ – French: *botte* /bɔt/ 'boot' or *beau* /bo/ 'pretty'; German: *sonne* /ˈzɔnə/ 'sun' or Sohn /ˈzoːn/ 'son'. Nevertheless, in German, the vowels do differ not only with respect to their quality but also with respect to their phonetic duration: lax vowels tend to be produced as short vowels, and tense vowels tend to be produced as long vowels (Becker 1998). In French, this additional distinction is not phonemic. Thus, we expected production difficulties regarding phonetic vowel duration in French learners of German. In what follows, we are going to pay special attention to the realization of the phonetic vowel duration in German L2 speakers with French as a first language.

Syllable-initial /h/ production

In the English as a Second Language (ESL) literature, L2 English productions of French learners have been analysed with respect to syllable-initial /h/ realizations (Janda and Auger 1992; John and Cardoso 2009; Kamiyama, Kühnert and Vaissière 2011). Janda and Auger (1992) studied syllable-initial /h/ realizations, deletions and insertions across different speech tasks for six learners of English with French as a first language. The authors discussed the results with respect to hypercorrection. John and Cardoso (2009) went a step further and analysed syllable-initial /h/ realizations, deletions and insertions with respect to the stress pattern of the syllable (stressed/unstressed), the word category (lexical word/function word) and the environment preceding the syllable initial /h/ (pause, vowel, consonant). Kamiyama, Kühnert and Vaissière (2011) were interested in /h/-deletions and their various realisations. They separated 'hard vowel onsets' from null or empty onsets. However, none of these papers compared syllable-initial /h/ duration between English native speakers and French learners of English. In German, one study carried out by Zimmerer and Trouvain (2015b) analysed French native speakers' productions of German words with syllable-initial /h/. The authors included both native speaker productions and non-native speaker productions in their dataset. They also analysed syllable-initial /h/ realizations with regard to the left context and segment duration. Findings showed that French learners of German tend to produce longer /h/ than native speakers.

Vowel duration contrast

Work on vowel duration contrasts often focuses on English as a foreign language where the vowel inventory includes vowels which differ both in duration and quality (Flege 1992; Flege, Bohn and Jang 1997; Levy 2015; Major 1987; Munro 1993). The study by Flege, Bohn and Jang (1997) especially showed that learners of English with different first languages tend to have comparable strategies in producing and perceiving L2 vowels. Specific production and perception difficulties, however, were directly related to the vowel inventory of their L1. German, just like English, also has vowels that differ in both duration and quality (Bennett 1968). Zimmerer and Trouvain (2015a) reported a perception study with German native listeners who judged long and short vowels produced in minimal pairs by French learners of German. They found that French learners of German have difficulties producing German vowels, and that these difficulties affect both short and long vowels, but especially short rounded vowels. The authors also reported that existing contrasts in the L1 (here French) such as /ø - œ/ are not always predictors for successful realizations in the L2 (here German).

Pronunciation difficulties that are related to conflicting orthographical conventions have not received a lot of attention in the literature. Dieling (1992) showed that Polish learners' phonetic errors in German can be conditioned by interferences from their L1 orthography. Rolffs (2003) reported that Turkish learners of German tend to produce German double consonants as geminates, like they would in Turkish. German and French orthographies also show differences in coding speech sounds. For instance, <z> is pronounced [ts] in German but [z] in French. In our study, production errors due to orthographic conventions in the languages were expected in the reading tasks.

Corpus studies can shed some light on how L2 pronunciation differs from L1 pronunciation. Most recorded corpora present elicited speech in the form of repeated and read speech, or semi-spontaneous assignments such as picture description and interviews (Detey, Racine and Kawaguchi 2011; Granger 2002; Meister and Meister 2015; Sönning 2014; Turco, Dimroth and Braun 2015). Non-scripted speech tasks that are closer to the challenges L2 speakers face outside the classroom are not very common.

Especially in German L2 pronunciation corpus research, studies are most often carried out on populations who share the same L1 (Lleó and Vogel 2004: L1 Spanish; Nossok 2007: L1 Belarusian; Zimmerer et al. 2014: L1 French). The advantage of homogeneous groups is that all the learners share the same phonemic system. As a consequence, each learner group has the same pronunciation difficulties in German, which restrains inter-speaker variation due to L1 background. In a pronunciation variety study as well as in a pronunciation class, student groups with a homogeneous L1 background permit a focus on pronunciation difficulties that are first-language specific. For example, if we compare French and English natives regarding German L2 pronunciation, French-specific problems with /h/-production are not at all relevant for English natives, whereas English natives may struggle to produce stable (i.e. non-diphthongized) vowels, which is not a problem for French native speakers.

We know that production and perception difficulties in a second language depend on the phonemic differences that exist between a speaker's first language and the second language he or she is learning (Best, McRoberts and Goodell 2001; Flege and Davidian 1984; Shoemaker 2014 etc.). For instance, the German language has a vowel duration contrast (e.g. Wiese 1996). That means that minimal pairs can be found that differ in meaning only by the change of vowel duration, e.g. *messt* /ˈmɛst/ 'you scale' or *mähst* /ˈmɛːst/ 'you mow'. The French language does not have a phonemic vowel duration contrast. Furthermore, the French language does not have a phonemic /h/ in its inventory whereas /h/ constitutes a frequent phoneme of the German language. According to Flege, MacKay and Meador (1999), L2 speakers have particular difficulties in producing phonemic contrasts in their L2 that they lack in their L1. With appropriate training, L2 learners should be able to produce those sounds and sound contrasts (Flege, Takagi and Mann 1995).

The present L2 production study includes three speech tasks with increasing production complexity: oral repetition, reading and picture description. We have recorded two corpora with comparable speaker populations (see the section on speech material).

Our study aims to investigate whether the production difficulties of L2 speakers depend on the complexity of the task. Regarding the vowel duration contrast, we are interested in whether the duration contrast production is more successful for some vowel pairs than others. Furthermore, we examine whether and how word-initial /h/ phonemes are realized across the three speech production tasks. We will also briefly discuss whether visual representations of speech (spectrograms) can help learners with their productions. First, we present an overview of the phonemic differences between German and French. Then, we present the speech materials followed by the methods and results sections of the study. Finally, the results will be summarized and discussed.

Differences between the phonemic systems of German and French

Here we present the major differences between the phonemic systems in French and German on a segmental level.

Vowels

In German, a vowel duration contrast: /iː-ɪ, ɛː-ɛ, eː-ɛ, aː-a, oː-ɔ, uː-ʊ, yː-ʏ, øː-œ/ exists that is not phonemic in French. In the German vowel inventory, only schwa /ə/ is an exception to the vowel duration contrast.

German also has three diphthongs: /aʊ̯/, /aɪ̯/ and /ɔʏ̯/, whereas there are no phonemic diphthongs in French. Standard German does not have any nasal vowels. Standard French counts three in its phonemic inventory: /œ̃/, /ɑ̃/ and /ɔ̃/.

Consonants

Regarding the consonantal system, the French consonants /ʒ/ and /ɲ/ appear in German in loan words only. The German consonant /ŋ/ does exist in French but only in English loan words (e.g. *parking*). German includes the following consonants that are not phonological in standard French: the word-initial /h/ fricative and the fricatives /ç/ *Ich-Laut* and /x/ *Ach-Laut* which tend to occur only in syllable and word-final positions.

In this study, we examine the vowel duration contrast, as well as the word-initial /h/ production in native and L2 German speech.

Speech material

In this section, the two speech resources that were used for the present study are presented. Both corpora were collected manually and follow an experimental design.

FLACGS

The *French Learners Audio Corpus of German Speech* (FLACGS corpus) was recorded to investigate differences between German speech in German native speakers and German L2 speakers with French as an L1 (Wottawa and Adda-Decker 2016).

All participants were recruited in Paris, France. Participation was on a voluntary basis. The recordings took approximately 45 minutes per participant.

French learners of German (FG)

Altogether 20 French learners of German, or FG (10 women and 10 men) were recorded. The women were aged between 20 and 30 years, the men between 24 and 32 (mean age of the FG group: 25.75 years). All FG as well as their parents had only French as their first language. They self-evaluated their competences in German based on the *Common European Framework of Reference for Languages* (CEFRL). In both gender groups, all levels were represented: A1/A2 up to C2. Furthermore, all participants had an equal or superior command of English, compared to their German proficiency.

German native speakers (GG)

Altogether 20 German native speakers, or GG (10 women and 10 men) were recorded. The women were aged between 22 and 47 years, the men between 20 and 45 (mean age of the GG group: 31.35 years). All GG as well as their parents had only German as their L1. Although the GG speakers were born in different parts of Germany, their productions can be rated as standard German, as there were no noticeable regional accents. Except for one female and one male participant who had no knowledge of the French language, all GG were highly proficient in French (B1/B2 up to C2+ according to the CEFRL). Their knowledge of English was equal or inferior to their proficiency in French. The great majority had lived in France for several years.

Tasks

The participants performed three tasks of increasing production complexity:

(1) Repetition task (audio): Participants heard short sentences over headphones, which they repeated immediately.

(2) Reading task (text): Participants read aloud the texts *Nordwind und Sonne* and *Die Buttergeschichte.*
(3) Picture description: The picture description task was the only task without linguistic information.

The *repetition task* aimed to investigate whether FG speakers are able to successfully produce lexical stress in different word positions, long and short vowel contrasts, as well as consonants and consonant clusters that are unusual or different in the French language. We defined a set of 55 German words illustrating the phenomena of interest.

Carrier sentences (*Er sagt ... klar und deutlich* and *Ich sage ... klar und deutlich*) including 55 distinct words in central position were recorded by a female native German speaker. The participants listened to all the spoken utterances in a randomized order over headphones and repeated them.

The material of the repetition task was composed of words with lexical stress in different positions (first syllable, last syllable, penultimate syllable and ante-penultimate syllable), minimal pairs with long and short vowels, e.g. *hüte* /ˈhyːtə/ 'hats' and *hütte* /ˈhʏtə/ 'hut', minimal pairs with a voiced or unvoiced plosive *glauben* /ˈglaʊ̯bən/ 'believe' and *klauben* /ˈklaʊ̯bən/ 'to cull'. Words that are difficult to pronounce because of their phonotactics for native French speakers: challenging consonants, clusters and glottal stops between vowels in adjacent syllables were included as well, e.g. *schächtelchen* /ˈʃɛçtəlçən/ 'small box' and *erobernde* /erˈʔoːbɛɐndə/ 'conquering'.

For the *reading task*, the participants were asked to read aloud two texts *Nordwind und Sonne* and *Die Buttergeschichte.* These two texts are reference material for German phonetics and have also been recorded in the Kiel corpus (Simpson, Kohler and Rettstadt 1997). Both languages, French and German, use the Latin alphabet. But the letters and letter combinations do not necessarily code the same sounds, e.g. *mantel* 'coat' is produced as [ˈmɑntl̩] by GG, while FG are more likely to say [mɑ̃ˈtɛl] as the letter combination <an> corresponds to a nasal vowel in written French. Conflicting orthographic conventions are possible sources of pronunciation difficulties (Dieling 1992). For instance the graphic <z> is pronounced /z/ in French but /ts/ in German. Another example is the graphic <au> which is pronounced as the vowel /o/ in French but as the diphthong /aʊ̯/ in German.

The aim of the reading task is twofold:

(i) check overall FG pronunciation difficulties, when reading;
(ii) focus on difficulties that may arise due to conflicting orthographic conventions between German and French.

Table 9.1. Summary of the FLACGS corpus.

NAME	*French Learners Audio Corpus of German Speech* (FLACGS)
LANGUAGE	German
SPEAKERS	40 speakers (20 male and 20 female) – 20 L1 German – 20 L1 French, L2 German (A2-C1/C2)
VOLUME	ca. 7 h of speech (35,250 words)
CONTENT	repeated, read and semi-spontaneous speech (picture description)
TRANSCRIPTION	manual using the German orthography
ALIGNMENT	MAUS-webservice (automatic) and manual checking

The reading task also allows us to compare prosodic patterns in different places of the utterance, e.g. to compare how word stress is realized in the beginning, the middle and the end of an utterance with respect to prosody.

The *description task* aimed to collect semi-spontaneous speech. All participants described the same picture. The picture that was chosen for the task showed a boy and a girl playing ball and running over a meadow. In the background, there was a house with flowers in the yard and some hills and mountains. We concentrated our analysis on isolated words like *haus* 'house', *mädchen* 'girl', *junge* 'boy' and *sonne* 'sun'. The image description is the only task where the participants did not have linguistic support (written sentences, spoken utterances) to help them with their speech production. Before the participants started the image description, we made sure they knew the names of the items and actions represented in the picture.

Table 9.1 summarizes the subset of FLACGS that is used to carry out the analyses.

ProFee-FLACGS

Study design

The *Progression and Feedback French Learners Audio Corpus of German Speech* (ProFee-FLACGS corpus) was recorded to investigate whether explicit pronunciation instruction helps German L2 learners to improve their German pronunciation.

Over a semester of 12 weeks, first-year university students majoring in English and German at *Université de Sorbonne Nouvelle – Paris 3* followed a stand-alone German pronunciation class. Two course sessions were occupied by written tests. The course programme included weekly speech assignments the students had to perform outside of the classroom. Four of these speech assignments were obligatory. For each sound file, the teacher filled out a feedback grid which was sent back to the students. A corrective feedback that was given after the actual recording was the least costly way to evaluate L2 pronunciation in a classroom setting (Olson 2014b). Research has also shown that feedback can help improve pronunciation (Olson 2014a).

German L2 learner groups

Participants were split up in two experimental groups: one whose teaching sessions were completed by spectrograms, and another group that was taught without this kind of visual illustration. In the following, the first group will be called AV (for audio and visual input) and the second group will be referred to as AO (for audio input only). The equipment of the classroom conditioned the choice, i.e. which group would obtain visual input and which one would only get audio input.

The AV group consisted of 15 participants (all female), who were between 17 and 23 years old, the AO group consisted of 15 participants (13 female and 2 male) who were between 17 and 19 years old. In the first class, participants self-evaluated their competence in German based on the *Common European Framework of Reference for Languages* (CEFRL). In both training groups, the following levels were represented: A2 up to C1/C2. In English, all participants indicated an equal or superior competence compared to their German level. In both training groups, all participants were French-dominant.

German native control group

The German native control group (referred to as CG in the following) consisted of 4 participants (3 female and 1 male) who were between 21 and 23 years old, and who attended the AO group. All participants in this group, as well as their parents had only German as L1. All native German speakers reported good knowledge of French (B1/B2 up to C1 according to the CEFRL). Their knowledge of English was rated equally high (B2 to C1). All of the CG had lived in France for at least one year before starting classes at university.

Even if the participants of the CG were born and raised in different regions of Germany, their productions could be considered as standard German, as none of them had a noticeable regional accent.

Students performed reading and picture description tasks over the semester. In this study, we will only consider the first picture description task students performed four weeks after classes began. This choice was made in order to increase the semi-spontaneous speech sample regarding word-initial /h/ and vowel duration contrast production.

Tasks

The tasks relevant for our investigations are picture description and reading. In this chapter, we focus on picture description only, which aimed to collect semi-spontaneous speech. All participants described the same picture to ensure a common vocabulary set in the collected speech. In the classroom, the teacher made sure that the students knew the names of the items and actions represented in the picture. This way, a common vocabulary set was also ensured. Table 9.2 summarizes the subset of the ProFee-FLACGS corpus that is used to carry out the analyses.

Table 9.2. Summary of the first semi-spontaneous speech task of ProFee-FLACGS.

NAME	*Progression and Feedback French Learners Audio Corpus of German Speech* (ProFee-FLACGS)
LANGUAGE	German
SPEAKERS	36 speakers (3 male and 33 female) – 4 L1 German – 32 L1 French, L2 German (A2-C1/C2)
VOLUME	ca. 1 h of speech (4,547 words)
CONTENT	semi-spontaneous speech (picture description)
TRANSCRIPTION	manual using the German orthography
ALIGNMENT	MAUS-webservice (automatic) and manual checking

The two speech resources can be explored in multiple ways. In this study, we focused on word-initial [h] productions and the acoustic vowel duration analyses.

Methods

Speech transcription and alignment

Firstly, an orthographic transcription of the recordings was made. For the repetition and reading task, the transcription consisted mainly in checking the recording for false starts or other deviations from the sentences (repetition task) and the texts (reading task). For the semi-spontaneous speech

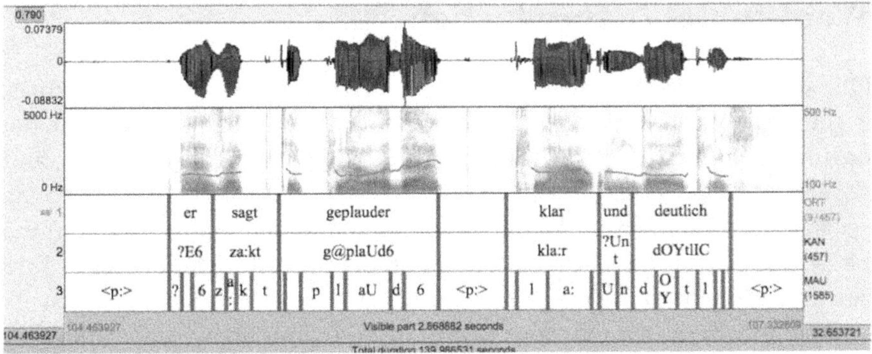

Figure 9.1. Example of the alignment generated with webMAUS.

part, a native German speaker made a faithful transcription of the recording manually. Secondly, the webMAUS (Munich AUtomatic Segmentation web service) (Kisler, Schiel and Sloetjes 2012; Schiel 1999) performed the alignment of the speech signal with its transcription. This aligner generates a TextGrid file that can be opened with Praat (Boersma and Weenink 2016).

MAUS uses orthographic transcriptions to segment the speech signal. The orthographic transcriptions were made manually and took hesitations, disfluencies and false starts into account. The TextGrids generated by MAUS comprise three tiers: the orthographic word, the canonical pronunciation of the word and the aligned phones (Figure 9.1).

The automatic alignment of each sound file was checked manually for boundaries and labelling. Phone boundaries of targeted phones and words were manually corrected if necessary. We also checked some aligned pronunciations, like for instance when MAUS had to perform a graph-to-phone conversion for words that were not included in its dictionary. Performing those adjustments took about 15 minutes for 1 minute of automatically aligned semi-spontaneous speech.

Statistical analyses

In the present study, we were interested in the duration of word-initial /h/ and short and long vowels in words with at least two syllables.

Statistical analyses were carried out with the R program (R Development Core Team 2008). As a statistical test, we privileged a two-way ANOVA with unequal sample sizes because of the high variance of tokens per task and per speaker in the semi-spontaneous speech tasks.

Word-initial /h/ production

One of the challenges faced by native French speakers learning German is the production of /h/. /h/ is frequent in the German language at the beginning of words or syllables and minimal pairs between /h/ and /ʔ/ are frequent: *haus* /ˈhaʊ̯s/ 'house' versus /ˈʔaʊ̯s/ 'out'. In French, the syllable-initial /h/ is not phonological. We mainly present results from the FLACGS corpus. In addition, we take the ProFee-FLACGS corpus into consideration for the semi-spontaneous speech part in order to increase its sample size. Semi-spontaneous speech productions show rather different results than repetition and reading.

In the FLACGS corpus, speech material from all three tasks (repetition, reading and picture description) was used to study:

(1) whether L2 German speakers (FG) produce /h/ in word beginnings or rather tend to replace them by empty onsets or [ʔ];
(2) whether FG produce /h/ with a similar duration compared to native German speakers' (GG) productions.

Regarding the type of realizations ([h], empty onsets, glottal stop), we expected native-like word-initial /h/ productions in the repetition task. Regarding the reading task, we expected longer [h] realizations in the FG group than in the GG group. This hypothesis is in line with the findings of Zimmerer and Trouvain (2015b) who also reported a high number of glottal stop realizations instead of [h] in L2 German speakers with French as a first language. The picture description task is supposed to be more difficult for L2 speakers. We thus expected both more /h/ omissions and longer segments when realized.

In order to decide whether the speaker produced [h], a glottal stop or an empty onset segment, a trained phonetician manually annotated the TextGrid files for /h/-productions. Figures 9.2, 9.3 and 9.4 illustrate how the decisions were made: if the spectrogram shows a noisy segment before a vowel, the speaker was recorded as having produced an [h] (see Figure 9.2); if the spectrogram shows a single (or sometimes multiple) bar right before the vowel as the result of a sudden air release, a [ʔ] was annotated (see Figure 9.3); if the word starts directly with a vowel that is not preceded by either the noisy portion or the bar on the spectrogram, an empty onset was marked (see Figure 9.4).

Table 9.3 displays all possible word-initial /h/ and its realizations by FG in the FLACGS corpus. First, we observe that word-initial /h/ production decreases with increasing complexity of the production task. The repetition task should have been the easiest task for L2 speakers, because they heard a

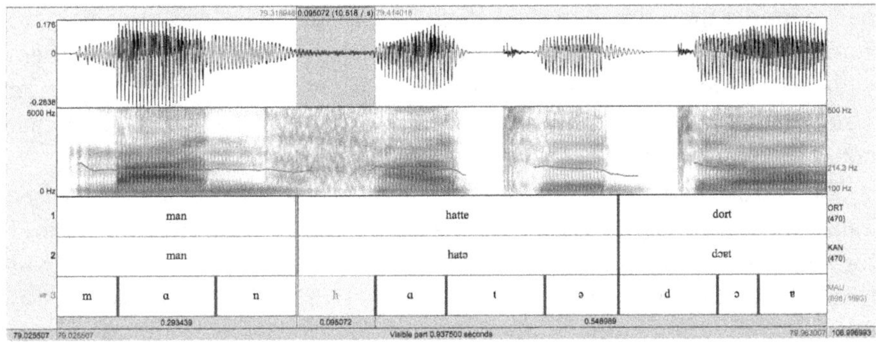

Figure 9.2. Transcription and alignment /h/-production: [h] (German L2 speaker).

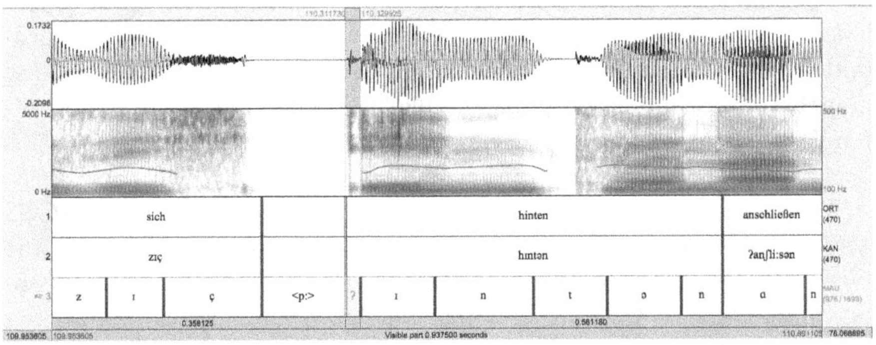

Figure 9.3. Transcription and alignment /h/-production: [ʔ] (German L2 speaker).

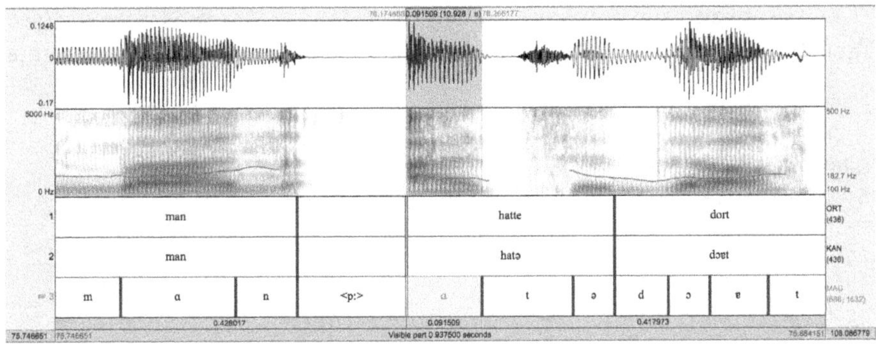

Figure 9.4. Transcription and alignment /h/-production: empty onset (German L2 speaker).

native model they aimed to reproduce. The reading task was already more complex, as participants did not have any auditory model to help them with their production. The most complex task was the picture description task. Participants were not provided with any linguistic information that could help them with their L2 speech production.

The results show that a surprisingly high number of word-initial /h/ (see Table 9.3) is actually produced by the FG group: at least three out of four for the most complex task, i.e. the picture description. Table 9.3 also shows that the production complexity of the task indeed has an impact on /h/ production accuracy: the highest number was obtained in the repetition task (85%) and the lowest in the picture description task. However, the difference of the canonically-uttered word-initial /h/ does not vary much between the reading (78%) and the picture description task (75%).

Furthermore, Table 9.3 confirms that word-initial /h/ is more likely to be replaced by empty onsets than glottal stops, except in the reading task where L2 German speakers produced one out of five instances of word-initial /h/ as a glottal stop. This result could be explained by conflicting grapheme-phoneme conventions between German and French. In written French, <h> are realized either as empty onsets or glottal stops. This decoding strategy might be transferred to texts written in German.

The numbers of /h/ realizations from the subset of the ProFee-FLACGS corpus are presented in Table 9.4. In order to assess improvement in the two learner groups, we compared productions of canonical /h/ in word beginnings after 4 weeks of training. The table summarizes the number of words with a canonical /h/ in the beginning and their realization in the three experimental groups: German native speaker control group (CG), the learner group in an audio-visual setting (AV) and the learner group with audio input only (AO).

We could observe that compared to the picture description task in the FLACGS corpus, the number of deletions and substitutions is very low (see Table 9.3). This result was most likely due to the fact that the participants

Table 9.3. Realizations of word beginning with /h/ in German L2 speakers across tasks in FLACGS.

Phone realization	*Repetition task*	*Reading task*	*Picture description*
[h] (canonical)	85%	78%	75%
[ʔ]	1%	20%	9%
empty	14%	2%	16%
Tokens	77	104	71

Table 9.4. Realization rates of word initial /h/ in ProFee-FLACGS.

	CG	*AV*	*AO*
Tokens	109	109	132
[h]	100 %	89 %	97 %
[ʔ] or empty	0%	11 %	3%

of the ProFee-FLACGS had already had four training sessions where their attention was drawn to substitution, insertion and deletion of segments in L2 German speech productions by native French speakers.

Both groups showed a very high number of canonical word-initial /h/ realizations. The rates reported in Table 9.4 are comparable or higher to those obtained for the repetition task in Table 9.3. These results suggest that increasing *awareness* is helpful for production accuracy with respect to the presence of the target phoneme in L2 speech.

Tables 9.3 and 9.4 do not inform us about the quantity of word-initial /h/ production of L2 German learners in comparison to native German speakers. /h/ is a fricative with very low energy. That is why we privileged a segment duration analysis rather than spectral analyses such as the centre of gravity or the intensity analyses of the segments.

The duration of word-initial /h/ production

Figure 9.5 shows the duration of [h] at the beginning of words in native German speakers (GG) and L2 German speakers (FG) in the FLACGS corpus. All words where [h] was produced in a different way (as [ʔ] or with an empty onset) were excluded from the plotted data in order to only compare actual [h] realizations of FG speakers to those uttered by the GG group.

In native German speakers, we observed that [h] is longer in the repetition task than in the other two tasks. This could be due to the prominent sentence position of the target words in the repetition task. In French learners of German, the prominent sentence position did not have the same effect on [h] durations compared to the other tasks.

We observed that in the repetition task, FG speakers behave native-like. The duration differences of [h] in word beginnings of the two groups were almost identical. Regarding the reading task, we saw that the difference between the duration of [h] in GG and FG speakers was more important: FG produce much longer [h] than GG. Regarding the picture description task, word initial /h/ produced by the FG group were globally longer than those produced by GG speakers.

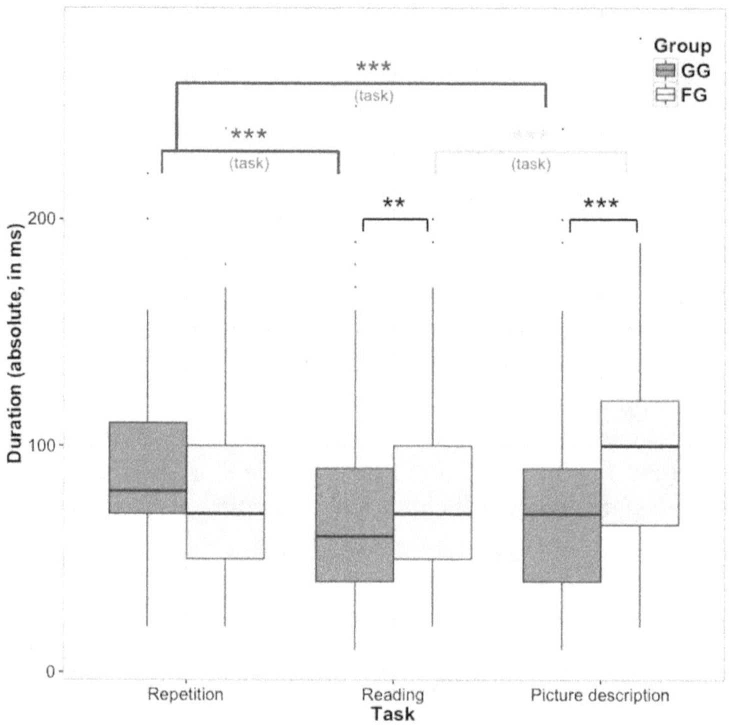

Figure 9.5. Duration of word-initial [h]: FLACGS.

To summarize Figure 9.5, French learners of German tend to produce longer [h] at the beginning of words than do German natives in reading and picture description. A possible explanation is that the French learners may aim to be unambiguous by insisting on the first segment of the word. These findings are in line with those reported by Zimmerer and Trouvain (2015b) for read speech.

Regarding the [h] production in a semi-spontaneous speech task, the ProFee-FLACGS corpus can give us some more insight. Compared to Figure 9.5, Figure 9.6 also shows the durations of [h] this time for the third experimental condition, i.e. the semi-spontaneous speech task. Figure 9.6 however contains overall more data points of uttered [h] in the two learner groups because the realization rates of canonical [h] productions were higher in this corpus subset than the FLACGS corpus with respect to the semi-spontaneous production task.

We observe that the duration of word-initial /h/ in both learner groups was significantly longer than in German native speakers. Two explanations could justify this result:

(1) increased awareness does not have an impact on the production accuracy, duration-wise;
(2) overall, the learner group produces longer fricatives than native German speakers.

The second possibility can easily be verified. We chose the fricative /f/ which is common to both languages and comparable to /h/. In Figure 9.7 the result of this analysis is plotted. Inferential statistics showed that duration differences between the AO learner group (mean: 80.98, sd: 45) and the native German speakers (mean: 72.45, sd: 35) are not significant. The AV group, however, produced longer [f] durations (mean: 96.24, sd: 54) than the other two speaker groups. This result can be explained by slower speech compared to the AO and CG groups. Nevertheless, Figure 9.7 indicates that L2 German speakers with French as an L1 do not generally produce longer fricatives than native German speakers, and that [h] production in L2 German speakers is different from L1 German speakers because they are not included in the French phonemic system. Thus, it seems to be the case such as suggested by Flege (1987) that /h/ is produced with familiar properties according to the L1 experience of the L2 German speakers.

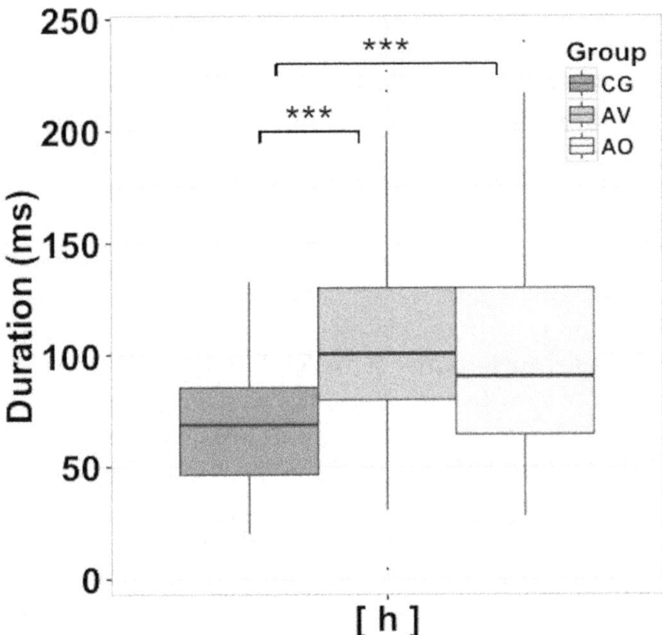

Figure 9.6. Duration of word-initial [h]: ProFee-FLACGS.

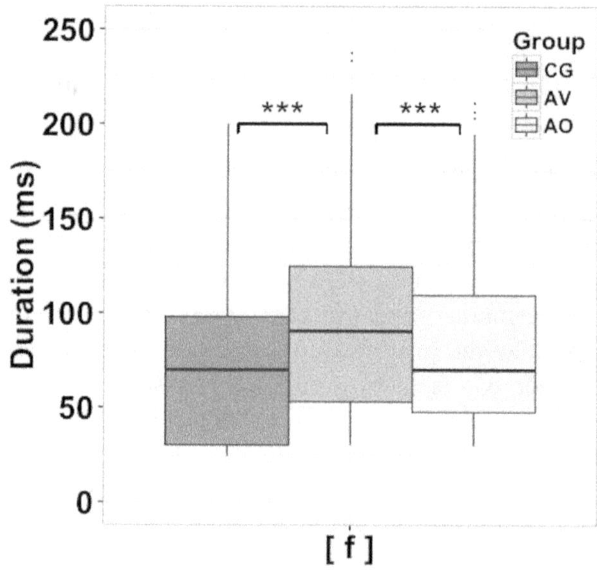

Figure 9.7. Duration of word-initial [f]: ProFee-FLACGS.

Vowel duration contrast

In French there is no vowel duration contrast such as in German. The vowel length contrast in German is not only a matter of duration but also a distinction between lax and tense vowels. Numerous minimal pairs can illustrate the phonological difference between those vowels: *lache* /ˈlaxə/ 'to laugh' versus *lache* /ˈlɑːxə/ 'puddle' and *bitte* /ˈbɪtə/ 'please' versus *biete* /ˈbiːtə/ 'to offer'.

Figure 9.8 illustrates the vowel duration contrast in native German speakers (GG). This figure was created with the data of the FLACGS corpus' repetition task. In this dataset, minimal pairs were presented that may be distinguished in terms of vowel duration. Figure 9.8 shows that in a controlled context (word repetition), native German speakers distinguished short and long vowels in terms of duration in minimal pairs. In a second step, we investigated whether this vowel duration contrast was also respected by L2 German learners with French as a native language.

Figures 9.9 and 9.10 illustrate the vowel duration contrasts in both the native German native speakers (in dark grey) and the L2 German speakers (in light grey). The figures show that both groups performed a vowel quantity contrast for the minimal pairs represented in Figure 9.9. This result suggests that L2 German speakers with French as an L1 are sensitive to

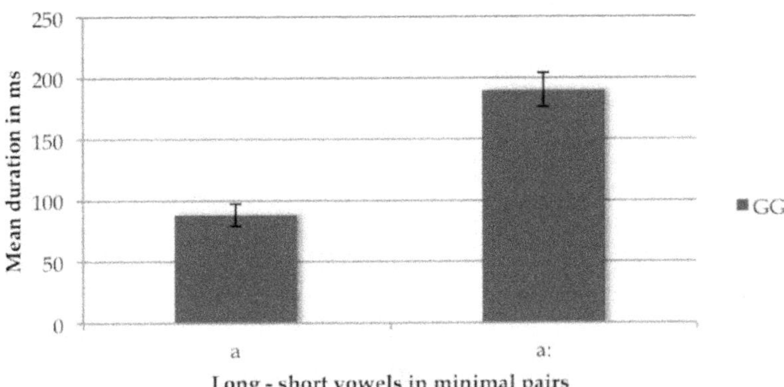

Figure 9.8. Vowel duration contrast in native German speakers.

vowel quantity and are able to reproduce this contrast that is not phonological in their native language.

Similar to the findings concerning word-initial /h/ (see the following section), L2 German learners behaved native-like when producing short and long vowels in the repetition task. As can be seen in Figure 9.9, vowel

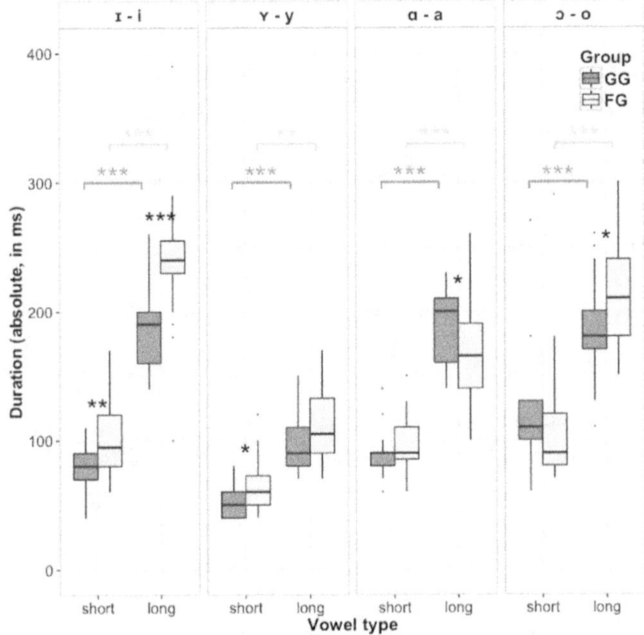

Figure 9.9. Vowel duration contrast: repetition task (FLACGS).

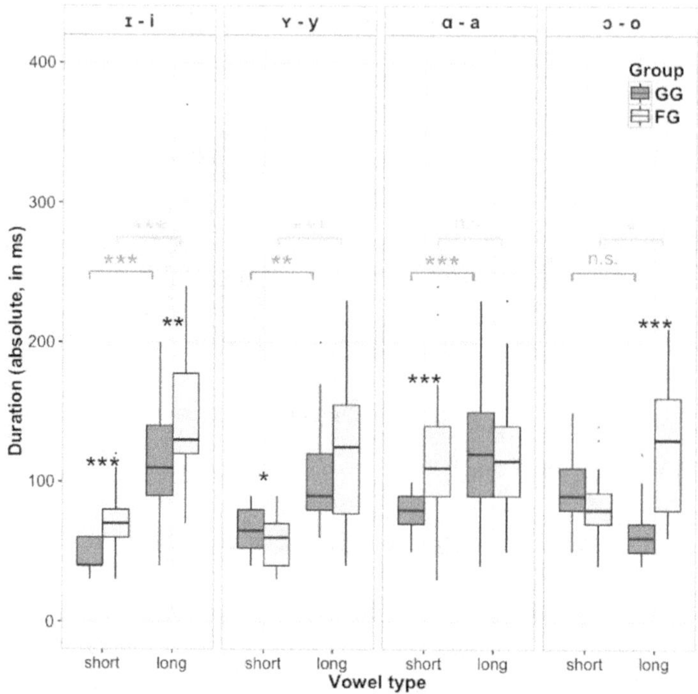

Figure 9.10. Vowel duration contrast: reading task (FLACGS).

duration values were almost the same in native German speakers and L2 German speakers. With respect to the reading task, slight differences could be observed between the German natives and the L2 German speakers, as illustrated in Figure 9.10. In particular for the short/long /a/-/a:/ vowel contrast, L2 German speakers tended to produce identical duration distributions while reading, which remained close to the duration distribution of the native German long /a:/ vowel. This suggests that French learners of German are not able to properly produce duration opposition in /a/ vs. /a:/ without any auditory input. It should be mentioned that the duration contrast /a/-/a:/ was well performed by the French learners of German in the repetition task, which shows that FG speakers are able to imitate the pattern in their oral productions. However, being able to reproduce vowel quantity patterns does not automatically entail that FG speakers have contrastive perception of vowel quantity. Especially for minimal pair production, a great number of participants reported that they thought they were repeating the same word.

In Figure 9.10, the /ɔ/-/ o:/ contrast plotted for the native German native speakers shows the following intriguing result: the short vowel [ɔ] is at least as long as its long vowel counterpart [o:] in the reading task. That might be a result of differences between canonical transcriptions of German words and their realization by native speakers, e.g. *schon* 'already' is transcribed as /ˈʃoːn/ (normative pronunciation) but often realized as [ˈʃɔn] (frequent variant). This may partly explain the observed results. Furthermore, we did not control for stress positions in the reading task, although sentence and word stress may have an impact on vowel duration.

The semi-spontaneous speech material (from the picture description task) collected in the FLACGS corpus did not allow us to carry out analyses on vowel pairs. In order to add some analyses of semi-spontaneous speech as well, target words from the ProFee-FLACGS corpus subset were carefully selected.

German is a language that has a lexical stress. This implies that not all syllables of a German word have an equal weight (Féry 1998): stressed syllables are unlikely to be reduced; they are longer and differ in fundamental frequency as compared to the other syllables of the word.

The selected material from the ProFee-FLACGS corpus were words with two or more syllables that are not function words and contain a short or a long vowel in the stressed word position. With these criteria, we made sure that the vowel duration was not compromised by segmental reductions that may appear in unstressed syllables (Kohler 1996). Furthermore, the short and long vowel distinction is most frequently made on stressed syllables in the German language.

In the ProFee-FLACGS corpus, we focused on four vowel pairs: /ɪ/-/iː/, /a/-/aː/, /ɔ/-/oː/ and /ʊ/-/uː/. As reported in Wottawa, Adda-Decker and Isel (2015), mid-front vowel pairs contrast more by vowel quality than by duration and were, hence, not considered here.

Table 9.5. Tokens of short and long vowels for each speaker group (ProFee-FLACGS).

Vowels	*4 weeks of training*		
	CG	*AV*	*AO*
[ɪ]	69	87	95
[iː]	68	118	83
[a]	75	100	93
[aː]	41	41	47
[ɔ]	46	22	23
[o]	33	40	34
[ʊ]	73	108	102
[uː]	12	22	21

Table 9.5 shows the number of tokens according to each speaker group and each target vowel. Even if the group of native German speakers (CG) counted fewer participants (only four) than the two learner groups, the number of tokens across the three speaker groups was fairly similar. Describing a picture in one's mother tongue requires less effort than in an L2. Thus, the speech productions of the CG group were more detailed and counted more variation regarding vocabulary and syntactic structures.

Figure 9.11 shows plots of the relative duration of the vowels (see the relevant part of the next section). From the top to the bottom, the vowel pairs /ɪ/-/iː/, /a/-/aː/, /ɔ/-/oː/ and /ʊ/-/uː/ are illustrated. In each box short vowels are plotted on the left and long vowels on the right-hand side.

Regarding the vowel duration contrast productions in semi-spontaneous speech (after 4 weeks of training in a stand-alone pronunciation class), we observed that the German control group (CG) showed significant duration differences of all four vowel pairs. Only for [a] and [aː], no significant difference in duration was found.

In the first learners group (AV: course material contained both audio and visual input), the duration difference between [ɪ] and [iː] is well marked; the

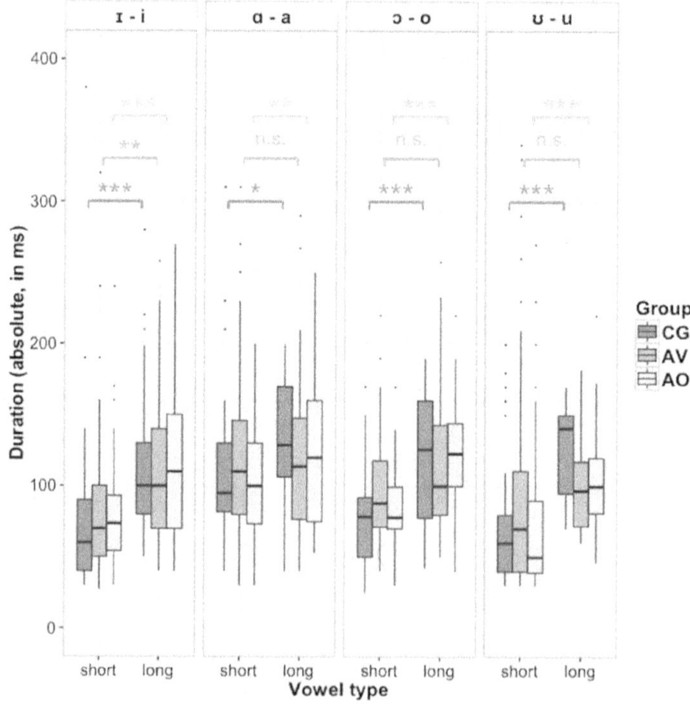

Figure 9.11. Vowel duration contrast: picture description (ProFee-FLACGS).

other three vowel pairs /ɑ/-/aː/, /ɔ/-/oː/ and /ʊ/-/uː/ did not show a duration difference for the AV group. However, the second learners group (AO: course material contained audio input only) marked the vowel quantity difference well for those three vowel pairs. This difference between the two learner groups suggests that the AO group behaves more native-like than the AV group. This group difference is probably due to speech competence differences within the groups.

With regard to the two other speech production tasks, it seems that the learners' performances in the semi-spontaneous task are comparable to those produced in the reading task. French learners of German realize vowel duration differences even in tasks without linguistic information. This successful production, however, seems to be linked to the proficiency speakers have in their L2.

Discussion

Evaluation of the chosen speech material

The *French Learners Audio Corpus of German Speech* (FLACGS corpus) recorded during 2014/15 presents three types of speech: repeated, read and semi-spontaneous speech by both German native and German L2 speakers.

The semi-spontaneous speech part had very heterogeneous outcomes: some L2 German speakers, especially those with a high linguistic competence level, were comfortable talking about the pictures for several minutes, while others, often those with a lower linguistic competence level (below B2), had to put much effort into realizing sentences that link the drawn objects and actions to one another. Hence, the speech material of the picture description task, although useful for studying /h/ realizations at word-initial position, cannot be straightforwardly used for studies such as the vowel duration contrast, because the collected speech material across all speakers is not rich enough.

Word-initial /h/ production

Overall, word-initial /h/ production seems to be less challenging than expected for French learners of German. This result stands in line with the findings of Flege and Hillenbrand (1984), who studied the production of French [u] and [y] in American native English speakers. The vowel /u/ exists in the vowel system of both languages, whereas the vowel [y] is part of the French vowel system only. The American native English speakers of the study achieved better native-likeness in producing the vowel [y] than [u], compared to native French speakers.

Our study included material from speech production, only. The data we obtained from the word repetition study alone did not inform us:

(1) whether participants did perceive the word initial /h/ and reproduced the word erroneously, or
(2) whether the word perception was erroneous and resulted in an erroneous production.

In order to investigate the link between perception and production, an additional perception study is necessary.

Across the three tasks, we could observe a clear distinction between the repetition task and the other two tasks. However, the difference of the canonically uttered word-initial /h/ did not vary much between the reading and the picture description task. In this line, it seems that the presence of auditory linguistic information helps most with word-initial /h/ production in matters of canonical production rates and segment duration.

Text (reading task) in comparison to no linguistic information (semi-spontaneous speech production) does not provide a considerable advantage to L2 German learners regarding word-initial /h/ production. We have to take into consideration that the French orthography also uses <h> in word beginnings, but the spoken words start with a vowel. Reading is a complex task especially in foreign languages. L2 readers are likely to mix up the contradictory orthographical conventions in order to assure fluent speech rate and a pleasant sentence intonation. Under this light, we might have to reconsider the complexity of the chosen speech production tasks and classify reading and semi-spontaneous speech tasks as equally difficult. The influence of both tasks is yet different: erroneous decoding due to contradictory orthographical conventions provokes different errors than semi-spontaneous speech (see Tables 9.3 and 9.4).

To summarize, German L2 speakers emphasize word-initial /h/ duration except when they are in a word repetition situation.

Vowel duration contrast

The vowel duration contrast production in L2 German speakers can be considered native-like for the repetition task.

Regarding the reading task, the L2 German learners with French as L1 realized vowel quantity surprisingly well. That could be due to orthographic cues. In German orthography short vowels are often followed by a double consonant, e.g. *sollte* /ˈsɔltə/ 'should'; and long vowels are often followed by a graphic <h> (*dehnungs-h*), e.g. *sohle* /ˈsoːlə/ 'sole'. Studies on the role of orthography in L2 learners, however, have shown that the information orthography provides is seldom used by L2 learners (Dieling 1983; Nimz 2016).

Our results showed the vowel duration contrast was realized for all examined vowel pairs except for the /a - aː/ contrast in the reading task. This result could suggest that French learners of German might only have one /a/-sound they can produce without any auditory input.

In the semi-spontaneous production task, we observed differences between the two learner groups, which were recorded for the ProFee-FLACGS corpus. The AO (audio input only) group seemed generally to constitute of more advanced L2 German learners than the AV (audio and visual input) group. That assumption could explain the differences in the vowel duration contrast for the vowel pairs /ɑ/-/aː/, /ɔ/-/oː/ and /ʊ/-/uː/. The AO group marked a statistically significant difference regarding vowel duration for these three pairs, whereas the AV group produced vowels with identical durations. The long vowels of the AV group for the pairs /ɑ/-/aː/, /ɔ/-/oː/ and /ʊ/-/uː/ shared the same duration distribution as the short vowels of the CG (native German control group).

A glimpse of the effects of increased awareness

The semi-spontaneous speech data extracted from the ProFee-FLACGS corpus gave us some insight on the effects of increased awareness in L2 German speech.

The results on word-initial /h/ and the vowel duration contrast production showed that increased awareness can help learners with their production rates of segmentals. In other words, both learner groups were less likely to replace or delete word-initial /h/ in their semi-spontaneous speech production compared to a population that was not particularly aware of pronunciation difficulties native French speakers might have in German.

However, production accuracy of target segmentals (word-initial /h/ and vowel durations) is not improved by increased awareness. French learners of both groups still produced statistically significant longer word-initial /h/ segments than the German native control group. The same trend can be observed in the vowel duration contrast. If awareness alone could help with the production accuracy, the AV (audio and visual input) group should perform better on the vowel pairs /ɑ/-/aː/, /ɔ/-/oː/ and /ʊ/-/uː/ than they do (see Figure 9.11).

Awareness has its limits regarding second-language pronunciation. Nevertheless, it does help learners to monitor their own speech productions more closely.

Conclusion and perspectives

In this chapter, we investigated the effect of task complexity on L2 German production in French natives. To this end, we recorded two speech corpora of French learners of German in three different tasks of increasing complexity: audio repetition, sentence reading and picture description.

The first corpus (FLACGS) totals an amount of 7 hours of German speech (20 French natives and 20 German natives, as control groups). The second corpus was collected as part of a stand-alone pronunciation class and results in a total of 4 hours from 36 speakers (32 French natives and 4 German natives). The presented results involved all the data of the first corpus and a 1 hour subset of the second corpus. All data were manually transcribed and automatically segmented using the WebMaus platform. As the study focused on the realizations of /h/ and vowel duration contrast, all these segments were manually checked for boundary accuracy. For word-initial /h/, the effective realizations were checked to decide between canonical [h], glottal stop or empty onset.

For /h/, we thus measured the respective realization rates of [h], [ʔ] and empty onset across the three tasks as well as the segment durations of realized [h].

For the vowels, we investigated whether the French natives were able to realize the vowel duration contrast by means of longer/shorter segment durations, as can be observed in German natives. In particular, we were interested in whether and how these durations vary across task complexity.

Our study reveals that L2 German speakers with French as a first language do not systematically replace word-initial /h/ by glottal stops or empty onsets. Interestingly, the results show that most of the word initial /h/ occurrences (87%) were well realized by the L2 German speakers in the auditory repetition task, and that their durations matched the [h] durations of the native German productions. Most of the other segments corresponded to empty onsets rather than to glottal stops. Rates of canonical [h] production in reading and picture description were smaller but still surprisingly high (at least 75%). In the picture description task, L2 German speakers tended to replace canonical word-initial [h] with empty onsets. In reading, however, L2 German speakers rather produced [ʔ] when /h/ was not realized, which could have been triggered by the orthographic representation of <h>. As expected, the word-initial [h] productions realized by the L2 German speakers were produced with longer segment durations in both the reading and the picture description task. As expected, increased *awareness* helps L2 German speakers with their canonical [h] productions. We observed fewer substitutions of word-initial /h/ in L2 German speakers in the picture description in the speech data of the second corpus, where the subjects were specifically trained towards correcting this pronunciation difficulty. Segment durations, however, are still longer for [h] in L2 German speakers than native German speakers after 4 weeks in a standalone German pronunciation class.

Regarding the vowel duration contrast, the results of the repetition task showed again that L2 German speakers were able to behave native-like in this task. The vowel duration contrast in minimal pairs was well separated for all the examined vowel pairs. This trend was also observed in the reading task. Only the /ɑ-aː/ contrast was not marked by an acoustic duration difference in L2 German speakers. While describing a picture, one of the two L2 German speaker groups was able to mark the vowel duration contrast, whereas the other group only marked duration differences for the /ɪ-iː/ contrast. These results are probably due to a lack in population homogeneity with regard to L2 proficiency. Hence, in order to better assess L2 speakers' progression over time, an examination of vowel quality could add more salient information than vowel duration only.

Overall, our work confirms that L2 production difficulties are linked to the task complexity, best pronunciation results being achieved for the audio repetition task. These results may then degrade when moving towards more complex production tasks, such as reading where conflicting grapheme-to-phoneme rules (as for <h>, which is mute in French and a fricative segment in German) may introduce specific difficulties, or for picture description where the speaker is the author of the produced message. Audio and visual feedback to the learners was globally judged as a welcome addition although it did not translate into a clear pronunciation benefit. Further studies are required to disentangle this question.

Acknowledgements

This work was made possible through a Sorbonne Nouvelle University PhD funding to the first author. It was also supported by the French Investissements d'Avenir – Labex EFL program (ANR-10-LABX-0083).

References

Becker, T., 1998, *Das Vokalsystem der deutschen Standardsprache*, Frankfurt am main: Peter Lang.

Bennett, D., 1968, 'Spectral form and duration as cues in the recognition of English and German vowels', *Language and Speech* 11, 64–85.

Best, C.T., McRoberts, G.W. and Goodell, E., 2001, 'Discrimination of non-native consonant contrasts varying in perceptual assimilation to the listener's native phonological system', *The Journal of the Acoustical Society of America* 109(2), 775–94. https://doi.org/10.1121/1.1332378

Boersma, P. and Weenink, D., 2016, *Praat: Doing phonetics by computer [Computer program]*, Version 6.0.15, http://www.praat.org/, retrieved March 23, 2016.

Detey, S., Racine, I. and Kawaguchi, Y., 2011, 'Assessing non-native speakers' production of French nasal vowels: A multitask-corpus-based study', *Working Papers in Corpus-based Linguistics and Language Education* 5, 277–93.

Dieling, H., 1983, *Zur Perzeption und Produktion von Vokalen im Fremdsprachenunterricht Deutsch (Anfänger)*, dissertation, Universität Halle-Wittenberg, Halle.

Dieling, H., 1992, *Phonetik im Fremdsprachenunterricht Deutsch*, Berlin and Munich: Langenscheidt Publishers.

Féry, C., 1998. 'German word stress in optimality theory', *The Journal of Comparative Germanic Linguistics* 2(2), 101–42. https://doi.org/10.1023/A:1009883701003

Flege, J.E., 1987, 'The production of "new" and "similar" phones in a foreign language: Evidence for the effect of equivalence classification', *Journal of Phonetics* 15(1), 47–65.

Flege, J.,1992, 'The Intelligibility of English vowels spoken by British and Dutch talkers', in R. Kent (ed.), *Intelligibility in speech disorders: Theory, measurement, and management*, pp. 157–232, Amsterdam: John Benjamins. https://doi.org/10.1075/sspcl.1.06fle

Flege, J.E., Bohn, O.S. and Jang, S., 1997, 'Effects of experience on non-native speakers' production and perception of English vowels', *Journal of Phonetics* 25(4), 437–70. https://doi.org/10.1006/jpho.1997.0052

Flege, J.E. and Davidian, R.D., 1984, 'Transfer and developmental processes in adult foreign language speech production', *Applied Psycholinguistics* 5(4), 323–47. https://doi.org/10.1017/S014271640000521X

Flege, J.E. and Hillenbrand, J.,1984, 'Limits on phonetic accuracy in foreign language speech production', *The Journal of the Acoustical Society of America* 76(3), 708–21. https://doi.org/10.1121/1.391257

Flege, J.E., MacKay, I.R. and Meador, D., 1999, 'Native Italian speakers' perception and production of English vowels', *The Journal of the Acoustical Society of America* 106(5), 2973–87. https://doi.org/10.1121/1.428116

Flege, J.E., Takagi N. and Mann V., 1995, 'Japanese adults can learn to produce English /ɹ/ and /l/ accurately', *Language and Speech* 38(1), 25–55.

Granger, S., 2002, 'A bird's-eye view of learner corpus research', in S. Granger, J. Hung, S. Petch-Tyson, S. (eds.), *Computer learner corpora, second language acquisition and foreign language teaching*, pp. 3–33, Amsterdam and Philadelphia: John Benjamins. https://doi.org/10.1075/lllt.6.04gra

Janda, R.D. and Auger, J., 1992, 'Quantitative evidence, qualitative hypercorrection, sociolinguistic variables – and French speakers' 'EADHACHES with English h/Ø', *Language and Communication* 12, 195–236. https://doi.org/10.1016/0271-5309(92)90015-2

John, P. and Cardoso, W., 2009, 'Francophone ESL learners' difficulties with English /h/', in M.A. Watkins, A.S. Rauber and B.O. Baptista (eds.), *Recent research in second language phonetics/phonology: Perception and production*, pp. 118–40, Newcastle, UK: Cambridge Scholars.

Kamiyama, T., Kühnert, B. and Vaissière, J., 2011, 'Do French-speaking learners simply omit the English /h/?', *Proceedings of the 17th International Conference on Phonetic Sciences*, pp. 1010–13, Hong Kong.

Kisler, T., Schiel F. and Sloetjes H., 2012, 'Signal processing via web services: The use case WebMAUS', *Digital Humanities Conference 2012.*

Kohler, K.J., 1996, 'Articulatory reduction in German spontaneous speech', *Proceedings of the 1st ESCA Tutorial and Research Workshop on Speech Production Modelling and 4th Speech Production Seminar*, pp. 1–4, Autrans: France.

Levy, H., 2015, 'Perception and production of vowel contrasts in German learners of English', in *Interspeech 2015*, ISCA, pp. 796–800.

Lleo, C. and Vogel, I. 2004, 'Learning new segments and reducing domains in German L2 phonology: The role of the prosodic hierarchy', *International Journal of Bilingualism* 8(1), 79–102. https://doi.org/10.1177/13670069040080010601

Major, R.,1987, 'Phonological similarity, markedness, and rate of L2 acquisition', *Studies in Second Language Acquisition* 9, 63–82. https://doi.org/10.1017/S0272263100006513

Meister, E. and Meister, L., 2015, 'Development and use of the Estonian L2 corpus', *Book of extended abstracts: Workshop on phonetic learner corpora*, pp. 45–47, satellite workshop of the 18th International Congress of Phonetic Sciences, Glasgow.

Munro, M., 1993, 'Production of English vowels by native speakers of Arabic: Acoustic measurements andaccentedness ratings', *Language and Speech* 36, 39–66.

Nimz, K., 2016, *Sound perception and production in a foreign language: Does orthography matter?*, PhD thesis, Humboldt Universität zu Berlin, Berlin.

Nossok, S., 2007, 'Ausspracheprobleme weißrussischer Deutschlernender und Schritte zur korrekten Aussprache', *Zeitschrift für Interkulturellen Fremdsprachenunterricht* 12(2).

Olson, D.J., 2014a, 'Benefits of visual feedback on segmental production in the L2 classroom', *Language Learning and Technology* 18(3), 173–92.

Olson, D.J., 2014b, 'Phonetics and technology in the classroom: A practical approach to using speech analysis software in second-language pronunciation instruction', *Hispania* 97(1), 47–68. https://doi.org/10.1353/hpn.2014.0030

R Development Core Team, 2008, *R: A Language and Environment for Statistical Computing*, ISBN 3-900051-07-0, Vienna, Austria: R Foundation for Statistical Computing, http://www.R-project.org.

Rolffs, S., 2003, 'Türkisch.', *Hirschfeld, Ursula/Kelz, Heinrich P./Müller, Ursula (Hg.) Phonetik International. Von Afrikaans bis Zulu. Kontrastive Studien für Deutsch als Fremdsprache. Waldsteinberg: Popp* (online: http://www. phonetik-international. de/letztes Sichtungsdatum 01.10. 2009).

Schiel, F., 1999, 'Automatic phonetic transcription of non-prompted speech', *Proceedings of the International Congress of Phonetic Sciences*, pp. 607–10, San Francisco, USA.

Shoemaker, E., 2014, 'The exploitation of subphonemic acoustic detail in L2 speech segmentation', *Studies in Second Language Acquisition* 36(4), 709–31. https://doi.org/10.1017/S027226311400014X

Simpson, A.P., Kohler, K.J. and Rettstadt, T. (eds.), 1997, *The Kiel corpus of read/spontaneous speech: Acoustic database, processing tools, and analysis results*, Kiel: IPDS.

Sönning, L., 2014, 'Unstressed vowels in German learner English: An instrumental study', *Research in Language* 12(2), 163–73. https://doi.org/10.2478/rela-2014-0001

Turco, G., Dimroth, C. and Braun, B., 2015, 'Prosodic and lexical marking of contrast in L2 Italian', *Second Language Research* 31(4), 465–91. https://doi.org/10.1177/0267658315579537

Wiese, R., 1996, *The Phonology of German*, Oxford: Oxford University Press.

Wottawa, J. and Adda-Decker M., 2016, 'French learners audio corpus of German speech (FLACGS)', *Proceedings of the 10th International Conference on Language Resources and Evaluation (LREC'16)*, pp. 3215–19, Portorož, Slovenia.

Wottawa, J., Adda-Decker, M. and Isel, F., 2015, 'Segmental difficulties in French learners of German', in E. Babatsouli and D. Ingram (eds.), *Proceedings of the International Symposium on Monolingual and Bilingual Speech 2015*, pp. 421–29, ISBN: 978-618-82351-0-6, retrieved from http://ismbs.eu/publications.

Zimmerer, F., Jügler, J., Andreeva, B., Möbius, B. and Trouvain, J., 2014, 'Too cautious to vary more? A comparison of pitch variation in native and non-native productions of French and German speakers', *Proceedings of Speech Prosody* 7, 1037–41, Dublin, Ireland.

Zimmerer, F. and Trouvain, J., 2015a, 'Perception of French speakers' German vowels', *Interspeech 2015*, pp. 1720–24, Dresden, Germany.

Zimmerer, F. and Trouvain, J., 2015b, 'Productions of /h/ in German: French vs. German speakers', *Interspeech 2015*, pp. 1922–26, Dresden, Germany.

Jane Wottawa is a certified high-school German teacher in France. Since 2014, she has been a PhD candidate at University Sorbonne Nouvelle – Paris 3 in the Laboratory of Phonetics and Phonology (LPP, UMR 7018). Her research interests are centred on foreign language learning with a special focus on speech production and perception. Her research is based on acoustic and phonetic analyses in L2 speech production as well as behavioural and neuroimaging methods in speech perception.

Martine Adda-Decker holds a MD in Applied Mathematics and a PhD in Computer Science from University Paris-Sud (Orsay) France. She has been a CNRS researcher since 1990. In 2010, she joined the Laboratory of Phonetics and Phonology (LPP, UMR 7018), her previous position was with the Spoken Language Processing group at LIMSI (UPR 3251), where she remains an associate researcher. Her research interests extend to man-machine communication, language and accent identification, multilingual speech recognition, acoustic-phonetic and lexical modelling, pronunciation variants, corpus phonetics, phonology and corpus-based studies. She has authored or co-authored over 150 peer-reviewed articles in the field, and regularly reviews papers for major Speech-related journals and conferences.

Frédéric Isel is Professor of Psycholinguistics at the University Paris Lumières – Paris Ouest Nanterre La Défense in France. His research is centred on the study of the neurodynamics of language processes involved in both word recognition and sentence comprehension. In particular, he investigates the role of linguistic prosody in lexical acess and parsing. He also studies second-language acquisition (SLA) and examines the link between language use and language control. His research employs both behavioural and neuroimaging methods.

10
The acquisition of second dialect speech: An acoustic examination of the production of Ecuadorian Spanish assibilated rhotics by Andalusian speakers of Spanish

Esparanza Ruiz-Peña, Diego Sevilla and Yasaman Rafat

Introduction

Despite the growing interest in second dialect (D2) speech acquisition (e.g. Babel 2009; Nielsen 2011), little is known about whether the same mechanisms that underlie second-language (L2) acquisition are also at work in D2 speech acquisition. While several models of L2 speech acquisition have been proposed (Best and Tyler 2007; Brown 1998; Colantoni and Steele 2007, 2008; Flege 1995), there is not much evidence that these models are also appropriate for D2 speech acquisition. Moreover, the disagreement on whether proximity/similarity makes a D2 more or less acquirable has not yet been resolved (e.g. Escure 1997; Siegel 2010). While some researchers believe that similarity between a first dialect (D1) and a D2 would make learning a D2 easier than learning an L2, others believe that similarity would actually be a hindrance. This study has three aims.

The first goal of the study is to test whether equivalence classification (Flege 1995) operates in the same way in D2 speech acquisition as in L2 speech acquisition. Flege's Speech Learning Model (SLM; ibid.) predicts that the smaller the acoustic-phonetic distance between the first language (L1) and the target language (TL) sounds, the higher the possibility of equivalence classification, i.e. mapping the TL sound on to the L1 sound. This hypothesis has also been formulated to say that 'old' sounds are not problematic for L2 learners, those that are 'new' will eventually be acquired by L2 learners, and those that are 'similar' would be mapped on to an existing L1 phonetic category, and they will be most difficult to acquire. The acoustic-phonetic distance between the L1 and the TL defines how L2 sounds may be mapped on to pre-existing L1 categories.

In this study, we will explore this hypothesis with respect to D2 acquisition of assibilated rhotics by determining whether assibilated rhotic production by Andalusian Spanish speakers pattern with English speakers' productions previously reported in Rafat (2015). Assibilated rhotics are rather interesting from an acoustic point of view. They cause difficulty for L2 learners because they are *r-like* sounds that also exhibit assibilation – a common variant of the trill in several varieties of Spanish (e.g. Bradley 1999; Colantoni 2001, 2006; Colantoni and Rafat 2013; Harris 1969; Lipski 1994; Quilis 1999). Though they characterize some varieties of Ecuadorian Spanish, they are not typically reported as a feature of Andalusian Spanish.

The second goal of this study is to determine whether knowledge of the target words affects D2 production. Therefore, the study includes an imitation task based on real words in Spanish and another based on nonce words that conform to Spanish phonotactics and phonological rules.

The third goal of this study is to determine if the social factor gender plays a role in the production of assibilated rhotics by Andalusian speakers. A number of studies such as Shockey (1984), Bortoni-Ricardo (1985), Foreman (2003), MacLeod (2012) and Rys (2007) among others have considered the role of gender in D2 imitation. However, the findings are inconclusive. Here, we will compare assibilated rhotic production by males and females in order to further investigate this effect.

Ecuadorian, Andalusian and English rhotics

While the tap (e.g. <caro> ['ka.ɾo]) and the trill (e.g. <perro> ['pe.ro]) are the two rhotic phonemes in Spanish, these phonemes can have other realizations. The assibilated rhotics in Spanish are characterized as a kind of strident fricative (e.g. Bradley 1999; Colantoni 2001, 2006; Colantoni and Rafat 2013; Harris 1969; Lipski 1994; Quilis 1999; Rissel 1989; Vásquez-Carranza 2006; Widdison 1998) and exist in several varieties of Spanish (e.g. Bradley 1999; Colantoni 2001, 2006; Colantoni and Rafat 2013; Harris 1969; Lipski 1994; Navarro Tomás 1980; Quilis 1999; Rissel 1989; Vásquez Carranza 2006; Widdison 1998) including Ecuadorian Spanish (e.g. Bradley 1999). While assibilated rhotics exist in a number of varieties of Spanish, the degree of assibilation may range from one variety to another (e.g. Lipski

1994). Moreover, the degree of assibilation may vary from token to token within an individual speaker (e.g. Rafat 2015).

Assibilated rhotics have been associated with sociolinguistic variables such as age, gender and social class (e.g. Adams 2002; Chela-Flores and Chela-Flores 2002; Gómez 2003; Matus-Mendoza 2004; Rissel 1989). For example, while Rissel (1989) reports that assibilated rhotics are the prestigious variants of rhotics in Mexico City, assibilation is stigmatized in other regions such as in Costa Rica (e.g. Adams 2002). In Ecuador, assibilated rhotics typically characterize the highlands (e.g. Sierra region). Within the Sierra region, they may be more abundant in some cities (Ambato or Riobamba) in comparison with others (e.g. Quito). They are stigmatized, in particular, by the educated upper-class people in the capital. They might also be considered *bad Spanish*, often associated with the speech of indigenous people. From an acoustic point of view, they are heavily assibilated.

Andalusian Spanish, on the other hand, is mainly characterized by a trill and a tap and their reduced forms (e.g. Blecua 2001). Moreover, Andalusian Spanish is generally characterized by a weakened articulation (e.g. Hualde 2005), and it includes sibilants such as [ʃ] as an allophonic variant of the fricatives such as [ʧ] (e.g. Carbonero 2001; Jiménez 1999). Neither English nor Andalusian Spanish have been reported to have an assibilated rhotic. Furthermore, whereas Spanish has two phonemes, namely the tap and the trill, English has an approximant phoneme with retroflexed and bunched variants (e.g. Delattre and Freeman 1968; Westbury, Hashi and Lindstrom 1999; Zhou et al. 2008).

The L2 production of assibilated rhotics

Rhotics have been categorized, in general, as difficult sounds for both L1 (Bosch 1983; Carballo and Mendoza 2000; Jiménez 1987) and L2 learners (Colantoni and Steele 2007, 2008; Face 2006; Major 1986; Rafat 2008; Reeder 1998; Waltmunson 2005). Moreover, the unity of rhotics as a class is questionable and they have often been reported to alternate with fricatives (Solé 1992, 1998, 2002). The fact that they have been diachronically grouped into the rhotic class has been attributed to their orthographic representation, such as the letter <r> by Maddieson and Ladefoged (1996). Because of their varied acoustic nature, assibilated/fricative rhotics provide an excellent opportunity for comparing equivalence classification in D2 and L2 acquisition. Assibilated/fricative rhotics have been compared to palato-alveolar sibilants because of their articulatory and acoustic similarity (Colantoni 2006; Hall 1997; Maddieson 1984; Solé 2002). On the other hand, they have traditionally been classified as rhotics (Maddieson and Ladefoged 1996; Quilis and Carril 1971). More recently, the data from Rafat (2015) has suggested that they might acoustically exhibit both assibilation and rhoticity. Because of their dual nature, it is likely that they might be categorized by learners as either a sibilant or a rhotic depending on the characteristics of the first language (ibid.) and/or first dialect.

Rafat (2015) studied the production of Mexican Spanish assibilated rhotics by native English speakers in auditory-only and auditory-orthographic conditions. The participants were presented with three words, one at a time, during training. In both conditions, the auditory input (spoken word) was accompanied by its corresponding image. In the auditory-orthographic condition, the participants were also presented with the written version of each word. The production/testing phase immediately followed the training phase, where the participants were tested on the same triplet that they had been presented with, word-by-word. During testing, the participants in the auditory-only condition were only presented with the images, but in the auditory-orthographic condition the participants were presented with both the images and the written words. The results showed two diverging patterns of production. In the auditory-only condition, in comparison with the auditory-orthographic condition, the participants exhibited a significantly higher rate of sibilant production, in particular /ʃ/ production (36.84% vs. 1.36%, respectively). In the auditory-orthographic condition, compared to the auditory condition, the participants produced a significantly higher rate of assibilated rhotics (23.13% vs. 0% respectively) and other rhotics (42.86% vs. 9.65%, respectively). In other words, rhotics were, for the most part, mapped on to sibilants in the auditory input, but they were mostly mapped on to rhotics in the auditory-orthographic input. Furthermore, a higher degree of assibilation in the rhotics resulted in a higher rate of assibilated rhotic production in the auditory-orthographic condition.

Rafat (2015) explained the results by proposing that rhoticity is the less salient feature of assibilated rhotics and exposure to the grapheme <r> together with the degree of assibilation modulate the rate of L2 assibilated rhotic production. Specifically, exposure to <r> makes the less salient feature of assibilated rhotics in the input more salient. Depending on the degree of assibilation in the input, exposure to <r> may either result in a higher rate of assibilated rhotic production in the participants, or it may result in transfer effects overriding the input, yielding a higher rate of English approximant rhotic production. In the current study, we will compare the D2 production of assibilated rhotics by Andalusian speakers with those reported in Rafat (2015).

Effect of extra-linguistic factors on D2 acquisition

The effects of several extra-linguistic factors such as age of acquisition (e.g. Bortoni-Ricardo 1985; Tagliomente and Molfenter 2007; Trudgill 1981), length of residence (e.g. Kerswill 1994; Tagliomente and Molfenter 2007; Trudgill 1981), social identity (e.g. Foreman 2003; Ivars 1994; Omdal 1994), degree of interaction in the context with other D2 speakers (Bortoni-Ricardo 1985; Tagliomente and Molfenter 2007), motivation and attitude (Kerswill 1994; Omdal 1994), and occupation (Bortoni-Ricardo 1985; Ivars 1994; Kerswill 1994; Noulijärvi 1994) have been studied in D2 acquisition. However, there is not much consensus in the literature with regard to the potential effects of many of these factors. Similarly to L2 studies, one of the most studied factors is age of acquisition (e.g. Berthele 2002; Bortoni-Ricardo 1985; Chambers 1992; Foreman 2003; Ivars, 1994; Kerswill 1994; Omdal 1994; Payne 1976; Rys 2007; Shockey 1984; Sibata 1985; Tagliomente and Molfenter 2007; Trudgill 1981; Wells 1973). Although it is generally believed that younger is better than older, various ages have been proposed as the cutoff point for mastery of a D2 in a native-like manner: 5 years (Tagliomente and Molfenter 2007), 8 years (Payne 1976) and 13 years (Chambers 1992).

There is also a growing body of literature on the effect of *social identity* on D2 acquisition. Foreman (2003), Ivars (1994) and Omdal (1994) considered the role of social/national identity in their studies. The results of these studies suggest that the individual's use of the D2 is affected by whether the individual identifies himself/herself with the D2 environment or with the native speakers of the target variety. Motivation and attitude have also been proposed to be related to social identity and to significantly affect D2 acquisition (e.g. Kerswill 1994; Omdal 1994; Rys 2007). For example, Kerswill (1994) and Omdal (1994) looked into the effect of attitude in Norwegian, where the D1 (Stril and Setesdal, both rural dialects) has a lower prestige than the D2 (Bergen and Kristiansand, both urban dialects), and found a significant correlation between the attitudes of speakers towards the target variety.

Another social factor studied in D2 acquisition is gender; however, the results with respect to this variable are contradictory. While some have not found a significant effect for gender in D2 acquisition (e.g. Ivars 1994; Kerswill 1994; Nycz 2011; Rys 2007; Shockey 1984; Vousten and Bongaerts, 1995; Wells 1973), others have found the opposite (e.g. Bortoni-Ricardo 1985; Foreman 2003; MacLeod 2012; Milroy and Milroy 1993; Noulijärvi 1994; Trudgill 1974). For example, Kerswill (1994) examined the effect of gender, among many other factors, in speakers of the rural Stril variety of Norwegian who had moved to Bergen city, where a different variety of Norwegian is spoken. Bergen (D2) and Stril (D1) varieties differ in terms of the pronunciation of some lexical items and morphological categories (gender, grammatical markets and prepositions), among others. The variables studied included the degree of use of Stril lexical items and morphological elements such as /hota/ 'remember' (Stril pronunciation) and /hʉskə/ 'remember' (Bergen pronunciation), the adjustment of a Bergen phonological feature (scwha lowering, with reference to the quality of the schwa vowel /ə/), and the production and perception of phonetic contrast, such as <melk> /mjɛlk/ (Stril pronunciation) and /mɛlk/ (Bergen pronunciation). Although the findings provided some evidence of the acquisition of the D2, such as younger speakers using more Stril and a positive correlation between the level of education and the use of D1, no significant differences were reported between males and females in terms of the D1 use.

Similarly, Nycz's (2011) sociolinguistic interviews were conducted with adults who were from Canada but had moved to New York City later on in life. This study focused on the linguistic and social factors which influence the acquisition/accommodation of the low back vowel distinction [o] / [oh] and the nonraising [aw] of English in the New York City area. The quantitative patterns showed that males tended to reduce Canadian raising (a production with lower nuclei before voiceless obstruents) and were less prone to embrace a strong [o] / [oh] contrast. Specifically, male participants and those from the Western Canadian provinces tended to cluster on the low-distance end of the low back vowel distance range.

Ivars (1994) found that younger females of the Närpes Finald variety of Swedish languages used more of the Eskilstuna D2 variant, which was attributed by the author to differences in the jobs occupied by men and women. She argued that the younger women/participants in the study were involved in service jobs that required more language skills; this made them more sensitive to the type of language/variant they used at work than men who held industrial jobs. Another study which shows significant difference between males and females was conducted by Nuolijärvi (1994). The study examined the effect of social factors on the loss of D1 dialectal features.

The participants consisted of migrants to Helsinki who had moved there as young adults from Ostrobothnia and Savo (Finland) between 1965 and 1974. The results showed that male participants maintained D1 features more consistently than women. Nuolijärvi, in line with Ivars (1994), concluded that young women readily adapt the speech of their new environment. In addition, Noulijärvi considered the possibility that women had 'more intense social control' than men, and that this was due to the type of their professional occupation.

MacLeod (2012) examined the degree of convergence on six phonetic/phonological differences between Buenos Aires Spanish and Spanish spoken in Madrid. She looked at both male and female speakers coming from Buenos Aires who had been living in Madrid for about 2 to 2.5 years. While the main goal of the experiment was to examine the effect of 'salience', she also looked into gender, and found that women converged on 63.2% of the tokens, while men converged on 53.8% of the same tokens, and the difference was significant.

The review of the studies above shows that gender may or may not affect D2 acquisition. Moreover, while on the surface gender may appear to explain some of the variation in D2 production, other aspects such as occupation may be the real reason for the differences evidenced (Bortoni-Ricardo 1985; Ivars 1994; Kerswill 1994; Noulijärvi 1994). The current study examines the effect of gender on D2 assibilated rhotic production by Andalusian Spanish-speaking participants.

Research questions and predictions

This study sought to ask the following questions:

(1) Does the production of assibilated rhotics by native Andalusian Spanish speakers pattern with that of native English speakers, to suggest that equivalence classification (Flege 1995) in D2 speech acquisition operates in the same fashion as in L2 acquisition?
(2) Does knowledge of the target words affect the production patterns of assibilated rhotics in native Andalusian Spanish speakers?
(3) Does gender play a role in the facilitation of the imitation and production of assibilated rhotics by Andalusian speakers?

The predictions are as follows. Firstly, if equivalence classification operates in the same way as in L2 speech learning, then, because Andalusian Spanish includes both rhotics and sibilants, similar to English, the

Andalusian Spanish speakers' patterns of assibilated rhotics will be similar to those of the English speakers reported in Rafat (2015). That is, assibilated rhotics will be mostly categorized as 'similar' sounds and, therefore, they will be produced as other types of rhotics or sibilants. Secondly, nonce words (e.g. Goldinger, 1998; Namy, Nygaard and Sauerteig 2002) provide a tabula rasa for novel exemplar coding in L2 speech (e.g. Pierce 2014). Consequently, it is predicted that production patterns will differ between the two tasks: the one utilizing real words and that utilizing nonce words. Specifically, it is hypothesized that knowledge of real words will make rhoticity more salient which will result in a higher percentage correct production of assibilated rhotics in the real words task, in comparison with the nonce word task. On the other hand, it is also hypothesized that there will be a higher rate of sibilant production in the latter task than in the former. Finally, based on assumptions and findings in studies like Bortoni-Ricardo (1985), Foreman (2003), MacLeod (2012), Milroy and Milroy (1993), Noulijärvi (1994) and Trudgill (1974), it is hypothesized that gender will play a role in the production of assibilated rhotics.

Method

Participants

The participants were 10 native Spanish speakers from Seville in Spain: 5 females and 5 males, aged between 26 to 62 years (mean age 37.7 years). Each had at least 12 years of education. None of the Spanish-speaking participants had contact with or heard the Ecuadorian variety of Spanish prior to the study. They all identified themselves as members of the upper middle class.

Procedures

The participants were required to perform each of the following five tasks twice: a picture-naming task, two imitation tasks (real words and nonce words) and two reading tasks (real words and nonce words). They were also required to complete a linguistic background questionnaire. Here, we will report the two imitation tasks. The Spanish-speaking participants were instructed to imitate as closely as possible the real Spanish words and Spanish-sounding nonce words produced by an Ecuadorian Spanish speaker. Both tasks were carried out using PowerPoint presentations during which the participants would hear a word once and had to immediately repeat it to the best of their ability. The inter-stimuli interval was three and a half seconds.

A digital audio recorder Olympus LS-7 Linear PCM was used with an unidirectional sound-cancelling microphone Olympus ME-52W to record the Spanish-speaking participants. Productions were recorded with a sampling rate of 44.1 KHz and 16 bits per sample. All audio files were stored in .wav format.

Stimuli

The data presented in this study were collected as part of a larger study consisting of a total of 529 Spanish stimuli and 155 fillers in the picture-naming task, the two imitation tasks and the two reading tasks. The present study has focused on a subset of the stimuli for the real word and nonce word imitation tasks. Each imitation task included a set of 110 target words and 36 fillers which were controlled for position in the word and stress. All the words were biysilabic, and the nonce words did not violate Spanish phonotactics. This study reports on 30 stimuli for each of the imitation tasks, which include words with an assibilated rhotic word-initially, e.g. <**r**isa> [ˈ**ř**i.sa] 'laughter'; intervocalically, e.g. <bi**rr**a> [ˈbi.**ř**a] 'beer'; and word-finally, e.g. <lico**r**> [li.ˈko**ř**] 'liqueur' (see Appendices I and II).

The stimuli were produced by a 33-year-old male Ecuadorian (Quito) Spanish native speaker. The speaker exaggerated the assibilation of the rhotics in order to make them more salient.

Data analysis

The analysis in the present study included 1,200 tokens. The productions of both the Spanish-speaking participants and those of the Ecuadorian Spanish speaker were phonetically transcribed by two of the authors of this chapter who are native speakers of Spanish, one being a native speaker of the Andalusian variety and the other of the Ecuadorian variety. The stimuli produced by the Ecuadorian Spanish speaker and the productions of the Andalusian speakers were also analysed acoustically in Praat (Boersma and Weenink 2012). Segmentation and labelling of the tokens were done manually based on spectrograms and waveforms. The following measurements were considered in order to determine the degree of assibilation: duration of the rhotic (ms), the F2 (Hz), the COG (HZ), intensity (dB) and relative intensity.

The duration of assibilated rhotics was measured from the beginning to the end of the frication noise. Relative duration was defined as the duration of the segment divided by the duration of the entire word. The measurements of COG were taken by capturing a 40 ms Hamming window and passing the sounds to a low filter under 15,000 Hz for the whole duration of the assibilated rhotics. Relative intensity was measured as the intensity of

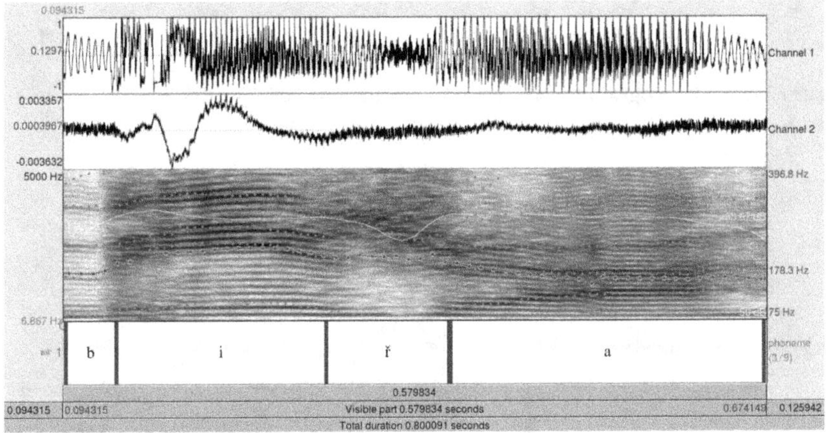

Figure 10.1. Spectrogram for <birra> ['bi.ra] 'beer'.

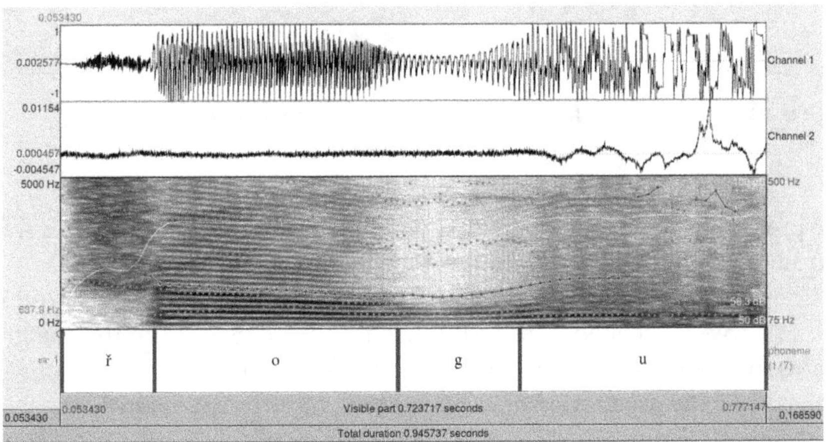

Figure 10.2. Spectrogram for <rogú> [ro'gu].

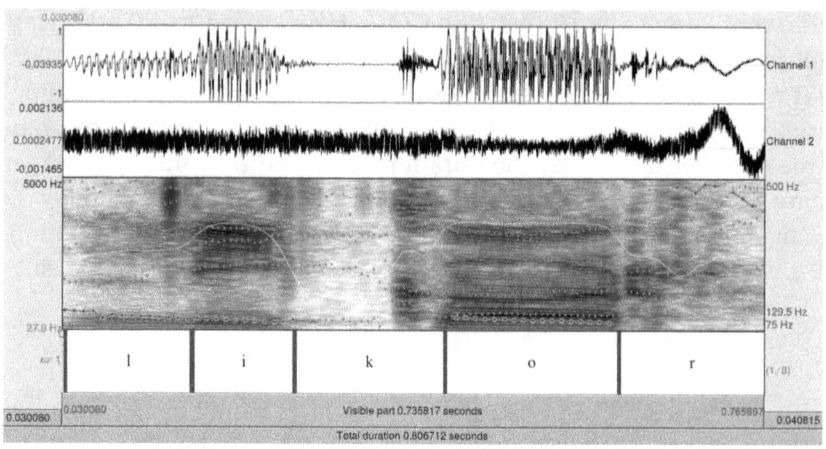

Figure 10.3. Spectrogram for <licor> [li.ˈkor] 'liqueur': trill production.

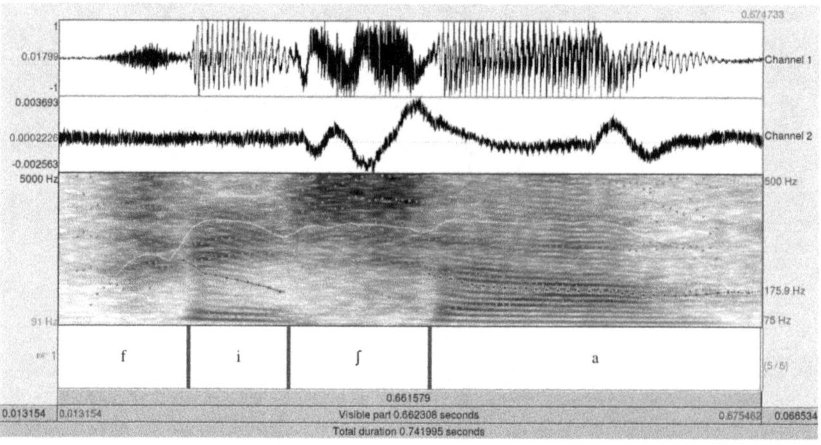

Figure 10.4. Spectrogram for <firrá> [fi.ˈʃa]: sibilant production.

the preceding vowel minus the that of the assibilated rhotic. The data were introduced into the programming language Python.

The above spectrograms provide some examples of the various productions that were attested in the data. Figures 10.1 and 10.2 are the spectrograms for the word <birra> [ˈbi.ra] 'beer' and <rogú> [ro.ˈgu] respectively, which show the production of an assibilated rhotic by the Spanish-speaking participants. Figures 10.3 and 10.4, on the other hand, are the spectrograms for the word <licor> [li.ˈkor] 'liqueur', which exemplify a trill and a sibilant

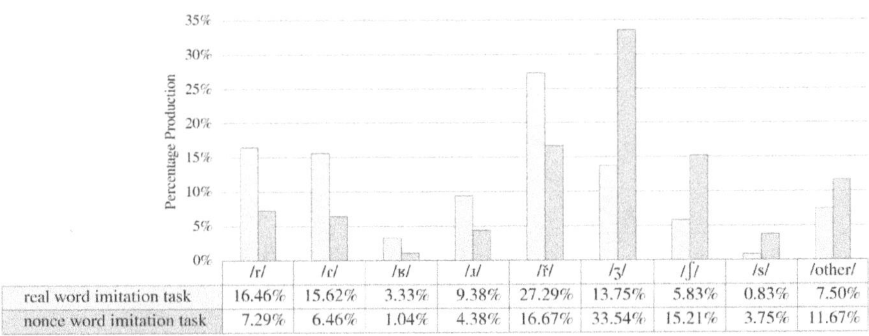

	/r/	/ɾ/	/ʁ/	/ɹ/	/ř/	/ʒ/	/ʃ/	/s/	/other/
real word imitation task	16.46%	15.62%	3.33%	9.38%	27.29%	13.75%	5.83%	0.83%	7.50%
nonce word imitation task	7.29%	6.46%	1.04%	4.38%	16.67%	33.54%	15.21%	3.75%	11.67%

Figure 10.5. Results for real word task.

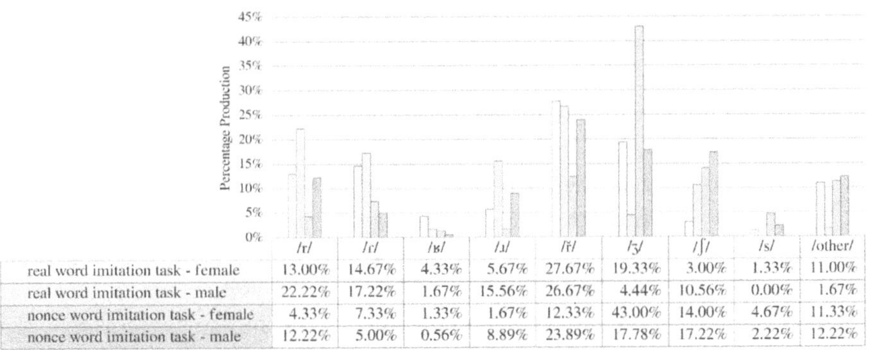

	/r/	/ɾ/	/ʁ/	/ɹ/	/ř/	/ʒ/	/ʃ/	/s/	/other/
real word imitation task - female	13.00%	14.67%	4.33%	5.67%	27.67%	19.33%	3.00%	1.33%	11.00%
real word imitation task - male	22.22%	17.22%	1.67%	15.56%	26.67%	4.44%	10.56%	0.00%	1.67%
nonce word imitation task - female	4.33%	7.33%	1.33%	1.67%	12.33%	43.00%	14.00%	4.67%	11.33%
nonce word imitation task - male	12.22%	5.00%	0.56%	8.89%	23.89%	17.78%	17.22%	2.22%	12.22%

Figure 10.6. Results for nonce task.

production in <firrá> - [fi.ˈʃa], that are representative of the real word imitation task and the nonce word imitation task, respectively.

The results provided in this section are based on the two imitation tasks with real and nonce words. For the real word task (see Figure 10.5), 88 tokens (16.46%) were produced as /r/, 88 tokens (15.62%) as /ɾ/, 16 tokens (3.33%) as /ʁ/, 82 tokens (9.38%) as /ɹ/, 163 tokens (27.29%) as /ř/, 79 tokens (13.75%) as /ʒ/, 38 tokens (5.83%) as /ʃ/, 7 tokens (0.83%) as /s/ and 30 tokens (7.0%) as other. In the nonce task (Figure 10.6), 36 tokens (7.29%) were produced as /r/, 33 tokens (6.46%) as /ɾ/, 5 tokens (1.04%) as /ʁ/, 57 tokens (4.38%) as /ɹ/, 99 tokens (16.67%) as /ř/, 189 tokens (33.54%) as /ʒ/, 4 tokens (15.21%) as /ʃ/, 22 tokens (3.75%) as /s/ and 43 tokens (11.67%) as other.

For the contingency tables, Chi-square tests were run. The results obtained in Figure 10.5 show that the imitation task based on real words

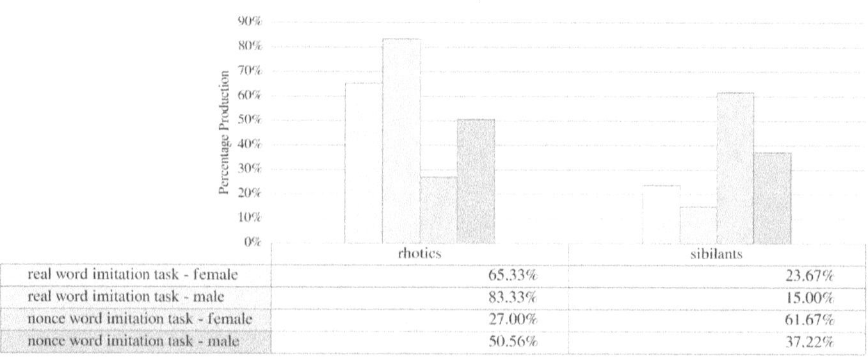

	rhotics	sibilants
real word imitation task - female	65.33%	23.67%
real word imitation task - male	83.33%	15.00%
nonce word imitation task - female	27.00%	61.67%
nonce word imitation task - male	50.56%	37.22%

Figure 10.7. Percentage of rhotic and sibilant production: male/female.

yielded a significantly higher rate of rhotics than sibilants (72.08% vs. 20.42%), while the task based on nonce words yielded a higher rate of sibilants [53.75% vs. 35.83%, $\chi^2(2) = 132.637, p < 0.05$]. Moreover, there was a higher rate of assibilated rhotic production in the real word imitation task (27.29%) in comparison with the nonce word imitation task (16.67%).

In order to examine the effect of gender on D2 assibilated rhotic production, we ran a Chi-square contingency test. Both the effects of gender and task were significant [$\chi^2(3) = 24.625, p < 0.05$]. Figure 10.6 shows that the rate of assibilated rhotic production was very similar in the real word imitation task: 27.67% vs. 26.67%, for male and female participants, respectively. Nonetheless, males (23.89%) outperformed females (12.33%) in the nonce word imitation task.

Figure 10.7 shows the results for percentage of rhotic and sibilant production in male and female participants for each task. The results show that, in the real word imitation task, male participants produced a higher rate of rhotics (83.33%) than female participants (65.33%), and female participants obtained a higher rate of sibilants (23.67%) than male participants (15.00%, $p < 0.05$; FET, the odds ratio is 0.496). These results are mimicked in the nonce word task in which male participants again produced a higher rate of rhotics (50.56%) in comparison with the females (27.67%), and female participants produced a higher rate of sibilants (61.67%) than the males (37.22%). The results of Fisher exact tests showed that the difference between male and female participants with respect to the rate of rhotic and sibilant production was significant ($p < 0.05$; FET, the odds ratio is 0.322).

An acoustic analysis of the asssibilated rhotic realizations, comparing the productions of the Andalusian Spanish-speaking participants with those of the Ecuadorian Spanish speaker with respect to intensity, place, duration and voicing was conducted (see Figures 10.8–10.10).

Figure 10.8 shows that the distributions of duration for both the Andalusian Spanish-speaking participants and the Ecuadorian Spanish speaker are similar at a significant level, as reported by a two-sample Kolmogorov-Smirnov Test (D = 0.195, p = 0.019). They also share a very similar mean (~177 ms). However, the duration values of the productions of the Andalusian Spanish-speaking participants ranged between 119 ms to 283 ms, while the ranges for the Ecuadorian speaker were between 90 ms and 390 ms. Moreover, variability was higher for the Andalusian Spanish-speaking participants than for the Ecuadorian speaker.

The distributions of F2 values (see Figure 10.9) were also similar but not at a significant level (D = 0.178, p = 0.084), exhibiting small differences in the median and interquartile ranges. The F2 medians were 2,077.3 Hz and 2,028.9 Hz for the Andalusian Spanish-speaking participants and the Ecuadorian Spanish speaker, respectively. Moreover, the means were different. The mean for the Andalusian Spanish-speaking participants was 2,064.2 Hz, while for the Ecuadorian Spanish speaker, it was 1,997 Hz. Generally, Andalusian Spanish-speaking participants produced higher and larger ranges of F2 values (1,236.1–2,785.9369 Hz) compared to the Ecuadorian Spanish speaker (1,411.7–2,729.5 Hz).

Figure 10.10 shows the distributions of centre of gravity (COG) of the assibilated rhotic in both groups. In this case, the plot shows that neither

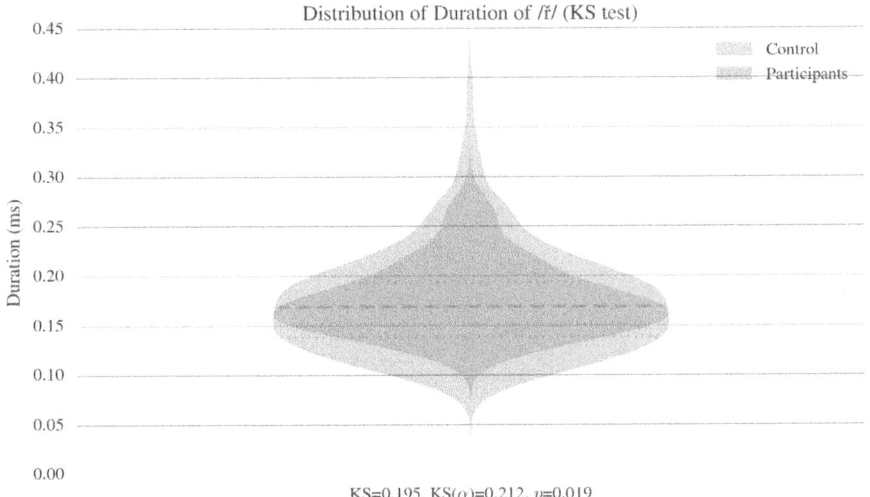

Figure 10.8. Distributions of duration.

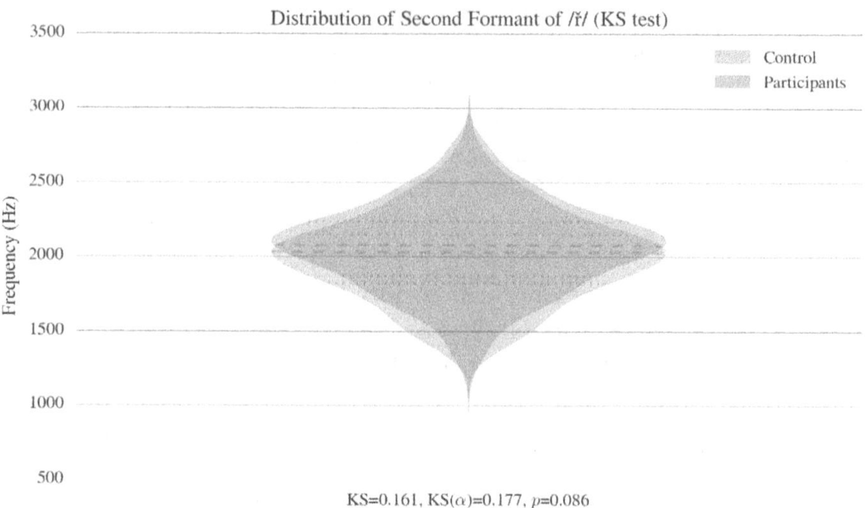

Figure 10.9. Distributions of F2 values.

the Ecuadorian Spanish speaker nor the Andalusian Spanish speakers were drawn from the same distribution. Moreover, the means were 1,030 Hz for the Andalusian Spanish-speaking participants and 616.94 Hz for the Ecuadorian Spanish speaker, being significantly different (D = 0.391, p = 0.000). Furthermore, the COG ranged between 35.7 and 3,774.1 Hz for

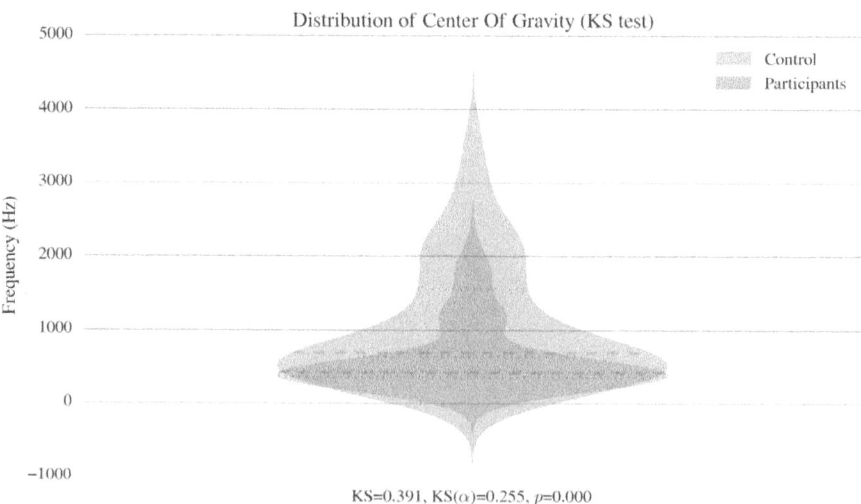

Figure 10.10. Distributions of COG.

the Andalusian Spanish participants, while it ranged between 182.6 and 2,192.6 Hz for the Ecuadorian Spanish speaker. These results suggest that Andalusian Spanish speakers do not produce the COG in a target-like manner.

Figure 10.11 contains the results of the study with respect to intensity. The distributions of both groups are different. An important aspect to highlight is that, although it looks like there is a shift of intensity values in the productions of the Andalusian Spanish participants towards those of the Ecuadorian Spanish speaker, the difference between the distributions was significant (D = 0.393, p = 0.000). The Andalusian Spanish-speaking participants produced the assibilated rhotic at a lower intensity than the Ecuadorian Spanish speaker. The intensity values ranged between 63.9 and 87.1 dB for the Andalusian Spanish speaker, while they ranged between 71.64 and 88.2 dB for the Ecuadorian Spanish speaker. Also, the mean for the Andalusian Spanish-speaking participants was lower at 79.7 dB than that of 82.14 dB for the Ecuadorian Spanish speaker.

Figure 10.12 reports on the relative intensity of the assibilated rhotics by the Andalusian Spanish speakers and the Ecuadorian Spanish speaker. The graph illustrates that the relative intensity of the assibilated rhotic by the Andalusian Spanish-speaking participants falls within the range of 0.93–19.74 dB, while the range for the Ecuadorian Spanish speaker is 1.13–14.72 dB. Both the Andalusian Spanish-speaking participants and the Ecuadorian Spanish speaker shared close values of intensity, based on their first quartile and median values (3.60 dB for the Andalusian Spanish-speaking

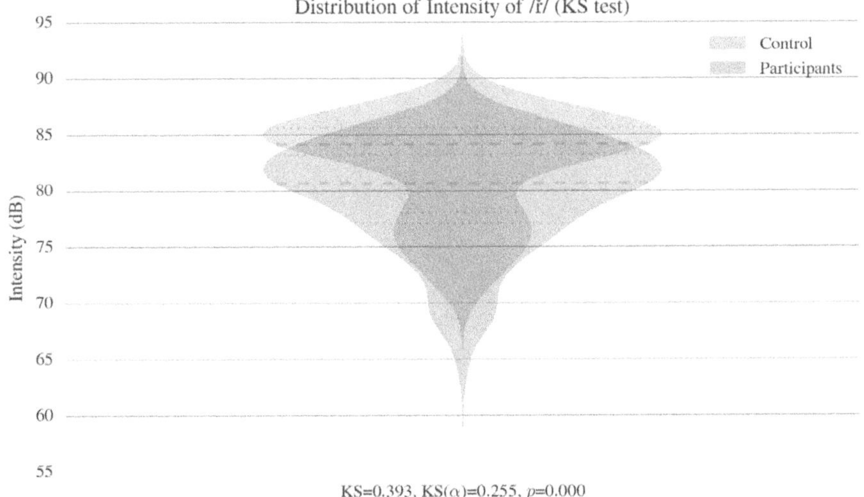

Figure 10.11. Distributions of intensity.

participants and 3.16 dB for the Ecuadorian Spanish speaker). Both groups, however, produced the same amount of assibilated rhotic [ř], between 0 and 5 dB. However their behaviours differed because the Ecuadorian speaker produced more assibilated rhotics at higher values of intensity (> 8 dB) than the Andalusian Spanish-speaking participants. Although the KS test reports the same distribution for the relative intensity ($D = 0.107$, $p = 0.487$), we cannot trust the finding that the Ecuadorian Spanish speaker and the Spanish-speaking participants behave alike. Regarding the mean, the Andalusian Spanish-speaking participants' average was 4.7 dB and that for the Ecuadorian Spanish speaker was 5 dB, meaning that they were not significantly different ($p = 0.487$).

The effect of gender was also considered with respect to duration, because it was shown earlier that the distributions in the Andalusian Spanish participants were not significantly different from those of the Ecuadorian Spanish speaker. With respect to duration, a KS test reported the same distribution (see Figure 10.13) for both female and male Andalusian participants, as well as for the Ecuadorian Spanish speaker. The mean duration was 173 ms for the female group, 177 ms for the male group and 176 ms for the Ecuadorian Spanish speaker. Furthermore, the medians of the three groups were similar: 173.5 ms for the female participants, 177.3 ms for the male participants and 176.3 ms for the Ecuadorian Spanish speaker. However, while there was a significant difference between the values for the male group and those for the Ecuadorian Spanish speaker ($D = 0.209$, $p = 0.04$), there was not a significant difference between the values of the

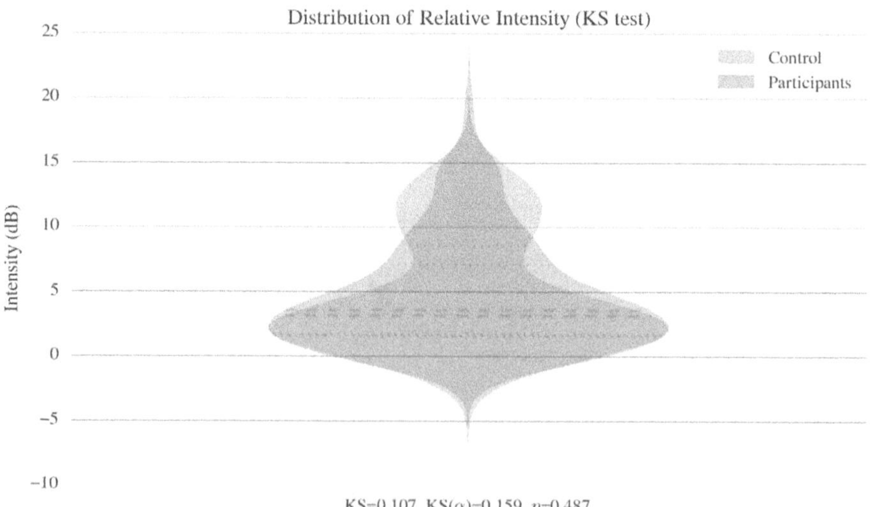

Figure 10.12. Distributions of relative intensity.

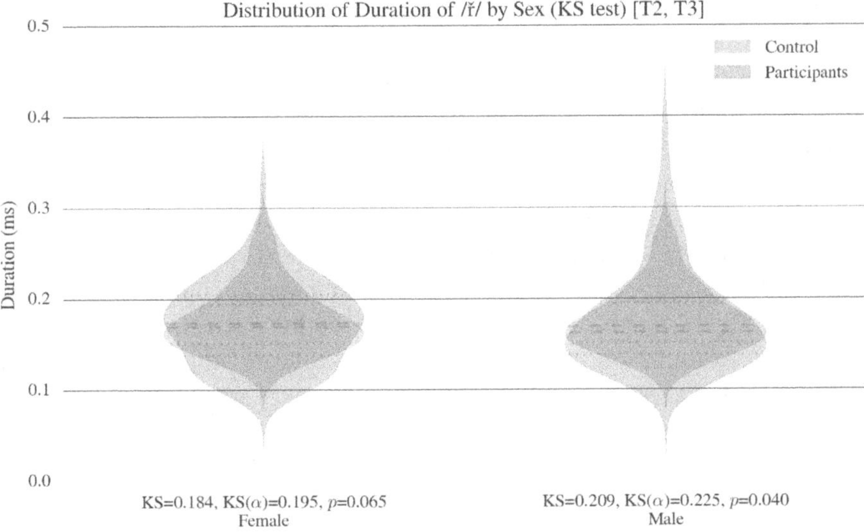

Figure 10.13. Distributions of duration: female/male.

female participant group and those of the Ecuadorian Spanish speaker ($D = 0.184$, $p = 0.065$).

Discussion and conclusions

Three hypotheses were tested in this study. Firstly, it was predicted that if equivalence classification operates in the same way as in L2 speech learning, then the Andalusian Spanish speakers' patterns of assibilated rhotics would be similar to those of the English speakers reported in Rafat (2015) because Andalusian Spanish includes both rhotics and sibilants, similar to English. That is, although a relatively small percentage of assibilated rhotics would be attested in the D2 production data, assibilated rhotics would be categorized as 'similar' sounds and produced as other types of rhotics or sibilants, for the most part. Secondly, it was predicted that real and nonce words would result in different patterns of production: specifically, that knowledge of real words would make rhoticity more salient and would result in a higher percentage production of assibilated rhotics in the real word imitation task, when compared to the nonce word imitation task. Furthermore, it was predicted that there would be a higher rate of sibilant production in the latter than in the former task. Lastly, gender would also affect assibilated rhotic production in the participants.

The results confirmed all the hypotheses of this study. There were striking similarities between the patterns that emerged here in the production of assibilated rhotics by the native Andalusian Spanish speakers and those reported for the native English speakers in Rafat (2015). In the real word imitation task, assibilated rhotics were acquired only at the rate of 27.29%. The results in Rafat (2015) showed that native English-speaking participants produced assibilated rhotics at a similar rate (23.13%). Moreover, as in Rafat (2015), the production patterns varied between the two tasks. In the real word imitation task, similarly to the audio-orthographic group in Rafat (2015), the participants produced L1-based rhotic sounds, for the most part. However, in the nonce word imitation task, similarly to the audio-only group in Rafat (2015), the bulk of the participants' productions consisted of sibilants. The fact that the results of both the real word and nonce word imitation tasks in the present study echoed the results of the audio-orthographic group and the audio-only group respectively in Rafat (2015) leads us to conclude that knowledge of words can affect equivalence classification in both D2 and L2 acquisition.

Rafat (2015) showed that assibilated rhotics exhibit various degrees of assibilation. She proposed that when assibilated rhotics are highly assibilated, exposure to the orthographic cue <r> can make rhoticity (i.e. the less salient cue of assibilated rhotics) more salient for learners and, thus, facilitate target-like productions. She also proposed that when rhotics are not heavily assibilated, exposure to <r> may result in L1-based transfer of the English rhotics or even result in L1 overriding the input. In the current study, knowledge of the target words and, more specifically, knowledge that words are produced with a rhotic in Andalusian Spanish, increased the salience of these rhotics (though rhoticity is their less salient feature) resulting either in a target-like production or in D1-based rhotic transfer, such as the production of a trill or a tap. When participants did not have knowledge of the words, however, because there was nothing in their L1 phonology to facilitate noticing rhoticity in the input and, given that assibilation is a more salient feature in assibilated rhotics than rhoticity, native Andalusian Spanish participants were more likely to map these sounds on to sibilants from their D1.

Although the overall patterns of D2 productions mirrored the production patterns of the L2 speakers in Rafat (2015), we must note that some differences were also noted. For example, whereas assibilated rhotics were mainly produced as /ʃ/ by the L2 auditory-only group in Rafat (2015), they were mainly produced as a /ʒ/ in this study. This might be because of the differences in the degree of voicing of assibilated rhotics of the Ecuadorian Spanish speaker in this study in comparison with the Mexican Spanish speaker in Rafat (2015). This hypothesis will have to be further explored in future work. There were also four instances where assibilated rhotics were produced as /l/ in the D2 production data. However, /l/ was never attested in the productions of the native L2 English-speaking participants in Rafat (2015). The /l/ production is very likely due to the fact that liquid neutralization is a characteristic of Andalusian Spanish (e.g. Ruiz-Peña 2013). In all, although equivalence classification may operate similarly in L2 and D2 learners, phonological processes in the D1 may also exert an influence in the productions of D2 learners. However, more data are needed before such findings can be generalized.

Furthermore, this study conducted an acoustic analysis of the assibilated rhotics produced by the Ecuadorian Spanish speaker and those of the native Andalusian Spanish-speaking participants. According to the auditory transcription of the results, 27.29% of the target assibilated rhotics in the real word imitation task and 16.67% in the nonce word imitation task were realized as assibilated rhotics by the participants; they were thought to have both rhotic-like and sibilant-like qualities. A visual analysis of the spectrograms also showed that these assibilated rhotics exhibited a high degree of frication. It has been argued earlier in the literature that manner is the most salient feature of rhotics (Ohala and Kawasaki 1984; Steriade 1999). Manner was also the most acquirable feature for the French voiced dorsal fricative [ʁ] in Colantoni and Steele (2007). An acoustic analysis of other features associated with assibilated rhotics, however, showed that not all acoustic parameters were produced in a target-like manner. When F2, COG, intensity and relative intensity were compared, duration was the most accurately produced parameter. Duration has also been shown to be a cue that Spanish L2 learners rely on when identifying new L2 vowels (e.g. Bohn 1995; Cebrian 2006; Escudero 2001). Escudero (2001) found that, while Scottish-English speaking learners of Southern English had native-like perception of the Southern British English /i-ɪ/ contrast, Spanish-speaking learners of English used duration to identify these L2 vowels.

The third hypothesis regarding the effect of gender was also confirmed. The male and female participants in this study exhibited two diverging patterns of assibilated rhotic production, in which the male participants had a significantly higher rate of rhotic production than female participants, and female participants had a significantly higher rate of sibilant production, compared to the males. Moreover, males outperformed females with respect to the rate of assibilated rhotic production in the nonce word imitation task. In a sense, the male imitation productions pattern more closely with those observed in the auditory-orthographic condition in Rafat (2015), and the female imitation patterns with those reported in the auditory-only condition, in general. It is possible that the female participants' D1 phonetic and phonological inventory differs from that of males, which subsequently leads to different patterns in mapping and categorization of D2 sounds. It is also possible that sibilants characterize female speech in Andalusian Spanish more than they do so in male speech and, therefore, the rate of sibilant production in D2 speech production of the assibilated rhotic might be correlated with the rate of lenition/sibilant production in D1 speech. However, these hypotheses have to be further tested. In short, the effect of gender on duration was also considered, and the results were significant. However, the differences between the male and female duration values were small and may not be discernible from an acoustic point of view.

In all, this study is important because it makes new contributions to our understanding of likely mechanisms that underlie the acquisition of D2 speech at the very beginning stages of acquisition. Firstly, there has been evidence of a very robust similarity in the production patterns between D2 and L2, suggesting that equivalence classification operates similarly in both cases. Secondly, just like knowledge of orthography (e.g. Bassetti and Atkinson 2015; Bassetti, Escudero and Hayes-Harb 2015; Rafat 2011, 2015, 2016), real words can modulate equivalence classification in L2 speakers (Pierce 2014) and, as seen here, knowledge of words can modulate equivalence classification in D2 learners. Consequently, based on the results of the acoustic analysis of the assibilated rhotics produced by the Andalusian Spanish-speaking participants here, it can be deduced that the framework of Flege's SLM cannot allow adequate predictions about the relative difficulty of the phonetic features of D2 sounds, though it may predict the overall patterns of equivalence classification and, hence, D2 production patterns. While, manner and duration were acquirable, other parameters such as F2, COG, intensity and relative intensity were not. Hence, evidence from the data suggests that D2 productions may also be additionally constrained by D1 phonological processes, although more data are needed to verify this. Finally, the effect of gender is interesting because difference in gender, in this study, results in two diverging patterns, which raise the question regarding the effect of D1 phonetic and phonological inventories on D2 imitation.

Although one of the strengths of this study lies in the fact that it is a very controlled one which tells us how equivalence classification may operate in the very beginning stages of D2 acquisition, it is not a naturalistic study. Future studies should include more naturalistic conditions, such as a conversation between speakers of the two varieties of Spanish, and/or the production data of Andalusian speakers who have been exposed to a variety of Spanish characterized by assibilated rhotics. Future studies should also examine other extra-linguistic factors and investigate the perception of D1 and D2 dialects on the dimensions of prestige, solidarity, social attractiveness and linguistic validity (Rindal 2010), as well as the degree of contact with other dialects, and place of residence. In this study, the participants did not report having had any contact with Ecuadorian Spanish. Additionally, although the Andalusian variety of Spanish is stigmatized (e.g. Ruiz-Peña 2013), Andalusian Spanish speakers are very proud of their variety of Spanish (e.g. Ariza 2008; Ruiz-Peña 2013). Alvar (1975) points out that there is 'dual linguistic awareness of both pride and inferiority'. However, after Franco's dictatorial regime came to an end, the Spanish nationalistic movements began to promote a positive sense of Andalusian identity. This study did not examine the effect of social context, but because of the issue of 'Andalusian identity', it is plausible that the participants were not the most amenable to imitating another variety of Spanish. It would be interesting to compare assibilated rhotic production by Andalusian speakers with that of speakers of another Spanish variety, who may relate differently to their D1, where D1 may not be such a strong identity marker. The perceived degree of prestige that Ecuadorian Spanish enjoys in the Spanish-speaking countries will have to be further investigated, as it may be another factor that contributes to the low accuracy in production of these assibilated rhotics. Furthermore, because this study is based on production data, the proposals regarding equivalence classification in D2 will need to be further validated by conducting a perception task. Finally, this chapter has focused on production and equivalence classification patterns at the very beginning stages of acquisition. Future studies should also consider a comparison of beginner, intermediate and advanced D2 and L2 learners.

Appendix I: List of real words and fillers for the real word imitation task

Table 10.1. List of real words per position and stress.

Position	*Stressed*	*Unstressed*
Word-initial	*remo* 'oar'	*rubí* 'ruby'
	risa 'laugh'	*ramón* 'Ramón'
	ropa 'cloth'	*rapé* 'shaved'
	rusa 'female Russian'	*robé* 'stole'
	ruta 'route'	*rocé* 'touch'
Word-medial/ intervocalic	*birra* 'beer'	*borré* 'erased'
	parra 'vine'	*moral* 'moral'
	tarro 'jar'	*cerró* 'closed'
	porro 'joint'	*carril* 'track'
	burro 'donkey'	*barrí* 'swept'
Word-final	*poder* 'can'	*dólar* 'dollar'
	calar 'penetrate'	*sonar* 'to ring'
	sabor 'flavour'	*fúcar* 'Fúcar/ Függer'
	licor 'liquor'	*lemur* 'lemur'
	pulir 'to polish'	*césar* 'Caesar'

Table 10.2. List of fillers for the real word imitation task.

gluten 'gluten'	*pilló* 'caught'	*fin* 'end'	*subí* 'went up'
lápiz 'pencil'	*biblia* 'bible'	*habla* 'speaks'	*maná* 'manna'
llanta 'rim'	*domé* 'tamed'	*folio* 'sheet'	*mote* 'nickname'
llave 'key'	*malla* 'net'	*mal* 'bad'	*callé* 'shut up'
gasto 'expense'	*gel* 'liquid soap'	*tos* 'cough'	*tabla* 'table'
fajó 'beat up'	*fuga* 'escape'	*jefe* 'boss'	*toldo* 'sunshade'
pez 'fish'	*tan* 'so'	*flaco* 'skinny'	
lomo 'loin'	*boté* 'threw'	*fumó* 'smoked'	
lobo 'wolf'	*beca* 'scholarship'	*plato* 'dish'	
mano 'hand'	*llamé* 'called'	*zafé* 'got out of'	

Appendix II: List of nonce words and fillers for the nonce word imitation task

Table 10.3. List of nonce words per position and stress.

Position	*Stressed*	*Unstressed*
Word-initial	*refo*	*rogú*
	rube	*refó*
	riga	*raní*
	renu	*rupá*
	raca	*ricú*
Word-medial/intervocalic	*firrá*	*porre*
	nerró	*hurri*
	murrí	*lerra*
	nurró	*tarre*
	carrí	*lirra*
Word-final	*liper*	*júpir*
	dafer	*létar*
	padur	*cásor*
	zater	*cáfor*
	jalor	*sígur*

Table 10.4. List of fillers for the nonce word imitation task.

zombón	*fueya*	*zop*	*mofsú*
loifu	*mif*	*abce*	*bliapa*
mul	*moltre*	*blaspo*	*tebó*
astog	*guybla*	*llejal*	*gaox*
jófa	*luhom*	*gafu*	*sot*
paxfí	*feheje*	*onmex*	
fezá	*temlla*	*omlan*	
jul	*julmú*	*dolpa*	
llopí	*moan*	*nat*	
fangué	*naami*	*bizú*	
		pizlo	

References

Adams, C., 2002, *Strong assibilation and prestige: A sociolinguistic study in the central valley of Costa Rica*, PhD thesis, University of California, Davis.

Alvar, M., 1975, *Hoja Informativa Literatura y Filología* número 28, Junio, Fundación Juan March.

Ariza, M., 2008, 'The sociolinguistics of Spanish in Extemadura', *International Journal of the Sociology of Language*, 109–20.

Babel, M., 2009, *Phonetic and social selectivity in speech accommodation*, PhD thesis, University of California, Berkeley.

Bassetti, B. and Atkinson, N., 2015, 'Effects of orthographic forms on pronunciation in experienced instructed second language learners', *Applied Psycholinguistics* 36(1), 67–91. https://doi.org/10.1017/S0142716414000435

Bassetti, B., Escudero, P. and Hayes-Harb, R., 2015, 'Second language phonology at the interface between acoustic and orthographic input', *Applied Psycholinguistics* 36(1), 1–6. https://doi.org/10.1017/S0142716414000393

Berthele, R., 2002, 'Learning a second dialect: A model of idiolectal dissonance', *Multilingua* 21, 327–44. https://doi.org/10.1515/mult.2002.014

Best, C.T. and Tyler, M.D., 2007, 'Nonnative and second-language speech perception: Commonalities and complementarities', in M.J. Munro and O.S. Bohn (eds.), *Second language speech learning: The role of language experience in speech perception and production*, pp. 13–34, Amsterdam/Philadelphia: John Benjamins. https://doi.org/10.1075/lllt.17.07bes

Blecua, B., 2001, *Las vibrantes del español: Manifestaciones acústicas y procesos fonéticos*, PhD thesis, Universidad Autónoma de Barcelona.

Boersma, P. and Weenink, D., 2012, *Praat: Doing phonetics by computer* (Version 5.3. 35) [Computer program], retrieved from: http://www.praat.org/.

Bohn, O.S., 1995, 'Cross language speech production in adults: First language transfer doesn't tell it all', in W. Strange (ed.), *Speech perception and linguistic experience: Issues in cross-language research*, pp. 279–304, Baltimore, MD: York Press.

Bortoni-Ricardo, S.M., 1985, *The urbanization of Rural Dialect Speakers: A sociolinguistic Study in Brazil*, Cambridge, UK: Cambridge University Press.

Bosch, L. 1983, 'El desarrollo fonológico infantil: Una prueba para su evaluación', *Anuario de Psicología* 28, 87–114.

Bradley, T.G., 1999, 'Assibilation in Ecuadorian Spanish', in J.M. Authier, B.E. Bullock and L.A. Reed (eds.), *Formal Perspectives on Romance Linguistics. Selected papers from the 28th linguistics symposium on romance languages*, pp. 57–71, Amsterdam: John Benjamins. https://doi.org/10.1075/cilt.185.06bra

Brown, C.A., 1998, 'The role of the L1 grammar in the acquisition of segmental structure', *Second Language Research* 14(2), 139–93. https://doi.org/10.1191/026765898669508401

Carballo, G. and Mendoza, E., 2000, 'Acoustic characteristics of trill productions by groups of Spanish children', *Clinical Linguistics and Phonetics* 14(8), 587–601. https://doi.org/10.1080/02699200750048125

Carbonero, P., 2001, 'Identidad lingüística y comportamientos discursivos', *Sociolingüística Andaluza 12*, Universidad de Sevilla.

Cebrian, J. 2006, 'Experience and the use of non-native duration in L2 vowel categorization', *Journal of Phonetics* 34, 372–87. https://doi.org/10.1016/j.wocn.2005.08.003

Chambers, J.K., 1992, 'Dialect acquisition', *Language*, 673–705.

Chela-Flores, B. and Chela-Flores, G., 2002, 'Old and new issues in Spanish dialectology: The Venezuelan data', *Dialectologia et Geolinguistica* 10, 31–39. https://doi.org/10.1515/dig.2002.2002.10.31

Colantoni, L., 2001, *Mergers, chain shifts and dissimilatory processes: Palatals and rhotics in Argentine Spanish*, PhD thesis, University of Minnesota.

Colantoni, L., 2006, 'Macro and micro sound variation and change in Argentine Spanish', in. J. Toribio. and N. Sagarra (eds.), *Selected proceedings of the 9th Hispanic Linguistic Symposium*, pp. 91–102, Somerville, MA: Cascadilla Press.

Colantoni, L. and Rafat, Y., 2013, 'Las consonantes róticas en el español argentino' [Rhotic consonants in Argentine Spanish], in L. Colantoni and C. Rodríguez Louro (eds.), *Perspectivas teóricas y experimentales sobre el español de la Argentina* [Theoretical and experimental perspectives on Argentinian Spanish], pp. 82–98, Madrid-Frankfurt: Iberoamericana/Vervuert.

Colantoni, L. and Steele, J., 2007, 'Acquiring /R/ in context', *Studies in Second Language Acquisition* 29, 381–406.

Colantoni, L. and Steele, J., 2008, 'Integrating articulatory constraints into models of second language phonological acquisition', *Applied Psycholinguistics* 29(03), 489–534. https://doi.org/10.1017/S0142716408080223

Delattre, P. and Freeman, D.C., 1968, 'A dialect study of American r's by x-ray motion picture, *Linguistics* 6(44), 29–68. https://doi.org/10.1515/ling.1968.6.44.29

Escudero, P., 2001, 'The role of the input in the development of L1 and L2 sound contrasts: Language specific cue weighting for vowels', in A. Do, L. Dominguez and A. Johansen (eds.), *Proceedings of the 25th annual Boston University conference on language development*, Vol.1, pp. 250–61, Somerville, MA: Cascadilla Press.

Escure, G., 1997, *Creole and dialect continua: Standard acquisition processes in Belize and China*, Amsterdam: John Benjamins.

Face, T.L., 2006, 'Intervocalic rhotic pronunciation by adult learners of Spanish as a second language', in C.A. Klee and T.L. Face (eds.), *Selected proceedings of the 7th conference on the acquisition of Spanish and Portuguese as first and second languages*, pp. 47–58, Somerville, MA: Cascadila Proceedings Project.

Flege, J., 1995, 'Second language speech learning: Theory, findings and problems', in W. Strange (ed.), *Speech perception and linguistic perception: Theoretical and methodological issues*, pp. 233–77, Timonium, MD: York Press.

Foreman, A., 2003, *Pretending to be someone you're not: A study of second dialect acquisition in Australia*, PhD thesis, Monash University, Melbourne.

Goldinger, S.D., 1998, 'Echoes of echoes? An episodic theory of lexical access', *Psychological Review* 105(2), 251–79. https://doi.org/10.1037/0033-295X.105.2.251

Gómez, R., 2003, *Sociolinguistic correlations in the Spanish spoken in the Andean region of Ecuador in the speech of the younger generation*, PhD thesis, University of Toronto.

Hall, T.A., 1997, *The phonology of coronals*, Amsterdam/Philadelphia: John Benjamins. https://doi.org/10.1075/cilt.149

Harris, J.W., 1969, *Syllable structure and stress in Spanish*, Cambridge, MA: MIT Press.

Hualde, J., 2005, *The sounds of Spanish*, Cambridge, UK: Cambridge University Press.

Ivars, A., 1994, 'Bidialectalism and identity', in B. Nordberg (ed.), *The sociolinguistics of urbanization: The case of the Nordic countries*, pp. 203–22, Berlin: De Gruyter. https://doi.org/10.1515/9783110852622.203

Jiménez, B.C., 1987, 'Acquisition of Spanish consonants in children aged 3–5 years, 7 months', *Language, Speech and Hearing Services in Schools* 18, 357–63. https://doi.org/10.1044/0161-1461.1804.357

Jiménez, R., 1999, *El andaluz*, Madrid: Arco/Libros, S.L.

Kerswill, P., 1994, *Dialects converging: Rural speech in urban Norway*, Oxford, UK: Clarendon Press.

Lipski, J.M., 1994, *Latin American Spanish*, New York, NY: Longman.

MacLeod, B., 2012, *The effect of perceptual salience on cross-dialectal phonetic convergence in Spanish*, PhD thesis, University of Toronto.

Maddieson, I., 1984, *Patterns of sounds*, Cambridge, MA: Cambridge University Press. https://doi.org/10.1017/CBO9780511753459

Maddieson, I. and Ladefoged, P., 1996, *The sounds of the world's languages*, Cambridge, MA: Blackwell.

Major, R.C., 1986, 'The ontogeny model: Evidence from L2 acquisition of Spanish r', *Language Learning* 36, 453–504. https://doi.org/10.1111/j.1467-1770.1986.tb01035.x

Matus-Mendoza, M.L., 2004, 'Assibilation of /r/ and migration among Mexicans', *Language Variation and Change* 16, 17–30. https://doi.org/10.1017/S0954394504161024

Milroy, J. and Milroy, L., 1993, 'Mechanisms of change in urban dialects: The role of class, social network and gender', *International Journal of Applied Linguistics* 3(1), 57–77. https://doi.org/10.1111/j.1473-4192.1993.tb00043.x

Namy, L.L., Nygaard, L.C. and Sauerteig, D., 2002, 'Gender differences in vocal accommodation: The role of perception', *Journal of Language and Social Psychology* 21(4), 422–32. https://doi.org/10.1177/026192702237958

Navarro Tomás, T., 1980, *Manual de pronunciación española*, Madrid: CSIC.

Nielsen, K., 2011, 'Specificity and abstractness of VOT imitation', *Journal of Phonetics* 39, 32–42. https://doi.org/10.1016/j.wocn.2010.12.007

Noulijärvi, P., 1994, 'On the interlinkage of sociolinguistic background variables', in B. Nordberg (ed.), *The sociolinguistics of urbanization: The case of the Nordic countries*, pp. 149–70, Berlin: De Gruyter. https://doi.org/10.1515/9783110852622.149

Nycz, J., 2011, *Second dialect acquisition: Implications for theories of phonological representation*, doctoral dissertation, New York University.

Ohala, J., and Kawasaki, H. 1984, *Prosodic phonology and phonetics*, Phonology Yearbook 1, 113–27. https://doi.org/10.1017/S0952675700000312

Omdal, H., 1994, 'From the valley to the city: Language modification and language attitudes', in B. Nordberg (ed.), *The sociolinguistics of urbanization: The case of the Nordic countries*, pp. 116–48, Berlin: De Gruyter.

Payne, A.C., 1976, *The acquisition of the phonological system of a second dialect*, PhD thesis, University of Pennsylvania.

Pierce, L., 2014, *Learning novel vowel contrasts: experimental methods in classroom applications*, PhD thesis, University of Illinois at Urbana-Champaign.

Quilis, A., 1999, *Curso de fonología y fonética españolas*, Madrid: Consejo Superior de Investigaciones Científicas (CSIC).

Quilis, A. and Carril, R.B., 1971, 'Análisis acústico de [r] en algunas zonas de Hispanoamérica', *Revista de Filología Española* 54(3), 271–316. https://doi.org/10.3989/rfe.1971.v54.i3/4.844

Rafat, Y., 2008, 'The acquisition of allophonic variation in Spanish as a second language', in S. Jones (ed.), *Proceedings of the Annual Conference of the Canadian Linguistic Association*, Vancouver, BC.

Rafat, Y., 2011, *Orthography-induced transfer in the production of adult novice English speaking learners of Spanish*, unpublished PhD thesis, University of Toronto.

Rafat, Y., 2015, 'The interaction of acoustic and orthographic input in the L2 production of assibilated/fricative rhotics', *Applied Psycholinguistics* 36(1), 43–64. https://doi.org/10.1017/S0142716414000423

Rafat, Y., 2016, 'Orthography-induced transfer in the production of English-speaking learners of Spanish', *The Language Learning Journal* 44(2), 197–213. https://doi.org/10.1080/09571736.2013.784346

Reeder, J.T., 1998, 'English speakers' acquisition of voiceless stops and trills in L2 Spanish', *Texas Papers in Foreign Language Education* 3, 101–18.

Rindal, U., 2010, 'Constructing identity with L2: Pronunciation and attitudes among Norwegian learners of English', *Journal of Sociolinguistics* 14(2), 240–61. https://doi.org/10.1111/j.1467-9841.2010.00442.x

Rissel, D.A., 1989, 'Sex, attitudes, and the assibilation of/r/among young people in San Luis Potosí, Mexico', *Language Variation and Change* 1(3), 269–83. https://doi.org/10.1017/S0954394500000181

Ruiz-Peña, E., 2013, *'Alma' o 'arma', evidencia de la neutralización/l//r/en la variedad dialectal andaluza de Sevilla*, Master's thesis, Western University.

Rys, K., 2007, *Dialect as second language: Linguistic and non-linguistic factors in secondary dialect acquisition by children and adolescents*, PhD thesis, Ghent University.

Shockey, L., 1984, 'All in a flap: Long-term accommodation in phonology', *International Journal of the Sociology of Language* 46, 87–95. https://doi.org/10.1515/ijsl.1984.46.87

Sibata, T., 1985, 'Conditions controlling standardization', in *Nihonnō hōgēn* [The Dialects of Japan], Tokyo: Iwanami Shotēn (trans. Motoei Sawaki, 1990).

Siegel, J., 2010, *Second dialect acquisition*, Cambridge, UK: Cambridge University Press. https://doi.org/10.1017/CBO9780511777820

Solé, M.J., 1992, 'Experimental Phonology: The case of rhotacism', in W.U. Dressler, H.C. Luschützky, O.E. Pfeiffer and J.R. Rennison (eds.), *Phonologica 1988*, pp. 259–71, Cambridge, UK: Cambridge University Press.

Solé, M.J., 1998, 'Phonological universals: Trilling, voicing and frication', *Berkeley Linguistics Society* 24, 427–42. https://doi.org/10.3765/bls.v24i1.1238

Solé, M.J., 2002, 'Aerodynamic characteristics of trills and phonological patterning', *Journal of Phonetics* 30, 655–88. https://doi.org/10.1006/jpho.2002.0179

Steriade, D., 1999, *The phonology of perceptibility effects: The P-map and its consequences for constraint organization*, unpublished manuscript, University of California, Los Angeles.

Tagliomente, S. and Molfenter, S., 2007, 'How'd you get that accent? Acquiring a second dialect of the same language', *Language in Society* 36, 649–75. https://doi.org/10.1017/s0047404507070911

Trudgill, P., 1974, 'Linguistic change and diffusion: Description and explanation in sociolinguistic dialect geography', *Language in Society* 3(2), 215–46.

Trugdill, P., 1981, 'Linguistic accommodation: Sociolinguistic observations on a sociopsycological theory', in C.S. Masek, R.A. Hendrick and M.F. Miller (eds.), *Papers from the Parasession on Language and Behaviour*, pp. 218–37, Chicago: Chicago Linguistic Society. https://doi.org/10.1017/S0047404500004358

Vásquez-Carranza, L.M., 2006, 'On the phonetic realization and distribution of Costa Rican rhotics', *Revista de Filología y Lingüística de la Universidad de Costa Rica* 32(2), 291–309.

Vousten, R. and Bongaerts, T., 1995, 'Acquiring a dialect as L2: The case of the dialect of Venray in the Dutch province of Limburg', in W. Viereck (ed.), *Verhandlungen des internationalen dialektolo-genkongresses Bamberg 1990*, pp. 299–313, Band 4, Stuttgart: Franz Steiner.

Waltmunson, J.C., 2005, *The relative degree of difficulty of L2 Spanish /d, t/, trill, and tap by L1 English speakers: Auditory and acoustic methods of defining pronunciation accuracy*, unpublished PhD thesis, University of Washington, Seattle.

Wells, J.C., 1973, *Jamaican Pronunciation in London*, Oxford, UK: Blackwell.

Westbury, J.R., Hashi, M. and Lindstrom, M.J., 1999, 'Differences among speakers in lingual articulation for American English /ô/', *Speech Communication* 26, 203–26. https://doi.org/10.1016/S0167-6393(98)00058-2

Widdison, K.A., 1998, 'Phonetic motivation for variation in Spanish trills', *Orbis* 40, 51–61. https://doi.org/10.2143/ORB.40.1.505038

Zhou, X., Espy-Wilson, C., Boyce, S., Tiede, M., Holland, C. and Choe, A., 2008, 'A magnetic resonance imaging-based articulatory and acoustic study of "retroflex" and "bunched" American English /r/', *Journal of the Acoustical Society of America* 123(6), 4466–81. https://doi.org/10.1121/1.2902168

Esperanza Ruíz-Peña obtained her MA in Hispanic Studies (Linguistics) from Western University in London, Canada, and currently she is in her last year of her PhD in the Hispanic Studies programme there. Her research focuses on sociolinguistics and dialectal phonetic variation. She has especially investigated the neutralization of /l/ for /r/ in Seville (Spain), the production of Ecuadorian assibilated rhotics by Spanish speakers who belong to a non-assibilated rhotic Spanish variety, and the bilingual advantage in the imitation of intonation patterns in English second-dialect learners.

Diego Sevilla obtained his MA in Hispanic Studies (Linguistics) from Western University in London, Canada. Fascinated by the field of linguistics, he decided to continue his studies and has been recently admitted by the Pennsylvania State University in the MA/PhD programme in Spanish Linguistics, where he will be working towards a dual PhD in Spanish and Language Science. His interests and research areas are mainly related to language contact, morpho-syntax and semantics.

Yasaman Rafat obtained her PhD in Hispanic Linguistics from the University of Toronto. She is currently a Professor of Hispanic Linguistics at the Department of Modern Language and Literatures at Western University in London, Canada, and is also affiliated with the graduate programme in Linguistics there. Her primary research interests include second-language speech acquisition, where she has examined the interaction between orthographic and acoustic input in second-language learners. She also works on bilingualism and first-language change, second-dialect acquisition, foreign accent, sound change and variation. The languages she has examined are Spanish, Farsi, English and Korean.

11
The perceptual weight of word stress, quantity and tonal word accent in Swedish

Åsa Abelin and Bosse Thorén

Introduction

Wherever migration or travelling takes place, people need to learn new languages. This learning entails a variety of interlanguages. Irrespective of whether you are a learner or a teacher of a language, you need to decide how to allocate time and effort into developing different sub-skills of the language. Four main skills are considered in second-language teaching and learning; listening, reading, speaking and writing. Proficiency in speaking requires sub-competences, such as pragmatic competence, fluency or making a clear pronunciation. Further, each of these sub-competences for speaking requires sub-skills. For example, to have a 'good' pronunciation, one needs to realize segmental features well: phonemes, phonotactics, assimilations, as well as prosodic features: rhythm and intonation.

In most cases, young children learning their first language (L1) as well as additional languages (L2s) acquire these pronunciation skills without formal training and often reach native-like speech also in additional languages. By contrast, adult learners of an additional language seldom reach native-likeness in their pronunciation of the language. However, ideally, they can still achieve a fluent, intelligible and well-received pronunciation of the language.

The present chapter is concerned with the pronunciation of Swedish as an additional language, and in particular three phonemic prosodic contrasts, namely word stress, quantity and tonal word accent. We attempt to find out, among these three prosodic contrasts, which is more crucial than the others for making one's speech intelligible. That is, if the second-language learner cannot acquire all of them perfectly, which of them should be given more priority in learning and teaching Swedish pronunciation? We also want to study whether or not a pronunciation that lacks or mispronounces one of these contrasts can still be well understood.

Here, we need to clarify two things for our study. Firstly, we exclude the aspect of segmental properties of pronunciation, focusing on the effect of deconstructing Swedish prosody, and looking at the three phonemic parts and their respective relevance to intelligibility. We, however, do not assume or suggest that either prosody or the aspect of segmental properties is more important for intelligible speech. Secondly, we use the term 'perceptual weight' in our study to make it clear that we are only concerned with intelligibility of pronunciation, leaving out other aspects of foreign accent. The degree of native-like pronunciation is not addressed in the study, nor is the question of attitudes towards foreign accented speech. According to Munro and Derwing (1995) certain aspects of foreign accent can decrease intelligibility to some extent, but the degree of foreign accent in general does not seem to correlate with further decreased intelligibility. We therefore believe that certain features in a foreign accent may be crucial to intelligibility, while others are not particularly so. In fact, Bannert (1980) suggested some phonological features of Swedish as more crucial for intelligibility than others. Likewise, Thorén (2008) discussed the importance of prioritizing among the different Swedish prosodic contrasts and their respective acoustic correlates for pedagogical purposes.

In our study, we measure the degrees of importance of the three Swedish prosodic contrasts for intelligible speech. To do this, we use Swedish native speakers' perceptions, by means of letting them listen to natural pronunciations of words mixed with distorted pronunciations. As mentioned earlier, the general purpose of our paper is not to suggest native likeness as the norm for acquiring Swedish pronunciation. Instead, we seek to shed more light on the relative importance of different phonological and phonetic features in order to develop '*lingua franca* core features'[1] for Swedish. Swedish is not as international as English is, but in the last half century Sweden has developed into a multi-accented speech community where a huge variety of different linguistic groups dwell together. In addition to the varieties of native dialects and accents, the country has now people with diverse accents, such as Finnish, Arabic, Turkish, Persian, Vietnamese and Somali, to name a few. According to Parkvall (2016), there are between 150 and 200 languages used as first languages in Sweden today. Therefore, arguing for intelligibility rather than native likeness as the ideal pronunciation goal

1 The concept of lingual franca phonetic core features was suggested by Jenkins (2002) in the context of using English as an international language.

(Derwing and Munro 2015) and focusing on phonetic core features in pronunciation (Jenkins 2002) are very much relevant to teaching Swedish as an additional language. Accordingly, we are in the line of developing criteria for assessing different pronunciations of the Swedish language in terms of intelligibility rather than the degrees of accentedness.

The research questions are as follows:

(1) To what extent does the distortion of stress pattern affect the intelligibility of Swedish words when measured against the perception of native listeners?
(2) To what extent does the distortion of quantity category affect the intelligibility of Swedish words when measured against the perception of native listeners?
(3) To what extent does the distortion of tonal word accent category affect the intelligibility of Swedish words when measured against the perception of native listeners?
(4) Among the distortions of the three prosodic contrasts, which ranks first, second and third, in terms of negatively affecting the intelligibility of Swedish words?

Theoretical considerations

General considerations in speech perception

A general question concerning this study is which type of perception model is relevant for the interpretation of our results. There are two issues involved in perception: what phonetic cues and what units of perception are there? In accordance with Marslen-Wilson and Welsh (1978), we believe that speech input activates words in a cohort from 'left-to-right' and that there is interactive activation from the lexicon (cf. McClelland and Elman 1986; Marslen-Wilson 1987). Prosody and especially intonation have not been addressed much in psycholinguistic modelling, but there are some important example studies. For instance, Zhou and Marslen-Wilson (1994) provided a model of spoken word recognition for Mandarin that incorporates both segmental and tonal layers.

Soto-Faraco, Sebastian-Galles and Cutler (2001) studied whether suprasegmental information can facilitate lexical access in Spanish, and the relation between segmental mismatch and mismatch of lexical stress. Experiments using intentional mispronunciations of truncated words showed that listeners process segmental and suprasegmental information in exactly the same way. Soto-Faraco et al. (2001) interpret the results to support a model of spoken-word recognition where the activation process is sensitive to all acoustic information relevant to the language's phonology.

In a study on Swedish tonal word accents, Abelin and Suomi (1997a) used a word-spotting design with two-syllable compounds having *accent I* or *accent II* where the first syllable of the compound was segmentally nonsense. The results of Abelin and Suomi (1997b) showed that the recognition of a morpheme in the second part of the compound is greatly facilitated (having shorter reaction times) when the first syllable is pronounced according to the *accent II* tone, as opposed to the *accent I* tone. Thus, the *accent II* tonal movement on a one-syllable nonsense word predicts that at least one more syllable follows. In a study on truncated *accent I* and *accent II* words with a slightly different purpose and design, Felder, Jönsson-Steiner, Eulitz and Lahiri (2009) concluded that both the perception of surface tonal contours and the identification of entire words are speeded up more by *accent I* than *accent II*. They also argued that *accent I* is governed by the underlying lexical structure with tonal specification.

Morphology, such as different inflectional forms, can affect processing as was shown by Söderström, Horne, Frid and Roll (2016), for example. They examined the perceptions of *accent I* and *accent II* in a mismatch condition where *accent I* words were followed by *accent II*-inducing suffixes, and *accent II* words were followed by *accent I*-inducing suffixes. It was found that *accent II*-inducing suffixes preceded by an *accent I* tone were more difficult to process compared to *accent I*-inducing suffixes preceded by *accent II*. This is interpreted to mean that there is a stronger relation between suffixes and *accent II* as compared to *accent I*, which could imply that *accent II* can indeed be very important for identification and comprehension in certain contexts.

Grosjean and Gee (1987) argue that stressed syllables are used to initiate lexical search. Also, Cutler and van Donselaar (2001) showed that Dutch listeners can effectively use stress placement in the recognition of spoken words, and that mismatching stress placement reduced word activation. With the exception of Abelin and Thorén (2015), we don't know of any similar studies on manipulation of stress placement or quantity in Swedish.

We thus have assumed that suprasegmental information affects speech perception and have investigated how mismatching stress placement, tonal word accent or syllable quantity affects processing. Listeners do use lexical information to restore degraded speech. The question here has been which prosodic phonological category is the most sensible to mispronunciation, for L1 Swedish listeners.

The three prosodic contrasts of Swedish

Standard Swedish has three prosodic phonological contrasts: stress placement, quantity and tonal word accent. Swedish word stress is determined by prominence contrasts between syllables that are mainly signalled by syllable duration (Fant and Kruckenberg 1994). Quantity contrast largely depends on the durational relation between the vowel of a stressed syllable and the following consonant, resulting in the two categories: /Vː C/ and /VCː/. Meanwhile, tonal word accent is mainly signalled by changes in the F0 contour and the timing of those changes in relation to the main stressed syllable of the word, for which related categories are: *accent I* (acute) and *accent II* (grave).

Stress contrast is traditionally regarded as a dynamic contrast, perceived as having varying prominence among syllables. According to Bruce (1977, 2012) and Elert (1970), word stress in Swedish is variable and words can have different meanings depending on where the main stress is placed, as found in *banan* [ˋbɑːnan] 'the path/course' and *banan* [baˊnɑːn] 'banana'. A great number of disyllabic trochaic-iambic minimal pairs exist. A smaller number of trisyllabic minimal pairs, such as *Israel* [ˋiːsrael] 'the state of Israel' and *israel* [ɪsraˊeːl] 'Israeli citizen', are also identified. Stress differences also create semantic contrasts on the sentence level in verb phrases containing either one of the verbs plus an unstressed preposition, as in ˈ***hälsa** på N.N.* 'greet somebody' or a verb plus an stressed particle *hälsa* ˈ***på** N.N.* 'visit somebody'. Just like in English, the perceived prominence of stressed syllables in Swedish relies more on temporal (duration) and tonal (F0) acoustic correlates than dynamic (intensity) ones (Fant and Kruckenberg 1994; Fry 1958). In Swedish in particular, duration is the most reliable correlate (Fant and Kruckenberg 1994), while in English, it is change in F0 that is the most reliable acoustic cue to stress (Fry 1958). This entails that a syllable perceived as stressed is always longer than the same sequence of segments in unstressed position, and that higher sound intensity may or may not contribute to the impression of syllable prominence. Although Fant and Kruckenberg (1994) also conclude that F0 gestures, voice source parameters and differences in vowel quality combine with duration to signal syllable prominence, dynamic dimension can still be a possible cue to the listener's perception. Some studies in the extant literature, however, regard the Swedish stress contrast as a temporally based one. For example, Thorén (2008: 109) found that word stress had to be signalled by at least temporal properties in order to be correctly perceived by native listeners. In addition to the main temporal/durational acoustic correlates of the perceived prominence contrasts, stress is allocated, along the timeline, to a word in a sequence of words and to a syllable in a sequence of syllables within the word.

In most regional varieties, quantity contrasts result in the two categories: /V:C/ as in *mäta* [mɛ:ta] 'to measure' and /VC:/ as in *mätta* [mɛt:a] 'measured (plural)'. Some studies report only /V:/ and /V/ in some South Swedish dialects (e.g. Gårding et al. 1974). In the latter case, the long vowel is mostly signalled by a diphthong in addition to pure duration. The quantity contrast is also accompanied by spectral differences between long and short vowel allophones. These differences are substantial for some vowel phonemes but very small for others. There is also a substantial variation between different regional varieties in this respect (cf. Behne, Czigler and Sullivan 1997; Bruce 2010; Hadding-Koch and Abramson 1964; Thorén 2003). Standard Finland-Swedish is known to have no or minimal spectral difference between long and short vowel allophones (Reuter 1971). There has been a debate regarding the Swedish quantity distinction, with some suggesting it is mainly a vowel distinction, some arguing it to be mainly a consonant distinction, and others saying it is equally based on vowel and consonant duration. It has also been suggested by Malmberg (1956), for example, that long and short vowels are separate phonemes, and that the mentioned durational contrasts in vowel and following consonants are there but are not phonemic per se. The present study, however, is not concerned with the refinement of theoretical accounts for the three contrasts; we merely aim to study their respective contribution to intelligibility.

A common proposal is that Swedish has two tonal word accent categories: *accent I* (acute), as in *tomten* [ˊtɔm:tən] 'the plot', and *accent II* (grave), as in *tomten* [ˋtɔm:tən] 'Santa Claus' (see Elert 1970), although only the grave accent can be considered as a real word accent. It is the only one of these two that predicts that the main stressed syllable and the following syllable belong to the same word (in a di- or polysyllabic word), thus having a cohesive function, and it is limited to the word, simple or compound. Word accent is connected with a primary stressed syllable. When pronounced in isolation, words usually carry sentence accent, and *accent II* then tends to involve two F0 peaks (see Bruce 2010 for regional variation in tonal patterns for *accent I* and *II*). The two lower prominence levels in a sentence stress perspective – unstressed and secondary stressed – do not result in any signalling of word accent. The non-focal but still stressed 'accentuated' level (see Bruce 1977) usually results in a tonal fall within the stressed syllable in *accent II* words. In focal position, a tonal rise is added to a following syllable. The tonal contour of *accent I* seems to depend more on sentence intonation than on the word proper, although alternative views have also been advanced (e.g. Felder et al. 2009). Standard Finland

Swedish lacks the word accent contrast, which is also neutralized in singing. Irrespective of which word accent category should be seen as specified or unspecified, they appear with different F0 patterns in accentuated and focal positions. The reader may refer to Bruce (1977) for an extensive account of the Swedish tonal properties on sentence and word level.

Intelligibility aspects of Swedish prosody

As mentioned before, the present study does not promote native-likeness for determining whether the prosodic features of a pronunciation are correctly or incorrectly signalled. It is only concerned with how much they affect intelligibility. This is in line with Derwing and Munro (2015), Abercrombie (1949) and others, who propagate a shift in the perspective from native-likeness to intelligibility as the goal of second-language learning, particularly for adult learners. Furthermore, as suggested by Jenkins (2002), we assume that some phonetic features of a language are more crucial for intelligibility than others. This idea is not completely new in the context of Swedish as an additional language. For example, Bannert (1980) suggested word stress, sentence stress, 'vowel quantity' and increased duration of stressed syllables as important goals in pronunciation teaching and learning. He also proposed that tonal word accent, complementary consonant length and some assimilations could be given less priority. However, his proposal was mostly based on his own and colleagues' intuition, lacking robust empirical evidence. Recently, Abelin and Thorén (2015) empirically confirmed Bannert's ranking concerning word stress and tonal word accent. In the present study, where investigating quantity contrast is also added, we do not separate 'vowel quantity' from the complementary consonant length, but we regard the quantity distinction as an entity involving the elements mentioned above. In future studies, we hope to look at the perceptual weight of segmental features, such as voicing, consonant clusters and some assimilations, and their respective contributions to intelligibility.

There is some structural evidence that word stress and quantity should play an more important role in the perception and comprehension of Swedish than tonal word accent. As mentioned above, the two former contrasts are present in all varieties of Swedish, which is not the case for tonal word accent. There are some jingles and joking sentences in Swedish where word stress is changed, resulting in total loss of intelligibility to the first-time listener. Gårding (1979: 13) describes what is assumed to happen when the native Swedish listener is confronted with a word that has distorted stress when produced by an L2 speaker (Translation from Swedish by the present authors):

> How about [ɕəláːre] (instead of [ɕɛ̀lːɐrə] 'cellar')? The word loses its identity. The listener searches for a similar word, i.e. <u>a word with the same stress pattern</u>, rummages around in the brain-lexicon, but finds no correspondence/equivalence. As you see [Gårding refers to a table] it is supposed to mean <u>*källare*</u> 'cellar'.

The prosodic features of Swedish, however, can be associated with the morphological structure of the words. As shown by Söderström, Roll and Horne (2012), the tonal word accent pattern of the first syllable of a word as well as stress placement may entail morphological information that makes a word easier or more difficult to process.

In our study we have not tested the effect of morphology, or the effect of other contexts such as syntactic, semantic or pragmatic.

We currently look at intelligibility from a native Swedish listener's perspective, but in future studies we want to look at intelligibility in all combinations of speakers and listeners, involving L1 speakers to L2 listeners, L2 speakers to L1 listeners, and L2 speakers to L2 listeners. L2 listeners and speakers should be understood as language users from diverse L1 backgrounds.

Although using an L1 speaker of Swedish for the production of distorted prosodic categories cannot mimic exactly how L2 speakers typically mispronounce the current prosodic categories, it still allows a higher degree of control with respect to the phonetic properties that are studied than using an L2 speaker.

Pedagogical considerations for Swedish L2 pronunciation

According to Gårding (1974) the prosody of an additional language is something that is particularly hard to be learned by the adult learner. A general account of second-language pronunciation learning at different ages is provided by Derwing and Munro (2015). They show that it is possible for adults to perceive and produce new segmental and prosodic features. Our study does not address how these adult learners should best be helped to achieve the prosody in an L2, but we want to find out whether and how the three Swedish prosodic contrasts differ with respect to their importance in making speech intelligible.

As Kjellin (1995) and Thorén (2008) suggest, the properties of stress and quantity can be combined to benefit teaching pronunciation of Swedish as a second language. Since both contrasts rely mainly on duration as perceptual cues, exaggeration of the duration of the stressed syllables, which thereby signals the prominence of syllables, can be utilized in teaching pronunciation. Furthermore, if lengthening of the stressed syllables is realized by lengthening the correct segment (vowel or following consonant), learners are assumed to have learned the realization of the intended quantity category. We can talk about killing two birds with one stone, i.e. we promote two prosodic contrasts by means of one measure – lengthening the correct segment in the correct syllable. Our previous study showed that stress is important for intelligibility, and if the present study shows that the quantity distinction is also important, teachers and learners can confidently combine the two prosodic contrasts by means of their shared acoustic cue, i.e. duration.

Outline of the study

In this study, we have carried out three experiments that involve all three Swedish phonemic prosody contrasts – stress, quantity and tonal word accent. The aim was to determine a ranking order for the three Swedish prosodic contrasts with respect to their relative importance for intelligibility. We prepared a number of disyllabic words: some are real words, some are nonsense words, and some are real words pronounced in the opposite phonological category, i.e. (1) changing the word stress category from trochaic to iambic and vice versa, (2) changing the quantity category from /V:C/ to /VC:/ and (3) changing the tonal word accent category from *accent I* to *accent II* and vice versa. We avoided minimal pairs to prevent creating another known word by changing category.[2] We are aware that this manipulation is somewhat crude and does not reflect all typical L2 realizations of stress patterns. For example, whereas we changed words to the opposite phonological category with typical Swedish clear realization of acoustic correlates, some L2 speakers may also typically produce unclear realizations, resulting in ambiguous prosodic categories, presumably due to insufficient awareness of the mentioned prosodic patterns. The method used in the study consists of three lexical decision experiments (1a, 1b and

2 See the discussion of Experiment 1, which acknowledges minor mistakes in this process.

2) with word stimuli in both the correct and opposite prosodic category. We measured degree of correct identifications, rejections and reaction times.

Experiments 1a and 1b

Material and design

The material for Experiment 1a consisted of three sets of intact words: 10 trochaic *accent I* words, e.g. bilen [ˈbiːlen] 'the car', 10 trochaic *accent II* words, e.g. gatan [ˋgɑːtan] 'the street', and 10 iambic words, e.g. kalas [kaˈlɑːs] 'party'; two sets of words with changed prosodic category: 10 originally trochaic words pronounced with iambic stress, e.g. låset* [loˈsɛːt] 'the lock', and 10 originally *accent II* words pronounced with trochaic stress and *accent I*, e.g. sagan* [ˈsɑːgan] 'the fairy tale'. As distractors, we presented 26 disyllabic non-words, with varying stress patterns or tonal accent categories. Likewise, the material for Experiment 1b consisted of three sets of intact words: 10 trochaic *accent I* words, e.g. köket [ˈɕøːkət] 'the kitchen', 10 trochaic *accent II* words, e.g. gatan [ˋgɑːtan] 'the street', 10 iambic words, e.g. kalas [kaˈlɑːs] 'party', 10 originally iambic words pronounced with trochaic stress, e.g. kanel *[ˈkaːnel] 'cinnamon', and 10 originally *accent I* words pronounced with *accent II*, e.g. degen *[ˋdeːgən] 'the dough'. The same 26 disyllabic non-words were used in both parts of this experiment. Thus, words with *accent I* were mispronounced with *accent II* and vice versa, and words with trochaic stress were mispronounced with iambic stress and vice versa. See Appendix I for the complete list of stimulus words.

All the trochaic words (with the exception of sälar 'seals') were nouns in the definite singular form, having excluded possible members of minimal phonological pairs.[3] The words were recorded by a male phonetician with a moderate Stockholm dialect. This means that his pronunciation cannot be traced with certainty to Stockholm but rather to a wider area in eastern Sweden. Recordings were made with a Røde NT3 condenser microphone to a laptop at a sampling frequency of 22,050 Hz in a silent studio at the University of Umeå, Sweden, and editing was made with Praat (Boersma and Weenink 2013).

3 We accidently included one word *[ˋjʉːrət], whose distorted form can be interpreted as a real word. This is described in detail in the general discussion.

There was some deliberation about how to treat vowel quality in the stressed and unstressed syllables, since these vary according to the degrees of stress and quantity category. We decided to choose vowels which do not vary so much in unstressed vs. stressed position or short vs. long allophones (e.g. /e/ rather than /a/) and keep the quality of the original word (e.g. not changing [e] to [ɛ] or [ə] in unstressed position) as much as possible. Each word was presented until self-terminated, in all cases just below 1,000 ms. At the same time, participants had 1,000 ms to react to each stimulus. Thus, the time allotted for reaction to the stimuli started when the word started and there was a 1,000 ms pause between each word. For building and running the experiment, the PsyScope software was used (Cohen, MacWhinney, Flatt and Provost 1993).

Procedure and participants

Two lexical decision tests were performed in Experiments 1a and 1b. In the first experiment, there were 18 female L1 speakers of Swedish, approximately 20–25 years of age, who were presented with the above described 76 words of Experiment 1a, one by one in random order. In Experiment 1b, there were 16 female L1 speakers of Swedish, approximately 20–25 years of age, who were presented with the above described 76 words of Experiment 1b, one by one in random order. The subjects were instructed to press one key on the keyboard if the word was a real word and another key if the word was a non-word. The subjects were instructed to decide, as quickly as possible, whether the word they heard was a real word or not. Reactions that were not registered within the 1,000 ms period were categorized as loss. The subjects had no reported hearing impairment.

Results

Accuracy

Figure 11.1 shows the main results of Experiments 1a and 1b. It turned out that the task was quite demanding, and that the loss in the experiment was large.

It is evident from Figure 11.1 that wrong stress placement produced more rejections than wrong tonal word accent in both Experiments 1a and 1b. Wrong tonal accent produced more acceptance than wrong stress placement in both experiments. An unpaired t-test showed a significant difference between the two groups ($p < 0.0001$). The difference in the number of 'yes' responses between *accent I* mispronounced as *accent I* and *accent II* mispronounced as *accent I* was not significant. There was no significant difference between the responses for trochaic pronounced as iambic and iambic pronounced as trochaic.

Figure 11.2 shows a comparison of the wrongly pronounced words with the correctly pronounced words. The correctly pronounced words are, as expected, the most robust; they exhibit smaller loss and they are more often assessed as real words. The words which were most frequently judged as non-words were the words with wrong stress placement. The difference in the number of 'yes' responses between correctly pronounced *accent I* words and *accent I* words pronounced with *accent II* was significant in an unpaired *t*-test ($p = 0.0233$). The difference in the number of 'yes' responses between correctly pronounced *accent I* words and *accent II* words pronounced with *accent I* was not significant. When comparing the numbers for loss, *accent II* pronounced as *accent I* showed more loss than the reverse condition.

The difference in the number of 'yes' responses between correctly pronounced trochaic words and trochaic words pronounced with iambic stress was significant ($p < 0.0001$). Likewise, the difference in the number of 'yes' responses between correctly pronounced iambic words and iambic words pronounced with trochaic stress was significant ($p < 0.0001$).

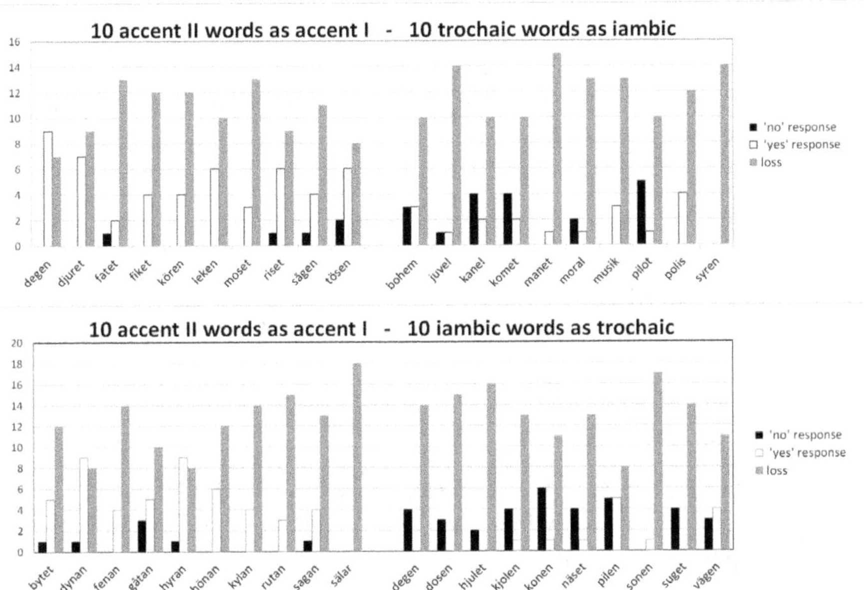

Figure 11.1. Results of Experiment 1.

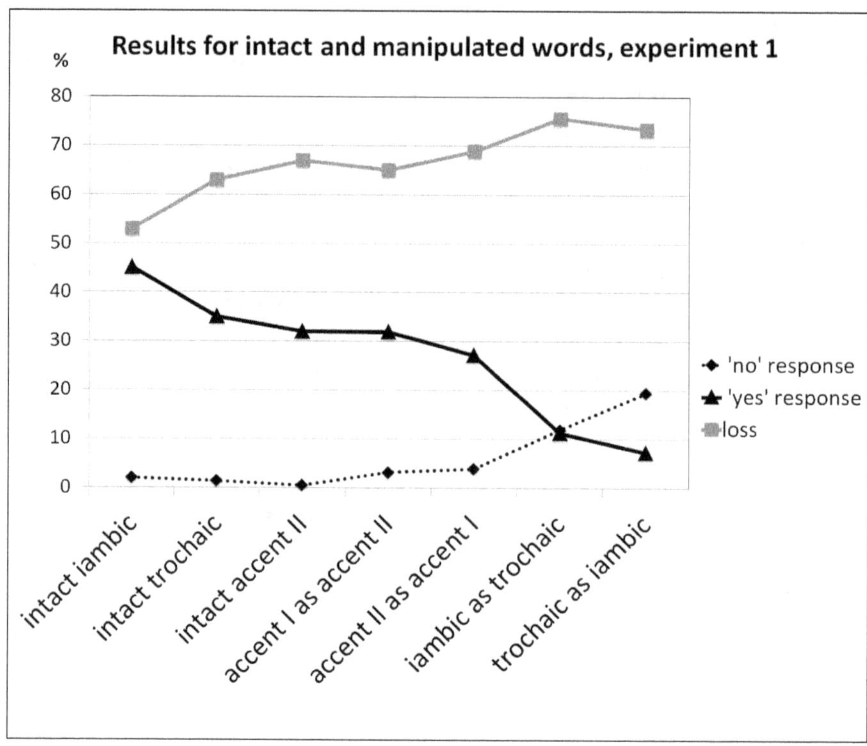

Figure 11.2. Comparison of wrongly and correctly pronounced words: Experiment 1.

There was a connection between loss and 'no'/'yes' responses. There was a negative correlation between number of 'yes' responses and loss ($r^2 = 0.8473$). Furthermore, the loss was greater where there were more 'no' responses.

Reaction times

It was not possible to compare reaction times in 'yes' responses' for word accent errors and stress placement errors, since there were so few 'yes' responses for the words with wrong stress placement.

Durations of sound stimuli

The durations of the sound stimuli were measured and we found that the wrongly pronounced trochaic *accent I* words pronounced as iambic were slightly longer. However, this did not correlate with reaction times.

In general, reaction times were longer than word durations, but not if 200 ms were deducted for motor activation. There was a tendency for less loss, and the 'yes' responses were more numerous when the durations were shorter.

Discussion

The results of Experiment 1 suggest greater perceptual weight in the case of the stress pattern when compared to tonal word accent.

There was a connection between loss and 'yes' responses, with negative correlation between the number of 'yes' responses and loss. Furthermore, the loss was greater where there were more 'no' responses. This could be due to the simple fact that 'no' responses generally have longer reaction times than 'yes' responses; thus, it could be that in some cases when a 'no' response is intended, the response time exceeds 1,000 ms. But the result could also be due to an inability to interpret the wrongly pronounced word. This is further explored in Experiment 2, which allowed for longer reaction times.

Although we checked the words for membership in minimal phonological pairs, one such case became apparent after the first presentation of our results. The word *djuret* [ˊjʉːrət] 'the animal', normally pronounced with *accent I* and here pronounced with *accent II* *[ˋjʉːrət], can actually be interpreted as the compound word *djurrätt* [ˋjʉːˌrɛtː] 'animal rights'. As shown in Figure 11.1, the mispronounced ˋ*djuret* showed the second highest number of 'yes' answers and relatively less 'loss' in this distortion category, indicating that it was recognized as a real word by just above half of the listeners. We do not, however, know whether listeners perceived the word as 'the animal' or 'animal rights'.

Conclusion

Participants identified correctly pronounced words as real words more easily and they produced smaller loss, more 'yes' responses and less 'no' responses than they did with the wrongly pronounced words. In terms of the degree of ease among the correctly pronounced words, the iambic category was the highest, the trochaic *accent I* category was next, and the *accent II* category was the lowest.

Among the incorrectly pronounced words, wrong stress placement produced larger loss, fewer 'yes' answers and more 'no' answers than wrong tonal word accent. When the 'yes' responses of mispronounced words were compared with the correctly pronounced words, we saw a highly significant difference between correctly pronounced stress and mispronounced stress, for both types of stress change. There was a significant difference in the amount of 'yes' answers between correct *accent I* and *accent I* as *accent II*, but not vice versa. This suggests that intelligibility of speech is more affected by wrong word stress placement than by wrong word accent.

In Experiment 2, we tested the perceptual weight of the third prosodic distinction of Swedish, quantity contrast, together with the two contrasts in Experiment 1.

Experiment 2

Material and design

A lexical decision experiment was performed, where 10 native Swedish listeners were exposed to 50 intact words representing combinations of trochaic, iambic, *accent I, accent II* as well as /V:C/ and /VC:/ categories. The test words were 10 originally trochaic words pronounced with iambic stress patterns, 10 originally *accent I* words pronounced with *accent II*[4] and 10 trochaic /V:C/ words pronounced as /VC:/. It was not possible to include all three contrasts in both directions since the experiment would become too large. 60 nonsense words with the same combinations of phonological categories served as distractors. See Appendix II for the complete list of stimulus words.

The words were recorded by the same person as in Experiment 1 and under the same technical conditions, except for the place of recording. This time the recording was made in a small room with provisional anti-echo treatment. Each word was presented until self-terminated, and all words lasted just below 1,000 ms. Participants had 1,500 ms to react to each stimulus (500 ms longer than in Experiment 1). Reaction times were measured beginning the moment the words started. Between each word, there was a 1,000 ms pause. For building and running the experiment the PsyScope software was used (Cohen et al. 1993). Participants were instructed to judge as quickly as possible whether the words they heard were real words or not. They were asked to press the 'yes' button if they heard a real word, and the 'no' button if they heard a non-word. The number of yes/no answers

4 As we had received comments on the first experiment that *accent II* words pronounced with *accent I* could be perceived as 'correct' pronunciations in some dialects, we chose to make the distortion from *accent I* to *accent II*.

and non-responses (answers that exceeded the reaction time limit) were counted and reaction times were measured.

Results

The results of Experiment 2 are shown in Figure 11.3. As in Experiment 1 participants identified correctly pronounced words as real words more easily and they produced more 'yes' responses, fewer 'no' responses and less loss than they did in the wrongly pronounced words. The results also show that participants tended to judge words as non-real to a higher degree when pronounced with distorted quantity than when pronounced with distorted stress and distorted tonal word accent. The frequency of non-responses (loss) and non-word decisions for distorted word stress was slightly lower than for distorted quantity but still much higher than for distorted word accent.

Through pairwise analysis of correct stress placement with distorted stress placement, correct quantity with distorted quantity, and correct

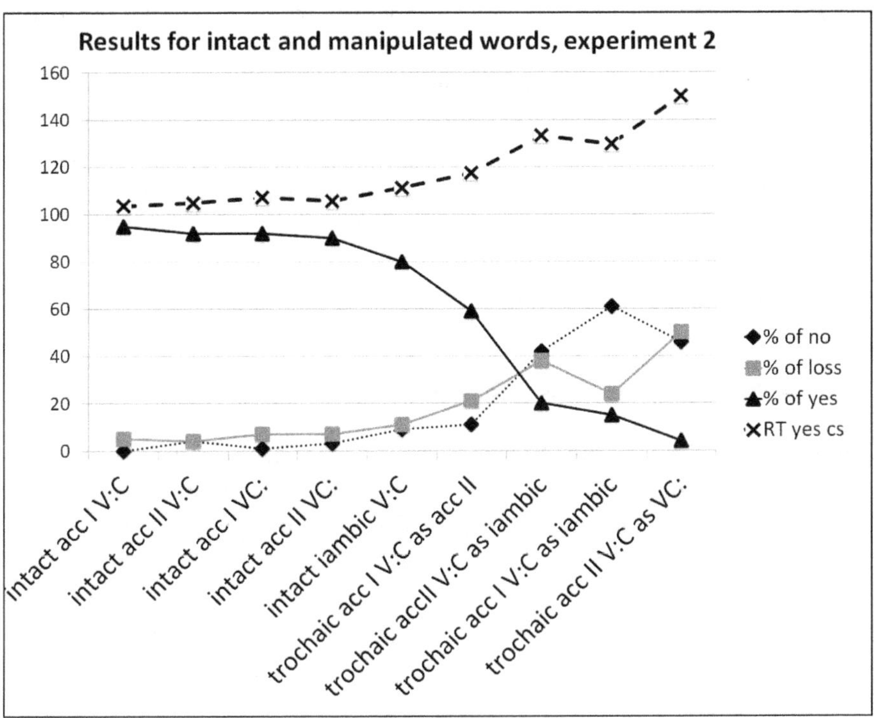

Figure 11.3. Comparison of wrongly and correctly pronounced words: Experiment 2.

tonal word accent with distorted word accent, we see that distorted quantity had the largest negative effect on word identification. There was a significant difference in the amount of 'yes' responses between correct and incorrect quantity (unpaired *t*-test, $p = 0.0001$). The difference in reaction times could not be calculated for wrongly pronounced quantity since so many subjects did not react within the allotted 1,500 ms. (The mean reaction time [RT] of 150 centiseconds for wrong quantity in the diagram is really a dummy, since reaction times were much longer and, thus, not measurable.) These long reaction times indicate great difficulties in processing. The difference in 'yes' and 'no' answers for trochaic pronounced incorrectly with iambic stress was also significant (unpaired *t*-test, $p = 0.0001$). The difference in 'yes' and 'no' answers for incorrect *accent I* as *accent II* was significant as well (unpaired *t*-test, $p = 0.002$), as was the difference in reaction time for correct trochaic words and trochaic words pronounced incorrectly with iambic stress (unpaired *t*-test, $p = 0.0001$). The difference in reaction time for incorrect *accent I* to *accent II* was also significant (unpaired *t*-test, $p = 0.0085$), though to a lesser degree as expected.

We can also see that reaction times show a negative correlation with 'yes' judgements (–0.967) and a positive correlation with 'no' judgements (0.875). In other words, those distorted words which produced more 'no' responses also had longer reaction times when they were judged as real words. Both 'no' responses and longer reaction times indicate difficulty in identification and, therefore, lower intelligibility of the mispronounced words.

The results of Experiment 2 show that loss is diminished when longer reaction times are allowed. Reaction times for 'yes' responses became possible to measure and the length of reaction times largely reflects the same order as the amount of 'yes' and 'no' answers.

Discussion and conclusion

The results of Experiment 2 indicate that distorted quantity is more detrimental to word identification than distortions of both word stress and tonal word accent. However, both word stress and quantity place themselves near each other and with some distance from word accent contrast with respect to listeners' sensitivity to changed category. Thus, the results from Experiment 1 were replicated, adding the results on quantity contrast.

General discussion

The results of this study suggest greater perceptual weight for quantity and stress pattern when compared with tonal word accent. Change in the quantity category was suspected to be less detrimental to word recognition than change in the stress pattern, but quantity turned out to be the most crucial of the three tested prosodic contrasts.

There was a negative correlation between the number of 'yes' and 'no' responses in both experiments. Furthermore, there was a negative correlation between reaction times and 'yes' responses in the second experiment. Altogether, these findings indicate that recognition of words with mispronounced prosody is difficult. We also saw that quantity errors were the most harmful to recognition and that tonal word accent errors were the least harmful, although not negligible.

These results could also be discussed in relation to the left-to-right cohort model of speech perception (cf. Marslen-Wilson 1987), but it is unclear how prosody can get accommodated in this model. One question is whether an early absence of stress placement would be more detrimental for recognition than a late absence. That is, would a trochaic word with changed stress-placement (which ought to have stress on the first syllable – and therefore lacking early durational and intonational cues) be more difficult to process than an iambic word with changed stress-placement (which ought to have stress on the second syllable)? There is some evidence of this in Experiment 1, but more studies on Swedish are needed for addressing this question. Similarly for *accent I* and *accent II*, there were slightly more errors for *accent II* as *accent I* than for *accent I* as *accent II*. If *accent I* is characterized as later peak and *accent II* is characterized as earlier peak in isolated pronunciation (cf. Felder et al. 2009 on Stockholm dialect) this indicates that an absence of correct tone movement on the first syllable in a disyllabic word is more disturbing than the presence of wrong tone movement on the first syllable in a disyllabic word. An alternative explanation is that it is the absence of high tone which causes more problems in perception. This indicates that the absence of a cue (for stress or tonal word accent) is more disturbing to the listener than the wrong presence of a cue (for stress or tonal word accent), but this needs to be further verified.

We can only speculate whether a change in the quantity category in either direction between /V:C/ and /VC:/ would have a more or less detrimental effect on word recognition, since we only included the direction from /V:C/ to /VC:/ in our study. We assume, however, first, that identification of the quantity category is processed from 'left-to-right', since vowel quality must be the first perceptual cue to the listener. Vowel duration and post-vocalic consonant duration are subsequently assumed to confirm or falsify the listener's original hypothesis. Establishing the quantity category is a first step, but word identification still remains to be done. Again, we can only speculate, but we assume that word identification is dependent on the number of known homophonic first syllables that are parts of real words. On the other hand, in a /VC:/ word, the post-vocalic consonant is revealed within the first syllable giving the listener one more cue to the entire word (or non-word). In the time frame within which this is done, the /V:C/ word reveals only the vowel. That could possibly result in intact /VC:/ words being easier to process than /V:C/ words. Our data, however, do not show any significant differences in this respect. But when we change either of the two categories into the other, and focus on word recognition rather than perception of the quantity category, the listener is likely to depend on the frequency of different stems that may agree with the perceived sequences.

The words of the present experiments were not checked for frequency or number of phonological neighbours. The reason they were not balanced for frequency was that it was difficult to find suitable words. We made a check for possible correlations between rankings of frequencies and rankings of reaction times and found no correlation between lower frequencies and longer reaction times. Söderström, Horne and Roll (2016) found that differences in processing of *accent I* and *accent II* stems can in part be explained by the density of the phonological neighbourhood of stems, due to lexical competition. In the present experiment, we cannot draw similar conclusions regarding lexical effects, since we do not have reliable data on phonological neighbourhoods.

What is puzzling is that, in our first experiment, the correctly pronounced iambic words were the words that had the least loss, the highest number of 'yes' responses and the lowest number of 'no' responses, which is in opposition to the result in Experiment 2. A post-check of frequencies for the stimuli words in the two tests did not provide any explanation for this.

In relation to studies concerning the effect of morphology, such as that of Söderström et al. (2012), a question arises whether *accent II* might be more important to comprehension when there are other errors as well, such as in the speech of learners of Swedish as a second language who may use the wrong suffixes in nouns or verbs. Adding further learner errors, such as word order mistakes or wrong lexical choices, complicates the picture further.

We are well aware that our experiment does not show high ecological validity since it tested deliberately mispronounced words, which were judged out of context. Furthermore, as mentioned above, L2 speakers do not typically change any of the mentioned prosodic categories into a clear realization of the opposite category, but rather into a generally unclear pronunciation with respect to the mentioned prosodic contrasts. We are therefore planning follow-up studies in more natural scenarios with combinations of L1 and L2 speakers and listeners.

Conclusion

We conclude that Swedish L1 listeners perceive and identify words with incorrect quantity category, incorrect stress placement and incorrect tonal word accent with greater difficulty than words pronounced with correct stress, quantity and word accent. Thus, correctly pronounced words are easier to identify (they produce smaller loss, more 'yes' responses and less 'no' responses, and entail shorter reaction times) than the wrongly pronounced words.

For the incorrectly pronounced words the results show that wrong quantity category and wrong stress placement produce fewer 'yes' answers, more 'no' answers and more loss than wrong tonal word accent. The study also shows that phonetic, phonological and psycholinguistic experimental methods combine well for dealing with pedagogical issues.

Pedagogical implication

Based on the results, we suggest that learners of Swedish as a second language benefit more from proficiency in temporal prosodic properties than in the choice of word accent category or precise realization of word accent category (cf. Thorén 2008). In fact, word accent categories are realized differently in different geographical regions, and some varieties do not utilize the contrast at all.

Since the second experiment implies that quantity and stress pattern in Swedish are more crucial to intelligibility than tonal word accent, we suggest that second-language learners of Swedish are specifically trained in perceiving and producing both the quantity distinction and the stress pattern. We can imagine a second-language learner of Swedish going to school outside the Stockholm (capital) region. Her teacher may use teaching material that describes the general Swedish stress and quantity patterns and, also, the Stockholm variety of the word accent contrast. In addition to this, the teacher may unintentionally introduce her own local accent, despite her effort to comply with the tonal patterns described in the material. Even if the teacher succeeds in mimicking the Stockholm tonal patterns, the learner will probably receive diverse input on tonal word accents from social interaction outside the school and from the media, as well. This may confuse her interlanguage system, not allowing her to discern what the 'correct' Swedish word accent patterns are. The results of the present study suggest that the learner in this hypothetical situation, who is very likely to represent actual learners, can minimize confusion and successfully acquire appropriate pronunciation, if the focus of teaching and learning is placed on the temporal prosodic properties rather than on tonal word accents.

In addition to a better foundation on what should be prioritized in teaching Swedish L2 pronunciation, teachers and learners of Swedish as a second language can draw on the findings of Fant and Kruckenberg (1994) and the suggestions by Kjellin (1995) and Thorén (2003, 2008) to lengthen the correct segment (vowel or consonant) in the stressed syllable, thereby promoting the significance in the signal of both stress placement and the quantity category of a given word. Teaching and learning can benefit from the finding that two important phonological contrasts share the same main acoustic cue, namely, duration.

Further experiments

We believe that future studies should examine the relative perceptual weights of segmental features like vowel quality, consonant features, phonotactic features and the role of assimilations and reductions; also intelligibility tests should involve phrases and sentences in addition to single words. Together with studies of L1 and L2 speakers and listeners, we intend to replicate the two experiments in this study with typically developing Swedish children aged around 4 to 6 years. We will then be able to see how children's word recognition is affected by non-standard prosody. The question is whether speech perception in children is more or less segmental than speech perception in adults, thus, addressing the effects in protolanguage. A study by Sundström, Samuelsson and Lyxell (2014) on word repetition and non-word repetition alluded to age-dependent differences regarding how prosody is stored and integrated with segments.

Appendix I

The categories of real/intact words, nonsense words and words with changed prosodic categories that are used in Experiment 1. The manipulated categories are shown in bold.

Intact real words			*Nonsense words*		
10 intact words trochaic *accent II* /V:C/	10 intact words trochaic *accent I* /V:C/	10 intact words iambic *accent I* /V:C/	26 Nonsense /V:C/, mixed *accent I*, *accent II*, trochaic and iambic		
bulan	bilen	baron	`blyran	`göpan	púret
bönan	boken	belag	búget	kadél	tö´ket
diket	bordet	besök	dában	`kafan	sirán
duvan	duken	cerat	`dyset	`kogan	vakós
dåren	dalen	dekal	fakén	kýgen	`tjoman
faran	fåret	filur	femól	linár	topít
gatan	fölet	metan	fúket	míben	
kakan	filen	minut	gáket	misýt	
leran	gåsen	raket	`garan	núgen	
ligan	huset	safir	golát	porít	

Changed phonological category			
10 **trochaic** *accent I* /V:C/ pron. as **iambic** *accent I* /V:C/	10 **iambic** *accent I* /V:C/ pron. as **trochaic** *accent I* /V:C/	10 **trochaic** *accent I* /V:C/ pron. as **trochaic** *accent II* /V:C/	10 **trochaic** *accent II* /V:C/ pron. as **trochaic** *accent I* /V:C/
degen	bohem	degen	bytet
dosen	juvel	djuret	dynan
hjulet	kanel	fatet	fenan
kjolen	komet	fiket	gåtan
konen	manet	kören	hyran
näset	moral	leken	hönan
pilen	musik	moset	kylan
sonen	pilot	riset	rutan
suget	polis	sågen	sagan
vägen	syren	tösen	sälar

Appendix II

The categories of real/intact words, nonsense words and words with changed prosodic category that are used in Experiment 2. The manipulated categories are shown in bold.

Intact real words					*Nonsense words*		
10 intact words trochaic *accent II* /V:C/	10 intact words trochaic *accent II* /VC:/	10 intact words trochaic *accent I* /V:C/	10 intact words trochaic *accent I* /VC:/	10 intact words iambic *accent I* /V:C/	20 non-sense words trochaic *accent I* /V:C/+ /VC:/	20 non-sense words trochaic *accent II* /V:C/+ /VC:/	20 non-sense words iambic *accent I* /V:C/
bulan	himmel	bilen	buggen	baron	buget	byran	bynet
bönan	hackan	boken	bussen	belag	dyset	garan	diran
diket	kaffe	bordet	dammen	besök	föket	höpar	dugåm
duvan	killen	duken	luggen	cerat	gaket	kalan	faken
dåren	soffan	dalen	lasset	dekal	kupet	nögat	femål
faran	villan	fåret	sucken	filur	tjygen	pagar	filås
gatan	mössan	fölet	missen	metan	lafen	tjipan	golöt
kakan	ärtan	filen	lacken	minut	miset	jöpat	henut
leran	bullen	gåsen	tuppen	raket	nugen	kafan	kadel
ligan	pannan	huset	lappen	safir	töben	säpan	linar
					sibben	möckan	matus
					byllet	våmmar	misyt
					dacket	faggar	mokut
					fippet	koggan	piret
					gåppen	paffan	porit
					marret	vuggan	potil
					nyppen	dibban	siben
					påffet	gåppan	siran
					rybben	jöllan	topit
					vellet	pyffan	vakos

Changed phonological category			
10 **trochaic** *accent I* /V:C/ pron. as **trochaic** *accent II* /V:C/	6 **trochaic** *accent II* /V:C/ pron. as **iambic** *accent I* /V:C/	10 **trochaic** *accent I* /V:C/ pron. as **iambic** *accent I* /V:C/	10 **trochaic** *accent II* /V:C/ pron. as **trochaic** *accent II* /VC:/
basen	logen	djuret	bön:an
bogen	medar	dosen	näs:an
degen	sagor	fyren	sön:er
diset	sätet	kilot	fån:en
fatet	sidor	kjolen	kål:or
gamen	kilar	låset	ler:an
sylen		näset	nit:ar
låret		polen	skid:an
piken		renen	tjäl:en
leken		rågen	våg:ar

References

Abelin, Å. and Suomi, K., 1997a, 'Swedish word accents and speech segmentation', in *Proceedings of FONETIK 97*, Umeå University.

Abelin, Å. and Suomi, K., 1997b, 'Prediction of Swedish tonal word accent', Department of Linguistics, University of Gothenburg (unpublished manuscript).

Abelin, Å. and Thorén, B., 2015, 'The relative weight of two Swedish prosodic contrasts', in E. Babatsouli and D. Ingram (eds.), *Proceedings of the International Symposium on Monolingual and Bilingual Speech*, pp. 3–7, Chania, Greece (ISBN: 978-618-82351-0-6).

Abercrombie, D., 1949, 'Teaching pronunciation', *ELT Journal* 3. https://doi.org/10.1093/elt/iii.5.113

Bannert, R., 1980, 'Svårigheter med svenskt uttal: Inventering och prioritering', in *Praktisk lingvistik nr 5*, Institutionen för lingvistik, Lunds universitet.

Behne, D.M., Czigler, P.E. and Sullivan, K.P.H., 1997, 'Swedish quantity and quality: A traditional issue revisited', in *Phonum 4*, Department of Linguistics, Umeå University.

Boersma, P. and Weenink, D., 2013, *Praat: Doing phonetics by computer*, retrieved from http://www.praat.org.

Bruce, G., 1977, *Swedish word accents in sentence perspective*, Vol. 12, Lund University.

Bruce, G., 2010, *Vår fonetiska geografi – Om svenskans accenter, melodi och uttal*, Lund: Studentlitteratur.

Bruce, G., 2012, *Allmän och svensk prosodi*, Lund: Studentlitteratur.

Cohen, J.D., MacWhinney, B., Flatt, M. and Provost, J., 1993, 'PsyScope: A new graphic interactive environment for designing psychology experiments', *Behavioral Research Methods, Instruments, and Computers* 25(2), 257–71. https://doi.org/10.3758/BF03204507

Cutler, A. and van Donselaar, W., 2001, 'Voornaam is not (really) a homophone: Lexical prosody and lexical access in Dutch', *Language and Speech* 44(2), 171–95. https://doi.org/10.1177/00238309010440020301

Derwing, T. and Munro, M.J., 2015, *Pronunciation fundamentals: Evidence-based perspectives for L2 teaching and research*, Amsterdam/Philadelphia: John Benjamins. https://doi.org/10.1075/lllt.42

Elert, C.-C., 1970, *Ljud och ord i svenskan*, Almqvist & Wiksell: Stockholm.

Fant, G. and Kruckenberg, A., 1994, 'Notes on stress and word accent in Swedish', *STL-QPSR* 2–3.

Felder, V., Jönsson-Steiner, E., Eulitz, C. and Lahiri, A., 2009, 'Asymmetrical processing of lexical tonal contrast in Swedish', *Attention, Perception, and Psychophysics* 71(8), 1890–99. https://doi.org/10.3758/APP.71.8.1890

Fry, D.B., 1958, 'Experiments in the perception of stress', *Language and Speech* 1, 126–52.

Gårding, E., 1974, 'Den efterhängsna prosodin', in U. Teleman and T. Hultman (eds.), *Språket i bruk*, Lund: Liber.

Gårding, E., 1979, 'Avvikande uttal – Analys och värdering', in *Praktisk Lingvistik 1*, Institutionen för lingvistik, Lunds universitet.

Gårding, E., Bannert, R., Bredvad-Jensen, A-C., Bruce, G. and Naucler, K., 1974, 'Talar skåningarna svenska?', *Svenskans beskrivning* 8, 107–17.

Grosjean, F. and Gee, J.P., 1987, 'Prosodic structure and spoken word recognition', *Cognition* 25, 135–55. https://doi.org/10.1016/0010-0277(87)90007-2

Hadding-Koch, K. and Abramson, A., 1964, 'Duration versus spectrum in Swedish vowels: Some perceptual experiments', *Studia Linguistica* 18, 94–107.

Jenkins, J., 2002, 'A sociolinguistically based, empirically researched pronunciation syllabus for English as an international language', *Applied Linguistics* 23(1), 83–103. https://doi.org/10.1093/applin/23.1.83

Kjellin, O., 1995, *Svensk prosodi i praktiken – instruktioner och övningar i svenskt uttal, speciellt språkmelodin*, Stockholm: Hallgren & Fallgren studieförlag.

Malmberg, B., 1956, 'Distinctive features of Swedish vowels: Some instrumental and structural data', in H. McLean et al. (eds.), *For Roman Jakobson*, pp. 316–21, The Hague: Mouton.

Marslen-Wilson WD., 1987, 'Functional parallelism in spoken word recognition', *Cognition* 25, 71–102. https://doi.org/10.1016/0010-0277(87)90005-9

Marslen-Wilson, W.D. and Welsh, A., 1978, 'Processing interactions and lexical access during word recognition in continuous speech', *Cognitive Psychology* 10, 29–63. https://doi.org/10.1016/0010-0285(78)90018-X

McClelland, J.L., and Elman, J.L., 1986, 'The TRACE model of speech perception', *Cognitive Psychology*, 18(1), 1–86. https://doi.org/10.1016/0010-0285(86)90015-0

Munro, M.J. and Derwing, T., 1995, 'Foreign accent, comprehensibility and intelligibility in the speech of second language learners', *Language Learning* 45, 73–97. https://doi.org/10.1111/j.1467-1770.1995.tb00963.x

Parkvall, M., 2016, *Sveriges språk i siffror: vilka språk talas och av hur många?*, Stockholm: Morfem.

Reuter, M., 1971, 'Vokalerna I finlandssvenskan – En instrumentell analys och ett försök till systematisering enligt särdrag', *Studier i nordisk filologi* 58, 240–49.

Söderström, P., Horne, M. and Roll, M., 2016, 'Word accents and phonological neighbourhood as predictive cues in spoken language comprehension', in *Proceedings of Speech Prosody 2016*, pp. 45–48, Boston.

Söderström, P., Horne, M., Frid, J. and Roll, M., 2016, 'Pre-Activation Negativity (PrAN) in brain potentials to unfolding words', *Frontiers in Human Neuroscience* 10. https://doi.org/10.3389/fnhum.2016.00512

Söderström, P., Roll, M. and Horne, M., 2012, 'Processing morphologically conditioned word accents', *Mental Lexicon* 7, 77–89. https://doi.org/10.1075/ml.7.1.04soe

Soto-Faraco, S., Sebastian-Galles, N. and Cutler, A., 2001, 'Segmental and suprasegmental mismatch in lexical access', *Journal of Memory and Language* 45, 412–32. https://doi.org/10.1006/jmla.2000.2783

Sundström, S., Samuelsson, C. and Lyxell, B., 2014, 'Repetition of words and non-words in typically developing children: The role of prosody', *First Language* 34(5), 428–49.

Thorén, B., 2003, 'Can V/C-ratio alone be sufficient for discrimination of V:C/VC: in Swedish? A perception test with manipulated durations', *Proceedings from Fonetik 2003*, Umeå University.

Thorén, B., 2008, *The priority of temporal aspects in L2-Swedish prosody: Studies in perception and production*, PhD thesis, Stockholm University.

Zhou, X. and Marslen-Wilson, W., 1994, 'Words, morphemes and syllables in the Chinese mental lexicon', *Language and Cognitive Processes* 9(3), 393–422. https://doi.org/10.1080/01690969408402125

Åsa Abelin is a Professor of General Linguistics at the Department of Philosophy, Linguistics and Theory of Science, University of Gothenburg. Her research interests lie within phonetics and psycholinguistics, in the areas of second-language acquisition, emotional prosody and iconicity in language. In particular, she has studied intelligibility, comprehensibility and attitudes to non-native accent as well as perception of emotional prosody, and sound symbolism and onomatopoeia in Swedish.

Bosse Thorén is a senior lecturer at Dalarna University, Sweden, and he also gives lectures to teachers of Swedish as a second language at seminars and workshops. His PhD at Stockholm University was about the priority of temporal aspects of the Swedish prosody. His research interests lie in describing Swedish and English prosodies and investigating the intelligibility of foreign-accented speech in relation to second-language learners. He seeks to suggest phonological core features of Swedish and English critical for crosscultural communication.

Synopsis on Interlanguage

The Authors and Editors

This concluding section comprises a synopsis of each contributed chapter in the section on *Interlanguage* (IL). Similarly to the *Synopsis on Protolanguage,* it states how each chapter has served the theme of the book; this second summary section was also put together combining write-ups by the contributing authors and the editors of the volume. There are 5 chapters under the section *Interlanguage*: one has addressed phonological skill in bilingual adults; another has examined the role of formal instruction and L2 exposure on the identification and discrimination of phonological contrasts by adult L2 learners in foreign language instruction settings; the next one has investigated the impact of production complexity on adult L2 learners' speech; the fourth has dealt with the under-represented theme of second-dialect acquisition (D2) in adults; and the last chapter has investigated the perceptual weight of phonemic contrasts in an L1 with interesting implications for the interlanguages in foreign language instruction settings, thus enhancing the focus of teaching practices. This array of IL studies arguably lacks a representative example study of child interlanguage from foreign language instruction settings. The present section continues by briefly describing each contributed chapter to the book with regard to IL.

7 Schwa productions in Spanish-English bilingual adults

Several studies have shown that a lag of even a few years in acquiring a second language (L2) tends to have dramatic consequences on both speech production and perception. Chapter 7 investigates the production of American English reduced vowels by early sequential Spanish-English bilingual adults. The central question is whether adult bilinguals would be able to develop native-like phonological patterns and maintain separate phonetic categories for the sounds of their L2 (English), or if starting a few years later would create impediments in the formation of new phonetic categories. The study acoustically examines the durations and quality of English reduced vowels in unstressed syllables produced by the sample of Spanish-English bilinguals. The analyses of vowels are done in two different prosodic environments, and word frequency was also measured, to examine the effect of these two factors on vowel duration and quality. The productions of bilinguals are compared to a control group consisting of monolingual English-speaking adults in order to determine the amount of deviation in both duration and formant frequencies. Through an analysis of multiple variables, the research contributes evidence that early age of acquisition of a bilingual speaker's L2 may result in a perceived native-like sound; however measurable differences suggest that their pronunciation is different from that of monolingual speakers. Their system is phonemically stable (native-like), but phonetically exhibiting non-monolingual aspects.

The study has provided further evidence supporting the view that the adult bilingual speaker is distinct from the adult monolingual speaker. In spite of their early sequential exposure to the L2, the speech of the bilingual adult speakers exhibits interlanguage characteristics. The fluent speech patterns of the participants in the study, that are phonemically native-like, are found to have reached a fairly fixed and steady state but are nevertheless not phonetically equivalent to the targeted adult monolingual speech; this is evidence of an interlanguage. The advanced age of the participants in the study by default precludes this study from being representative of research on protolanguage that has more likely than not fossilized.

8 Identification and discrimination of initial voiceless stops by Catalan and Portuguese learners of English: The role of formal instruction and L2 exposure

Due to the interplay of several factors, including L1 attunement and L2 experience and the quantity and quality of the L2 input received, native speakers of Romance languages who learn English as a second language (L2) encounter certain difficulty when perceiving English voiceless stops. The purpose of Chapter 8 is twofold: (a) to examine whether the L2 learners' perceptual knowledge of their L2 falls closer to their native language or to the target language, and more specifically (b) to further investigate the effect of length of formal instruction and language exposure (i.e. the amount of outside classroom L2 input) on the non-native perception of the English voiceless stops /p, t, k/ by Portuguese and Catalan learners of English. A total of 63 learners of English as a Foreign Language (EFL) were divided into three experimental groups (an advanced group and two upper-intermediate groups, differing in their L1) and were asked to identify and discriminate between naturally produced tokens, contrasting word-initial voiceless aspirated and unaspirated stops. The results showed that the more advanced Portuguese learners outperformed the intermediate Portuguese learners, which seems to indicate that formal instruction plays a role on the development of the learners' interlanguage. Furthermore, comparison between the performance of the two upper-intermediate groups revealed that, despite the comparable VOT patterns in both languages, the upper-intermediate Portuguese perceivers outperformed the Catalans, which may be accounted by the effect of a greater exposure to the L2 outside the classroom. Overall, the advanced learners' perceptual competence in the L2 was found to be closer to the native perceivers than that of the intermediate learners.

This chapter enhances existing knowledge on interlanguage with regard to the perceptual phonetic skills of adult L2 learners. It also complements interlanguage phonology literature by providing more empirical evidence that IL phonology becomes increasingly native-like as a result of greater experience and length of formal instruction in the L2.

9 The impact of production complexity in German L2 by French native speakers: Focus on /h/ and vowel duration contrast

Research on foreign language speech production often focuses on repeated speech and read speech. Only a few studies have investigated the role of the complexity of speech production tasks on the abilities to produce sounds in a foreign language. Chapter 9 aimed to fill this gap by presenting a phonetic study on the L2 production of unknown contrasts in the native language. A contribution of the study is its focus on a pair of languages so far under-represented in interlanguage studies, namely German (second language, L2) and French (first language, L1). Speech production in a second language may reveal specificities of both phonetic systems with respect to sound production and co-articulation. As a result, L2 speech production is considered to be an interlanguage. The authors have investigated the phonetic skills of adult L2 learners, which may contribute to better understanding phonemic awareness in IL. They collected relatively large speech corpora composed of speech productions by native speakers of French who were late learners of German. More specifically, the speakers were asked to produce unknown contrasts in French, such as the long/short vowel contrast or the syllable-initial /h/, in three different experimental tasks with increasing complexity, i.e. audio repetitions, read texts and image descriptions. The effect of the complexity of the production tasks on the production accuracy was measured. The results of the study show that both increasing L2 speech production complexity and conflicting grapheme-phoneme conventions in the two languages have an impact on production accuracy in L2 speech. Moreover, the L2 learners tended to achieve native-like productions when provided with a native German auditory input. Awareness of pronunciation differences between one's first and second language can help with the amount of correct sound production, but it has very limited impact on the accuracy of the produced sounds. Taken together, results show that German L2 productions by French native adults are affected by the complexity of the production task: the less accurate productions by French native speakers were obtained in the most complex production task (i.e. picture description). This finding suggests that L2 production performances are task-related, and that L2 learners' production accuracy can benefit from an auditory model.

10 The acquisition of second dialect speech: An acoustic examination of the production of Ecuadorian Spanish assibilated rhotics by Andalusian speakers of Spanish

The main goal of Chapter 10 was to inform on likely similarities between second-dialect (D2) acquisition of speech and second-language (L2) acquisition of speech; this has been achieved by investigating whether equivalence classification in D2 acquisition of speech by native participants operates in the same fashion as in second-language acquisition. The hypothesis is that second-dialect acquisition behaves like an interlanguage. Specifically, the study compares the acquisition of Ecuadorian Spanish assibilated rhotics by native Andalusian Spanish-speaking participants to the native English-speaking participants' L2 Spanish productions reported in an earlier study. Assibilated rhotics are common across several varieties of Spanish. These sounds may be characterized both by rhoticity and assibilation. Because of their varied acoustic nature, assibilated rhotics provide an excellent opportunity for comparing equivalence classification in D2 and L2 acquisition. In this study, the D2 production patterns of Ecuadorian assibilated rhotics by native Andalusian-speaking participants are found to echo the L2 production patterns of Mexican Spanish assibilated rhotics by native English-speaking participants. Specifically, the results show that at the very onset of acquisition assibilated rhotics are mapped on to either rhotics or sibilants, for the most part. Knowledge of words seems to modulate equivalence classification. Furthermore, an acoustic analysis of the productions of assibilated rhotics by the participants shows that not all the acoustic features measured are equally acquirable. This study also contributes to our understanding of D2 speech learning by showing that male and females exhibit two diverging patterns in the production of assibilated rhotics, thus indicating that D2 learning is constrained by similar factors operating in speech production and variation in general. Overall, the results presented in this chapter are supportive of the hypothesis that D2 acquisition shows evidence of an interlanguage system reminiscent of that in L2.

11 The perceptual weight of word stress, quantity and tonal word accent in Swedish

The study presented in Chapter 11 aims at ranking the perceptual weight among the three phonemic prosodic contrasts of Swedish, namely word stress, quantity and tonal word accent. In two experiments, native Swedish subjects were presented with several disyllabic sequences, intact words, nonsense words and words that were distorted with respect to the three prosodic contrasts. The distorted words were not members of minimal pairs. In addition to intact words and non-word distractors, subjects heard originally trochaic words pronounced with iambic stress pattern and vice versa, originally /V:C/ words pronounced as /VC:/, and originally *accent I* words pronounced with *accent II* and vice versa. Listeners were asked to decide whether the words were real or not. The results of the study show that words with changed word accent category are rather easy to identify, words with changed stress pattern harder to identify, and that changed quantity category causes the most problems.

This study was instigated by the following question in the back of the authors' minds: What do we want to safeguard in an interlanguage that is not likely to reach native-like level? Interlanguages are the products of typical development in learners of target language *X* who have *Y* as L1. When teaching the pronunciation of an additional language, teachers should know which properties ought to be given high or low priority. The present study shows how the three prosodic phonemic contrasts, specific to the Swedish language, can be very different with respect to their importance for intelligibility. Tonal word accent (a contrast regarded as exotic and hard to learn) is interestingly proven to have the lowest perceptual weight of the three prosodic contrasts, whereas the most crucial contrast for the purposes of intelligibility is shown to be quantity. The results on the perceptual effect of different stress placement have led to a speculation on the possibility of a universal, which has profitable and interesting implications for scholars in second-language acquisition, as well as direct inferences for improving teaching practices in L2 instruction settings.

Index

accent 8, 14, 202, 203, 205
  foreign 8, 14, 202
  native-like 203, 205, 222
accuracy 326
acquisition 4–5
affective filter 5
age of acquisition (AOA) 165, 202, 205, 290, 343
allophony 76, 95, 232, 249, 282, 321
  place assimilation of nasals 76, 90, 96–97
  spirantization 76, 90, 96–97
articulation disorder 27, 35, 37
atypical development 2, 12, 29, 42

bilingual enhancement effect 167
bilingualism 9, 10, 14, 77
  adult 207
  early 50–51, 202–05
  late 202
Broca's area 6

case study 13, 27–48, 59,109–38
categorical perception 5
CEFRL 260
center of gravity (COG) 295, 299
chaos vii, 8
cleft lip/palate 38
coarticulation 5
consonants 70, 110
  allophonic contrast 232
  assibilated rhotic 287–89
  clusters 110–12
  coda 49, 52–54, 56–57, 64–68, 70
  correctness 31–33, 35, 39–40, 44–45
  duration 295, 299, 305
  fricatives 110
  glottal fricative 255, 256, 269–70
  labials 110
  quantity VC 320, 321, 334
  rhoticity 289, 298, 303, 304, 305
  sibilance/stridency 287, 289, 298, 303, 304
  voice before place 42–44
  voice onset time (VOT) 49, 55, 76, 81, 84, 91, 233
  voiceless stops: in English 233; in Portuguese 233; in Spanish 233
corpus/corpora
  CHILDES 80
  COCA 209
  EXMARaLDA 80
  FLACGS 260
  HNC 170
  HZSK 80
  Kiel 261
  PAIDUS 52, 80
  PEDSES 80
  PhonBLA 80
  ProFee-FLACGS 262
critical period 2, 7–8, 11, 14, 205, 206
crosslanguage phonetic (dis)similarity 231
crosslinguistic interaction 49–52, 56, 61, 69–70, 77, 79
  acceleration 51–52, 58, 77, 78, 81, 89
  bidirectional transfer 78, 86, 88
  delay 51, 54, 58, 77, 78, 81, 82–83, 93
  fusion/merger 78, 81
  order of acquisition 79, 81, 87–88, 94
  transfer 10, 51, 55, 77, 78, 81, 89, 96

developmental stages 116
distortion of phonological categories 317–18, 322–23
dominance 69, 80, 92, 168, 205, 207
dynamic systems theory 8, 11

elicited speech 7, 35, 113, 157, 233, 238, 257
English 27–48, 109–38, 201–30
equivalence classification 286–88, 292, 303, 305, 306

error 328, 333
extra-linguistic factors
gender 291–92, 298, 302, 305–06
social identity 290, 307

F2 295, 299
first language acquisition (FLA) 5, 10, 50, 59, 62–63
Flege, James 59, 205, 231, 235, 286, 292, 306
formant frequency 205–07, 218–22
fossilization 14
frequency 53, 57, 64, 67
French 61, 64–65, 255–85
fundamental difference hypothesis 10

German 49–75, 52–56, 60–66, 76–108, 255–85
Greek 109–38, 162–91
gross inclusion 42–43
group study 9, 29–46, 56, 63, 66, 146, 168, 207, 237, 299, 263, 326

Hungarian 139–61

Ingram, David 2, 6, 7, 12, 27–48
initial stage 306
intelligibility 164, 317, 318, 322, 330, 335
intensity 295, 301
interference 10, 14
interlanguage (IL) 2, 13–15, 231, 342–46
input 7, 9, 69

Jakobson, Roman 2, 12

L2 experience 235
L2 exposure 236
L2 instruction 9, 10, 236, 346
L2 pronunciation 323, 336
language contact 76, 77, 79, 98
learning 4–5
explicit 4
implicit 4
length of residence (LOR) 9, 208, 290
Lexical Restructuring Model 165, 181
lexicon 6–7, 62, 69
child/adult 7
lexical abilities 63
lexical decision 324, 326, 330
logical problem of acquisition 7
longitudinal 8–9, 109, 112

macrostructure 165
Major, Roy 8, 10
mapping 286–87, 304, 306
markedness 2, 110
maximal contrast 29–30, 37
microstructure 165, 167
MLU 166
monitor hypothesis 4
monolingualism 5, 10, 50, 59, 62–63, 202–06, 222–24
multilingualism 4

narrative structure 166
nativeness 7, 8, 9, 11
nonce vs. real word production 287, 293–94, 297, 304, 309

Ontogeny Phylogeny Model 8
Optimality Theory 92
orthography 257, 303, 304
transparent 162, 167

PCC 32, 163, 164, 167, 168, 170
pedagogical 317, 323, 335
Perceptual Assimilation Model 232
perceptual training 233, 235, 259
perceptual weight 317, 329, 330, 333
phonemic awareness (*see* phonological awareness)
phonetic distance 286–87, 291
phonological
awareness 164, 167, 170, 174
delay 12, 30
disorder 12, 28, 30–31, 35, 42
representations 167
phonotactics 111
PMLU 32, 163, 164, 168, 171
Portuguese 234–54
PPC 163
PRIMIR 63
principle of least effort 6
prosody 76, 316–20, 322
intonation 76
prefinal phrases 85
resyllabification 76
rhythm 76, 77, 85–86
stress 76
unfooted syllables 81–83
Proto-Indo-European (PIE) 2
protolanguage (PL) 2, 12–15, 192–98
PVC 163
PWP 32

quantity 320, 322, 335

reaction time 325, 329, 330, 331
reading
  comprehension 170, 174
  word 170, 174
realize, realization 316, 324, 335

saliency 304, 305
second dialect (D2) 6, 9
  acquisition 286, 288, 290, 304, 206
second language acquisition (SLA) 3, 10, 50, 59
segments 76, 316, 317
Selinker, Larry 13–14
sonority 110
  distance 110–11
Spanish 49, 52–58, 60–61, 76–108, 201–30
  Andalusian 287, 288, 303, 306–07
  Catalan 231–54
  Ecuadorian 287–88, 304, 305
Speech Learning Model (SLM) 59–60, 203, 231–32, 249, 286, 306
speech motor control 62–63
speech perception 5, 233, 318–19, 333
speech production 5, 6, 286, 303
spontaneous/naturalistic speech 7, 58, 80, 118, 147, 257
stochastic processes 98
stress
  primary 201–02, 206
  secondary 201, 206, 223
  stress 1 206, 208, 223–24
  stress 2 206, 208, 222–24
stress-timed languages 77, 92, 201, 203
Swedish 314–40
  as an additional language 318, 322
  as a second language 324, 334, 335
syllable-timed languages 60, 77, 92, 201, 203

task 258
  categorical discrimination 239, 245
  description 260–62
  doze 170
  identification 241
  imitation 287, 293, 297, 305, 309: real words 293, 305; nonce 293, 305
  lexical decision 326
  motor-based 62
  narrative 165
  naturalistic 58, 118, 147; quasi-naturalistic 157
  non-scripted speech 258
  perceptual 234, 235
  phonological awareness 167
  picture-naming 58, 293
  reading 208, 233, 235, 238, 257, 260: real words 293; nonce 293
  repetition 258, 336
  semi-spontaneous speech 264
  single-word 147: real 293; nonce 293
tonal word accent 318, 320, 324
  accent I 320, 324
  accent II 320, 324
TOWRE 170

vowels 32, 139–40, 205
  diphthong 52, 163, 259, 261, 321
  full vowel 201–04
  in English 201
  in German 54, 84, 203, 259
  in Greek 162
  in Hungarian 142–45
  in Spanish 52, 54, 88, 96, 203
  Pairwise Variability Index 85–86
  phonemically long vowels 139, 144
  phonemically short vowels 139, 144
  schwa 201–02, 204, 206, 222–23
  vowel duration 139–41, 202–04, 206–07, 223, 257, 272
  vowel epenthesis 87, 115, 116
  vowel inventory 257
  vowel length 54, 76, 77, 54, 84, 140, 272
  vowel quality 139, 257
  vowel quantity 139, 140, 320, 321, 334
  vowel reduction 60, 201–07, 222–23

webMAUS 265
Weinreich, Uriel 10
Wernicke's area 6
whole word
  acquisition 31
  measures 163, 166
  proportion of proximity 164, 169, 172
  proportion of variation 164, 167, 169, 172
word
  complexity 31–35, 39–40, 44
  frequency 206–07, 209, 223
  stress 318, 320, 322: trochaic 320, 325; iambic 320, 325